For Philip —
I hope you enjoy!
[signature]

Visions of Mahayana Buddhism

Then Sudhana respectfully circumambulated the enlightening being Maitreya and said, "Please open the door of the tower, and I will enter." Then Maitreya went up to the door of the tower containing the adornments of Vairochana, and with his right hand snapped his fingers; the door of the tower opened, and Maitreya bade Sudhana to enter.

The Flower Ornament Scripture

Dedication

For the scholars of Buddhism who dive so deep
into the ocean of Dharma, and salvage precious treasure.

Visions of Mahayana Buddhism

Awakening the Universe to
Wisdom and Compassion

by
Nagapriya

indhorse Publications

Published by
Windhorse Publications
38 Newmarket Road
Cambridge CB5 8DT
United Kingdom

© 2009 Nagapriya Wright
All rights reserved

Cover design: Marlene Eltschig
Cover image © Corey Hochachka/Design Pics/Corbis
Printed in the United Kingdom by Bell & Bain, Glasgow

Quote on half-title:
Cleary, Thomas (trans.). 1993. *The Flower Ornament Scripture: A Translation of the Avatamsaka Sutra*. Boston: Shambhala, 1489 (adapted by author).

Permission has been granted for the use of all images, as noted on Image Descriptions.

All effort has been made to procure permission to quote or use the following:
Page xii: Map from BuddhaNet: http://www.buddhanet.net/e-learning/buddhistworld/sbmap02.htm [accessed 25.05.09].
Pages 36, 67, 68, 69: Thurman, Robert A.F. 1976. *The Holy Teaching of Vimalakīrti: A Mahāyāna Scripture*. University Park: Pennsylvania State University Press.
Page 195: Poem by Bashō: Bownas, Geoffrey and Thwaite, Anthony (trans. and eds). 1998. *Penguin Book of Japanese Verse* (rev. edn). London: Penguin, 111.
Page 199: Poem by Ikkyū: translation by James Sandford originally appeared in 1981. *Zenman Ikkyū*. Decatur: Scholars Press, 14.

ISBN 978 1899579 97 6

The right of Nagapriya Wright to be identified as the author of this work has been asserted by him in accordance with the Copyright, Designs and Patents Act 1988.

About the Author

Nagapriya was born in 1969 and brought up in South Gloucestershire, England. He first came into contact with Buddhism while studying philosophy at Leeds University and in 1992 entered the Western Buddhist Order. Since then he has taught Buddhism in a wide range of contexts in the UK and mainland Europe.

Nagapriya's study and writing interests have evolved from early Buddhist thought and practice to East Asian developments, especially Pure Land and Buddha-nature conceptions of Awakening. You can visit his homepage and blog at www.nagapriya.com. He lives in Greater Manchester, England.

Nagapriya's first book, *Exploring Karma and Rebirth*, was released in 2004 and is now available in five languages. He has also published several articles in the *Western Buddhist Review* and is currently its Reviews Editor.

Acknowledgments

Although in the Mahayana scheme of things this book is a drop in the cosmic ocean, at times the writing of it felt like an epic quest that was never going to end. To choose another metaphor, at times I felt like a snake trying to swallow a buffalo, staggering about under the weight of the meal that I was trying to digest. Many people have helped bring this book to print; some have offered encouragement, some academic input, others literary suggestions, and still others precious spaces to write in. In light of the Tiantai notion of mutual inclusion, this book reveals everyone I have ever known and everything I have ever read or learnt.

In writing the book, I found myself regularly humbled by the dedication, care, and illumination that so many scholars of Buddhist ideas, practices, and cultures have brought to their enterprise, often with little recognition. In large measure, this book is a product of their painstaking efforts.

Francesca Tarocco invited me to lecture on Mahayana Buddhism at the University of Manchester and so sparked the initial idea for this book. She also contributed generously with her knowledge and enthusiasm. Bodhipaksa, Jnanasiddhi, Ratnaguna, Shuddhabha, and Subhadassi generously read parts of various drafts and offered valuable comments. David Loy, Robert Morrison (Sagaramati), Alan Sponberg (Saramati), and Ian Reader all gave valuable academic input. My editor, Maitripushpa, helped to improve the book significantly in its later drafts, including preparing the glossary and index, and also soothed my frayed nerves. Without her help, the book may never have been finished.

Martin Corder, David Stockdale, and Subhadassi offered me places to write in over the course of the project. My thanks go also to those who allowed me to use their photographs to illustrate the book. Finally, I must thank Windhorse Publications who kindly agreed to publish this and the hardworking team there who responded cheerfully to my many anxious emails and phone calls.

Table of Contents

List of Features and Illustrations

Illustrations

Map

Images (*following page 116*)

Abbreviations and Conventions

AMF   *The Awakening of Mahayana Faith*
AN   *Aṅguttara-nikāya*
AP   *Aṣṭasāhasrikā-prajñāpāramitā-sūtra*
CWS   *Collected Works of Shinran*
DN   *Dīgha-nikāya*
MN   *Majjhima-nikāya*
MMK *Mūlamādhymakārikā*
SMS   *Saṁdhinirmocana-sūtra*
SN   *Saṁyutta-nikāya*
T   *Taishō shinshū daizōkyō*

Any venture into the world of Mahayana Buddhism inevitably involves stumbling into a heap of new terms from a range of Asian languages. Sanskrit is widely regarded as the *lingua franca* of Buddhism and this convention has been followed here. But for many readers Sanskrit diacritical marks will mean little; consequently, terms are rendered in simplified forms to aid pronunciation and diacritics used only when a word or phrase is first mentioned, as well as in footnotes. A number of Sanskrit terms, like Mahayana and nirvana, are treated as English words and so do not require diacritics. Where appropriate, quotations have also been modified to reflect this approach.

There are two main systems for transliterating Chinese into English: Wade-Giles and pinyin. The Wade-Giles system has been widely used in the past by Western academics but pinyin is now preferred and so I use this throughout. This may mean that names previously familiar for some readers are rendered rather differently. In the case of book and article titles, conventions follow that of their authors. Where individuals have chosen to render their own names according to the Wade-Giles method, this preference has been respected.

The rendering of Japanese terms follows the Hepburn system, except where a word has been absorbed into English (notably koan). The Revised Romanization of Korean has been preferred in place of the more established McCune-Reischauer system, in part due to its adoption by the Korean government and in part because it avoids potentially confusing diacritic marks.

To reduce the proliferation of terms in many languages, the titles of traditional Buddhist writings, including scriptures and commentaries, and technical terms have generally been rendered into English with the original Sanskrit (Sk.), Chinese (Ch.), Japanese (Jp.), and Korean (Kor.) words in brackets or footnotes. T. numbers (referring to the *Taishō shinshū daizōkyō*, the listing of the standard modern Mahayana canon) are also used where appropriate to assist in identification.

With regard to gender-inclusive pronouns, for simplicity, 'he/his/him' has been used throughout to mean 'he/his/him' or 'she/hers/her'. It should also be noted that when speaking historically about the Buddhist clergy, this has, more often than not, signified men.

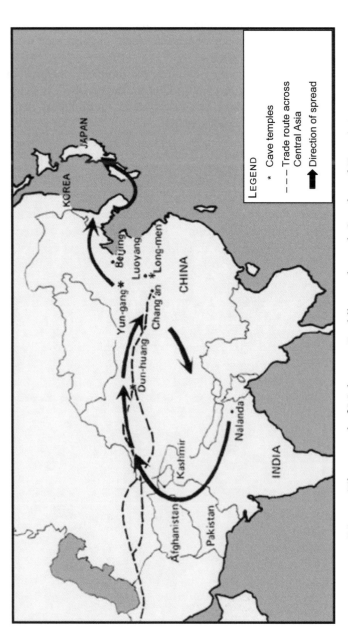

Map 1: The spread of Mahayana Buddhism through South and East Asia
Courtesy: BuddhaNet

Prologue

I first came across Mahayana Buddhism when I was about ten years old. I began following a comic — and rather bizarre — TV serial about a Chinese Buddhist monk en route to India. The show was called *Monkey* and was based on the 16th-century Chinese epic *Journey to the West*.[1] The epic itself was inspired by the historical pilgrimage of Xuanzang (c.600–64 CE),[2] who undertook this long, dangerous, and difficult journey in search of missing scriptures. The narrative drew specifically on Buddhist themes and, amidst the slapstick battle scenes and general comic mayhem, pinches of Dharma were sprinkled in. 'The Buddha taught: "Whatever you do, you do to yourself. We want so much when we need so little. But the illumined man wants for nothing."'[3] All this delivered in a suitably grave, 'oriental' accent.

In the very first episode Monkey meets the Cosmic Buddha who appears in female form and is huge. The arrogant Monkey wagers with the Buddha that he can fly off her hand. He then summons a cloud, flies away and, believing he has reached the end of the universe, stops at five pillars to relieve himself, then scribbles some graffiti to prove he has been there. Feeling very pleased with himself, he looks round to discover that he is still standing on the Buddha's hand and has just desecrated her fingers! With adult eyes, I can see that this is a comic reference to the Buddha-nature teaching but I can't recall what I made of it then.

With all its craziness, who knows what Buddha seeds *Monkey* planted in my febrile mind?[4]

---

[1] *Xiyou ji*; the story evolved over a long period but a definitive version was written down by Wu Cheng'en (1500?–1582). An abridged version has been translated into English: Waley 1973.

[2] Also written Hsuan-Tsang.

[3] From Episode 2: 'Monkey Turns Nursemaid'. See *Monkey* 2002.

[4] I am not the only one to be affected by my childhood exposure to *Monkey*. In 2007, the musician Damon Albarn (b. 1968) launched an opera entitled *Monkey: Journey to the West*, partly inspired by his memories of the show.

Introduction:

Portals, Pilgrimage, and Psychic Salvage

MAHAYANA MEANS THE 'GREAT WAY' or 'Great Vehicle' and refers to a powerful current of Buddhist thought, practice, art, and culture that began to flow in India around the beginning of the Common Era, and which continued for the next thousand years and beyond, spreading throughout Asia. It still flows today. It has produced literature on a colossal scale, given birth to a spiritual ideal that may be the most magnificent ever conceived, and inspired art and architecture which, where not destroyed, stand as wonders of the world. Mahayana Buddhism embodies an explosion of the spiritual imagination which continues to reverberate through the cosmos.

This book seeks to open a portal, or even a series of portals, into this imaginative universe. But these portals disclose not just the doctrines that underpin Mahayana traditions, for ideas are condensations of spiritual imagination which may function as sets of directions — or even maps — guiding us towards the imaginative spaces that produced them. Just as C.S. Lewis' wardrobe functioned as a doorway into the magical dimension of Narnia,[1] so the teachings of Mahayana Buddhism enable us to step across the imaginative threshold into its transcendent realm. They thus serve a liminal function, connecting us to a world of expanded significance, an immersive environment where we may soak in the rain of Mahayana wisdom.

A second metaphor that may help in reading this book is that of pilgrimage. A pilgrimage is a religious odyssey, which may follow a rigorous and perhaps dangerous itinerary through unknown and even unimagined terrain. As it is in many other religious traditions, pilgrimage is a time-honoured ritual practice within Buddhism and can be seen as a form of 'exteriorized mysticism'. The faithful may travel vast distances and willingly endure many hardships to reach a site that holds religious significance, and which may inspire profound transformation. Xuanzang himself journeyed from China across to India at a time when the fastest forms of transport were the donkey, camel, and ox cart.

By means of his or her journey, the pilgrim may follow a symbolic itinerary towards Awakening.[2] A pilgrimage can function as a means of

---

[1] Lewis 1950.

[2] The term 'Awakening' is used to translate the Sanskrit *bodhi*, often rendered as

purification, of reconnecting with cherished values and aspirations, and may culminate in a spiritual rebirth. More generally, through visiting sanctified places, we may recall the life and world of the people who created them, and how they lived out their ideals. We may thus reinvigorate the spiritual universe of the ancestors who trod the path before us.

Sadly, much of the past has not been preserved in stone, in images, not even in ruins, and so has been lost beyond recovery. So many visionary ideas, compassionate gestures, and records of Awakening have vanished forever, perhaps burnt at the hands of some spiteful vandal or simply left behind by changing fashion, then buried by the sands of time.

Thankfully, other aspects of the past have been recorded in writing, preserved on scraps of silk or parchment, or etched in rock, sometimes in languages and scripts long since dead. Through deciphering and piecing together the clues these texts have left, we may reawaken some long forgotten insights, of ways of living and being that once stirred the imagination of vibrant spiritual communities.

Such material enables a different kind of pilgrimage, not across continents into foreign lands but into the recesses of the imagination to discover the spiritual treasure that may lie within. In the course of such a journey, we may stumble upon new visions, ideas, practices, and customs and, in doing so, be transformed by them. For the recovery of forgotten texts, teachings, and practices is not just a matter of piecing together physical remains — like gluing together the fragments of a manuscript — but also of psychic salvage, of plumbing the depths of the imagination to rediscover what lies buried there.

History does not always reward the most creative or radical thinkers by remembering them. It is often the opposite; those willing to compromise and toe the line endure. Those more daring and creative thinkers are, for this very reason, sometimes suppressed since they represent a threat to the established order. As their missions fade, their memories may be forgotten. But one of the joys of studying Buddhist historical materials is that it allows us imaginatively to revive some of these figures, and even to hear their voices as they preach their unique vision of the Dharma.

Delving through these particular archives, we are enabled to make our own pilgrimages — pilgrimages of the imagination — into the amazing world of Mahayana Buddhism, a world that dazzles with the radiance of perfect wisdom and cosmic benevolence. And just as the universe is said to be expanding into space, so through study, reflection, and imagination we may expand our own minds and, in doing so, be lifted into a higher state of awareness. In reading this book, I hope that you may enter some spaces of thought, imagination, and being that you never knew were there.

'Enlightenment'. It is used as a general term to signify the Buddhist goal (as variously understood).

Approaching Mahayana Buddhism

It is often said that the first question to be answered in writing an auto-biography is what to leave out. The same may be true for any kind of general survey, since the potential material for inclusion is vast. Inevitably, the content must be highly selective and, perhaps just as certain, this content will reflect the prejudices, interests, and limitations of the writer. This is certainly true here.

There are judgements to be made about what counts as mainstream and what is marginal, about what is legitimate and what is spurious, about what is creative and what is decadent. Moreover, there is the question of which historical instant of any given phenomenon to describe. After all, Mahayana Buddhism is not some static entity but a constantly unfolding universe. In describing features of this universe, we are obliged to view snapshots which represent only moments in time and space, and may fail to do full justice to the 'line of flight' of a particular tradition or idea.

Rather than attempt a comprehensive overview of Mahayana Buddhism — which could run to many volumes — the book aims instead to evoke, and even revive, some of its central (and sometimes peripheral) motifs. So, while Mahayana Buddhism spread broadly throughout Central, South, and East Asia, not all its traditions are covered here. Instead, the focus is on its Indian origins and elaboration, then on developments in China, Korea, Japan, and ultimately the contemporary West. Innovations in other parts of Asia were judged beyond the scope of this work. The most notable absence is a detailed account of Tibetan Buddhism, which draws signifycantly from Mahayana teachings and practices. This was a deliberate choice, owing partly to the vast array of material already published on Tibetan Buddhism and partly to its Tantric orientation.

The book adopts a broadly chronological approach on the assumption that situating innovations within their specific historico-cultural context creates gateways to understanding their meaning and significance. Exploring the dynamic interplay between cultural environment, received ideas, and spiritual needs is key to unlocking the door to the Mahayana imagination. But the focus here is not on ideas alone. Rather, the book discloses how the Mahayana vision has been embodied in a wealth of practices, institutions, and forms of life.

In approaching these forms of life, it seems important not to shy away from events and practices that have been incorporated into Mahayana Buddhism but which appear to challenge — and even undermine — its most cherished principles. Religious traditions are often messy, inconsistent, and even self-contradictory; rather than airbrush out unflattering blemishes, it may be salutary to allow our gaze to be drawn to them. So while my general attitude towards Mahayana culture is appreciative, this is not incompatible with measured criticism. I find it both sobering and instructive to reflect that, from time to time, even the most sublime aspirations can be hijacked. Mahayana Buddhism has laid out a dazzling vision — or series of visions — of the profound possibilities of human experience. At the same time, these possibilities have been compromised by human failings. Sustaining such a vision in the face of human frailty is perhaps the key challenge of the creative life.

The Structure of the Book

Broadly speaking, the book is divided into two sections. Chapters 1–6 examine the origins of Mahayana Buddhism and then explore some of its fundamental concepts, images, and practices. Chapters 7–12 chart how these concepts, images, and practices have been articulated and developed in East Asia, especially China, Korea, Japan, and finally the contemporary West. Having said this, there is much cross-referencing between different sections of the book and you may find yourself wanting to follow a particular thread, rather than working systematically through each chapter.

To complement the main narrative, the book includes a series of features that highlight specific aspects of Mahayana culture. There is no profound plan governing the content of these but rather a studied arbitrariness; some things just grabbed my interest. Many of the features reveal specific details of thought and practice not normally treated in general works; as such, they function as snapshots of Mahayana life.

Besides this, the book includes a glossary of key terms to assist in recapping the technical ideas covered in the main body. References to further reading are made throughout the text and all cited works are catalogued at the back. In addition, there is a further reading section which offers general suggestions for taking your knowledge of key themes deeper.

1
Entering the Mahayana Imagination

ENTERING THE MAHAYANA IMAGINATION can lead into a dimension that is beyond time, an eternal present where anything and everything is possible, a world of the untrammelled imagination. Here, thought opens out into an infinite inner space beyond the routine of the ordinary mind, so burdened as it is by day-to-day concerns. In many forms of the Mahayana, events unfold on a mind-boggling scale: numbers are huge, distances are vast, timespans are incalculable, imagery is extravagant, and ambitions are epic. It is a world of inner freedom, of myth and creative fantasy. It is characterized by beauty, compassion, even ecstasy. A miraculous episode from a Mahayana scripture called the *Sutra of Golden Light* illustrates this point.[1]

In this text, a devout Buddhist called Ruchiraketu (Ruciraketu; Beautiful Comet) is wrestling with a knotty question concerning the Buddha's lifespan. As he grapples with his problem — and contemplates the Buddha — Ruchiraketu's house starts to expand in all directions, growing infinitely vast and, at the same time, transforming into a glittering, jewelled palace.

In each of the four directions, jewelled lotus-thrones appear and seated on each of these is a resplendent Buddha. Besides this, Ruchiraketu's entire home town begins to radiate celestial light. Still more fantastic, 'the triple-thousand great-thousand world-sphere and world spheres equal to the grains of sand of the Ganges River in all the ten directions became filled with light'.[2] Divine flowers rain down and strains of heavenly music can be heard. Moreover, all those with ailments are miraculously healed, all those in want are satisfied, all those suffering are relieved.

Entering the transcendent dimension of the Mahayana means expanding your own 'house', awakening your creative imagination and, in doing so, being transformed by it. The spiritual vitality of Mahayana Buddhism rests in large part on the power of images, symbols, and myths as agents of individual and collective transformation.

This chapter traces a general impression of Mahayana Buddhism. The Mahayana is not a single, unitary institution but rather a field of spiritual creativity that has inspired a vigorous family of traditions. Having situated

---

[1] *Suvarṇaprabhāsottama -sūtra*, T.663; Emmerick 1990: 3–4.
[2] Emmerick 1990: 4.

Mahayana Buddhism within a broader Buddhist context, the chapter goes on to outline some key Mahayana themes, filled out in later chapters, and characterizes it in terms of a number of distinctive moods. Finally, the historical spread of the Mahayana across Asia is sketched out.

Triyana: The Three Ways of Buddhism

It has been usual to divide Buddhism into three distinct strands or 'ways': Hinayana (Hīnayāna; Little Way); Mahayana (Mahāyāna; Great Way); and Vajrayana (Vajrayāna; Diamond Way).[3] These three strands (triyana: triyāna) are often related to three stages or phases of historical development, each of which originated in India and diversified as it spread further afield. While at first glance this seems like a neat scheme, it legitimizes a none too subtle polemic against the so-called 'Hinayana', implying that it is a less complete means to Awakening than the other two ways. Moreover, some interpret the scheme as a progressive hierarchy with Vajrayana at the top. Putting aside these sectarian readings, the triyana model nevertheless remains a useful starting point.

The first main phase of Buddhist development is usually placed between the time of the historical Buddha (c.484–404 BCE) and the beginning of the Common Era (although it continued to develop after this).[4] Owing to the demeaning connotations of the term 'Hinayana', the sects that evolved during this period are now often referred to as Nikaya Buddhism (nikāya here refers to a division within the sangha or Buddhist spiritual community).[5] These early sects spread across India and later gained considerable influence throughout Asia.

The sole surviving descendent of Nikaya Buddhism is known as Theravada (Theravāda; Doctrine of the Elders) and is widely followed in South and Southeast Asia, including Sri Lanka, Thailand, Burma, Cambodia, and Laos.[6] It has also begun to take root in Western cultures. Sadly, Nikaya Buddhism has been more or less extinct in its birthplace of India for centuries. The geographical distribution of Theravada has led to its being dubbed 'southern Buddhism' by some modern scholars.

The signature image of Theravada is the saffron-robed, shaven-headed monk walking sedately with his alms bowl held in his outstretched hands. This tradition is broadly conservative in outlook and, among other things, emphasizes the renunciation of worldly desires, scrupulous observance of

---

[3] The term yāna is also often rendered as 'path' or 'vehicle'.
[4] The precise dates of the Buddha's life are a matter of much scholarly conjecture and will probably never be definitively settled. Other estimates place his dates at 566–486 BCE.
[5] For a discussion of this term, see Hallisey and Keown 2007: 549–58. The terms 'mainstream Buddhism' and 'early mainstream Buddhism' are also widely used to refer to these sects.
[6] For a study of Theravada Buddhism, see Gombrich 2006.

monastic discipline, and the pursuit of ethical purity. Its ultimate aim is to realize nirvana: release from the endless cycle of birth, death, and rebirth. The Theravada reveres exclusively a specific body of eminent texts known as the Pali Canon.[7]

The second phase of Buddhism is the Mahayana. This probably began to emerge around the beginning of the Common Era, perhaps a little earlier, and is widely believed to have supplanted Nikaya Buddhism. However, it now seems likely that Mahayana remained a minority interest within India for several centuries, even as it had considerable success further afield in Central Asia and then China where it morphed into many different forms. Its early lack of success was a cause of some resentment and we will see later how, in their battle for prestige, converts, and patronage, Mahayana followers disparaged Nikaya teachings. While continuing to emphasize many of the teachings and practices of Nikaya Buddhism, the Mahayana re-envisioned the imaginative context of the individual's quest for liberation, scripting it into a spiritual drama of universal awakening that may unfold over myriad lifetimes. Its rhetoric emphasized the centrality of compassion for all beings as the guiding force of all spiritual endeavour.

The third phase of Buddhism was the Vajrayana or 'Diamond Way', also known as the Tantra.[8] Probably influenced by similar developments within Hinduism, Buddhist Tantric texts began to emerge around the 5th century, although this tradition did not become significant before the 7th century. Tantra incorporates shamanic practices and principles, framing them within a complex synthesis of Mahayana philosophy. It focuses on the invocation and manipulation of psycho-cosmic energies through the use of mantras, visualization, sacred gestures (*mudras*) and diagrams (*maṇḍalas*) in order to bring about ritual mastery and spiritual transformation. It emphasizes secrecy and individual initiation as means of safeguarding the power of its ritual practices, which is why it is also known as esoteric Buddhism. Key to the Tantra is the claim that its practices accelerate the path to Buddhahood, enabling the accomplishment of Awakening in just one lifetime.

Tantric Buddhism spawned a bewildering array of transcendent beings, including 'wrathful' Buddhas, animal-headed protectors, and other luminous figures with multiple heads, arms, and legs. These beings are often the focus of complex and detailed patterns of visualization, invocation, and ritual service.

This form of Buddhism was successfully exported to Tibet and other Himalayan kingdoms, to Mongolia, and to Russia. In time, it was also transmitted to other parts of Asia, most notably Japan, where it informed

---

[7] For a summary of the Pali Canon and related literature, see Pagel 2001.
[8] For an overview of Tantric Buddhism, see Williams with Tribe 2000: 192–244.

the Shingon and Tendai traditions. Owing to the Tibetan diaspora following the Chinese invasion of Tibet in 1951, the magic dust of Tantra has now been scattered across the globe. Tibetan Tantric Buddhism is probably the most visible form of Buddhism in the Western world, partly owing to the high profile of HH the Dalai Lama, who is the spiritual and political leader of the Tibetan people.

1.1 Mahayana Time

Time in Mahayana scriptures is measured in *kalpas* (aeons), or even *mahākalpas* (great aeons). It is almost impossible to grasp how long these periods of time really are. One early scripture illustrates this by means of an image. If there were a solid stone mountain a *yojana* in height (four to nine miles), and it was stroked once every 100 years with a piece of fine cloth, it would wear away before an aeon came to an end.[9] According to one text, it takes 3000 million million great aeons to accomplish the Mahayana path to Awakening.[10]

The Mahayana Family: Six Marks of Mahayana Buddhism

While many have heard of Buddhism, 'Mahayana' is not a widely known word. Yet it is a distinction that is as significant within Buddhism as is Catholicism in the context of Christianity, or Sunni within Islam. Moreover, it is likely that you have already encountered Mahayana Buddhism, even if you were not aware of it at the time. If you have ever visited a Zen garden, seen a picture of HH the Dalai Lama, flicked through Jack Kerouac's *The Dharma Bums*, or listened to *Bodhisattva Vow* by the Beastie Boys, you have been touched by the light of the Mahayana. What is the nature of this light?

Not surprisingly, the Mahayana shares many features with Nikaya and Tantric Buddhism. So what is distinctive about it? It would be wrong to think that there was a single, uniform Mahayana since it is more of an umbrella concept, which shelters a diverse range of teachings, texts, practices, cultures, and languages. As with any general term, it simplifies great complexities, glossing over distinctions that have been of vital significance to those who made them. Nevertheless, in order to make sense of these rich deposits of Buddhist creativity, we need some organizing principles. There are a number of recurring themes that make it possible to link Mahayana Buddhism's diverse incarnations together. The notion of 'family resemblances' may be helpful here. While family members do not

---

[9] SN 2.181–2.
[10] See Harvey 2007: 163.

look exactly alike, they are nevertheless linked by recurring features, which may reappear in unique patterns across many generations. Mahayana Buddhism could be seen as such a family. What resemblances *are* found here? What *are* the marks of Mahayana Buddhism? First, there is a distinctive literature which coalesced in a Mahayana 'canon'. Secondly, there is an emphasis on the universality of the goal of Awakening; in principle, it is for all beings, not just a monastic elite. More than this, Awakening is pursued in a spirit of compassion, the aim being not just to liberate oneself but *all* beings from suffering. Thirdly, there is an emphasis on the transhistorical presence of the Buddha, and the consequent possibility of multiple Buddhas throughout time and space. Fourthly, there are a number of emblematic doctrines, especially shunyata (*śūnyatā* or 'emptiness', 'consciousness-only', and the concept of Buddha-nature. Fifthly, distinctive practices emerged, including new forms of meditation, ritual, and devotion. Finally, there is an emphasis on the unity of Buddhism, underpinned by the principle of skilful means (*upāya-kauśalya*), whereby Mahayana traditions were able to see their own teachings as the culmination of earlier developments. Let's look at these six features in more detail.

1 The Mahayana canon

While there is no definitive Mahayana canon, no set Bible, there is a body of texts whose themes, stories, and doctrines run like seams of gold throughout the history of Mahayana thought and practice. These texts are generally more elaborate than their Nikaya Buddhist counterparts, which some of their creators hoped to supersede.[11]

A leading example of a Mahayana scripture is the *Lotus Sutra*, the nucleus of which was written in India around the 1st century CE.[12] It later became a celebrated text throughout East Asia, inspiring a number of doctrinal developments and spiritual movements over a period of many hundreds of years. It is still widely read and studied today and continues to influence the lives of millions of Mahayana Buddhists.

Some Mahayana scriptures have been described as 'transcendental science fiction'[13] and 'a kind of literature of the fantastic'[14] because they draw us into a world of incalculable dimensions, a cosmos that defies imagining. Whereas in the early Buddhist scriptures there were just humble monks — and perhaps a few favoured lay people — listening to the

---

[11] This theme is exemplified in, for instance, the parable of the magic city found in the *Lotus Sutra*. For a discussion of this, see pp. 43–44. See also Hurvitz 1976: 130ff.

[12] *Saddharma-puṇḍarīka-sūtra*, T.262.

[13] Sangharakshita 1995: 23.

[14] Harrison. 1995: 68.

Buddha's discourses, now there may be myriad beings who travel from incalculable world systems and appear miraculously in order to hear the Buddha's spiritual message. Not merely texts to be read, some Mahayana sutras are more like dramas in which we can *participate* as they unfold a visionary universe before us. These texts may transport us to a magical inner space where our imaginative powers are given free rein; they thus serve not only as extended metaphors for the liberated mind but actively work on freeing it.

But given how many Mahayana scriptures there are — and there are hundreds — it is important to recognize that they are not all uniform. Besides the fantastic imagery of scriptures such as the *Lotus Sutra*, there are other texts which are more restrained, precise, and, in some cases, philosophically abstruse.

1.2 Nikaya Buddhist Canons

The historical Buddha wrote nothing. Instead, his teachings were collected, edited, and transmitted orally for several hundred years. This oral character is evident in the use of repetition, stock formulae, and other structural features that aided memorization and recitation. The mnemonic patterns in which the teachings were embedded allowed many generations of disciples to remember and transmit them before they were eventually written down.

As the Buddhist tradition grew and spread, a number of versions of what became known as the Tripitaka (three (*tri*) baskets (*piṭaka*)) emerged. This comprises the sutra (*sūtra*), vinaya (*vinaya*), and abhidharma (*abhidharma*) pitakas. Sutras (scriptures) are mostly teachings of the Buddha, often set in a narrative context; the vinaya concentrates on monastic discipline; and the abhidharma emphasizes philosophical analysis.

Each of the canons had a common core but over time linguistic and sectarian factors led to differences. The only complete canon produced by the early Buddhist traditions that survives is the Pali Canon, which was preserved by the Theravada monks of Sri Lanka. While this corpus lays claim to be the 'word of the Buddha', it is impossible to know how faithfully it records the Buddha's teachings.

The advent of new sutras marked a shift from the 'closed' textual canons of Nikaya Buddhism, to which new teachings could not be added, to the more 'open' tradition of the Mahayana. Mahayana Buddhism expanded its conception of what could count as authentic Buddhist teaching and this enabled it to innovate and so evolve. There was now room for continuing revelation, including the possibility of teachings being passed on by transcendent Buddhas in the context of meditative experience. The impact of these possibilities will be considered in later chapters.

2 Universal compassion: The bodhisattva ideal

In Mahayana cosmology, the conduct of the individual Buddhist is placed within a universal, mythic context. Spiritual practice is no longer simply an individual, historical matter but a cosmic event, which has significance for all beings. The aim is not just to awaken oneself but, in a spirit of compassion, to liberate the entire cosmos. Moreover, Awakening is not something to be achieved within the present lifetime alone; it becomes an epic quest pursued through numberless rebirths until all beings have been liberated. This new ideal was embodied in the bodhisattva ('awakening being'), the Mahayana saint.[15]

Some later traditions emphasized the possibility of accomplishing this ideal rapidly, even in the present lifetime, while others regarded it as so rarefied that mere mortals could not hope to accomplish it at all through their own efforts. Instead, the bodhisattva path is fulfilled vicariously by a spiritual superhero who, out of supreme compassion, transfers its benefits to less able beings.

3 The transhistorical or cosmic Buddha

While the Buddha of early Buddhism was very special, even unique, he was decidedly human. In Mahayana thought, however, he emerged as a cosmic force, a transhistorical reality that manifests at different times, in different places; he embodies the principle of Awakening. Specific, iconic forms of the Buddha became objects of devotion, aspiration, and petition. He evolved into a celestial being of pure wisdom and compassion with untold powers and abilities. The Buddha expanded to become an eternal, cosmic reality, perpetually reawakening in the universe for the good of all beings.[16]

4 Distinctive systems of ideas

Mahayana Buddhism encompasses several great systems of thought, intricate in their complexity and profound in their aspirations. These systems include Madhyamika (Mādhyamika), which emphasized that all things lacked an independent nature and were consequently 'empty' (shunya: *śunya*) or interdependent; Yogachara (Yogācāra), which highlighted the role of mind in determining our experience; and notions of Buddha-nature, which underlined that all beings have the potential to become Awakened. New ideas often developed to resolve problems inherent in earlier ones; this means that they are often relational in

---

15 This ideal and those who pursue it are discussed more fully in Chapters 3 & 4.
16 Chapter 4 explores the concept of the cosmic Buddha in more detail.

character and that ideas often conflict. In still later systems, dissonant ideas were sometimes reconciled and harmonized in new configurations of thought, such as those found in Pure Land, Chan, and Tiantai Buddhism.[17]

1.3 The Hidden Library at Dunhuang

In 1907, the explorer M. Aurel Stein was engaged in the last of several journeys through Central Asia in search of artefacts and cultural treasure on behalf of the British government. When he arrived at the spectacular complex of rock-cut cave-temples near Dunhuang, northwest China, his hopes of finding anything important were fading. But, after gaining the confidence of a self-appointed guardian of the caves, he learnt that a treasure trove of manuscripts and paintings had been walled up in one of the caves, untouched for a thousand years. Stein eventually succeeded in carrying off some 50,000 manuscripts, paintings, and other materials, including the oldest known printed book: a version of the *Diamond Sutra*. Much of this is now held by the British Museum.

These discoveries, together with material lifted by other archaeologists, have made a significant contribution towards the rewriting of Central Asian Mahayana Buddhism, including Chan and the largely forgotten Three Stages Sect (*see* Feature 6.1). The finds included texts in languages that have long been extinct, some of which took years to decipher. The value of the Dunhuang finds for Buddhist cultural history could be likened to the discovery of Tutankhamen's tomb in the context of Egyptian studies.[18]

---

5 New practices

While Mahayana Buddhism continued to observe many of the practices of Nikaya forms, it sometimes gave them a new twist. For instance, while meditation remained important, the Mahayana introduced new approaches, such as the visualization of cosmic Buddhas or the Chan practice of 'no mind' (*wuxin*), and embedded them within innovative theoretical frameworks. In addition, Mahayana Buddhism also inspired new forms of practice, such as text worship, elaborate devotional rites, and the celebrated koan of Zen Buddhism. Finally, as Mahayana teachings entered new cultural environments, they combined with local customs to produce distinctive forms of practice at both the elite and popular levels. In China,

---

[17] These various approaches are discussed throughout chapters 5–12.
[18] A highly readable account of the race to secure ancient treasures in central Asia, including the Dunhuang finds, is Hopkirk 2006.

for instance, bridge-building attracted the efforts of charitable monks, while in Japan funeral services became central to the life of the local temple.[19]

6 The unity of Buddhism: Skilful means

Skilful means is one of the leading ideas of Mahayana thought, yet it is basically a restatement of the anti-dogmatic outlook of early Buddhism.[20] First, it refers to the compassionate activity of Buddhas and bodhisattvas expressed through giving appropriate teachings, and even through magical apparitions. Secondly, it functions as a transmoral principle that appears to justify not only breaches of the monastic code but even transgressions of basic Buddhist ethics. Finally, it may be used as an interpretive framework or hermeneutic that unifies the seemingly disparate teachings of Mahayana Buddhism and even Buddhism in general.

In a famous parable of early Buddhism, the Buddha compared his teachings to a raft.[21] Their purpose is to ferry us across the river of life's challenges to the far shore of Awakening. Beyond this they have no meaning. Another way of putting this is to say that Buddhist teachings are pragmatic: they function as tools to enable us to reach salvation. This deceptively simple claim has far-reaching consequences. One way of understanding this could be to say that teachings should be evaluated in terms of their outcome, not their origin. The measure of a teaching is thus practical, not theoretical: does it lead in the direction of freedom or doesn't it?

According to Mahayana Buddhism, the Buddhas formulate a range of teachings to address the unique needs of beings and so lead them all towards Awakening; these are skilful means. While on the surface teachings may appear different, on a deeper level they serve the same function and are inspired by the same spiritual wisdom. All Buddhist teachings are united in their common aim of initiating Awakening. This point of view is put forward in the *Lotus Sutra*, which uses a number of parables to illustrate how skilful means works. The most famous of these is the Parable of the Burning House.[22]

In this story, there is a rich man with a great deal of land, many houses and servants. His own house is big and rambling but only has one gate. The house is tumbling down, yet nevertheless many people live there, including the rich man's many children. A fire breaks out in the house and,

---

[19] Many such cultural practices are discussed throughout chapters 5–12.
[20] For a detailed study of skilful means, see Pye 2003.
[21] MN I.134.
[22] See Hurvitz 1976: 58–61.

seeing it, the man thinks, 'I can easily get out of this burning house but my children can't. They are playing games, oblivious of what's happening!' So he calls to them, letting them know that they are in danger and that they must get out immediately. But the children are so absorbed in their games they ignore him. Knowing that time is short, the man devises a plan to entice the children from the house. He tells them that there is a special present waiting for each of them outside the gate: goat-drawn carts, deer-drawn carts, or ox-drawn carts. Perhaps these wouldn't inspire the modern child but it works here — they all come out and are saved. But instead of giving what he promised, the father gives each child an identical cart, even more special than the ones he had promised.

The basic meaning of this parable is that the Buddha addresses the individual on his own terms, presenting the truth in a way that each can understand. In spite of the diversity of teachings, ultimately everyone will attain to the same Awakening through the Buddha's skilful means.

In one elegant move, skilful means binds all Buddhist teachings into a harmonious unity. Not only this, but in the *Lotus Sutra* they are ranked according to a hierarchy, naturally with Mahayana teachings placed at the top. In this way, skilful means is used to confer legitimacy and authority upon teachings that might otherwise be dismissed as bogus.

This is important because Mahayana sutras were not widely accepted at first. Their unpopularity is even acknowledged in the sutras themselves. The *Lotus Sutra*, for instance, dramatizes the hostility towards its Mahayana message by describing an episode where hundreds of monks walk out when the Buddha announces that he has a new teaching to proclaim — the new teaching being the Mahayana.[23] In addition, sutras often warn that this new teaching is difficult to grasp and that many people will not understand it and may even revile it. The unpopularity of Mahayana texts stemmed from the fact that they not only incorporated teachings absent from Nikaya scriptures but included still others that appeared to contradict and even criticize them. In order to build spiritual credibility and gather support, the Mahayana needed to establish legitimacy for its new teachings. This legitimacy is grounded at least partly in the principle of skilful means.

But the parable of the burning house raises an important question: does the father act dishonestly in offering the children different carts but then giving them all the same kind? The sutra's answer is an emphatic 'No'; there is no dishonesty because all the children get safely out of the house. This apparent disregard for conventional ethics is a further key aspect of skilful means. Other texts describe how, out of compassion, Buddhas commit what appear to be serious offences to prevent others from suffering.

---

[23] See Hurvitz 1976: 29.

Not only may they break rules of monastic discipline but even basic ethical precepts.

In the *Sutra on Jnanottara's Questions*, for instance, the Buddha recounts how, in a previous life, he accompanied 500 traders on a sea voyage in search of treasure.[24] Along with the traders travelled an evil robber; the Buddha, with his magical powers, foresaw that the robber would kill all the traders in order to grab all the treasure for himself. The Buddha agonizes over how he can both save the lives of the 500 *and* prevent the robber from falling into hell as a consequence of such evil conduct. He concludes that the only way to save everyone concerned is for him to kill the robber (and so transgress the fundamental principle of non-violence in the process). So this is what he does. The Buddha then explains that he was able to avoid the painful consequences of this highly unethical act because his action was a skilful means, motivated by wisdom and compassion.[25]

Such episodes must have shocked readers — and they were meant to. A Buddhist killing another human being? This transgresses the most basic ethical obligation of non-harm — but such stories were intended not as prescriptions. Rather they illustrated that for Mahayana Buddhists, concern for others is paramount; their first thought is not to help themselves but to benefit others. Moreover, it indicates that compassion overrides everything else, so that if a conflict arises between following monastic etiquette and benefiting others, there is no contest. In Mahayana Buddhism, compassion is trumps. Implicit in this is a critique of Nikaya Buddhism, which — true or not — Mahayana texts portray as exclusively preoccupied with personal salvation, and somewhat obsessed with matters of monastic decorum.

Skilful means does not establish an obvious hierarchy of teachings; consequently, whoever applies it may use it to promote the orthodoxy and supremacy of his own sutra or message, at the expense of some other teaching. For instance, the *Nirvana Sutra* uses it to support a claim that there is a real self — a doctrine that flatly contradicts the basic Buddhist teaching of no-self.[26] As long as it can be grounded in the aspiration towards Awakening, skilful means may legitimate any new doctrine or practice. It is thus an anti-dogmatic and uncompromisingly soteriological principle.

At the same time, it appears to offer scope for rationalization. Couldn't someone use skilful means to rationalize selfish and destructive behaviour,

---

24 *Jñānottara-bodhisattva-paripṛcchā-sūtra*, T.310. For a translation of this scripture, see Chang 1991: 427–68.
25 Chang 1991: 456–7.
26 *Mahāyāna-mahāparinirvāṇa-mahā-sūtra*, T.374. See http://www.nirvanasutra.net/, chapter 12.

or else dredge up some crackpot teaching and claim that it is Buddhist because it 'helps me'? Crucially, in Mahayana Buddhism skilful means is underwritten by the twin principles of wisdom and compassion. Strictly interpreted, skilful means is the province of highly developed spiritual beings whose actions are informed by deep spiritual insight and guided by the warmth of their compassion for all beings.[27]

Moods of the Mahayana

With this framework of marks or family resemblances of Mahayana Buddhism in mind, it is also possible to see that through its specific teachings, practices, and cultural forms, Mahayana Buddhism evokes distinctive atmospheres, even *moods*. A mood could be described as an immersive environment that envelops everything, infusing our experiences with a particular ambience, colour, or emotional tone. For our present purpose, we can identify four prominent moods: the fantastic, the elusive, the contemplative, and the devotional. Let's muse over these in turn.

1 The fantastic

The first — and perhaps most seductive — mood of Mahayana Buddhism is the fantastic. It is evoked through the flamboyant imagery and epic drama that exude from the pages of many Mahayana scriptures. A passage from the popular scripture known as the *Vimalakirti Sutra* illustrates this point.[28] In this text, Shariputra (Śāriputra), an historical disciple of the Buddha, is used as a 'stooge' to highlight the superiority of the Mahayana perspective.[29] For example, at one stage, Shariputra becomes concerned as it approaches noon that the assembled array of cosmic beings has not yet taken lunch, it being against Buddhist monastic rules to eat after midday. (This was no doubt a regular preoccupation of the hungry monk.) The hero of the scripture, Vimalakirti (Vimalakīrti), who functions as a personification of the Mahayana, points out that Shariputra should be more concerned with liberating his mind than with eating.

After this somewhat comic rebuke, Vimalakirti then performs a magical feat, enabling the assembly to see a remote universe called Most Excellent of All Fragrances, located beyond as many universes as there are sands in 42 Ganges rivers.[30] In this infinitely distant universe, there resides a great Buddha called Fragrance Accumulation who teaches entirely through the

---

[27] For a discussion of this point, see Keown 1992: 152ff.

[28] Vimalakīrti-nirdeśa-sūtra, T.475. For a translation of the scripture based on the Tibetan version, see Thurman 1976.

[29] This section refers to chapter 10 of the translation; see Thurman 1976: 78–83.

[30] The Sanskrit name for this universe is *Sarvagandhasugandhā*; this translation is by Sponberg 2007b: 803.

dispersal of beautiful aromas.[31] Vimalakirti then despatches a magical incarnation to collect the remains of that Buddha's lunch. Fragrance Accumulation kindly pours out some of his food, which is saturated with all perfumes, into a small vessel; 90 million of his followers volunteer to accompany the incarnation back to Vimalakirti's house with the meal.

Upon their instantaneous arrival, Vimalakirti creates 90 million lion-thrones for them to sit on. The food spreads perfume throughout 100 universes and countless beings are cleansed in body and mind. But some of the more earth-bound disciples become worried that there will not be enough food to go round. The magical incarnation reassures them.

> If all living beings were to eat for an aeon an amount of this food equal to Mount Meru[32] in size, it would not be depleted. Why? Issued from inexhaustible morality, concentration, and wisdom, the remains of the food of the Buddha contained in this vessel cannot be exhausted.[33]

After all the assembly has had its fill, the food remains undiminished and an exquisite bliss descends on all those present, as divine perfume pours forth from every pore of their skin.

2 The elusive

Besides the cosmic psychedelia that lights up episodes like the one just summarized, the Mahayana can also be a world of intricate, dense, even scholastic philosophy. Its labyrinthine pathways may lead into a world of head-scratching befuddlement, of paradox, and of seeming self-contradiction. Trying to get to grips with Mahayana philosophy can seem like grasping at mist or scooping up the ocean with a teaspoon; it eludes all the conceptual tools we might use to capture it. This passage from the celebrated *Heart Sutra*, a Perfect Wisdom text, is typical of this elusive profundity.

> [F]orm is emptiness and the very emptiness is form; emptiness does not differ from form, form does not differ from emptiness; whatever is form, that is emptiness, whatever is emptiness, that is form, the same is true of feelings, perceptions, impulses, and consciousness.[34]

Such seemingly opaque utterances fill the pages of an entire class of Mahayana literature and may leave the unwary reader (and even the

---

[31] The Sanskrit name of this bodhisattva is *Sugandhakūta* and is translated in various ways eg 'Pinnacle of Excellent Fragrances'. (Sponberg 2007a: 157)

[32] Mount Meru is a mythical mountain and in Indian mythology is regarded as the sacred axis of the universe.

[33] Adapted from Thurman 1976: 81.

[34] *Hṛdaya-sūtra*, T.251; see Conze 1988: 103.

informed one) completely baffled. This is in fact part of their purpose, thus enabling a new kind of understanding to arise, one that transcends the exclusively rational.

3 The contemplative

In contrast to its dense, seemingly meandering philosophy, Mahayana Buddhism may also evoke a mood of exquisite stillness, simplicity, and immediacy. This is especially true of some Chinese and Japanese forms, now widely known as Zen, which exude quietness, contemplation, and spaciousness. It is a world of glowing particulars in which everything is illuminated, disclosing a deeper, numinous reality. In this world, the everyday is celebrated as beautiful, poignant, and revelatory as the following passages illustrate.

> Supernatural power and marvellous activity —
> Drawing water and carrying firewood.[35]

> A monk said to Zhaozhou,
> 'I have just entered the monastery. Please teach me.'
> 'Have you eaten your rice porridge?' asked Zhaozhou.
> 'Yes, I have,' replied the monk.
> 'Then you had better wash your bowl,' said Zhaozhou.
> With this the monk gained insight.[36]

> Damei asked Mazu, 'What is the Buddha?
> Mazu answered, 'This very mind is the Buddha.'[37]

The spiritual dimension is not far off, *kalpas* and millions of light years away, but always immediately and intimately present, the true character of each moment. Consequently, we need not necessarily set out on some marathon quest to find Awakening — just observe the world around us and enter the stillness and clarity inherent within our own minds. In this way, we may awaken here and now. In the words of the Zen mystic, Dōgen:

> When even for a short period of time you sit properly in *samādhi* [meditation], imprinting the Buddha-seal in your three activities of deed, word, and thought, then each and every thing throughout the dharma world is the Buddha-seal, and all space without exception is enlightenment.[38]

---

[35] Attributed to Layman Pang (active late 8th century): cited in Faure 1991: 111.
[36] From *The Gateless Gate* (*Wumen guan*), T.2005, case 7. Adapted from the translation in Sekida 2005: 44. Zhaozhou (Jp. Jōshū, 778–897) was a Chinese Chan master.
[37] From *The Gateless Gate*, case 30: Sekida 2005: 98. Mazu (Jp. Baso, 709–88) was a Chinese Chan master.
[38] *Bendōwa*, translated in Waddell and Abe 2002: 11.

4 The devotional

Finally, Mahayana Buddhism may evoke a mood of joyful devotion, spiritual receptivity, and humble faith.

> I worship the Buddhas, who are like oceans of virtues, mountains gleaming with the colour of gold... I go for refuge to those Buddhas and with my head I bow down to all those Buddhas.[39]

This is often accompanied by a solemn appraisal of one's individual failings and a coming to terms with human fallibility. In some traditions, notably Pure Land Buddhism, this results in a shift of the locus of Awakening away from the individual practitioner towards a transcendent Buddha. Rather than a personal accomplishment, Awakening thus becomes a priceless gift which may inspire overwhelming gratitude, as the following passage makes clear.

> When I consider deeply the Vow of Amida [Buddha], which arose from five kalpas of profound thought, I realize that it was entirely for the sake of myself alone! Then how I am filled with gratitude for the Primal Vow, in which Amida resolved to save me, though I am burdened with such heavy karma.[40]

This may inspire an unwavering commitment to serve the needs of the Buddhas always, to surrender one's individual will and place it at the service of universal salvation. In this way, the devotee becomes a channel through which the Buddhas accomplish their compassionate mission.

The Spread of Mahayana Buddhism

Mahayana Buddhism can be seen as a current of spiritual energy; while its source was India, it swelled as it flowed throughout Asia, depositing spiritual sediment on its course and absorbing cultural and spiritual riches to be scattered further downstream. Its precise source is a matter of debate, since what we know of its origins is limited. Scholars are not sure how it emerged or why, as most surviving evidence comes from Mahayana sources alone and these cannot be trusted for historical accuracy. We do know that this current began to flow west, reaching as far as Persia, and north, where it entered Russia. The Mahayana current also turned eastward, irrigating Central Asia, then China, Korea, Japan, and Vietnam. Finally, it reached as far south as Indonesia and Malaysia.

It left its mark on the countries through which it flowed, marks which, even where Buddhism died out as long as a thousand years ago, are still

---

[39] Emmerick 1990: 14.
[40] CWS: 679.

visible: in gigantic statues etched into cliff faces, in rock-cut temples decorated with Buddhist imagery, in customs, even in language and lifestyle.

The great current of Mahayana Buddhism was carried to all corners of Asia along the course of a river. What was this river? Not the Brahmaputra, not the Ganges, not even the Indus but a river of silk: the Silk Route. The Silk Route refers to a network of pathways crisscrossing Asia, connected by caravans of camels, donkeys, traders, and even pilgrims.[41] Rather than one continuous path, the Silk Route was a vast web of relay stations and so it was rare for anyone to traverse the entire span. Buddhist pilgrims, such as the Chinese monk Xuanzang who travelled from China all the way to India, were the exception rather than the rule.

1.4 The Kamakura Buddha: c.1252–62 CE

One of the most iconic Buddhist images ever created is the Great Buddha (*Daibutsu*) of Kamakura, Japan (*see* Image 1). Cast in bronze and gold, this sculpture is more than 11 metres high and weighs some 120 tonnes. It depicts the cosmic Buddha Amida in a distinctive, 'hunched' sitting posture, which reflects Chinese artistic influence.

When originally constructed, the Daibutsu was sheltered by a wooden temple building. In 1498, this was destroyed by a tsunami; since then, the Buddha has sat exposed to the elements. The consequent discoloration has lent its surface a blue-green patina. Like many colossal Buddha statues of Japan, money to build it was gathered through public donations.

Thus, there was no system in this dissemination of the Mahayana, no master plan; there was no Pope or central leader directing missionaries. Rather, the Mahayana was carried piecemeal into different parts of Central and East Asia. Sometimes later developments were deposited on the banks of new cultures before earlier ones; some developments were not carried forward at all; and sometimes the tradition that reached its final destination — say China — had already been transformed on its journey. Doctrines and practices were constantly reformulated, added to, misunderstood, creatively reinterpreted or just plain made up as they were laid down in new cultural fields. While the Mahayana was born in India, it grew up in Central and East Asia, and arguably reached its maturity in China and Japan.

---

[41] Some scholars and explorers consequently refer to this network as the silk *roads*, in the plural.

In subsequent chapters, our pilgrimage will navigate the course of Mahayana development, pausing to take in some of the main sites and holy places along the route. The journey may at times be tough and seemingly circuitous but, by maintaining a strong resolve, we may eventually find ourselves at the threshold of the Mahayana Treasure Tower and — should we choose to — we may step across it.

2

Tracking the Great Vehicle: The Origins of the Mahayana

FOR A MOVEMENT THAT NURTURED such heroic ambitions, the Mahayana had modest beginnings, so humble in fact that there is no evidence of a significant body of Mahayana devotees in India before the 5th or 6th century CE. This was some six centuries or so after its first texts were written, a time lag that at first glance is puzzling. While scholarly understandings of the origins of Mahayana Buddhism have undergone radical revision in recent decades, it is probably also true to say that there is much that we will never know for certain.

This chapter traces the emergence of this nascent Mahayana Buddhism and, in particular, introduces the abundant spiritual literature that it created. Reflecting on how and why Mahayana Buddhist teachings and texts emerged, in what context, and with what success, we see that a number of widely held assumptions about its early history now seem highly unlikely, and that an accurate portrait of its earliest phase of development may resist capture. Moreover, there is probably no single origin of Mahayana Buddhism, since it emerged as a 'loosely bound bundle'[1] of diverse influences with some overlapping features. But before the particular concerns and focus of early Mahayana Buddhism can be introduced, it is necessary to sketch out a general picture of the religious world that gave birth to it.

Ancient India and the Growth of Buddhism

The first texts that are generally classed as Mahayana were probably written around the beginning of the Common Era. This was some 500 years after the historical Buddha began his ministry or, in traditional terms, 'first turned the Wheel of the Dharma' in the Deer Park at Rishipatana, northeast India. Over that period, Buddhism had devolved into many sects, each with its own canon, ordination lineage, and philosophical system. This early flowering is now often called Nikaya Buddhism but, as noted above, for the Mahayana it was contemptuously dubbed the 'Hinayana': the Little Way. This was because, according to Mahayana polemics, these sects

---

1 Schopen 2003: 492.

focused on individual salvation alone and lacked the compassionate urge to strive for universal liberation which the Mahayana advocated. There is no way of knowing whether or not this characterization of Nikaya Buddhism is accurate, although it is fair to say that it placed less *explicit* emphasis on altruism.

The historical Buddha, Siddhartha Gautama (Siddhārtha Gautama), emerged from a tradition of wandering holy men (*śramaneras*) and his first committed followers initially adopted this lifestyle. Far from being the well-groomed, neatly laundered monk (*bhikṣu*) of picture postcards, these first followers may at times have looked more like vagrants, perhaps in dirty rags, with beards and matted hair. But the wandering lifestyle was soon superseded as the primary expression of Buddhist spirituality. The emergence of the rainy period retreat, when monks settled in one place for a period of about three months, paved the way for permanent monastic establishments, which owned buildings and other property. While it is not known how far settled monasticism had developed before the Buddha's death, it was not long before it became the standard form of Buddhist practice, and it has remained so into modern times.

The Buddha and his sangha (spiritual community) also attracted lay followers who supported the ascetic wanderers by giving alms in the form of food, clothing, and shelter. This resulted in a two-tier religious community, although movement between these tiers was not uncommon. In general, the monks were the full-time practitioners and the lay followers were less committed devotees carrying on regular village or town-based lifestyles. This division between monastic and lay followers has remained central to most Buddhist traditions, including most Mahayana sects, ever since.

The decisive period in the history of early Buddhism began in 268 BCE with the ascent of Ashoka (Aśoka) to the throne of Magadha, a powerful state in what is now northeast India and where Buddhism had taken root. After an initially bloody campaign of expansion, Ashoka converted to Buddhism and began to sponsor missions to propagate its teachings throughout his empire and beyond. These missions carried Buddhism as far afield as Sri Lanka, where it remains to this day, and Gandhara (in modern Pakistan and Afghanistan), where it was later swept away by Islam. Not only this, but Ashoka also supported a huge programme of stupa (*stūpa*) building — supposedly 84,000 of them! A stupa is a form of burial monument, in which the relics of a revered monk, or perhaps even the Buddha, may be interred. Stupas thus became focal points for Buddhist devotion and helped to establish a sacred Buddhist landscape. (*see* Feature 2.2 and Images 13 & 15)

Around the time of Ashoka, the sangha had splintered into at least five sects and this fragmentation continued up to the period when the Mahayana sutras began to appear — and even beyond. By the time of the

Common Era, there were as many as 18 or more Buddhist sects.[2] Thus there was an increasingly complex early Buddhist scene. This complexity should alert us that the emergent Mahayana cannot be characterized as rejecting some monolithic Buddhist organization; while it roundly criticized the doctrines and practices of some early schools, it conserved and even developed others.

While the early schools followed distinct *vinayas* (clerical codes) and disagreed on some important points of doctrine, they all shared the same spiritual goal: nirvana. For the early Buddhists, life was understood as a painful cycle of birth, death, and rebirth and attaining nirvana (literally 'blown out') meant liberation from this. The ideal Buddhist was the *arhat* ('worthy one') who had extinguished all negative habits and who understood, in the words of one classic formula, that 'Birth is destroyed, the holy life has been lived, what had to be done has been done, there is no more coming to any state of being'.[3] The arhat was no longer subject to the process of rebirth, although what happens to him at death is said to be one of the 'undeclared' questions.[4] To many eyes, what seems like an aspiration to cease to be will seem peculiarly negative, and it was in part this emphasis on escape from a painful world that the Mahayana sought to redress. It was also very much an individual goal which doesn't, at least superficially, seem to reflect much compassion for those not yet liberated.

While the goal of the monk was nirvana — attained through the vigorous application of ethics, meditation, and wisdom — the goal of the lay person was a better rebirth, which might then provide ideal conditions from which to 'go forth', become a monk, and live the classic Buddhist life. This meant that a good deal of the lay person's spiritual practice focused on the accumulation of merit (*puṇya*). It still does. Merit can be understood as a kind of spiritual capital gained through giving to the monastic sangha, listening to discourses, observing festivals, and practising the Buddhist ethical precepts. According to the doctrine of karma, merit may then be 'transferred' to the individual's future life. The lay person then is not so much concerned with attaining liberation in this life but with preparing for its possibility in a future one.[5]

---

2 For a discussion of these sects, see Warder 2000: 272–8, 287ff.
3 Found, for instance, at MN III.20.
4 SN IV.374 ff.
5 Karma is a principle that governs human ethics; our actions of body, speech, and mind transform our selves, colour our world, and influence how others respond to us. Central to this is our intention, which may be skilful (*kauśalya*) or unskilful (*akauśalya*). Skilful karmas are rooted in generosity, love, and understanding, while unskilful karmas are rooted in their opposites. In practice, our intentions are often mixed. Many Buddhists believe that skilful conduct will result in a favourable rebirth in the life to come. For an introduction to Buddhist understandings of karma, see Nagapriya 2004.

While it is true that the historical Buddha and some of his disciples are credited with supernormal powers, the overwhelming tone of the early Buddhist scriptures is human; there is an atmosphere of real people living believable lives at a specific time and place. Their spiritual ambition — to become arhats through the attainment of nirvana — was seen as a practical, human goal, achievable within the present lifetime. The ideal practitioner lived a life of renunciation, perhaps of solitude, dedicated to the single-minded pursuit of self-liberation. This arhat ideal was the preserve of the monastic elite, the chosen few.

The contrast between this earth-bound flavour of early Buddhism and that of classic Mahayana sutras couldn't be more profound. I am reminded of the movie *The Wizard of Oz*. Early Buddhism represents the opening scenes, shot in black and white, which depict Dorothy living a humdrum life in Kansas with her dog Toto. But she is then swept up by a tornado and transported to a glorious technicolor world where she skips and sings along the yellow brick road, meeting all sorts of fantastic creatures on her way and having magical adventures. The classic Mahayana world is something like this; it is by comparison a world of scintillating light and exquisite colour, of visionary drama and magical display. How can we account for this dramatic transformation?

The Emergence of the Mahayana

The exact origins of the Mahayana may never be known. Given that it became extinct in India and parts of Central Asia as long as a thousand years ago (*see* pp.115–16), its early records have long since been lost, destroyed by later civilizations, or otherwise buried by the sands of time. At present, we don't know precisely when the first Mahayana texts were created, where they were authored, by whom, or in what institutional context. Moreover, it is unlikely that there was any single event that signalled the emergence of this new spiritual current. A chronological perspective inevitably compresses events which may take place over decades, even hundreds of years, and therefore makes them appear more revolutionary and less evolutionary than they often are. Instead, then, let us suppose a steady period of gestation, of the gradual development and refinement of new ideas, distinctive practices, particular imagery, and literature. Imagine a largely forgotten proto-Mahayana that laid the ground for the glittering array of later Mahayana creations.

In tracing the origins of the Mahayana, historians have two main sources to draw on: texts and archaeological finds. First, there is a vast body of texts, which have collectively become known as the Mahayana sutras, along with a mountain of commentaries and sub-commentaries on these. However, none of the sutras is individually authored, nor are they dated. Aside from the survival of the sutras themselves, there is precious little written evidence confirming that the Mahayana even existed as a movement at that time. For instance, Faxian, a Chinese Buddhist pilgrim who travelled across Central Asia to India and Sri Lanka between 399 and 414 CE, left a record of his journey which offers valuable glimpses of the state of Buddhism at the end of the 4th century.[6] What is strange is that Faxian failed to note any Mahayana activities in India, yet he travelled there around four centuries after scholars believe the first Mahayana texts were written.

The second form of evidence is archaeological, especially epigraphical material, which has been studied more intensively in recent decades.[7] This consists of inscriptions, such as donative messages on statues, stupas, or in caves. In addition, there are Buddha images, monastic ruins, and other archaeological residues of Buddhist life that we can draw on to piece together an impression of the early Mahayana.

The Evolution of Mahayana Scriptures

Mahayana Buddhism produced a vast body of literature. While a good deal of this dates from its Indian period, the production of sutras, commentaries, and apocrypha continued for hundreds of years.[8] The Chinese Mahayana Canon stands as the largest body of religious literature ever created by human beings. As with nearly everything concerning the Mahayana, its scale is staggering. This is without even counting the many sutras that have been lost to the historical record, others that survive only as fragments, and still others that have been deemed spurious.

Not only did the Mahayana inspire a vast number of texts but many of these texts exist — or existed — in more than one recension since they often evolved over long periods of time. Typically, later recensions will be longer since, over time, sutras tended to accrete more material. It is as though a sutra exerted a gravitational influence, sucking in more material and so growing larger. One of the largest Mahayana texts, the *Flower Ornament Sutra*, exceeds 2000 pages in English and, as it developed, swallowed up several other sutras whole.[9]

Besides this, many of these texts survive in several ancient languages and not always in their original tongue. In the process of translation, sutras

---

[6] For a translation of this record, see Legge 2006.

[7] See, for instance, Schopen 2005.

[8] The concept of apocrypha is a difficult one in Buddhism, especially in relation to Mahayana Buddhism. Since there has never been a formal process of closing the canon, whether something is counted as a genuine scripture or as apocrypha may be a matter of dispute. This area is considered in Buswell 1990.

[9] *Avataṃsaka-sūtra*, T.279, incorporates the *Daśabhūmika-sūtra* and the *Gaṇḍavyūha-sūtra*. For a translation, see Cleary 1993.

often evolved; some material was omitted and new passages incorporated, perhaps to update the text in the light of doctrinal developments or to adapt it to a new cultural context. The earliest versions of Mahayana sutras that survive may in themselves consolidate two centuries of development.

Visionary Literature: The Style of Mahayana Scriptures

The style of the classic Mahayana scriptures is elaborate when compared with the Nikaya texts. This is in part due to the shift from the oral tradition that produced and preserved much of the early Buddhist canons to the literary tradition which played a major role in the development of Mahayana scriptures. While the form of the early scriptures was shaped for ease of memorization, and often for collective recitation, Mahayana scriptures, being primarily written documents, exhibit greater literary creativity. Consequently, Mahayana sutras tend to be longer, more elaborate, and more innovative than their Nikaya counterparts. All of these elements owe something to the emergence of writing as a means of preserving spiritual teachings. While plundering many of its structural elements, these new texts creatively recast the earlier material, often situating it in the context of visionary dramas that unfold in 'a universal sacred space that was at once everywhere and yet nowhere in particular'.[10] Many of the Mahayana sutras thus become visual extravaganzas, commonly emphasizing what is *seen* above what is *heard*.

It has been suggested that besides creating an aesthetically rich and symbolically charged visual universe, the imagery of Mahayana sutras also serves a legitimizing and even polemical function.[11] While the Nikaya Buddhists could only *hear* the transmitted teachings of the Buddha, the followers of the Mahayana might also *see* him in a glorious, immaterial light-body, and even receive new revelations.

The opening of the *Flower Ornament Sutra*, for instance, describes in lavish detail a scene where incalculable numbers of Buddhas and bodhisattvas appear from distant galaxies and make all kinds of magical offerings to the Buddha. But his historical disciples — such as Shariputra and Maudgalyayana — are seemingly unaware of the jaw-dropping scenes unfolding before them. The sutra explains that this is because they lack the necessary roots of goodness and, in particular, lack compassion for others.[12] The ability to witness the visionary dramas that unfold within Mahayana sutras confirms a higher spiritual attainment; the Mahayanist participates in an expanded universe, a world of limitless creative possibilities, whereas the 'mere disciple' is stuck in humdrum reality.

---

10   McMahan 1998: 272.
11   McMahan 1998: 269.
12   Cleary 1993: 1146-50.

A leading scholar has suggested that two of the most distinctive characteristics of Mahayana sutras are the concept of *samādhi* (vision-world) and the related practice of creative visualization.[13] It may be that the purpose of a sutra is not simply to describe a vision-world but to *create* it through functioning as a template for visualization. The sutras do not necessarily depict something that is already there but are 'blueprints for something to be constructed in the mind'.[14] They are not just to be read but performed, like the script for a play or the score for a piece of music. They are dramas in which the reader participates.

To 'read' a Mahayana sutra, then, is not just to follow the words but to enter the vision-world that the text evokes. A sutra records the directions for an imaginative journey, and the pilgrim progresses through its stages on his unique path of inner transformation. It may be that, far from representing a new programme for practical conduct, the Mahayana path was, to a significant degree, an exercise in creative visualization; not just a fantasy but a rigorous discipline of meditative visualization resulting in profound personal transformation. The bodhisattva path may thus 'constitute a kind of dream, a dream deliberately engaged in, of unlimited power, bliss and freedom from the shackles of ordinary reality, of purity and perfection'.[15]

Any given sutra may have represented only a tiny literate constituency, perhaps a small study group. Preservation in writing allowed new insights to endure and be taken up at later times by future practitioners. Consequently, there was a greater possibility that individual insights would survive than there had previously been, when their preservation depended on collective memory. Writing allows for individual virtuosity, even idiosyncrasy, enabling the minority to consolidate its spiritual legacy for posterity. This may well explain why so many Mahayana scriptures survive from a time when Mahayana practice was only a marginal interest; they are not a testament to the popularity of Mahayana forms of religious practice but rather to the durability of writing.[16]

Mahayana Scriptures and the Problem of Authenticity

Mahayana Buddhism may have originated as an attempt to shift the focus of religious practice back from devotion and giving towards doctrine,

---

13 Harrison 2003.
14 Harrison 2003: 122.
15 Harrison 2003: 146.
16 A satirical take on this theme is found in Will Self's novel *The Book of Dave: A Revelation of the Recent Past and the Distant Future* (2007). The story focuses on a text written by a mentally-ill London cabdriver to his estranged son, which remains buried for hundreds of years but is rediscovered after a period of cata–strophic flooding and inspires a new religion. For instance, certain parts of the book are treated as 'hymns', whereas in reality they represent sections of the famed 'knowledge' of London cabbies.

although this did not last long. It quickly replicated the functions of relic worship through text cults, which centred on devotion to specific Mahayana scriptures.[17] The emergence of these scriptures signals a shift from a closed scriptural tradition to one of continuing revelation. But from the outset the promoters of these new texts faced the problem of legitimacy. How could these emerging sutras, with apparently innovative teachings, be accepted as authentic?

The legitimacy of Nikaya Buddhist scriptures had rested on the claim that they embody 'the word of the Buddha' (*buddhavacana*).[18] According to tradition, after the Buddha's death his teachings were orally collated and then authenticated through formal councils. The canon was then closed, which meant that no new scriptures could be admitted. Since Mahayana scriptures were not included, they were regarded as inauthentic by those committed to this understanding of buddhavacana.

However, Mahayana Buddhists claimed that their scriptures too embodied the word of the Buddha; many of their texts adopted the format of early Buddhist works, with teachings usually being attributed to the Buddha. While this structural imitation could be dismissed as a dishonest tactic to establish authority for spurious teachings, the creators of these texts probably saw it rather differently. Rather than as authors in the modern sense, they may have regarded themselves as more like messengers, receiving and then transmitting a new teaching from a higher source.

The Nikaya canons themselves had recognized the authenticity of 'inspired speech' (*pratibhāna*), which enabled the utterances of a disciple to be embraced as Awakened speech (usually when authorized or certified by the Buddha himself). This possibility is expanded upon in Mahayana scriptures, as the following passage makes clear.

> Whatever … the Lord's Disciples teach, all that is to be known as the Tathagata's [the Buddha's] work. For in the dharma demonstrated by the Tathagata they train themselves, they realise its true nature, they hold it in mind. Thereafter nothing that they teach contradicts the true nature of dharma. It is just an outpouring of the Tathagata's demonstration of dharma.[19]

This shows that teachings given by Awakened masters other than the Buddha may also be regarded as buddhavacana.

---

[17] See Schopen 1975. This seminal article has been reprinted in Schopen 2005. See also Schopen 2003: 497. Note: the term cult is used throughout this book not in the contemporary, pejorative sense to signify some exclusive — and often dubious — religious group; rather, it identifies a specific form of religious belief and practice associated with a cultic focus such as a book, image, or transcendent figure.

[18] For a more detailed examination of *buddhavacana*, see MacQueen 1981.

[19] AP, 4; Conze 1994: 83.

Moreover, the Mahayana scriptures need not be read as grounding their authorship in the *historical* Buddha.[20] A recurring feature of Mahayana scriptures is the presence of the Buddha as a transhistorical reality who may be encountered in dreams, within meditation, or through visionary experiences, in the context of which he continues to reveal the Dharma. In addition, some texts exalt Awakened gnosis, or 'Perfect Wisdom' (*prajñapāramitā*), as the 'mother of the Buddhas'.[21] It is through their attainment of perfect wisdom that the Buddha or Buddhas gain authority and, consequently, anyone else who possesses this wisdom merits that same authority. Through the presence of perfect wisdom, the Buddha lives on: 'as long as the perfection of wisdom is current in the world the Tathagata [Buddha] still abides, the Tathagata still teaches the dharma'.[22] Besides this, 'One should consider those beings who hear ... the perfection of wisdom ... as living in the presence of the Tathagata'.[23] In short, wisdom itself is the ground of authenticity, rather than a specific person or text.

Passages like these indicate a tension between differing models of practice and different conceptions of the Buddha. One conception regards the Buddha as a continuing individual presence whose relics may be worshipped via stupas, or who may reveal himself in the context of meditation. The second conception, embodied in the Perfect Wisdom literature (*see* Chapter 5), suggests a more abstract Buddha, embodied in the Dharma, who continues to be accessible through individual realization. This second conception appears to follow a maxim attributed to the historical Buddha: 'One who sees the Dharma sees me; one who sees me sees the Dharma.'[24] Both of these models became significant in Mahayana Buddhism, consolidating into Buddha cults and text cults respectively.

Mahayana scriptures may have been revealed through the inspired speech of dharma-preachers (*dharmabhānaka*). The dharma-preacher probably fulfilled several key functions. First, he was a guardian of the scripture to which he was devoted, and may well have possessed a manuscript of it. Secondly, he was a repository and voice for it, since he had it memorized and could recite it for the faithful — he was a talking book.[25]

---

[20] See MacQueen 1982.
[21] AP, 254; Conze 1994: 172.
[22] AP, 529; cited in MacQueen 1982: 53.
[23] MacQueen 1982: 53.
[24] SN III.120. Here, *dharma* is given for *dhamma*, the Pali form of the Sanskrit *dharma*.
[25] This kind of scenario is nicely illustrated in Ray Bradbury's (b. 1920) science fiction novel, *Fahrenheit 451*, published in 1953. In a dystopian future, all books have been banned. A few outcasts, resistant to the prevailing authority structure, take it upon themselves to memorize entire books, of which they become the guardians, able to recite them upon request until such time as printing is once again allowed.

Finally, he was a source of spontaneous, inspired speech and so could fire the enthusiasm of his congregation.[26]

Inspired speech could be understood in two ways. First, it could be seen as a result of channelling the Buddha's presence, whereby the dharma-preacher functioned as a divine messenger. Secondly, the dharma-preacher may have personally realized the truth of the Dharma, enabling him to communicate his inspiration spontaneously to others. The words of the dharma-preacher are guaranteed, or certified, by Perfect Wisdom and, consequently, what he revealed under its inspiration may be considered buddhavacana. Mahayana sutras thus embody a new understanding of buddhavacana, one that allows for continuing revelation through the medium of inspired preachers pouring forth their spiritual enthusiasm. The written sutras, at least in part, represent consolidations of such processes.

2.1 The Creation of the Mahayana Canon

The emergence of a distinct Mahayana canon can be traced to the production of sutra catalogues, which began in China in the late 4th century CE. These catalogues sought to differentiate between 'authentic' and 'spurious' Mahayana sutras in order to safeguard the integrity of Buddhist teachings and bolster their authority. However, the corpus of texts accepted as authentic include a number that are clearly of Chinese origin, again reinforcing the fluidity of what is categorized as 'canon'.

For centuries, scriptures were handcopied. The first printed Mahayana canon was sponsored by the Chinese government and was completed in 983 CE. The monumental task of carving 130,000 wood blocks took 12 years. A number of versions have followed but the standard modern canon is the *Taishō shinshū daizōkyō* published in Tokyo in the 1920s and 1930s. The *Taishō* comprises 55 volumes of around a thousand pages each, along with a supplement of 45 additional volumes, which include Japanese works, newly discovered material, catalogues of iconography, and bibliographies.

The Mahayana canon includes not only sutras but also centuries of commentarial writings. It also incorporates early Buddhist canonical material, although it regards this as incomplete. Unlike Nikaya canons, it is not 'closed', which means that there is no doctrinal reason why further material could not be added over the coming centuries.[27] (*see also* Feature 2.3)

---

[26] MacQueen 1982: 55 ff.
[27] For more on the production of Buddhist scriptures, see Mizuno 1982.

The Character of Early Mahayana Buddhism

How and why the Mahayana emerged, and what it looked like in its earliest phases, have all been matters of scholarly dispute and may always remain so. The majority of opinion has shifted dramatically in recent decades as more Mahayana sources have been put under the microscope and previous judgements have been interrogated more thoroughly. Given that a number of outdated assumptions about the nature of the early Mahayana continue to prevail, it may help to situate the latest thinking in relation to previous theories by giving brief consideration to six topics.

1. The relationship between the Mahayana and Nikaya Buddhist ideals
2. The structure of the Mahayana community
3. The scale of the Indian Mahayana movement
4. Mahayana forms of worship
5. The institutional context of the early Mahayana
6. The nature of the bodhisattva in the Mahayana

1 The relationship between the Mahayana and Nikaya Buddhist ideals

When we consider traditions that we are not familiar with, we are bound to frame them through our own cultural lens. The Mahayana may be a case in point. It has been represented by some scholars as a kind of Buddhist reformation, a protest against a corrupt 'Hinayana', with the aim of restoring the original message of the Buddha. On this reading, Nikaya Buddhism is seen as having lost its spiritual vitality; it had become stuffy, one-sidedly monastic and scholastic, and lacking in generosity and compassion. The arhat ideal is seen as having become too inward looking, even spiritually selfish. In contrast to this, the Mahayana's message is feted as a return to the spirit of early Buddhism — a restatement of the importance of compassion in Buddhist practice, and of the belief that all of us can gain Awakening, regardless of our present spiritual condition.

However, since this reading is drawn from Mahayana accounts of its own origins, it cannot be confirmed independently. Not only this, but the term 'Hinayana' as used in Mahayana texts does not necessarily refer to a particular school or body of doctrine but, according to one scholar, 'whomever we, the speakers, do not at the present moment agree with doctrinally or otherwise here in our discussion'.[28] To assume that the 'Hinayana' of Mahayana polemics is identical with the Nikaya Buddhism of the time — in itself not a monolithic entity — is to be seduced by the Mahayana's own rhetoric. It may well be that the degenerate 'Hinayana' is a

---

[28] Silk 2002: 367.

straw man, knocked down to establish the credibility of Mahayana teachings, which were rejected (if not simply ignored) by mainstream Buddhist schools of the time.

Evidence suggests that use of the pejorative term 'Hinayana', in contrast to the affirmative term 'Mahayana', didn't emerge before the 3rd century CE.[29] Before this characterization, it appears that the arhat ideal and the Mahayana's bodhisattva ideal co-existed reasonably harmoniously. In an early Mahayana scripture known as the *Inquiry of Ugra*, for instance, the arhat and bodhisattva ideals are both accepted as legitimate, although clearly distinct, ideals.[30] Here, the bodhisattva ideal is *not* advanced for everyone (as it is in classic Mahayana doctrine) but only for the exceptional few; for everyone else, the arhat ideal is recommended. Moreover, when he eventually becomes a Buddha some time in the distant future, the bodhisattva will teach others the arhat and *not* the bodhisattva path.

While the arhat ideal was seen as attainable within the present lifetime, in its classic formulation the bodhisattva ideal was believed to take many lifetimes to accomplish. So why bother? It is usual to point to the compassionate motivation of the bodhisattva to liberate others from suffering but in early accounts of this ideal, it seems that personal ambition was a key motivator; imagine the glory in becoming the highest kind of being in the universe: a world-redeeming Buddha.[31]

2 The structure of the Mahayana community: Lay revolution or monastic conservatism?

The distinguished scholar Etienne Lamotte and others have interpreted the incipient Mahayana as a lay reaction to monasticism.[32] This again resonates with the notion of a Buddhist reformation breaking free of the shackles of a corrupt and inward looking clergy. The bodhisattva is portrayed as someone who transcends the confines of the monastic code, who breaks free of the stuffy literalism of monkish rules. This ideal of an apparently lay bodhisattva who is not only on a par with his monastic counterparts but in fact their spiritual superior is beautifully, and at times comically, illustrated through the figure of Vimalakirti in his eponymous scripture.

---

29 Harrison 1987: 80. See also Nattier 2003: 172–4.
30 See Nattier 2003.
31 Nattier 2003: 145–7.
32 Hirakawa Akira is another scholar supporting this approach. For a succinct discussion of Hirakawa's position, which is elaborated in Japanese works, see Nattier 2003: 89–93. For a critique of both Lamotte and Hirakawa's view, see Silk 2002: 376–82.

He wore the white clothes of the layman, yet lived impeccably like a religious devotee. He lived at home, but remained aloof from the realm of desire, the realm of pure matter, and the immaterial realm. He had a son, a wife, and female attendants, yet always maintained continence. He appeared to be surrounded by servants, yet lived in solitude. He appeared to be adorned with ornaments, yet always was endowed with the auspicious signs and marks. He seemed to eat and drink, yet always took nourishment from the taste of meditation. He made his appearance at the fields of sports and in the casinos, but his aim was always to mature those people who were attached to games and gambling ... He understood the mundane and transcendental sciences and esoteric practices, yet always took pleasure in the delights of the Dharma. [...]

To train living beings, he would appear at crossroads and on street corners, and to protect them he participated in government. To turn people away from the Hinayana and to engage them in the Mahayana, he appeared among listeners and teachers of the Dharma. To develop children, he visited all the schools. To demonstrate the evils of desire, he even entered the brothels. To establish drunkards in correct mindfulness, he entered all the cabarets.[33]

This is surely no ordinary layman! In fact, it would perhaps be more accurate to say that Vimalakirti appears in the *guise* of a layman. He is more like a powerful magician than a lay person, able to move freely in any sphere of society as a means towards helping beings to make spiritual progress. His spiritual virtues are so developed that nothing can corrupt his mind. More than an individual, Vimalakirti is the personified spirit of the Mahayana, at least as imagined by some of its writers.

The *Vimalakirti Sutra* was to become very popular in East Asia, and remains so, at least in part because it appears to elevate the position of the lay bodhisattva. But this representation of a bodhisattva as a layman is the exception rather than the rule; in most Mahayana sutras, the bodhisattvas are monks and the position of the lay bodhisattva is subordinate to them.[34] Besides this, the female state was regarded as less advantageous for making spiritual progress and the title of bodhisattva is generally withheld from them.[35] For all its apparent revolutionary universalism, early Mahayana Buddhism appears to conform to the belief that women are spiritually disadvantaged.

Far from being a lay movement, the early Mahayanists were almost certainly monks. It has been suggested that they upheld and promoted the

[33] Thurman 1976: 20–1.
[34] See Nattier 2003, especially 75–8.
[35] See Nattier 2003: 96-100.

ideal of the forest ascetic and re-emphasized the importance of meditation as against the mainstream of settled monasticism where its role was declining.[36] One leading scholar has argued that, far from being a revolutionary, popular movement, the earliest Mahayana was most likely monastic and conservative, concerned with reviving principles and practices that may have fallen into neglect.[37]

2.2 The Stupa or Pagoda

The stupa (or pagoda as it is known in East Asia and parts of Southeast Asia) began as a burial mound or reliquary but in time developed into a complex architectural monument. According to tradition, the Buddha requested that when he died a stupa should be made and his remains placed inside.[38] In time, stupas became objects of ritual worship because they were seen to be pervaded by the charisma of the saint or Buddha whose relics were held there.

It was common for wealthy people, including monks, to pay for the construction of stupas as a means of gaining merit for themselves. For the everyday pilgrim, the stupa was an object of worship to be reverenced, entreated, and even given gifts. Above all, the pilgrim circumambulated the stupa in a clockwise direction, usually chanting and sometimes prostrating all the way round, repeating this many times.

As the Mahayana developed in China, Indian relics became highly prized and many stupas (pagodas) were built to house them. Pilgrims travelling to India sought not only Buddhist texts and teachings but also relics. High demand led not only to the 'discovery' of local Chinese relics but also to relic trading and even theft.[39]

One of the most famous of all Buddhist stupas is the one at Borobudur on the island of Java, which was completed in the 9th century CE (*see Image 15*). This huge construction, erected using approximately 55,000 cubic metres of lava-rock, functions as a pilgrimage route, leading the pilgrim higher and higher towards the summit of Awakening. Its various walls are decorated with scenes from the *Gandavyuha Sutra* depicting the pilgrimage of Sudhana. (*see* pp.131)

---

3 The scale of the Indian Mahayana movement

Until recent decades, it was believed that when the Mahayana emerged, it supplanted Nikaya Buddhism, then the mainstream Buddhist movement in

---

[36] See Harrison 1995 for example.
[37] Schopen 1999, reprinted in Schopen 2005.
[38] DN II.141–2.
[39] Kieschnick 2003: 37.

India. However, this picture of a large-scale Indian Mahayana is now widely discredited. From the 2nd century CE onwards, Mahayana Buddhism became increasingly influential in China, as well as in various Central Asian states. Before very long, the Mahayana became the dominant form of Buddhism in China and several Silk Route states. Given this apparently widespread influence in Central and East Asia, scholars have tended to assume that Mahayana Buddhism must also have been influential in India.[40]

It seems that this was not so. There is no evidence for the Mahayana being a significant influence in India before the 5th or 6th century CE. In other words, the Mahayana was a minority movement in its country of birth for its first 500 years or so. It may be that Mahayana followers proselytized beyond India not because of their relative success but because of their marginality.[41] The volume of literature that the Mahayana generated in its Indian period has undoubtedly contributed to an exaggeration of its influence there.

4 Mahayana forms of worship

Hirakawa Akira, an influential Japanese scholar, has argued that the early Mahayana focused on stupa worship, which he identifies as a specifically lay form of Buddhist practice frowned upon by monks.[42] This theory has been decisively discredited since it is clear that stupa worship was already a wide-spread activity within Nikaya Buddhism. The study of donative inscriptions has shown that not only lay people but monks and nuns regularly sponsored the erection of stupas, believing that in doing so they would benefit spiritually.[43] As noted above, the Emperor Ashoka is thought to have sponsored the building of 84,000 stupas across his vast territories.

Gregory Schopen has argued that, far from fostering devotional practices, in its earliest phases of development, the Mahayana critiqued them, aiming to restore the principle of *emulation* of the Buddha, not simply of devotion to his relics or image.[44] The *Perfection of Wisdom in 8000 Lines*, for instance, explicitly argues for the reverence of Awakened realization above that of physical relics.[45]

While the impetus of early Mahayana may have been to 'send monks back to their books', this was soon eclipsed by the spread of text worship and the later absorption of the stupa cult and relic worship into Mahayana

[40] Schopen 2000, reprinted in Schopen 2005.
[41] Schopen 2005: 17.
[42] Hirakawa 1990: 270–74.
[43] Schopen 1997: 31–2.
[44] Schopen 1999: 307–8.
[45] *Aṣṭasāhasrikā-prajñāpāramitā-sūtra*, T.227–8; AP, 94–5: Conze 1994: 116–17.

practice.[46] These developments were connected with the development of a sacred geography, which established physical sources of spiritual blessing. Sutra worship, as opposed to the study of doctrine, became a leading feature of Mahayana Buddhism, as is illustrated, for instance, in Nichiren Buddhism where the *Lotus Sutra* became the primary object of veneration (*see* p.206ff).

Mahayana texts associated the recitation, copying, and memorization of sacred scriptures with accruing spiritual virtue, which in part may have been a survival tactic to help ensure its teachings were not neglected. Ironically, then, while proto-Mahayana Buddhists may have rejected worship in favour of emulation and doctrinal study, Mahayana Buddhism survived and thrived owing to its incorporation of devotional themes, including devotion to cosmic Buddhas, stupas, relics, and texts.

2.3 The Rock-cut Canon

In the early 7th century, a Chinese monk began carving a small selection of scriptures on limestone slabs at Yunzhu monastery to the southwest of modern Beijing.[47] He intended to inscribe just a few key texts — there was no master plan — yet more than five centuries later monks were still adding to his legacy.[48] Today 14,620 slabs survive, mostly carved on both sides, which incorporate hundreds of texts, some known only through these inscriptions. Beside this, many of the carvings represent the oldest datable versions of their texts. Some of the slabs are almost two metres long, 3–4 inches thick, and weigh several hundred pounds.

To protect the slabs from erosion, nine caves were excavated on neighbouring Mt. Baidai; the slabs were then placed inside and the caves sealed. Most of these precious records remained undisturbed until the middle of the 20th century, when rubbings were taken. Once these were complete — a process that took three years — all slabs were replaced and the caves sealed once more.

There was no systematic order to the carving, and some especially valued texts — like the *Heart Sutra* — were inscribed several times. Once a year, on the Buddha's birthday, newly finished slabs were interred. Typically, carvings were sponsored by groups of donors as means to generate merit.

---

[46] See Schopen 2003: 497.

[47] This account is based on Lancaster 1989.

[48] The bulk of the carvings were complete by the end of the 12th century but there were some Ming additions, notably a translation of the *Gandavyuha Sutra*. (Lancaster 1989: 151)

5 The institutional context of the early Mahayana

Both Hirakawa and Lamotte believed that the early Mahayana established new institutional forms and represented a distinct, coherent movement.[49] However, this claim now seems doubtful. Part of the problem here is the assumption that the term 'Mahayana' refers to a single, unified phenomenon. It is perhaps better seen as a heuristic: a useful umbrella term for finding our way through a particular body of texts, doctrines, and practices. As a descriptive term, 'Mahayana' did not emerge until some several centuries after the first so-called Mahayana sutras.[50] In some respects then, the term 'Mahayana' has been used retrospectively to confer a sense of order and unity upon something that was much less organized and coherent when it first emerged.

It is worth noting that the Mahayana in India never developed a distinct monastic vinaya but rather relied on the vinayas already developed by existing Buddhist sects. This means that the authors of the Mahayana sutras were most probably monks ordained within Nikaya sects, rubbing shoulders with other monks who upheld the arhat ideal. So it seems more likely that Mahayana represented a particular *orientation* to practice, and a specialist area of interest — at least in its early phases — rather than the radical critique of the arhat ideal that it eventually evolved into.

6 The nature of the bodhisattva in the early Mahayana

More than anything, the Mahayana is associated with the bodhisattva ideal and, in particular, celestial or cosmic bodhisattvas like Avalokiteshvara (Avalokiteśvara), who may be called upon to offer both spiritual or material support.[51] However, in its earliest incarnations, the bodhisattva ideal was something that individual practitioners aspired to accomplish. The 'celestial' bodhisattvas were not the initial focus of interest but became important only later on. The same goes for cosmic Buddhas. Owing to the emphasis on devotion towards transcendent figures in East Asian Mahayana Buddhism, it has been assumed that early Indian Mahayana shared this same characteristic. But few of the figures who were to become central to the East Asian tradition were significant in India, and even then, only relatively late on. The earliest Mahayanists were interested not in *worshipping* Buddhas — they aspired to *become* Buddhas. Even when, centuries later, celestial Buddhas and bodhisattvas became the objects of cult worship, this aspiration to emulate the Buddhas of the past remained.

---

[49] See note 32 above.
[50] Schopen 2003: 493.
[51] See Chapters 3 and 4.

A Tentative Sketch of the Early Mahayana

Given the many gaps in the historical record, scholars can only try to piece together the scraps they have to form some impression of the early phases of Mahayana development. What did it look like? First, the Mahayana emerged firmly from *within* the Nikaya tradition. Its earliest forms arose not as rejections of Nikaya Buddhism but to shift emphasis in relation to practice. In particular, it may have rejected the emphasis on stupa worship in favour of an emphasis on doctrinal study, only later incorporating devotional elements such as the worship of texts as well as cosmic Buddhas and bodhisattvas.

Mahayana sutras may be the products of cloistered monks, but they could also have been written by small groups of forest renunciate-type practitioners, given how some Mahayana sutras revere this lifestyle. Overwhelmingly, these texts do not exalt a lay ideal but primarily continue to emphasize monasticism. In addition, the early Mahayana movement was probably a fragmentary, somewhat nebulous phenomenon and attained coherence only after a long period of gestation. Above all, though, the Mahayana was for several centuries no more than a minority influence within Indian Buddhism. Nevertheless, many of the main doctrinal and practical forms of Mahayana Buddhism were established during its Indian phase and these were to transform the spiritual landscape of East Asia forever.

3

Pilgrims Through Cosmic Space:
The Bodhisattva Ideal

THE BODHISATTVA IDEAL, which embodies the aspiration to guide all beings to Awakening, is the jewel in the Mahayana crown. This chapter evokes its cosmic scope and outlines its main features. After highlighting the key moment in the life of the bodhisattva — the arising of the bodhichitta (*bodhicitta*) — which transforms the workaday individual into a cosmic superhero dedicated to the salvation of all beings, it then traverses the traditional ten stages (*bhūmis*) of the bodhisattva career, alongside the six (or ten) perfections (*pāramitās*), which provide the framework for the bodhisattva's ethics and offer a visionary template for his spiritual journey. More practically, we can then evaluate how this ideal could be approached today, reflecting in particular on how far it can be seen as a guide for individual spiritual practice.

Moving on from the arhat of Nikaya Buddhism to the bodhisattva ideal of the Mahayana is to be transported from a terrestrial to a cosmic stage, from the commonplace to the fantastic. The life of the ideal Buddhist now unfolds within a universal context, nothing less than the salvation of all beings. The bodhisattva participates in a cosmic process: the Awakening of the entire universe. No longer is he some humble monk begging food from the village but an intrepid pilgrim on a quest through infinite time and infinite space, a cosmic adventurer who will never rest until the Dharma has been proclaimed for all.

The bodhisattva's spiritual life plays out within a mythic dimension, a realm where celestial beings may travel across world systems in a split second, a realm of innumerable Buddhas, of mind-boggling miracles, of infinite worlds and immeasurable numbers. The bodhisattva ideal embodies what may well be the most dazzling vision of spiritual life ever conceived. Its scope is so colossal as to be overwhelming.

In Chapter 2, we saw that the ideal of early Buddhism was the arhat, the worthy one, who has overcome greed, hatred, and delusion, who has achieved nirvana and so is released from the painful round of birth, death, and rebirth known as samsara (*saṃsāra*). While this achievement may seem very lofty in itself, according to Mahayana polemic it was rather too inward-looking and self-regarding; it didn't take proper account of the needs of other beings and failed to recognize that the life of the practitioner is intimately connected not only to those around him but also to the entire cosmos. It is not clear how far the arhat ideal really undervalued compassion but it is caricatured as such in Mahayana texts. In contrast, Mahayana sutras affirm the compassionate motivation that inspires the bodhisattva — although it is impossible to know how far this emphasis is simply rhetorical and how far it described how Mahayana practitioners really lived. It seems likely that this rift between the supposed selfishness of the arhat and the compassion of the bodhisattva was exaggerated as the Mahayana sought to proclaim a distinct spiritual message. Some of the earliest proto-Mahayana texts appear to present the two ideals as peacefully co-existing.[1]

Unlike the arhat, the bodhisattva does not crave escape from the rounds of birth and death but instead, motivated by compassion, he or she *aspires* to be reborn again and again in order to guide all beings to Awakening before entering the final resting place of nirvana. In reality, this task is endless; since there are infinite numbers of beings, the bodhisattva's work is never done. The Mahayana mission, then, strives for the salvation of the entire cosmos.

While the bodhisattva ideal is rightly regarded as the emblem of the Mahayana, it was already present in texts belonging to Nikaya Buddhism.[2] In accounts of the historical Buddha's life, for instance, he is regularly described as a bodhisattva before his final Awakening and in classical Buddhist art it was common to depict him as a bodhisattva. There is a class of early Buddhist literature, known as Birth Stories (*jātakas*), that narrates what are said to be the previous lives of the Buddha in which — as a bodhisattva — he performs heroic and compassionate deeds as he progresses on the path to Buddhahood. In some of these texts, he even takes the form of an animal.[3] In the previous chapter, we saw that the bodhisattva ideal in the earlier literature was reserved for the exceptional few, like the historical Buddha; according to the classic Mahayana vision, it is the *universal* goal.

But if the bodhisattva ideal is the highest goal, why bother with the arhat ideal at all? Another way of putting this would be to say: if arhatship was the accepted goal of Nikaya Buddhism, how could Mahayanists make their own goal seem legitimate and even compelling? One resolution to this problem is offered in the *Lotus Sutra* by means of a number of parables, including the Parable of the Magic City, summarized here.[4]

---

1   See Williams 2008: 27-9.
2   For a more detailed account of these sources, see Samuels 1997.
3   For an introduction to this class of literature and a translation of some celebrated stories, see for instance Shaw 2006.
4   See Hurvitz 1976: 148–9.

Suppose there is a steep, difficult road. A great many seekers want to travel it because they have heard that there is a horde of jewels to be found at its end. There is a guide who knows the way to this treasure but he is aware of how difficult it is to get there. He offers to lead the way. Before too long, the seekers find it tough going and lose heart. They want to turn back. The guide, being a resourceful man, thinks, 'These people are about to throw away a priceless opportunity. How can I encourage them to keep going?'

Using magical powers, the guide conjures up a city just ahead. The exhausted travellers are overjoyed, enter the city and quickly regain their spirits. The guide then announces, 'Come on! The treasure is not far now. The city I conjured up was just to give you a rest, nothing more.'

The arhat ideal is the magic city taught by the Buddha so that people would not be dispirited at seeing how far the true goal — the bodhisattva goal — was to travel. This parable exemplifies the teaching of *ekayana* (*ekayāna*) or One Way: the one way being the bodhisattva's way, the only true path. So the claim of the *Lotus Sutra* is that there is just one goal — the goal of the bodhisattva — and all other goals are provisional teachings to help beings to progress to the point where they can embrace this one, exalted ideal.

The Bodhisattva Path

In a number of Mahayana sutras, the bodhisattva path is dramatized as a mythic quest or pilgrimage. Perhaps the most celebrated of these quests is recorded in the final chapter of the *Flower Ornament Sutra* (known as the *Gandavyuha Sutra*), which tells the epic tale of Sudhana's search for Awakening. Sudhana, a young man, is picked out by a cosmic bodhisattva, Manjushri (Mañjuśrī), as being someone special, someone who aspires to the Mahayana way.[5] As a result, Sudhana conceives the desire to gain Awakening. In a hymn of praise, Sudhana then asks Manjushri to guide him on the bodhisattva path. Manjushri advises him to seek spiritual benefactors who will help him along his way.

Over the next 300 or so pages, Sudhana makes a marathon pilgrimage during which he meets many spiritual benefactors — 53 in all — who offer him all sorts of advice about how to follow the bodhisattva way. In essence, they describe sublime meditation states, cosmic in scope, which they have realized. It is hard to do justice to the richness of the imagery since much of its impact depends upon repetition but it can be hinted at by means of a

[5] For more on Manjushri, see pp.78–9.

short passage which describes Sudhana's meeting with his sixth spiritual benefactor, Saradhvaja (Saradhvāja), who is dwelling in meditation.

Sudhana saw an inconceivable miraculous display of the liberation of enlightening beings coming forth from every pore of the ecstatic body of Saradhvaja, who had attained such profound tranquillity, silence and objectlessness. With this miraculous display of the medium of liberation, Saradhvaja filled the cosmos moment to moment with endless varieties of mystic projections, to perfect all beings...[6]

3.1 Shantideva's Bodhisattva Training Manual

The *Bodhicaryavatara*, or *A Guide to the Buddhist Path to Awakening*, is an 8th-century Sanskrit poem which presents an uncompromising and inspiring vision of the bodhisattva path. It became a definitive training guide, especially in Tibetan Buddhism, and is still revered and studied today.[7] Given that it belongs late in the evolution of Indian Mahayana Buddhism, the *Guide* presents the bodhisattva ideal in a mature form.

The text is structured around the six perfections (generosity, ethics, patience, energy, meditation, and wisdom) and offers practical guidance, as well as plenty of encouragement and admonition, on how to nurture and sustain each virtue. The whole is set within a passionately devotional mood. It culminates in a presentation of highly complex Mahayana philosophy of the Madhyamika orientation.[8]

Its author, Shantideva (Śantideva; fl. 685–763 CE), was a monk associated with the great Buddhist monastery of Nālandā in northeast India. According to legend, Shantideva was regarded as a backsliding monk who lazed around doing nothing. His fellow monks decided to humiliate him by inviting him to recite scriptures before the monastic assembly, believing that he would prove incompetent. Instead, Shantideva is said to have recited a new text, the *Guide*. When he reached the wisdom chapter, he ascended into the air and disappeared, although his voice could still be heard ringing in the ears of his detractors.

---

6 Cleary 1993: 1197, modified by author.
7 For instance, passages from the *Bodhicaryavatara* were sprinkled liberally into the screenplay of the movie *Kundun* (1997), directed by Martin Scorsese, which charts the early life and flight from Tibet of the Fourteenth Dalai Lama, Tenzin Gyatso. For a contemporary commentary by a Tibetan geshe, see Gyatso 2007.
8 See Chapter 5 for more on the Madhyamika.

The Arising of the Bodhichitta

The crucial moment in the life of the aspiring bodhisattva is the arising of the bodhichitta or the 'Awakening Mind'. This term describes a profound transformation that takes place in the mind and heart of the would-be bodhisattva. It inspires him to abandon the aspiration for freedom for himself alone and to embrace instead the cause of universal Awakening. He comes to see his spiritual career in the context of the liberation of all beings and pledges to bring this liberation about. Much more than a thought of Awakening or even a desire for it, the arising of the bodhichitta consists in an existential transformation, enabling the aspiring bodhisattva to dedicate his efforts to the benefit of others. According to Mahayana sources, someone in whom the bodhichitta has arisen becomes worthy of worship just like the Buddhas.

The bodhichitta is regarded as supremely precious and is praised in the most lavish terms. The *Bodhicaryavatara* (*Bodhicaryāvatāra*, hereafter '*Guide*'), a poetic evocation of the bodhisattva path, eulogizes it like this.

> This is the elixir of life, born to end death in the world.
> This is the inexhaustible treasure alleviating poverty in the world.
>
> This is the supreme medicine, curing the sickness of the
> world, a tree of shelter for weary creatures staggering along
> the road of existence.[9]

But it would be wrong to think of the bodhichitta as an individual attainment or possession; rather, the individual is *possessed by* the bodhichitta.

> The bodhicitta is a will at work in the universe, in the direction of
> universal redemption ... We may even think of the bodhicitta as a sort
> of 'spirit of Enlightenment', immanent in the world and leading
> individuals to ever higher degrees of spiritual perfection.... something
> vast, cosmic, sublime, which descends into and penetrates and possesses
> those who are receptive to it.[10]

Given its precious and remarkable qualities, it is not surprising that arousing and fulfilling the bodhichitta is central to the Mahayana vision. But how does the bodhichitta arise? In many Mahayana sutras, beings experience the arising of the bodhichitta when listening to a Dharma teaching by a Buddha or bodhisattva. In Sudhana's case, he is so inspired by the teachings of the bodhisattva Manjushri that the urge towards Awakening on behalf of all beings spontaneously arises. Elsewhere,

---

9 Santideva 1995: 3:28–9: 22.
10 Sangharakshita 1999: 38–9.

Mahayana texts recommend specific practices for generating the bodhichitta. Shantideva's *Guide* exemplifies a devotional practice called the *anuttarapuja* (*anuttarapūjā*) or 'supreme worship'.

The purpose of supreme worship (often referred to simply as puja (pūjā) is to evoke a series of spiritual moods, using visualization and the recitation of devotional verses. Its exact form varies but it is commonly divided into seven stages.

1. Praise of the Buddhas
2. Worship of Buddhas and bodhisattvas
3. Confession (of individual failings)
4. Rejoicing in merits of beings
5. Requesting the teaching
6. Begging the Buddhas not to abandon beings
7. Dedication of the merits of practice to all beings[11]

Through speaking (and acting) *as if* already a bodhisattva, one aims to call up an aspiration that matches the profound altruism of the puja's contents. Initially, then, one engages in the puja in an aspirational way; one would like to be in possession of — or possessed by — the bodhichitta but isn't yet. When practised collectively, the puja amounts to a mutual promise to accomplish its cosmic aspirations.

Puja also generates spiritual 'merit' (punya) for those who practise it, and it is customary to dedicate this to the benefit of all beings. This is a hallmark of the Mahayana, since practice is undertaken not for one's own sake but to help all beings to gain Awakening.[12] This constant remembrance of the universal context in which practice is pursued undercuts any tendency toward spiritual materialism or pride.

In addition to this devotional approach, there are also specific meditation practices concerned with generating the bodhichitta. Shantideva describes a practice called 'exchanging self for other', which consists in prioritizing the needs and sufferings of others above one's own.[13] Its purpose is to shatter one's own pride, envy, and self-centredness and develop empathy for others by imaginatively 'trading places' with them. More developed versions of this practice are found in various Tibetan schools where it is known as *tonglen* or 'sending and receiving'. Here one imagines receiving the sufferings of all beings and sending back joy and happiness to them.[14]

---

11 For a more detailed account, see Santideva 1995: 9–13.
12 This form of practice is also important in Vajrayana Buddhism.
13 Santideva 1995: 8:120–73: 99–103.
14 For a more detailed account of *tonglen*, see for instance Kongtrul 1993. Kongtrul

Once the bodhichitta has arisen, the bodhisattva is effectively the servant of all beings, even their slave. Shantideva sums up this situation of radical altruism.

> Just as the earth and other elements are profitable in
> many ways to the immeasurable beings dwelling throughout space,
>
> So may I be sustenance of many kinds for the realm of
> beings throughout space, until all have attained release.[15]

The Bodhisattva Vow

When the bodhichitta arises, the bodhisattva declares his vow (*praṇidhāna*) or, more usually, a series of vows (although in practice these vows are proclaimed by the aspiring bodhisattva). The vow may be understood as the public expression of the arising of the bodhichitta and amounts to a cosmic promise not just to gain Awakening for oneself but to rest only when all beings have been spiritually liberated. There are a number of different lists of vows found in Mahayana sutras, including the celebrated 48 vows of the bodhisattva Dharmakara (Dharmakāra; *see* pp.71–2) and the ten vows of Samantabhadra but perhaps the most well-known and simplest formula is that of the Four Great Vows.

1. May I deliver all beings from difficulties (compassion)
2. May I eradicate all defilements (ethics)
3. May I master all dharmas (wisdom/skilful means)
4. May I attain complete Enlightenment (liberation)[16]

It is worth pausing to compare the scope of these vows with the vinayas of Nikaya Buddhism — which also constitute sets of vows. Usually, anyone undertaking the bodhisattva vows will already be a monk and so will already be following a vinaya. The bodhisattva vows, then, represent a further aspiration and discipline. But it is plain that the character of even this short list of vows is radically different from a vinaya. A vinaya focuses mainly on the appropriate conduct and decorum of the monk or nun; for instance, it prohibits him to eat after midday, to engage in sexual activity, and specifies how long hair should be worn.

Rimpoche describes the practice in the following way.
[A]s you breathe in, imagine that black tar collecting all the suffering, obscurations, and evil of all sentient beings enters your own nostrils and is absorbed into your heart. Think that all sentient beings are forever free of misery and evil. As you breathe out, imagine that all your happiness and virtue pour out in the form of rays of moonlight from your nostrils and are absorbed by every sentient being. With great joy, think that all of them immediately attain buddhahood. (14–15)

15 Santideva 1995: 3:20–1: 21.
16 These vows are found in the *Liuzu tanjing* (T.2008), known in English as the *Platform Sutra* or the *Sutra of Huineng*. For a translation, see Price and Wong 1990: 102.

3.2 Mahayana Ordination

In India, there was no specifically Mahayana ordination; instead, monks of Mahayana orientation were ordained within Nikaya traditions but may then have undertaken additional bodhisattva precepts.

When Mahayana teachings were transmitted to China, those adopting monastic lives were not formally ordained for almost two centuries. This was because the texts that governed monastic procedures (vinaya) were not available. In time, ordination and other principles of etiquette were consolidated through the adoption of a text called the *Four Part Vinaya* (*Sifen Lü*, T.1428), compiled by an Indian school known as the Dharmaguptakas. A specifically Mahayana ordination tradition emerged only with the advent of the Tendai sect in 9th century Japan (*see* pp.177–8)

Ordination was not simply a technical procedure. Daoxuan (596–667), a Chinese Vinaya master, infused ordination with a mystical flavour through the institution of 'ordination platforms' (*tanchang*). For Daoxuan, the ordination platform, together with the ceremonies enacted upon it, 'represented a profound source of religious charisma'.[17] He came to believe that the Buddha, as a living presence, guaranteed the integrity of the ordination ritual. In ritual terms then, monks were ordained *by* the Buddha himself.[18]

The mid-5th century *Brahma Net Sutra* offers the possibility of both self-ordination and visionary ordination.[19] If one is without a master, then, following a structured process of repentance and visionary experiences, in front of images of Buddhas and bodhisattvas, one may ordain oneself. More radically, one may even receive the bodhisattva precepts from a Buddha or bodhisattva in the context of a vision.[20]

The bodhisattva vows are concerned not so much with specific behavioural requirements but rather with broad, even open-ended aspirations or obligations. Most significantly, they incorporate an altruistic dimension, placing the spiritual career of the bodhisattva in the context of the spiritual welfare of all beings. The task of the bodhisattva is not just to liberate himself but to lead other beings to Awakening. More than this, the bodhisattva vows are unrelentingly cosmic in scope; not only does the bodhisattva wish to deliver beings from this world and this time but also all

---

17 McRae 2005b: 71. Charisma may here be understood as the spiritually uplifting and transformative influence exerted by a teacher, place, or object. The transmission of charisma could be seen in terms of blessing.
18 McRae 2005b: 90.
19 *Fan wan jing* (T.1484); for a translation, see Batchelor 2004.
20 See Yamabe 2005. See also Feature 10.3.

beings at all times, anywhere, and everywhere in the cosmos. Truly a tall order.

Imagine if you have vowed to lead the entire universe to Buddhahood and then you don't manage it; perhaps you lose heart or get distracted along the way. For the Mahayana, this is the most terrible thing conceivable: a backsliding bodhisattva, falling away from the highest of aspirations. It is one thing making a rash promise when drunk on inspiration but quite another sticking to it in the sober light of day when inspiration has waned. This was a danger that Shantideva keenly appreciated; he devotes an entire chapter (chapter 4) to shoring up the bodhisattva on the 'morning after'. His main approach seems to be to strike terror into the heart of the aspiring bodhisattva by threatening endless torments to anyone who should fall back.

> It is taught that a man who has only thought about giving
> in his mind, but does not actually do so, becomes a hungry
> ghost, even if the gift were only small.

> How much worse will it be for me, having proclaimed
> aloud the unsurpassed happiness with great enthusiasm?
> After breaking my word to the entire world, what would be
> my future birth?[21]

It really doesn't bear thinking about — but Shantideva forces us to do so. He drives the point home by highlighting that a backsliding bodhisattva doesn't just deprive one or two people of some trifling pleasure but the entire universe of the most precious thing imaginable — complete Awakening. More positively, Shantideva encourages the bodhisattva to reflect on the precious opportunity that life offers to make spiritual progress and, given the rarity of the human birth, urges him to seize the day.[22]

The Six Perfections and the Ten Stages

The classic bodhisattva career fulfils six (sometimes ten) perfections (*paramitas*) and progresses through ten stages (*bhumis*) to complete Awakening.[23] Each perfection is linked to a specific bhumi, which may explain why the scheme of six perfections was expanded. But this does not

---

21 Santideva 1995: 4:5–6: 25.
22 Santideva 1995: 1:4–13: 5–6.
23 The classic version of this system is laid out in the *Ten Stages (Dasabhumika) Sutra*, part of the aforementioned *Flower Ornament Sutra*; for a translation, see Cleary 1993: 695ff. The account given here is largely based on that text. The text takes a leisurely 100 or so pages to traverse the bhumis. There is no substitute for reading the whole thing since the imagery has a cumulative effect.

mean that as the bodhisattva progresses through each stage he leaves the previous perfection behind; it is perhaps more a matter of emphasis. As a set, the perfections function as a template for Mahayana ethical conduct and may be practised at increasingly higher and more subtle levels.[24]

Correlation of Six/Ten Perfections and the Ten Stages	
Perfection (Paramita)	Stage (Bhumi)
Generosity (dāna)	Joyful (pramudita)
Ethics (śīla)	Immaculate (vimala)
Patience/forbearance (kṣānti)	Illuminating (prabhakārî)
Vigour/energy (vīrya)	Blazing (arciṣmati)
Meditation (samādhi)	Difficult to conquer (sudurjayā)
Wisdom (prajñā)	Face-to-face (abhimukhî)
Skilful means (upāya-kauśalya)	Far-going (dūrangama)
Vow/resolve (praṇidhāna)	Immovable (acalā)
Strength/power (bala)	Good mind (sādhumatî)
Knowledge (jñāna)	Cloud of Dharma (dharmamegha)

Much of the content of this scheme is not unique to the Mahayana. The six perfections, for instance, can be seen as an amplification of the Threefold Way of Nikaya Buddhism: ethics, meditation, and wisdom.[25] Not only this, versions of the perfections are found in Nikaya Buddhist canons.[26]

In textbook summaries of the bodhisattva path, the six perfections are often described in some detail while the bhumis get short shrift. Given their cosmic properties, they may seem rather distant, even fanciful, impossibly remote from the practical concerns of life. But to regard the bhumi scheme as charting an achievable series of ever more exalted spiritual states is probably a mistake. It may be more useful to see them as describing a

---

[24] For a detailed, contemporary account of the six perfections, see Sangharakshita 1999.

[25] Śila, samādhi, and prajñā. See Sangharakshita 1987: 462.

[26] See Samuels 1997. The fact that the six perfections do not originate with Mahayana teachings may help to explain why compassion — seemingly at the heart of the bodhisattva's path — is not among them. It is an omission that appears puzzling — at least to me.

visionary itinerary, which may be pursued in the context of meditation. Dwelling upon the fantastic dimensions of each bhumi stimulates the creative imagination and inspires a sense of inner freedom. The complete scheme, correlating the perfections with the bhumis, could be seen as a symbolic portrayal of the bodhisattva's path. For this reason, we will look at them here in some detail.

1 Generosity and the 'joyful' stage

The first bhumi is joyful (pramudita). This is associated with making the bodhisattva vow described above and with many other attainments, including generating compassion for suffering beings and having visions of trillions of Buddhas. During this stage, the bodhisattva specifically practises generosity (dana).

It is no surprise that the bodhisattva's practice begins with generosity since this is the cardinal Buddhist virtue. For the ordinary Buddhist, this usually meant donating money or goods to monks, a monastery, or a stupa, perhaps even sponsoring the erection of a sculpture or funding some other good work. At the more elite level, giving meant teaching the Dharma and this was normally the province of monks. In addition to these two forms of giving, four other kinds are often mentioned: fearlessness; education and culture; life and limb; and merit.

In one Perfect Wisdom text, the epitome of giving is described in terms of a 'threefold purity'. 'Here a bodhisattva gives a gift, and he does not apprehend a self, nor a recipient, nor a gift; also no reward of his giving.'[27] This implies that giving has become the spontaneous outpouring of the bodhisattva's spiritual attainment, without calculation, without self-conscious deliberation.

2 Ethics and the 'immaculate' stage

The second bhumi is immaculate (vimala) and represents a condition of moral purity. Naturally, then, it is associated with the practice of ethics (shila). During this stage the bodhisattva fulfils ten ethical precepts.

To abandon killing/violence	To abandon harsh speech
To abandon stealing	To abandon useless speech
To abandon sexual misconduct	To abandon covetousness
To abandon speaking falsely	To abandon ill-will
To abandon malicious speech	To abandon false views[28]

---

[27] From the *Perfection of Wisdom in 800 Lines*: Conze et al 1999: 137.
[28] For a detailed account of these ten precepts, see Sangharakshita 2005.

While abandoning these ten wrong actions, the bodhisattva cultivates their opposites and encourages others to do the same. The ethical code described here is in itself not a Mahayana creation since it was also promoted within the arhat ideal. However, for the Mahayana, ethical practice takes place within an enlarged, even universal context. The bodhisattva is not practising ethics simply to benefit himself but in order to benefit all beings. This means that when he breaks a precept, he doesn't just harm himself but the entire universe.

> One should do nothing other than what is directly or
> indirectly of benefit to living beings, and for the benefit
> of living beings alone one should dedicate everything to
> Awakening.[29]

The bodhisattva does not regard his ethical accomplishments as personal attainments, since this may encourage conceit, but instead places them in the service of all beings. Rather than harvesting any benefits gained for himself, he dedicates them to the Awakening of all beings. This also means that if he acts unethically — and therefore fails to generate merit — he is not only heaping up suffering for himself but also denying beings what he has promised them through his vow. In this way, the consequences of a bodhisattva's poor conduct are amplified.

In order to prevent ethical lapses, Shantideva encourages reflection on the severe consequences. 'For one who does not act skilfully and heaps up evil too, even the idea of a good rebirth is lost for hundreds of billions of aeons.'[30]

3 Patience and the 'illuminating' stage

The third bhumi, the illuminating (prabhakari), is associated with meditation and the purification of the mind. Its connection to the third perfection, patience (kshanti), seems tenuous. At this stage, with a mind full of kindness, compassion, joy, and equanimity, the bodhisattva travels to the farthest reaches of the cosmos, leaving no corner untouched by his radiant mind. He also experiences all manner of miracles and develops magical powers.[31]

Patience is a multi-faceted virtue encompassing not only forbearance but also love, humility, endurance, and forgiveness. Patience would seem an especially important virtue for the bodhisattva. After all, he has embarked upon a path that is likely to take billions of lifetimes to complete. Shantideva writes at length about how suffering and adverse circumstances

---

[29] Santideva 1995: 5:101: 43.
[30] Santideva 1995: 4:19: 26.
[31] See Cleary 1993: 724–5.

are blessings in disguise since they offer the opportunity to develop equanimity.[32]

> The virtue of suffering has no rival, since, from the shock
> it causes, intoxication falls away and there arises compass-
> sion for those in cyclic existence, fear of evil, and a longing
> for the Conqueror [Buddha].[33]

One rather comical representation of a bodhisattva with powers of forbearance is the story of 'Never Disparaging' (Sadāparibhūta) in the *Lotus Sutra*. Never Disparaging was so-called because whenever he met a monk or nun, he would exclaim, 'I profoundly revere you all! I dare not hold you in contempt...You are all treading the bodhisattva-path, and shall succeed in becoming Buddhas!'[34] So smug and irritating did monks and nuns find his piety that they would throw stones at him but still he would not condemn them. According to the story, Never Disparaging went on to become the Buddha. The monks and nuns who had resented him all fell into the worst of hells, although after this, owing to the powers of the Buddha, they gained complete Awakening.

4 Vigour and the 'blazing' stage

The fourth bhumi is blazing or fiery (arcismati), so called because the bodhisattva radiates energy like the sun. Amongst other things, it is associated with overcoming the belief in a permanent self (atman: ātman). At this stage, the bodhisattva practises the perfection of vigour or energy (virya). However, virya is not energy in general but rather energy that is directed towards Awakening.[35] This is significant because busyness is considered a form of laziness as it results in the neglect of spiritual practice. For the bodhisattva, energy directed exclusively towards worldly accomplishments is laziness.[36]

As with patience, this perfection blends together several key qualities. In particular, it incorporates the qualities of vigilance (apramāda) and determi-nation (dhṛti). The quality of vigilance is seen as especially important in guarding awareness so as to prevent ethical lapses; this includes guarding the precious bodhichitta. Virya also incorporates urgency; the bodhisattva has

---

[32] Santideva 1995: 6: 50ff.

[33] Santideva 1995: 6:21: 51.

[34] Hurvitz 1976: 280.

[35] Santideva 1995: 7:2: 67.

[36] According to the Tibetan commentator Gampopa (1079-1153), 'Gross laziness is addic-tion to such evil and unwholesome practices as subduing enemies and hoarding money. They have to be abjured because they are the cause of real misery'; cited in Sangharakshita 1999: 229, n.140.

been granted the precious opportunity of human life and will die all too soon.[37] He should therefore make the most of this precious chance by progressing on the bodhisattva path before it is too late.

Given that he has committed himself to guiding all beings in the universe to Awakening, the bodhisattva is likely to need superhuman powers of tenacity and resilience. Shantideva sums up the vitality of the bodhisattva in the following way.

> So, even at the conclusion of one task, one should plunge
> straight away into the next, as does a tusker [elephant],
> inflamed by the midday heat, immediately on coming to a
> pool.[38]

For the bodhisattva, helping beings is not a chore but play (*līlā*). The more he helps people, the more joyous he feels, and the more energy he has.

5 Meditation and the 'difficult-to-conquer' stage

The fifth bhumi is difficult-to-conquer (sudurjaya). At this stage the bodhisattva's ethical awareness is so thoroughly and securely developed that his mind is unlikely to be corrupted. He now has the quality of unwavering attention which enables him to reflect on teachings concerning the nature of truth. This stage is linked with the perfection of meditation. Specific Mahayana meditation practices are described at various places in this book, but a few general points are relevant here.

As it was in Nikaya Buddhism, meditation became a key feature of Mahayana practice, especially at the elite level of monks and nuns. However, Mahayana traditions expanded the range of meditation practices and placed them within the context of the bodhisattva path. In particular, the Mahayana emphasised the visualization (*sādhana*) of celestial Buddhas and bodhisattvas, as well as their Pure Lands or paradises. Distinct forms of meditation also emerged in China, especially in the context of Chan/Zen.[39]

Mahayana texts caution against the danger of becoming attached to meditative accomplishments. For instance, one Perfect Wisdom text warns:

> Those of great might who dwell in the four Trances [*dhyāna* or
> superconscious states]

---

[37] The fragility and preciousness of the human opportunity is graphically expressed in a well known illustration. Suppose a yoke were thrown into the sea, and it was carried every which way by the wind. Suppose also that a blind turtle were to poke his head up above the surf just once every hundred years. Once a human being has fallen into an evil realm, it is likely that the turtle will surface with his head through the yoke before the evil doer regains the human state. (MN III.169)

[38] Santideva 1995: 7:65: 73.

[39] See Chapter 4 for sadhana and Chapters 8 and 11 for Chan and Zen.

Do not make them into a place to settle down into,nor into a home.
But these four Trances ... will in their turn become
The basis for the attainment of the supreme and unsurpassed
enlightenment.[40]

The implication of this passage is that meditative absorptions should not
be regarded as personal attainments to be indulged in but should instead be
placed at the service of beings. Whether real or imagined, the target of this
implicit attack is a perceived self-gratification and complacency within
Nikaya Buddhist practice at the expense of compassion.

6 Wisdom and the 'face-to-face' stage

The sixth bhumi is face-to-face (abhimukhi). At this stage, the bodhisattva
encounters reality directly and fulfils the perfection of wisdom (prajna),
gaining deep insight into dependent origination (pratītya-samutpadā), the
fundamental Buddhist philosophical principle (see Feature 5.2). Within the
six perfections scheme, this stage represents the culmination of the bodhisattva path and many Mahayana sutras dedicate their attention to praising
its virtues. An entire genre of sutras is specifically concerned with perfect
wisdom.[41]

It is through the arising of perfect wisdom that the other five perfections
are consummated; without it, they are 'eyeless'.[42] Despite its rhetoric of
compassion, then, the Mahayana continued to value wisdom above all other
qualities. At this stage, the bodhisattva apparently enters the nirvana of the
arhat.[43] But given that, at least according to the *Lotus Sutra*, nirvana is a
'magic city', this does not really make sense. This anomaly may reflect the
fact that there were conflicting views on the status of nirvana within
Mahayana sources.

The stages beyond the sixth stage can be considered distinctively Mahayana, as opposed to belonging to Nikaya Buddhism. If it were possible,
accounts of the final four stages are still more extravagant, which makes it
difficult to do justice to their splendour. The states described become
increasingly transpersonal and their descriptions seem calculated to defy the
imagination. For this reason, they will be dealt with more briefly.

7 Skilful means and the 'far-going' stage

The seventh bhumi is the far-going (durangama). At this stage, the bodhisattva is Awakened but does not pass into final nirvana because he chooses

[40] *Ratnaguṇasaṁcayagāthā* XXIX:1: translated in Conze 1994: 63.
[41] See Chapter 5.
[42] See, for instance, *Ratnaguṇasaṁcayagāthā* VII:1–2: translated in Conze 1994: 23.
[43] Cleary 1993: 759.

to be reborn to help beings. This complex situation is described in the *Ten Stages Sutra*.

> In the seventh stage they enter and emerge from extinction [nirvana] in each mental instant, but they may not be said to actually experience extinction.... Just as a person with good knowledge of the characteristics of the waters of the ocean ... is unscathed by the ocean waters, in the same way enlightening beings [bodhisattvas] ... abide in the sphere of ultimate reality ... yet do not experience extinction.[44]

The bodhisattva experiences an exquisite tension: owing to his wisdom, he is continually pulled towards nirvana but, at the same time, his compassion for beings tugs him *back* into the suffering world.[45] As a conesquence, the bodhisattva remains in the world but not of it as exemplified, for example, by the miraculous figure of Vimalakirti.[46]

3.3 The Sacrifices of the Bodhisattva Ever Weeping

The lengths of self-sacrifice to which bodhisattvas are willing to go to fulfil their practice are portrayed symbolically in Mahayana sutras. For instance, in the *Perfect Wisdom in 8000 Lines*, Sadaprarudita (Sadāprarudita, 'Ever Weeping'), being poor and having nothing to give, tries to sell his own body in order to honour the Bodhisattva Dharmodgata. Māra, the Evil One, mischievously decides to obstruct Sadaprarudita so that he can't find a buyer. At this, Sadaprarudita lives up to his name as he breaks down in tears.

Then Shakra (Śakra), king of the gods, intervenes to test out how serious Sadaprarudita is about selling his body. He offers to buy his heart, blood, and bone marrow. Overjoyed, Sadaprarudita pierces his arm with a sword to let out his blood. He then cuts flesh from his thigh and strides up to the foot of a wall in order to break the bone. At this point, a merchant's daughter intervenes and offers to give Sadaprarudita whatever he needs to honour Dharmodgata.[47]

In the expanded set of perfections, at this stage the bodhisattva perfects skilful means (upaya-kaushalya). The addition of skilful means to the scheme underlines its importance within Mahayana thought. The bodhisattva has by now developed the agility to adapt his method of teaching to each and every individual being. He is not attached to any particular

---

44 Cleary 1993: 759.
45 See Nagao 1991: 23ff.
46 See pp.35–6.
47 For the full story, see Conze 1994: 277–300.

doctrine or form of words and may even use magical displays to free the minds of others. Besides this, he is prepared not only to break the monastic code but also to commit what on the surface seem like unskilful actions, all with the compassionate aim of helping beings.[48]

8 The vow and the 'immovable' stage

The eighth stage is known as immovable (achala) because the bodhisattva can no longer fall back from his aspiration to perfect Awakening. His spiritual practice is now effortless, like a boat on the ocean carried by the wind.[49] The irreversibility of this stage draws comparison with stream entry (*srotāpatti*) in Nikaya Buddhism.[50] However, for the Mahayana the eighth bhumi signifies irreversibility from a more exalted spiritual goal. Here the bodhisattva is constantly in the presence of all Buddhas and is able to appear anywhere and everywhere in the cosmos to teach beings. This stage is associated with the perfection of the *vow* described above.

9 Power and the 'good mind' stage

The ninth stage is known as good mind (sadhumati). By now, even if all the beings of a billion worlds were to appear at the same moment and all ask a question, each with countless nuances, the bodhisattva would be able to answer them all in a single utterance.[51] He is able to teach all beings according to their unique characters and needs and so fulfils the perfection of power (bala). He directs his compassionate attention to all beings simultaneously, and is able to listen to the teachings of all Buddhas throughout infinite time and space at the same time.

10 Knowledge and the 'cloud of dharma' stage

Finally, the tenth stage is cloud of dharma (dharmamegha). In this stage, the bodhisattva whips up a great wind of radiance and covers everything with a dense cloud of virtue and knowledge; he rains down the elixir of immortality and extinguishes the afflictions of all beings. In doing this, he accomplishes the perfection of knowledge (jnana). The full details of this stage are said to be beyond retelling.

However, even at this head-spinning summit, to compare the bodhisattva with a Buddha would be like picking up a few pebbles and asking, 'Which is bigger, the endless realms of the earth or these few pebbles?'. Even if in each of the ten directions there were as many lands as atoms in infinite worlds and these were filled with bodhisattvas who have reached

---

[48] See pp.15–18 for more on skilful means.
[49] Cleary 1993: 767.
[50] See Sangharakshita 1987: 201–2 on stream entry.
[51] Cleary 1993: 785.

this stage, their accomplishments over endless aeons would not amount to the tiniest fraction of a moment of the Buddha's knowledge![52]

How Credible is the Bodhisattva Ideal?

As you can see from some of the luxuriant imagery just described, accounts of the career of the bodhisattva read more like superhero stories found in comic books than as practical examples to be emulated. The cosmic context of the bodhisattva's path seems impossibly remote from everyday needs, obligations, and aspirations. According to one account, the bodhisattva is prepared to endure unimaginable suffering for thousands of aeons in order to benefit even one being. As each of us lives through our regular day, making a cup of tea, writing an email, changing our clothes, what bearing do the riotous imagery and sublime aspirations of the bodhisattva have upon our life? When stubbing a toe on the doorstep and then feeling sorry for ourselves, the bodhisattva path seems little more than an escapist fantasy. Can it be taken seriously as a human goal?

Whatever its limitations may be, the arhat ideal of Nikaya Buddhism seemed achievable; according to early Buddhist texts, it was realised by many of the Buddha's disciples. It was framed in human terms and lived out on a historical, comprehensible scale; it was a goal that relates to *this* life, here and now. In contrast, a key feature of the bodhisattva ideal is that, by definition, it can never be fully accomplished since there will always be more beings to save.

Templates of bodhisattva conduct like the *Guide* seem to suggest that the ideal was taken seriously and pursued as an individual goal by Mahayana followers. But given our present cultural and spiritual imaginary, to think of ourselves as literally following the bodhisattva path may lead us not towards spiritual Awakening but rather into grandiose self-delusion.

The bodhisattva ideal is perhaps better understood as a myth and the bodhisattva himself as a spiritual symbol. It embodies the spirit of the compassionate life and frees our imagination from the routine of daily life. We could regard the bodhisattva as a transpersonal, redemptive force at work in the universe.[53] This force is something that we may be able to recognise and draw on within our own lives and we may even become a channel for some of its compassionate influence. The bodhisattva myth then may be something in which we can *participate*, a visionary context through which we can understand our modest spiritual efforts. The bodhisattva ideal lifts the life of the struggling, individual Buddhist above everyday cares into a world of infinite dimensions that confers dignity,

---

[52] Cleary 1993: 798.
[53] For more on this way of understanding the bodhisattva, see Sangharakshita 1999: 64-5.

value, and purpose. Placing our lives within this cosmic narrative is in itself transformative, even profoundly so. Collectively, our conduct may evoke the compasssionate intensity that is symbolised by the bodhisattva.

Mahayana texts present the bodhisattva as the ideal Buddhist, to which all should aspire. But over time the bodhisattva became an increasingly exalted and transhistorical figure. This led to the emergence of cosmic bodhisattvas who became fitting objects of worship and devotion. We will turn to these next.

4

Visions of Awakening:
Buddhas, Bodhisattvas, and Buddha-fields

IT IS WIDELY UNDERSTOOD THAT there is no God in Buddhism, no creator of the universe who sustains life and to whom beings are subject. Yet within Mahayana Buddhism there is a pantheon of celestial beings revealed through a bewildering array of forms, functions, and powers. Quite a few of these have inspired individual cults, becoming the objects of devotion, penitence, petition, and even coercion. This chapter introduces some of the transcendent figures that came to populate the Mahayana imagination and explores their significance, including their iconographic representations. It also contemplates the notion of buddha-fields (*buddhakṣetras*), the 'spiritual universes' through which their boundless compassion reverberates.

While in early Buddhism the principal focus was a single Buddha — Siddhartha Gautama — in Mahayana Buddhism there are many, even innumerable Buddhas. Moreover, Mahayana Buddhas are luminous, transcendent figures who may manifest in all places at all times; they have untold spiritual virtues and incomprehensible magical powers. Less individual personalities, they are forces of cosmic liberation; ranging across incalculable world systems, they tirelessly bestow spiritual wisdom and worldly blessings upon all beings.

Besides these cosmic Buddhas, there is a host of angelic beings known as bodhisattvas who serve as missionaries of compassion, fuelled by their unwavering determination to release all beings from suffering. In the germinal Mahayana tradition, emphasis seems to have been placed upon the individual pursuit of the bodhisattva career, which implies that at least some exceptional beings must have progressed a long way down this path and, consequently, were reaching out to less capable beings with a compassionate hand. Over time, there was a shift of attention away from the individual accomplishment of the bodhisattva path towards its fulfilment by proxy. Although in doctrinal terms not as spiritually accomplished as Buddhas, transcendent bodhisattvas nevertheless aroused widespread devotion, inspiring a number of distinctive cultic traditions which helped to define Mahayana spirituality.

Many of the glittering stars of this Mahayana firmament are depicted — or embodied — in icons, images and sculptures which themselves have become sources of power, blessing, and even miracles. Images of transcendent figures are regarded not just as symbols but as living entities which exemplify Awakening in the world. Specific images may even inspire a legend or cult and may consequently attract throngs of pilgrims hoping for blessing, healing, and even the fulfillment of mundane goals. Images are activated through consecration, sustained through ritual service, and may be injured or even 'killed' through accidental or deliberate damage. How and why did these forms of religious practice evolve?

Recollecting the Absent Buddha

The historical Buddha, Siddhartha Gautama, also known as Shakyamuni, lived in northeast India around the 5th century BCE. Perhaps not surprisingly, after his death the absent Buddha became a focus of devotion and longing. In particular, a cult of relics emerged centred on the worship of stupas (*see* Feature 2.2). In contrast to the abundance of images found today, it seems that in early Buddhism the Buddha was not represented in human form at all, although the reasons for this are not clear.[1]

In the absence of icons, stupas rapidly became cult objects and stupa worship became an important part of Nikaya Buddhist experience. The stupa was believed not only to hold the relics of the Buddha but his very presence was seen as alive and active within it.[2] In other words, through worshipping the stupa, Buddhists encountered the essence of the Buddha himself; they were blessed by his Awakened presence. Such practice reflects a belief that the Buddha not only transcended his physical body but that he was not really dead; the essence or reality of the Buddha was something beyond his fragile human form. This paved the way for the concept of the Buddha as a transhistorical presence, and later for cosmic Buddhas who were not tied to earthly bodies but who might be encountered through the spiritual imagination.

This development was further encouraged by the evolution of a meditation practice known as Recollection of the Buddha (*buddhanusmṛti*).[3] The recollection of and reflection on the Buddha's qualities is recorded in early scriptures, and so must have developed fairly early on.[4] At some stage, this practice gained in importance and became associated with the visualization of the Buddha in the context of meditation practice. More than this, the

---

[1] On this point, see Huntington 1990.

[2] For a fascinating exploration of this theme, see Schopen 1997: Chapter 7.

[3] An insightful consideration of buddhanusmrti in the early Mahayana tradition can be found in Harrison 1978.

[4] See, for instance, the six *anussatis* (remembrances) found at AN V.328–332; this list includes recollection of the Buddha. See also *Sutta-nipāta* 976–1031.

notion emerged that the Buddha might hand out teachings within this visionary realm.

The *Sutra on the Samadhi of Seeing All Buddhas*, for instance, describes how the meditator hears the preaching of the Buddhas while in the vision-world of 'seeing the Buddhas of the present'.[5] He is urged to accept what he hears, to retain and memorise it; on leaving the vision-world, he is to put it into practice and teach it to others.[6] This possibility provides a justification for the appearance of Mahayana sutras. It rests on the conviction that meditation is an authentic means by which the Buddha can continue to reveal new spiritual insights to those ready to receive them. This new relationship between the meditator and the visionary Buddha is described in the following terms.

> The Buddhas, Lords, also show their faces and proclaim their names to that bodhisattva even in his dreams, and cause that bodhisattva to hear the Dharmas of the Buddhas. Further … undeclared, unobtained words of the Dharma come within the range of hearing of that bodhisattva, and he acquires them; by the power of that Samadhi that bodhisattva hears those dharmas.[7]

Some Buddhist Cosmology

Cosmic Buddhas began to appear in Mahayana literature around the 1st century CE, perhaps before, although it is worth noting that most of the associated cults did not develop fully for several centuries. Even in early Buddhism, there was an understanding that there was more than one Buddha. In order to explain this, we must touch on a little Buddhist cosmology.

According to Buddhist cosmology, the universe is cyclical; it goes through periods of development and degeneration. The same is also true of the Dharma. In each world cycle, there is a period before the emergence of the Dharma, a period where the Buddha appears to teach the Dharma, and then a period of decline and decay. Linked with this cyclical view is the notion that Shakyamuni (Śakyamuni, the present Buddha) is not unique but belongs to a long line of Buddhas.[8] Besides this, there will be a future Buddha called Maitreya, who became the focus of a devotional, even millenarian cult.[9]

---

[5] *Pratyutpanna-buddha-saṃmukhā-avasthita-samādhi-sūtra*, T.417; translated by Harrison in Lokaksema et al. 2006.

[6] Harrison 1978: 54.

[7] Harrison 1978: 54.

[8] See *Buddhavaṁsa* and also the *Mahāpadāna Sutta* (DN II.1–54).

[9] See *Cakkavattisīhanāda Sutta* (DN III.75).

Even within Nikaya Buddhism, then, there was a belief in multiple Buddhas reaching back into the primordial past. Mahayana cosmology expanded this vision of the universe; rather than there being just one world system, there are innumerable, extending endlessly through all directions of space. Moreover, there are Buddhas in each of these different world systems, not just in our own.

The Buddha in the Lotus Sutra

A key question for early Buddhists was this: if the Buddha was so compassionate, why did he die and so stop teaching? Surely beings still need the Dharma and if he was still around then many more people could become Awakened. Chapter 16 of the *Lotus Sutra* offers a Mahayana resolution. Here the Buddha declares that he has been Awakened for an incalculably long period of time.[10] This is a great revelation. The Buddha did not awaken just recently but an immeasurably long time ago — so long ago that we may as well think of him as eternal. This introduces the idea that the Buddha is a transpersonal, cosmic influence — a quite different conception from the historically rooted Buddha found in the earliest scriptures.

The Buddha of the *Lotus Sutra* also reveals:

> I have been constantly dwelling in this Saha ['enduring'] world sphere, preaching the Dharma, teaching and converting; also elsewhere, in a hundred thousand myriads of millions of nayutas of asamkhyeyas of realms (I have been) guiding and benefiting beings.[11]

This suggests that there is in fact only one Buddha but that this Buddha can manifest at different times, in different places, and in different guises. Moreover, he is an *active* force perpetually reaching out to beings in different worlds.

But the question remains: if the Buddha is eternal and teaches the Dharma all the time, why did he die? Surely this means that he can no longer teach the Dharma in this world. A mortal Buddha who only survives for 80 years seems rather at odds with the spectacular conception of him portrayed in the *Lotus Sutra*. The text resolves this problem by means of a parable.

There is a doctor who has many children. The doctor goes on a journey out of town and, while he is away, the children drink various poisons and go out of their minds. The father returns to discover what has happened

---

10   See Hurvitz 1976: 241.
11   Hurvitz 1976: 238.

and, skilled in the making of potions and medicines, he administers anti-
dotes to those children who are sane enough to take them. But some of the
children are so out of their minds they refuse to take the medicine.
Distraught, the father does not know what to do.

Before long, the father hits upon a plan. He decides to tell the children
that he is dying and leaves some medicine for them to take after he has
gone. He then secretly disappears and sends word that he is dead. The
children, on hearing this sad news, come sufficiently to their senses to take
the medicine and are cured.[12]

According to this line of thought, even the Buddha's death was a skilful
means to help beings gain Awakening. He is in fact present even now and
may be encountered in visionary meditation experience. Such a belief allows
for the possibility of many Buddhas; although they are essentially one in
nature, they may have different names and appear at different times and in
different places.

The Buddha's Three Bodies

The conviction that the Buddha transcended his physical body and historical personality gave rise to the notion that he had more than one kind of
body. Even in early Buddhism, a distinction was made between the Buddha
as a human individual (*nirmāṇakāya*) and the body of his teachings
(*dharmakāya*). For instance, the Pali Canon records the Buddha as saying
'He who sees the Dharma, sees me'.[13] In addition, dharmakaya signified the
qualities of a Buddha: those things that distinguished him from ordinary,
unawakened people. In Mahayana Buddhism, the notion that the teachings
were the true Dharma body was expressed in text worship. Through
listening, reading, or worshipping Dharma texts, the Buddha's spiritual
essence could be absorbed.

By around the 4th century CE, a formal theory of Three Bodies or
trikaya (*trikāya*) had emerged, which systematised differing understandings
about the nature of the Buddha. The most exalted body is the dharmakaya
or 'body of truth'. In the trikaya doctrine, the dharmakaya becomes a metaphysical concept; it is the 'Buddha in Eternity', beyond form and so beyond
representation. It is the essence of Awakening. In some later texts, the
dharmakaya is equated with the *dharmadhātu* or 'realm of reality'. This
signifies the entire cosmos as ultimately grounded in the Awakened mind; it
implies that the Buddha is the essence of reality — there is a Buddha in
every atom. This understanding of the nature of the Buddha became very
influential in East Asian thought, especially in the Huayan tradition (*see*
pp.130–4). In the words of the *Flower Ornament Sutra*:

---

12 See Hurvitz 1976: 239–41.
13 SN III.120, modified by author.

> Just as space pervades the ten directions,
> Like form but not a form, existent but not existent,
> Omnipresent, without bounds,
> In beings' bodies and lands, in all times,
> So does the true body of Buddhas
> Pervade all phenomena,
> Invisible, ungraspable,
> Yet manifesting bodies to teach beings.[14]

Next is the *sambhogakāya*, a luminous, apparitional body, or the 'Buddha in Heaven'.[15] This is revealed through the manifestation of cosmic Buddhas. These transcendent beings may be encountered in states of meditative absorption, visions, or in buddha-fields (*see below*). Such a belief guarantees the possibility of continuing revelations of the Buddha's wisdom. These cosmic Buddhas embody Perfect Wisdom and benevolence and consequently offer spiritual illumination, blessings, and even mundane aid to all beings. A number of these became objects of individual devotional cults.

The final, and most materialized, body is the *nirmāṇakāya* or 'Buddha on Earth'. This is equated with the historical Buddha Shakyamuni — the Buddha in this world. For some schools, this Buddha was no more than a phantom, a magic show. Out of compassion, he incarnated as an ordinary mortal and demonstrated the ideal spiritual life to inspire others but was fully Awakened all along. The Buddha on Earth is also revealed through images and sculptures, which are not just dead matter but icons, animated by a transcendent presence. They are living sources of blessing and spiritual knowledge.

The Buddha-field

Imagine a world where there is no suffering, no negative emotions, where all wishes are fulfilled, a world of scintillating light, of radiant colour, and of untold jewels; it is a world of transcendent beauty and purity. This is a buddha-field or Pure Land. It is a Buddhist utopia — the closest thing to a Buddhist heaven — an idyllic realm where conditions for spiritual growth are perfect, free of the hassles and constraints of life as we know it. Here everyone practises the Dharma joyfully and progresses effortlessly towards complete Awakening.[16]

---

[14] Cleary 1993: 987.

[15] It is often rendered 'body of mutual enjoyment' but I don't think this expresses its meaning very well. In my analysis of the trikaya here, I have borrowed terminology from Griffiths 1994.

[16] As noted below, some buddha-fields are regarded as impure and so do not conform fully to this utopian vision.

Mahayana sutras record many such buddha-fields, all with very similar characteristics. One of these is called Great Joy (*Abhirati*) and is connected with the Buddha Akshobya (Akṣobhya), one among a number of cosmic Buddhas who inspired individual followings. In the *Akshobya Sutra*, Abhirati is described as a land of peace and bliss where all gain joy from hearing the Buddha's teachings.[17] There is a fragrant breeze that carries to those who like it but not to those who don't. There is no darkness in Abhirati because Akshobya has an ever-shining light which illuminates everything.[18] This and other buddha-fields are described in lavish and sometimes garish imagery.

A buddha-field is the sphere of influence of a particular Buddha and sometimes of a bodhisattva. It is created through the fulfilment of a bodhi-sattva's great vows and embodies his incalculable stock of merit, generated through aeons of spiritual practice. Each buddha-field is dedicated to the benefit of all beings. In this sense then the buddha-field is an incarnation of a Buddha's compassion. It is a field of grace (*adhiṣṭhāna*) radiating a Buddha's wisdom in all directions, blessing all those touched by its light.

The notion of a buddha-field represents a shift away from the idea that Awakening is exclusively our own responsibility to be strived for through individual effort and towards the idea that Buddhas and bodhisattvas are reaching out to us, exerting a liberating influence by drawing us towards them through the power of their immense spiritual virtue. This way of thinking inspired the development of Pure Land devotion.[19]

Another way of thinking about a buddha-field is as a kind of cosmic sangha, a perfect spiritual community in which all members relate to one another compassionately. For instance, in the *Vimalakirti Sutra,* the Buddha declares:

> Noble sons, a buddha-field of bodhisattvas is a field of living beings.
> Why so? A bodhisattva embraces a buddha-field to the same extent that
> he causes the development of living beings ... a buddha-field of
> bodhisattvas springs from the aims of living beings.[20]

This suggests that a buddha-field should not be understood in a literal way, as some sort of physical world, but rather as a spiritual dimension that may interpenetrate the ordinary world, a field of collective spiritual practice. This possibility is further underlined in the *Vimalakirti Sutra* when Vimalakirti performs a miracle by bringing Akshobya's buddha-field into our world, known as Saha (Sahā, 'Enduring').

---

[17] The full name of the sutra is the *Akṣobya-tathāgatasya-vyūha-sūtra* (T.313) and it has been translated from Chinese in Chang 1991: 315–38.

[18] Chang 1991: 320ff.

[19] See Chapters 8 and 10.

[20] Thurman 1976: 15–16.

Although the universe Abhirati had been brought into the universe Saha, the Saha universe was not increased or diminished; it was neither compressed nor obstructed. Nor was the universe Abhirati reduced internally, and both universes appeared to be the same as they had ever been.[21]

Buddha-fields are sometimes divided into pure and impure. An impure buddha-field is one in which not all beings are practising the Dharma, whereas a pure buddha-field, like Abhirati, is full of bodhisattvas pursuing the highest goal. Our own little universe, Saha, despite being under the influence of Shakyamuni, is an impure buddha-field. This seems to have raised a problem for Mahayana thinkers.

4.1 Women in Mahayana Buddhism

Buddhism has generally judged the female state as less advantageous than the male, and Mahayana traditions have often endorsed this prejudice.[22] For instance, when he embarked on the bodhisattva path, the Medicine Buddha made 12 great vows, one of which was to guarantee a male rebirth for any women disgusted with the afflictions of the female form. Amitabha (Amitābha) made a similar vow, and consequently there are no women in his paradise of Sukhāvatī.[23] But this position is not universal. The buddha-field of Akshobya, for instance, is described as a sanctuary for women and children, where they are 'safe and unsullied'.[24]

Despite Mahayana beliefs such as the universality of Buddha-nature, nuns and lay women have generally been subordinate to monks and widely disparaged as lacking in spiritual aptitude. Moreover, since most Buddhist history has been written by men, the role of women within Mahayana traditions has been poorly chronicled. Nevertheless, despite overwhelming male dominance, exceptional women were sometimes able to attain influential positions.[25]

According to the *Vimalakirti Sutra*, a buddha-field is pure insofar as the mind of the Buddha who created it is pure.[26] If Shakyamuni created our buddha-field, and that buddha-field is impure, does this then mean that Shakyamuni's mind was not pure? This question is placed in the mouth of

---

21 Thurman 1976: 94.
22 For a discussion of the role of women in Buddhism, see Gross 2001.
23 See Gomez 1996: 74.
24 Chang 1991: 323.
25 For a study of influential women in Chinese Chan, see Hsieh 1999.
26 Thurman 1976: 18.

Shariputra, who is regularly cast as the epitome of Nikaya Buddhism in Mahayana sutras, and so may reflect a contemporary critique of the Mahayana's spiritual cosmology. The Buddha's response is to say that it is not his fault that the world appears impure. In reality, it *is* pure but not all beings can see this owing to their spiritual limitations. Those who possess a pure mind see a buddha-field as pure. The Buddha sums up the situation like this.

[L]iving beings born in the same buddha-field see the splendor of the virtues of the buddha-fields of the Buddhas according to their own degree of purity.[27]

This suggests that the real way to enter a buddha-field is to purify our minds. In addition, if a buddha-field equates with the purity of the Buddha's mind, then by purifying our minds and entering a buddha-field, we also participate in the Buddha's mind. Ultimately, we are already in a buddha-field but we do not know it. A buddha-field then is not a remote heavenly abode but the Awakened mind itself, which actively seeks to communicate with our unawakened minds.[28] It is a dynamic and even personal force, constantly trying to break through to us.

An Array of Cosmic Buddhas and Bodhisattvas

The Mahayana sky glitters with hundreds of thousands, even untold numbers of glorious Buddhas and bodhisattvas. While hundreds of these have attracted individual names, only a few dozen are sufficiently individualized to warrant distinct iconographic features and mythic biographies. An even smaller number have inspired lasting devotional followings and so, by way of introducing cosmic Buddhas and bodhisattvas as a whole, we will concentrate on a few of the most widely revered who have inspired the most enduring cults. It is worth noting that while there is usually a degree of continuity in relation to their functions, representations, and mythic biographies, Buddhas and bodhisattvas often went through significant transformations as they embedded in new cultures. Selecting just a few figures for discussion inevitably means excluding others who are also prominent stars in the Mahayana firmament.[29]

Amitabha/Amida

Without doubt the most important cosmic Buddha is Amitabha (Amitābha), whose name means Boundless Light, and who encapsulates the

---

27 Thurman 1976: 19.
28 Williams 2008: 227.
29 For a discussion of other Buddhas, see Vessantara 2008b. For an overview of bodhisattvas, see Vessantara 2008a.

spirit of universal compassion. He is also known as Amitayus (Amitāyus), meaning Boundless Life, and in East Asia these qualities were combined in the figure of Amituo (China) or Amida (Japan), where his cult became one of the most influential forms of Buddhist practice. So central did Amitabha become to East Asian Buddhism that it would be fair to say he eclipsed the historical Buddha.

4.2 Visualising the Pure Land

The *Visualization Sutra* outlines a series of exercises which evoke the spiritual world of Sukhavati and culminate in an encounter with the Buddha Amitabha (here known as Amitayus). The visualization guidelines are very detailed and incorporate sumptuous imagery. In brief, one begins by visualising the setting sun. Then, one visualises water in every direction, which then freezes and transforms into precious stones to form the 'earth' of the Pure Land. This ground is criss-crossed with golden cords and emits light of 500 colours.

Next, one visualises enormous jewel trees with leaves 25 *yojanas* in length and breadth (a yojana may be somewhere between four and nine miles). These trees have golden blossoms, which spin like fire-wheels. From the blossoms appear fruits which transform into jewelled canopies, reflecting the buddha-fields of the entire cosmos. Then, one contemplates the jewel ponds and heavenly musicians.

Next one visualizes a lotus-flower throne, each petal of which has the colour of 100 jewels, and is at least 250 yojanas in length and breadth. Upon the lotus-throne one visualises the golden figure of Amitayus, flanked right and left by bodhisattvas. The light of Amitayus blazes in all directions and in seeing him, one sees all the Buddhas of the cosmos.

Finally, one visualises oneself being reborn in Sukhavati inside a lotus blossom. As the petals of the lotus open, one's body emits coloured light and one can hear the Buddhas and bodhisattvas preaching the Dharma.

Amitabha is sometimes depicted as golden in colour, sometimes as dark red — the colour of the setting sun — and sits in meditative contemplation, radiating light throughout the cosmos. There are two key sutras — the shorter and longer *Sukhavati Sutras* — that describe Amitabha, his cosmic vows, his past practice as a bodhisattva, and his buddha-field called Sukhavati (Blissful).[30] This buddha-field has become more widely known than any other, to the point where it is commonly referred to as *the* Pure Land.

---

[30] Shorter *Sukhāvatī-vyūha-sūtra*, T.366; longer *Sukhāvatī-vyūha-sūtra*, T.360. For translations of both the sutras from Sanskrit and Chinese, see Gomez 1996.

The two Sukhavati sutras, which are among the most important sacred writings for East Asian Buddhism, were probably written in northwest India after 100 CE but are better known through their Chinese translations. A third sutra, popularly known as the *Visualization Sutra*, recounts a series of contemplative visions which disclose aspects of the Pure Land and Amitabha himself. This text was composed sometime later, perhaps in Central Asia or China.[31] Collectively, these texts have come to be known as the three Pure Land sutras.

Both the longer and shorter sutras focus on the figure of Amitabha and describe his Pure Land. The *Longer Sutra* lends him a mythic biography through the story of the bodhisattva Dharmakara (Dharmakāra) who, aeons ago, practised the Dharma under the guidance of a primordial Buddha. So inspired was Dharmakara that he vowed not just to gain Awakening for himself alone but to create a miraculous land where all can gain Awakening; in other words, to accomplish the bodhisattva ideal.[32] He pledged to create not just any buddha-field but one that distils the qualities of *all* other buddha-fields in one. He then spent five cosmic ages gathering these together. The Pure Land that he finally assembled is the embodiment of his untold merit (*see* Image 7).

Dharmakara made a series of 48 cosmic vows which guarantee all kinds of wonderful outcomes once he has gained full Awakening.[33] These vows are framed in a somewhat paradoxical way. In essence, Dharmakara declared that he only wanted to gain Awakening if the vows are all fulfilled. Perhaps the most celebrated of these is the 18th vow, the so-called Primal Vow.

> May I not gain possession of perfect awakening if, once I have attained buddhahood, any among the throng of living beings in the ten regions of the universe should single-mindedly desire to be reborn in my land with joy, with confidence, with gladness, and if they should bring to mind this aspiration for even ten moments of thought and yet not gain rebirth there.[34]

---

31 *Guan wu-liang-shou jing* (T.365). It is also known by a 'reconstructed' Sanskrit title of the *Amitāyur-dhyāna-sūtra*. For an online translation by Hisao Inagaki, see http://www12.canvas.ne.jp/horai/contemplation-sutra.htm. This site also offers Inagaki's translations of the two Sukhavati sutras.

32 See Gomez 1996: 64ff, 162ff.

33 The Sanskrit text has only 47 vows but given the authority that the Chinese text has gained, 48 will be taken as the standard.

34 Gomez 1996: 167. Note: I have abridged the vow to remove the 'exclusion clause' which withdraws the promise of the vow from those who have committed any of the 'five heinous crimes': killing one's father; killing one's mother; killing an arhat; injuring a Buddha; and causing schism in the sangha. The exclusion is at odds with the *Visualization Sutra*. See also Chapter 10, notes 53 and 66.

The *Longer Sutra* makes it clear that Dharmakara *did* go on to gain full Awakening, since he became the Buddha Amitabha, and consequently all of the vows *have* been fulfilled, including the eighteenth. This means that rebirth in the Pure Land is assured for those who follow the guidance of the vow. Many of the other vows offer similar guarantees.

The vows, and the sutras as a whole, represent a shift away from the individual fulfilment of the bodhisattva path towards a spiritual outlook that places confidence in the grace of a cosmic Buddha. The medium of Amitabha's grace is his infinite light; through its influence, beings not only feel joy but also begin to act ethically. Thus his light exerts a transforming impact on those blessed by its all-pervading rays. This transforming impact is conceptualised in terms of a transfer of merit from Amitabha to all beings. Since Amitabha pursued the bodhisattva ideal for many aeons, he has a lot of merit to go around — in fact, an infinite amount. By means of his measureless light, this merit is constantly gifted to all beings.

Although the Amitabha myth is a sacred narrative originating in India, it seems that his cult did not gain widespread support there.[35] It was in China, and then Japan, that Pure Land Buddhism, with Amitabha Buddha at its heart, grew into a distinct tradition.[36]

The Medicine Buddha: Bhaisajyaguru

A cosmic Buddha who gained wide popularity throughout Asia is Bhaiṣajyaguru (Healing Master), also known as Bhaiṣajyaraja (Healing King). This figure is most commonly known as the Medicine Buddha and is believed to confer not only spiritual but also health-giving benefits. The historical Buddha himself was compared to a surgeon, and the figure of the Medicine Buddha elaborates on this symbolism.[37] Chapter 23 of the *Lotus Sutra* records some of the feats of devotion of the bodhisattva Healing King and this may well have inspired his elevation to Buddhahood and cult status.[38] The most notable of these actions was to dowse himself with all kinds of perfume and to drink fragrant oils before setting himself alight as an offering to the Buddha. His glow illuminated innumerable worlds and he continued to burn for 1200 years.[39]

The Medicine Buddha is often depicted as the colour of lapis lazuli — an intensely blue gemstone believed to have healing properties. In his right

---

[35] For a detailed discussion of this point, see Schopen 2005: 154–89.

[36] See Chapters 8 and 10.

[37] *Sallakatta*, literally 'barb-remover'. See, for instance, *Sutta-nipāta* 560 and MN I.429. The latter makes use of an extended analogy of a surgeon removing a poison arrow with the Buddha teaching his Dharma.

[38] Hurvitz 1976: 293–302.

[39] Hurvitz 1976: 294–5.

hand he grasps a healing jar, also made from lapis lazuli, and with his left he sometimes holds a sprig of the myrobalan plant, or else it grows out from his healing jar. The Medicine Buddha radiates light of a lapis lazuli hue in all directions, blessing beings not only with good health but with wisdom. In the *Bhaisajyaguru Sutra*, he makes a series of 12 vows, a number of which promise worldly benefits, including restoring those with ailments or disabilities to health and providing material goods to those who need them.[40] Beyond this, the Medicine Buddha vows to lead beings to Awakening.

The sutra emphasises the value of reciting the Medicine Buddha's name, or even simply hearing it, promising ethical transformation to those who do so. This will enable people not only to become generous but also eventually even to give life and limb in the service of others. Simply through hearing the Medicine Buddha's name, all bad deeds are erased. In other words, the supreme merit of the Medicine Buddha dispels bad karma.

4.3 Self-Immolation in Mahayana Buddhism

While the story of the Medicine Buddha incinerating himself is richly symbolic, it seems to have inspired literal self-burning among Mahayana followers as an offering and proof of devotion. Apocryphal texts offer further justification for this practice, which seems to breach the basic Buddhist principle of *ahimsa* (non-harm).[41] For instance, at least until recently, perfumed cones were burnt on the shaven heads of the initiates during the monastic ordination ceremony in Chinese and Korean Buddhism, which left a series of scars (commonly nine), symbolizing their willingness to give life and limb for the Dharma.

In addition, it has not been uncommon for Mahayana Buddhists to burn off a finger or toe or to brand a limb in the belief that this will generate merit. For instance, the famous 20th century Chinese Buddhist Xu Yun burnt off one of his fingers in the conviction that it would produce merit that he could transfer to his departed mother.[42]

Still more dramatic is the practice of auto-cremation as a ritual offering to the Buddha, which was absorbed into Chinese Buddhism from indigenous traditions. A dedicated few regarded burning themselves alive as a route to holiness.[43]

---

40 *Bhaisajyaguru-sūtra*, T.450. For a translation, see Birnbaum 2003b.

41 See Benn 1998.

42 Luk 1988: 42–3. Justification for this practice is found in the *Surāngama-sūtra*, T. 945; see Benn 1998: 300.

43 For a detailed study, see Benn 2007.

While it seems that the Medicine Buddha's cult was not widespread in India, it became prevalent in Central Asia, and remains popular in China to this day, where he is known as Yaoshifo. He is also influential in Tibet as Sangye Menla. In Chinese temples, it is common to see images of Shakyamuni flanked by Amitabha and the Medicine Buddha, underlining his exalted status.

Cosmic Bodhisattvas

During the formative Mahayana period, the bodhisattva ideal was regarded as a practical path to be pursued by the committed individual and, to some extent, has remained so. But the emergence of cosmic bodhisattvas, who transcend the normal bounds of time and space, was perhaps inevitable for two reasons. First, it is a logical outcome of the ideal itself: if there are beings dedicated to pursuing Awakening on behalf of all beings, then they will be making efforts to help others towards Awakening even now. If this is the case, then it may be possible to enter into relationship with them. Secondly, Mahayana texts became so saturated with phantasmagoric imagery, colossal scales, and incomprehensible timespans that the bodhisattva ideal became increasingly mythical, perhaps no longer something to be individually attempted but rather a transcendent vision to be revered. The expectations that Mahayana sutras place on the prospective bodhisattva are superhuman; it would hardly be surprising if many people felt not only daunted but even crushed by its ambitions.

Paul Harrison has suggested that in early versions of Mahayana sutras the cosmic bodhisattvas are little more than cardboard cut-outs serving a literary function as mouthpieces for Mahayana teachings.[44] Rather than these texts offering evidence of bodhisattva cults, he argues that they were more likely the inspiration *for* such cults. So a transcendent figure may have begun life as little more than a name in a text and yet grown and consolidated in the Mahayana imagination to eventually inspire widespread devotion.[45]

In many respects, a cosmic bodhisattva is not so very different from a cosmic Buddha and, as time passed, the distinction became less and less clear-cut. For instance, at times some figures are portrayed as a bodhisattva, while at others as a Buddha. However, in principle there are important differences. First, cosmic bodhisattvas are represented differently. Cosmic Buddhas are more or less modelled on early images of the Buddha, whereas

---

[44] Harrison 2000.

[45] The Bollywood movie *Jai Santoshi Maa* (1975) serves as an interesting analogy. The goddess Santoshi Maa was little known before the release of this very popular film, yet her depiction in it inspired widespread devotion towards her across India, principally among women. (Thanks WB.)

cosmic bodhisattvas are generally presented as youths dressed in royal finery (*see* Images 8, 9, 10 & 16). This hints at their future role as 'spiritual monarchs', since the role of a Buddha was regularly compared with that of a king. Secondly, Buddhas are fully awakened and bodhisattvas are only on the path *towards* Awakening; however, this distinction becomes increasingly difficult to sustain in relation to cosmic bodhisattvas. Thirdly, bodhisattvas do not normally preside over a buddha-field. Finally, bodhisattvas are depicted as directly intervening in human affairs, sometimes to offer material as well as spiritual aid, whereas Buddhas usually remain more distant, transcendent figures.

In iconographic representations, cosmic bodhisattvas tend to be placed in positions subordinate to Buddhas, typically flanking a Buddha on either side. The relationship between cosmic Buddhas and bodhisattvas is sometimes characterised in terms of the contemplative and dynamic aspects of Awakening; the Buddhas represent depth, wisdom, and stillness, whereas the bodhisattvas exemplify energy, compassion, and dynamic engagement with the problems of the world. Some traditions came to believe that cosmic bodhisattvas even incarnate on earth, a belief that is embodied in institutions such as HH the Dalai Lama (whose followers believe he is a manifestation of Avalokiteshvara (Avalokiteśvara) or Chenrezig, as he is known in Tibet). They are also embodied through icons.

While Mahayana sutras record the names of thousands of bodhisattvas, only a few of these developed discernible identities and a handful have inspired significant followings. These include Maitreya, Avalokiteshvara, Manjushri, and Kshitigarbha (Kṣitigarbha).[46]

Maitreya

Mention has already been made of Maitreya who is destined to become the future Buddha. Maitreya's status is somewhat ambiguous since he is sometimes regarded as a bodhisattva and sometimes as a Buddha. Interest in Maitreya developed fairly early on in the development of Buddhism and his cult was probably well established by the beginning of the Common Era. It continued to be popular, both in Nikaya and Mahayana Buddhism, achieving particular significance in Central Asia. In China (as Mile), Maitreya's influence was supplanted by the growth of Amitabha devotionalism but he later regained popularity in Japan (as Miroku) before being superseded there as well.

Maitreya currently awaits in the Tushita (Tuṣita) heaven until it is time for him to descend and become the next Buddha. Although the Tushita heaven is not technically a buddha-field, it is possible to visit it in

---

[46] Together with Samantabhadra ('Universally Worthy'; Ch. Puxian, Jp. Fugen), the latter three bodhisattvas make up the Four Great Bodhisattvas of East Asian Buddhism.

meditation and to be reborn there. Xuanzang, for instance, described a meditation practice that he observed which was directed towards rebirth alongside Maitreya.[47]

There are some similarities between the myth of Maitreya and Christian narratives of the coming Messiah. Maitreya is regarded as a saviour whose coming will usher in a golden age of the Dharma, when untold numbers of people will turn towards Buddhist practice, thus establishing a Pure Land on earth. In China, such beliefs inspired a number of marginal and short-lived movements which rebelled against the government with the aim of creating appropriate conditions for Maitreya's terrestrial rebirth.[48]

In art, Maitreya is often depicted not in meditation pose but seated on a throne like a monarch, and this regal image was reproduced in monumental sculptures throughout East Asia, some of which still survive. But the custom of producing gigantic Maitreya statues is not just a thing of the past. The Maitreya Project is an ambitious contemporary venture which aims to cast a colossal 152-metre bronze statue of Maitreya and to install it at Kushinagar, northern India, which is traditionally believed to be the birthplace of the Buddha.[49]

Avalokiteshvara

Avalokiteshvara, whose name means 'Lord Who Looks Down', became the best known and most popular cosmic bodhisattva in East Asian Buddhism (*see* Image 16), as well as in Tibet, and is seen as the embodiment of compassion. His significance was first recorded in the *Lotus Sutra*, chapter 25, which has also circulated widely as an independent text. The other main Indian source for Avalokiteshvara is the *Karandavyuha Sutra*, a later composition which introduces the celebrated mantra *oṁ maṇi padme hūṁ*, closely associated with this bodhisattva.[50]

In the *Lotus Sutra*, Avalokiteshvara is seen as a figure who can intercede on behalf of ordinary people in order to change the course of worldly events. For instance, the sutra promises that whoever calls upon him will be saved from shipwrecks, fires, murderers, and other worldly disasters. This function of offering practical aid enhanced his appeal.

Avalokiteshvara is depicted in many forms, perhaps the most striking of which boasts a thousand arms and eleven heads. The eleven heads enable him to look in all directions to see what beings need and the thousand arms reach out to all corners of the cosmos offering help of all kinds. This mani-festation of Avalokiteshvara could be regarded as an imaginative embodiment of the principle of skilful means.

---

47 Cited in Sponberg 1986.
48 This theme is considered in Overmyer 1976.
49 For more information on this, see www.maitreyaproject.org [accessed: 08.03.09]
50 T.1050. For a discussion of this text, see Schopen 2005: 278–98.

There is a poignant legend that tells of how Avalokiteshvara came to look like this. On surveying the world and all the many sufferings of beings, he was overwhelmed by sorrow and despair, fearing that he would be unable to fulfil his bodhisattva vow. The stress of this emotion caused his head to splinter into ten pieces and his body to shatter into a thousand fragments. Amitabha, taking pity on Avalokiteshvara, made him anew. From each of the head-fragments, Amitabha made a new head and from each of the body-fragments he made an arm. He then remade the bodhisattva, placing his own head on top.

4.4 The Saikoku Kannon Pilgrimage

Many pilgrimage routes have emerged in the course of Mahayana Buddhist history. One of the more popular is the Saikoku Kannon pilgrimage, which centres on 33 temples dedicated to Kannon (Avalokiteshvara) in western Japan.[51] As a round trip, it is some 1500 miles, but it is now common to visit the temples in a series of day excursions from Kyoto.

At each temple, the pilgrim deposits a *fuda* in a special offertory box. This is normally a slip of paper with a prayer or invocation inscribed on it. In addition, he or she may make a donation, offer incense and candles, strike the temple bell, and say a prayer or recite a sutra.

Pilgrims also carry with them a 'pilgrim's book' (*nokyōchō*), which is inscribed and stamped (for a small fee) at each temple (*see* Image 11). Completed pilgrimage books are regarded as repositories of spiritual merit, even as passports to the Pure Land. As a consequence, they are sometimes mounted on lavish silk hangings.

The Saikoku pilgrimage inspired over 200 similar routes, including one that incorporates it into a 100-temple mega-pilgrimage.[52]

In China, Avalokiteshvara became known as Guanyin ('The one who observes the sounds of the world') and eventually changed gender. The female Guanyin is widely represented in flowing white robes and is associated with fertility.[53] Guanyin has been incorporated into the sacred geography of China with the identification of his/her birth place as Mount Putuo, a tiny island in the Bay of Hangchow, southwest of Shanghai. This has become one of the key Chinese Buddhist pilgrimage sites. Known as Kannon in Japan, this bodhisattva also became very important there.

[51] For a very informative, pictorial record of this pilgrimage, see http://www.taleofgenji.org/my_saigoku_pilgrimage.html.

[52] MacWilliams 1997: 377.

[53] For a study of Guanyin in China, see Yu 2001.

Owing to their spiritual kinship, Avalokiteshvara is often depicted flanking Amitabha, forming a triad with another great bodhisattva known as Mahasthamaprapta (Mahāsthāmaprāpta, 'Possessor of Great Power').

Manjushri

Manjushri (Manjuśri, Gentle Lord) is known as the bodhisattva of wisdom and is especially associated with the Perfect Wisdom tradition. In Indo-Tibetan traditions, he is depicted as wielding the flaming sword of wisdom, which cuts through ignorance. With his left hand, he clutches a wisdom scripture to his heart or holds a lotus which supports the text. He is sometimes shown as honey-coloured, sometimes as white.

Manjushri appears in a number of Mahayana sutras, including the *Vimalakirti Sutra* where he is the only bodhisattva brave enough to call on the ailing Vimalakirti to ask after his health (all the others are too scared of being made a fool of!). When Manjushri goes to see Vimalakirti, they pursue a heady discussion about the nature of reality, which culminates with a thunderous silence.[54]

The *Manjushri Sutra* describes Manjushri's practice as a bodhisattva and the qualities of his buddha-field, called Wish-Fulfilling Accumulation of Perfect Purity.[55] While it is rare for a bodhisattva to preside over a buddha-field, this anomaly shows how religious innovation does not always conform to doctrinal orthodoxy. The sutra compares this buddha-field with Amitabha's Sukhavati and, in a gesture of spiritual one-upmanship, points out that it is infinitely superior.

This sutra chronicles Manjushri's progress along the bodhisattva path, including his attainment of the tenth bhumi. In addition, '[h]e perfected every Dharma of the Buddha-stage but he never thought: "I shall become a Buddha!"'[56] This passage seems to show an awareness of the ambiguous position of Manjushri; he has all the attainments of a Buddha yet is still a bodhisattva.

In China, Manjushri is known as Wenshu and is sometimes depicted seated in meditation upon a lion — a beautiful and striking image (*see* Image 9). China engendered a spectacularly successful Wenshu cult focused on Mount Wutai, a set of snowy peaks in Shanxi province, which was at least partly validated using scriptural passages that link Manjushri with a snow-covered mountain. Chinese monks identified this mountain as Wutai and by the 7th century, it had become an international pilgrimage site

---

54 See Thurman 1976: 42ff.
55 The sutra's full Sanskrit title is *Manjuśri-buddha-kṣetra-guna-vyūha*, T.310; see Chang 1991: 164–88.
56 Chang 1991: 176.

helping to establish China as a central Buddhist realm. Mount Wutai remains a sacred place today.[57]

Known as Monju in Japan, Manjushri also became popular there and is represented in a number of forms. In the guise of the 'sacred monk', his image is enshrined in Zen meditation halls where he is revered both as a senior monk and as a protector. He has a personal attendant who offers him incense and tea daily, and monks bow to him whenever they enter or leave the meditation halls as well as chant for his wellbeing.[58]

Kshitigarbha

Kshitigarba (Kṣitigarbha) or 'Earth Store' (Ch. Dizang, Jp. Jizō) was not a significant figure in Indian Mahayana but became popular in Central Asia and also in China and Japan where he has fulfilled a wide range of spiritual and worldly functions.[59] While he is known through a number of scriptures, a detailed, mythic biography is recorded in the *Sutra of the Past Vows of Dizang Bodhisattva*, which was at least partly composed in China.[60] In keeping with similar bodhisattva 'histories', the sutra recounts some of the bodhisattva's exemplary past lives, which show a particular concern with the afterlife sufferings of ancestors. In one of these lives, Kshitigarbha or Dizang takes rebirth as a young woman who, with the help of past Buddhas, descends into hell to relieve the torment of her dead mother, and then vows to liberate all beings suffering as a result of their evil deeds.

Academic analysis of the sutra has suggested that it offers an account of late medieval Chinese death and afterlife rites.[61] A further scripture, the *Sutra on the Bodhisattva Dizang*, accentuates his role in relation to the dead, casting him as a judge of those in the underworld, a saviour who offers respite to tormented spirits, and a guide who directs the dying towards a Pure Land.[62]

These scriptural precedents, as well as folk stories, helped confirm Dizang as Lord of the Underworld, whereby he became the focus for rituals concerning departed relatives which aimed to improve their afterlife prospects through merit transfer. In accordance with this role, his image is often set up in memorial halls. Kshitigarbha/Dizang has also been incorporated into the sacred landscape of China, where Mount Jiuhua in Anwei province is regarded as his spiritual home and has become a popular pilgrimage site.

---

[57] For a discussion of the evolution of Wutai Shan into Manjushri's sacred mountain, see Sen 2004: 77-86.
[58] Foulk 2008: 61. This practice originated in Chinese Chan.
[59] For a detailed study of Dizang, see Ng 2007.
[60] *Dizang pusa benyuan jing*, T.412; for a translation, see Hua 1974.
[61] Ng 2007: 115.
[62] *Foshuo Dizang pusa jing*, T.2909.

In art, Kshitigarbha is often shown in the guise of a standing, shaven-headed monk.[63] In his left hand, he holds a wish-granting gem, the light of which illuminates even the darkest corners of hell, and with his right he supports a walking staff with jingling rings, which alerts small creatures to his approach so that he doesn't step on them. He looks very much like a pilgrim and this may be why he is regarded as a protector of travellers. Kshitigarbha is also sometimes depicted as a more conventional bodhisattva wearing a princely crown and garments.

In Japan, known as Jizō, this bodhisattva fulfils many and varied functions. As Mizuko Jizō, he is regarded as a guardian of dead children, especially those who have died prenatally and aborted fetuses.[64] There are special child and fetus cemeteries packed with Jizō figures (*see* Image 2), often dressed in red caps and bibs and decorated with toys and keepsakes. A famous and moving example is at the temple of Zōjōji in Tokyo.

Other forms of Jizō include Bound Jizō, Sweating Jizō, and Sixfold Jizō.[65] Sixfold Jizō is actually a group of six Jizō images, which symbolize his willingness to help beings in each of the six realms. Another form is Substitute Jizō, who releases a victim from affliction by volunteering to suffer himself. Stories tell of people suffering from, for instance, an eye disease who wake up having dreamed of Jizō to discover that their complaint has healed by being transferred to a Jizō enshrined nearby. Many pilgrimage routes have grown up around Jizō, especially sixfold circuits, underlining his compassion for the six realms.

In What Sense Are Buddhas and Bodhisattvas Real?

Having met some key personalities of the Mahayana imagination, you may be wondering in what sense, if at all, they really exist. Do Buddhas and bodhisattvas amount to anything more than the flights of fancy of a few giddy monks? And can they really help us? Certainly, in their ethereal forms, they do not belong to the world of the physical senses as commonly understood but rather to the inner world, the world of the spiritual imagination.

We have perhaps become accustomed to dismissing the imagination as fanciful, illusory, not as a faculty that may behold truth. But at other times

---

[63] A well known Western representation of this form of Kshitigarbha was created by the French painter Odilon Redon (1840–1916). Entitled 'The Buddha' (c.1908), it hangs in the Musée D'Orsay, Paris.

[64] LaFleur 1994.

[65] An example of how an icon may be coerced into fulfilling the mundane wishes of devotees is the Bound (*shibarare*) Jizō. Petitioners bind these figures with string in order to 'force' them to restore the health of an ill person, or perhaps to help recover lost or stolen property. If the wish is fulfilled, then the image is set free. A famous example is at Rinsenji, Tokyo.

and in other cultures, a more elevated concept of the imagination has been widely accepted, one that sees it as a medium of authentic experience and understanding. In writing about spiritual experience in Sufism, the Iranologist Henry Corbin describes how the Imagination (capital I) holds sway over an 'intermediate world' between matter and spirit. Through the power of the Imagination, 'spirits are materialized and bodies spiritualized'.[66] This enables the spiritual imagination to see the visionary via the ordinary as well as to consolidate the spiritual world into images.

4.5 A 'Living Buddha': The Zenkōji Icon

Zenkōji, a temple in Nagano, Japan, is the focus of a remarkable cult centred on a hidden icon, which may not even exist. The icon comprises a triad of images with Amida being the principal figure, and it is regarded as a 'living Buddha', constantly gifting both salvation and practical benefits to the faithful.

By the 13th century, the temple had become a renowned pilgrimage site attracting flocks of worshippers, some of whom might spend the entire night before the shrine in the belief that the icon would answer their prayers. The hidden icon inspired a series of 'replicas', which gave rise to a network of Zenkōji cult temples throughout Japan. It is through the replicas only that the icon may be seen.

Secret images are a common feature of Japanese Buddhism. Many temples have sacred statues or paintings that are sealed away for decades, or even centuries, to be displayed only on the rarest occasions.[67]

According to the medieval Islamic mystic Ghazali (d. 1111), this makes the imagination superior to the rational mind as a means of grasping spiritual truths.[68] The imagination makes these truths accessible by translating them into images. Such images then represent portals into spiritual understanding, which may be more reliable than ideas alone.

Buddhas, bodhisattvas and buddha-fields represent a consolidation of the spiritual imagination of Mahayana Buddhism. This world of light, image, and myth is not in conflict with the world of ordinary experience but is rather a further — and enlarged — dimension within which our lives unfold. The aim of Mahayana imagery is to affirm this dimension and unveil it before us. Stepping into it does not mean rejecting our current worldview but opening ourselves to a different kind of experiencing, what

---

[66] Corbin 1997: 182.
[67] McCallum 1995.
[68] Hughes 2002.

in Buddhism is called samadhi or a vision-world. It is not just a question of relaxing into an escapist fantasy but of expanding our consciousness to inhabit a spiritual dimension that reveals meaning through visionary forms.

Besides the ethereal presences of Buddhas and bodhisattvas, they also manifest in more material forms through physical images, including paintings and sculptures. Not just symbols, these images are widely revered as icons, sacred forms which in themselves materialize the spiritual realm. A consecrated image is not merely a 'representation' of a transcendent figure any more than our own bodies 'represent' us; they are us. The material form is a *living being* exerting wonder-working and even redemptive powers.[69] Entering into relationship with these images through devotion and ritual service has been — and still remains — a central form of religious practice within Mahayana Buddhism, which answers the need for the spiritual to manifest through the material.

---

[69] See Sharf 2001.

5

Jewels from the Deep:
Perfect Wisdom and the Madhyamika

BESIDES UNVEILING A VISIONARY UNIVERSE of scintillating light, opulent colour, and infinite dimensions in which transcendent beings communicate the Dharma through their luminous forms, the Mahayana nurtured a philosophical tradition that is often meticulous in its reasoning, and whose insights may be as elusive as they are profound. In this and the following chapter, we steer into this philosophical deep, tracing some of the intricate currents of thought that pulse through it. In particular, we examine some of the problems that arise from using philosophical thought as a tool for grasping the subtle nature of reality.

This chapter introduces the Perfect Wisdom texts and the Madhyamika (Mādhyamīka) or Middle School, which embodies the fundamental, philosophical perspective of the Mahayana.[1] It explores the key notion of shunyata or 'emptiness' and shows how this new idea arose as a restatement of the early Buddhist teaching of dependent origination. Rather than being a positive claim about reality, emptiness can be viewed as a tactic for deconstructing the philosophical views of others in order to show that they are not warranted. The chapter goes on to assess some of the problems associated with this style of thought, in particular the danger that it may undermine the instrumental role of concepts in the enterprise of spiritual transformation, and run the consequent risk of dissolving away the practical path before Awakening has been accomplished.

Before going further, a note of caution about the term 'philosophy'. We should not assume that intellectual reflection within Mahayana Buddhism rests on the same assumptions or serves the same purpose as it does in the Western imagination. Commonly, philosophy is divided into two branches.

Ontology: the study of what there is in the universe
Epistemology: the study of what can be known and how we can know it

It is true that these activities are present in Mahayana thought but their underlying aim is to foster Awakening.

---

[1] Some scholars prefer 'Madhyamaka' to designate the school and 'madhyamika' to denote a follower of it.

In other words, the aim of thought is not to arrive at a final description of reality but to bring about the transformation of the individual. So, even where Mahayana philosophy appears to put forward some authoritative account of experience, it is placed at the service of spiritual Awakening. In my view, all Buddhist thought is ultimately grounded in the concern for liberation, and so is often pragmatic. This is illustrated in the well-known early Buddhist parable of the raft.[2] The Buddha compares his teachings to a raft used to ford a river; the purpose of the raft is to get from one place to another, and this is its only function. Once on the other side, the raft should be abandoned. Similarly, Buddhist teachings are not ends in themselves but tools, strategies that foster the process of Awakening.

The Perfect Wisdom Texts

The beginning of the Mahayana, at least as a textual tradition, is connected with the emergence of Perfect Wisdom (Prajnaparamita; Prajñāpāramitā) literature around the beginning of the Common Era. Perhaps as many as 200 years later, this literature spawned the teachings of Nagarjuna (Nāgārjuna; c. 2nd century CE), widely revered as the greatest thinker in Buddhist history, who systematized its insights and inspired the Madhyamika school.

Responses to the Perfect Wisdom literature vary wildly: some people see it as sublime, hard to fathom, and deep, while others dismiss it as verbal diarrhoea, no better than nonsense. At times, it can certainly be a challenging read. The Perfect Wisdom sutras comprise a family — perhaps even a dynasty — of texts composed over a period as long as a thousand years. The family includes more than two dozen texts that vary in length, interest, and significance. It includes some of the earliest formulations of Mahayana thought and the group as a whole has been deeply influential.

The formation of Perfect Wisdom texts began in the 1st century BCE. Generally accepted as the first Perfect Wisdom text, the *Perfect Wisdom in 8000 Lines* originates from this period, although it continued to expand for as many as 200 more years.[3] A further text, the *Ratnagunasamcayagatha* (*Ratnaguna* for short), is also believed to date from this time and covers similar themes.[4]

During the period 100–300 CE, longer sutras emerged, the largest of which is the *Perfect Wisdom in 100,000 Lines*. Mercifully, this was followed by a period of consolidation which produced much shorter texts including the *Heart Sutra*, probably the best-known Perfect Wisdom text and still

---

[2] MN I.134; see p.15.
[3] *Aṣṭasāhasrikā-prajñāpāramita-sūtra* (Ch. *Daoxing banruo jing*, T.227–8).
[4] *Ratnaguṇa-saṁcayagāthā*, T.229. For a translation of both these texts, see Conze 1994.

widely used in liturgies and study.[5] The *Diamond Sutra*, especially revered within the Chan tradition, may also date from this phase but could be much older.[6] The creative phase of this literature ended around 600 CE.

The Perfect Wisdom texts can be rambling but also terse, devotional yet arcane, seemingly absurd and yet profound; they incorporate dense philosophical reflection as well as imaginative flights of fancy. They especially have a knack of pulling the rug from beneath your feet, leaving you tottering and bewildered, not sure what to make of it all. This is their intention, which makes their message hard to sum up.

Above all, these texts stress the supremacy of the quality of perfect wisdom: prajna-paramita. We have already seen that this is one of the six perfections and, in some schemes, is regarded as the culmination of the bodhisattva path (see pp.50–9). In later tradition, Prajnaparamita was even envisioned as a goddess and revered as the 'mother of all Buddhas'. 'Prajna' means wisdom but it is not knowledge or understanding in the ordinary sense; rather, it is a direct, nondual insight into the nature of experience. It is the type of understanding achieved by a Buddha. However, there are different levels of prajna and, in some contexts, it was understood as an intellectual ability to analyse experience into constituent parts. For the Mahayana, prajnaparamita became a synonym for Awakening itself — a condition of mystical intuition beyond description.

The Abhidharma Context for Perfect Wisdom

In order to unearth the concerns and emphases of the Perfect Wisdom texts, of Nagarjuna, and of the Madhyamika that he inspired, we need to take a few steps back into Buddhist history. Everything arises in dependence upon conditions and new Buddhist teachings and schools are no different. So what gave rise to this new flowering of the Buddhist imagination?

The emergence of the Perfect Wisdom literature is best understood as a response to the Abhidharma tradition of Nikaya Buddhism. This was both a method of classifying and analysing experience and a body of literature that recorded this. While it may not have developed very far within the Buddha's lifetime, it certainly became popular afterwards. Many Nikaya Buddhist schools incorporated some version of the Abhidharma tradition into their canons. It was not a school as such, more a particular *style* of inquiry, and so its specific content varied.

A basic method of Abhidharma thought and practice is to analyse a given phenomenon into constituent parts in order to gain deeper insight

---

5 This text is known by the Sanskrit title *Prajñāpāramitā-hṛidaya-sūtra*, T.251.
6 See Schopen 2005: 25-62. For a translation of the *Heart Sutra* and the *Diamond Sutra* (*Vajracchedikā-prajñāpāramitā-sūtra*, Ch. *Jingang banruo boluomi jing*, T.235–6), see Conze 1988.

into the truth that there is no enduring self (atman). For instance, we might analyse the human person into five constituents (*skandhas*): body, feeling, perception, volitions, and consciousness.[7] By pursuing this set of analytical reflections, often in the context of meditative absorption, the Abhidharmika aimed to gain spiritual insight into the true nature of the human being. Over time, the analytical categories became more precise and were termed 'dharmas'. So far, so good.

5.1 *Prajnaparamita*: Text as Goddess

In the Perfect Wisdom texts, the source of spiritual illumination, *prajna*, is conceived as feminine, even as the mother of the Buddhas.[8] This source is seen as supremely worthy of worship, more so than relics or even Buddhas. The Perfect Wisdom tradition exalted the worship of its own texts as the supreme means of generating merit and, some centuries later, this devotional momentum evolved into a goddess cult.

It is not certain when the first images of Prajnaparamita were created but many survive from the Pala period (8–12th centuries CE). Typically, she is depicted as a queen, seated in meditation with one hand in the gesture of giving, the other holding a lotus which supports a book. In other portrayals, she is shown with four arms. She is usually described as golden in colour, seated on a white lotus throne.

It is not clear how widespread the cult of Prajnaparamita became but images have been found at all the major monastic sites of northern India.[9] She is also known in Tibetan Buddhism. Further south, an exquisite image dating from around 1300 CE was recovered in east Java.[10]

As the Abhidharma developed, some of its exponents — but by no means all — began to harden the analytical categories that had been envisaged. Dharmas came to be regarded as irreducible, atomic constituents of reality. In other words, from a practical method for promoting spiritual insight, some Abhidharmikas developed an ontological theory. One example of this is the Sarvāstivāda school, whose name — 'all exists' — rather gives the game away. Dharmas were seen as truly existent, the building blocks of reality that underlie appearance, akin to the notion of atoms within classical scientific theory.

---

[7] *rupa, vedanā, samjñā, samskāra, vijñāna.*
[8] *Ratnagunasamcayagatha* XII:1-2; Conze 1994: 31.
[9] Kinnard 1999: 142.
[10] Klokke et al 2003: 146-7.

But the notion that dharmas are irreducible existents is problematic since it contradicts the fundamental Buddhist doctrine of dependent origination (pratitya-samutpada), which declares that everything arises in dependence upon conditions and, when those conditions cease, those things cease. Some Abhidharmikas resolved this problem by adopting a theory of two levels of truth. First of all, there is conventional truth (*saṁvṛiti-satya*), which is ordinary, everyday reality, where we think in terms of a self and of objects like tables and cars as real. Yet at the level of ultimate truth (*paramārtha-satya*), these things are not real but only names created by human thought. Underlying these names are dharmas — and these *are* truly real.

Different schools posited various lists of dharmas: 75, 82, even 100. Many of the dharmas classify types of mental states — positive and negative — which reflect a concern with mental cultivation and meditation. Through analysing experience into its constituent dharmas, the Abhidharmika aimed to gain prajna or understanding. But, according to the Perfect Wisdom texts, this doesn't go far enough. These texts teach the *perfection* of wisdom, which involves seeing the unreality of the dharmas themselves. This message was preached relentlessly by means of a massive literary output.

5.2 Dependent Origination

Dependent origination (*pratitya-samutpada*), sometimes known as 'conditionality', is the basic philosophical insight of Buddhism as formulated by the early tradition. In general terms, it states that all things arise in dependence upon conditions, and, when those conditions cease, things themselves cease.[11] It is illustrated in many Buddhist teachings, including the three marks of existence. First, since nothing exists independently of conditions, everything lacks enduring identity (*anātman*). Secondly, this means that everything is impermanent (*anicca*). Finally, because our desires are often not in harmony with conditionality, we suffer (*duḥkha*). These truths are fully realized by the Awakened mind.

While dependent origination is widely understood to govern the way in which the ignorant mind works, it also underpins the possibility of spiritual transformation. It is precisely *because* we do not have a fixed identify that we can change for the better and so become Buddhas. No matter how enmeshed in negative habits we are, conditionality offers the possibility of creative transformation.[12]

---

11 See, for instance, SN II.28.
12 This is explored in the *Upanisā Sutta* (SN II.29).

The Philosophy of Perfect Wisdom

Before getting too embroiled in the complexities of Perfect Wisdom thought, it is important to emphasize the role that it functions within the context of a spiritual path. Without this understanding, it can seem impossibly remote from the needs and concerns of the struggling human being. Early Perfect Wisdom sutras are just as keen to promote the bodhisattva as the ideal spiritual person as they are to dive into the philosophical deep. For instance, the bodhisattva is characterized in the *Ratnaguna* in terms of renunciation and non-attachment. These are traditional Buddhist virtues but with a difference: in this context, it is not just material things that the bodhisattva renounces but also concepts, theories, and even the idea of a spiritual path. The *Perfect Wisdom in 8000 Lines* begins:

> No wisdom can we get hold of, no highest perfection,
> No Bodhisattva, no thought of enlightenment either.
> When told of this, if not bewildered and in no way anxious,
> A Bodhisattva courses in the Well-Gone's [the Buddha] wisdom.
>
> In form, in feeling, will, perception, and awareness
> Nowhere in them they find a place to rest on.
> Without a home they wander, dharmas never hold them,
> Nor do they grasp at them...[13]

The bodhisattva uses concepts but is not attached to them. He does not mistake them for reality. More than this, he develops the same attitude towards even the terms and assumptions of the spiritual path. Concepts like the bodhichitta, bodhisattva, and wisdom have a conventional meaning only; they are not ultimately real and should not become objects of attachment. This caution against becoming over-reliant on concepts and mistaking them for real, independent things is a constant refrain throughout the Perfect Wisdom literature. Another way of putting this is to say that the Perfect Wisdom texts are constantly alert to the danger of literalism in the use of language. But why should this be a problem?

On a psychological level, perfect wisdom is concerned to guard against dogmatism — the kind of attitude that insists that it is correct and every other view must be wrong. This is a concern since it leads to conceit as well as sectarian argument, even aggressive opposition. Not only this, it is an expression of delusion. An intellectual grasp of the Dharma is seen as just as dangerous as no grasp at all; perhaps even more so since it offers the temptation to settle down in this understanding and so fail to achieve true wisdom.

---

[13] Conze 1994: 9.

Shunyata or Emptiness

In philosophical terms, the message of the Perfect Wisdom texts can be summed up in one word: *shunyata*. Shunyata is best understood as a restatement of dependent origination, especially as articulated through the concept of anatman — the idea that no things have an enduring essence or 'self'. It is sometimes rendered as 'emptiness', other times as 'nothingness', even as 'voidness'. Partly owing to these unfavourable translations, it is often taken as a nihilistic claim that nothing really exists, that life is some kind of collective figment of the imagination, even that our individual personalities are some kind of hallucinogenic delusion. But the term must be understood in context. It serves a deconstructive function, aiming to undo a perceived error in Abhidharma thinking, which was to see dharmas as ultimately real. It is framed in negative language not because it seeks to deny human experience but in order to eradicate a mistaken way of seeing things.

For the Perfect Wisdom texts, all dharmas are *empty* as regards their 'own-being' (*svabhāvaśūnya*). This means that they are not ultimate *facts* but only conceptual constructs; they are not ultimately real. But then a further step is taken. Since all dharmas are empty, this means that they do not really exist at all. The *Perfect Wisdom in 8000 Lines* expresses it like this.

> Just so a Bodhisattva, who courses and dwells in perfect wisdom, comprehends that all dharmas are like an echo. He does not think about them, does not review, identify or perceive them, and he knows that those dharmas do not exist, that their reality does not appear, cannot be found, cannot be got at.[14]

The Perfect Wisdom texts extend the scope of shunyata to cover everything; all things have the nature of emptiness, which also means that no things exist absolutely. This leads to some surprising and paradoxical assertions.

> [A] Bodhisattva, a great being, leads countless beings to Nirvana, and yet there is not any being that has been led to Nirvana, nor that has led others to it.[15]

Given this apparent denial of of everyday realities, it is perhaps not surprising that shunyata is sometimes read as a disavowal of the world of concrete experience. Moreover, the theme of illusion is pursued relentlessly throughout the Perfect Wisdom texts; not only are beings like illusions but

---

14 Conze 1994: 147.
15 Conze 1994: 90.

Perfect Wisdom, Awakening, *everything* is like an illusion. This is illustrated through a number of similes. For instance, the *Diamond Sutra* tells us:

> As stars, a fault of vision, as a lamp,
> A mock show, dew drops or a bubble,
> A dream, a lightning flash, or cloud,
> So we should view what is conditioned.[16]

But the Perfect Wisdom tradition created as many problems as it solved. If everything is emptiness, and there is no person, no object, no Awakening — no anything — why strive for Awakening at all? The discrepancy between a scrupulous renunciation of all conceptual constructs and the practical needs of individual spiritual life seems to have created a serious difficulty. This problem was never fully resolved and the Perfect Wisdom texts were seen by some as nihilistic, undercutting the basis for leading a spiritual life. This critique played a role in the development of more affirmative models of reality and the human person as found in Yogachara and Buddha-nature thought, which offered a corrective to one-sided under-standings of shunyata.[17]

Despite its rhetoric of repudiation, the Perfect Wisdom literature does not really dismiss the reality of the phenomenal world. Experience is *likened* to an illusion, not equated with it. The difficulty is that the texts do not discriminate between different levels of conversation. While, from its own point of view, to say that a being is no more real than a dream is correct (since they are both dependently arisen and shunya), this does not mean that they have equal value or significance. It is really not the same thing to act unethically in a dream as it is in waking life; the consequences are very different.

The Perfect Wisdom texts adopt shock tactics to jolt us into re-examining our relationship with experience. In making dramatic claims such as denying that there is any such thing as Awakening, every assumption is called into question, there is nothing left to hold on to — and this is the whole point. But to some degree these tactics backfired. In emphasizing the ontological at the expense of the epistemological and ultimately soteriological — what ultimately *is* (or isn't!) above a structured route towards realizing this — the Perfect Wisdom texts may seem to theorize the spiritual path away. Regarded in a positive light, these texts may offer a perspective from the farther shore of Awakening; negatively, they can appear to dismantle the raft even as we are crossing the river, leaving us floundering mid-stream. They fail to distinguish between when

---

[16] *Vajracheddika Sutra*, 32; see Conze 1988: 68.
[17] See Chapter 6.

they are speaking on the ultimate level and when they are speaking conventionally, and this invites the criticism that their position is ultimately nihilistic.

5.3 The Case of Tibetan Buddhism

Buddhism became popular in Tibet from around the 7th century CE. By this time, esoteric or Tantric practices had been absorbed into Indian Mahayana Buddhism and it was this hybrid tradition that was enthusiastically received. It mixed Mahayana philosophy and practice with magical beliefs and rituals. This combined well with Tibet's indigenous shamanic religion.

As a consequence, while sharing many Mahayana characteristics, Tibetan Buddhism is usually classed as a separate tradition, known as the Vajrayana ('Diamond Vehicle'). It became popular throughout the Himalayan region and spread to Mongolia, parts of China, and even Russia. Shingon, a distinctive form of esoteric Buddhism that flourished in Japan, shares many features with the Vajrayana.

Tibetan Buddhism incorporates a number of shamanic elements including the use of oracles, an emphasis on preparation for death, and the use of post-mortem rituals designed to assist the departing spirit in the afterlife. It has developed a unique procedure for ecclesiastic succession based on the idea that important masters are reborn over many lifetimes and that their *tulku*[18] should inherit their position. In addition, the discovery of hidden Dharma treasures or *termas*, such as teachings or ritual objects, has helped to shape the pattern of Tibetan Buddhism.

The Tibetan tradition is itself diverse. For example, the Gelugpa tradition is strictly monastic and emphasizes philosophical study while in the Nyingmapa tradition, teachers often function more like shamans than conventional Buddhist clergy and may not live monastically.

Since the Chinese invasion of Tibet in the 1950s, a diaspora community has established exile monastic centres in India and has begun to spread the Tibetan form of Buddhism throughout the world.[19]

Nagarjuna and the Madhyamika

Some of the insights of the Perfect Wisdom literature may have inspired Nagarjuna, whose writings later gave rise to a philosophical school known

---

[18] Literally, tulku means 'apparent body' and refers to any person believed to be the rebirth of a deceased master.
[19] For more on Tibetan Buddhism, see Powers 1994.

as the Madhyamika, which emphasized the teaching of shunyata. The centrality of shunyata to Nagarjuna's thought is made clear by the following passage.

For him to whom emptiness [shunyata] is clear
Everything becomes clear.[20]

The precise relationship between Nagarjuna and the Perfect Wisdom sutras is not known but there seems to be a good deal of overlap between them. This is reflected in a legend that tells how Nagarjuna was invited to visit the nagas (nāgas), or serpent deities, in their underwater kingdom. While he was there, Nagarjuna discovered the Perfect Wisdom sutras, which had been lost since being taught by the Buddha. The nagas made a gift of these scriptures to Nagarjuna so that he could share their wisdom with humanity.

Whereas the sutras were not systematic and tended to make unargued assertions, Nagarjuna pursued a more logical, analytic approach. Much of his writing is very technical and at times his arguments are difficult to follow. His intentions have proved notoriously difficult to recover and scholastic debate has raged for centuries over what he really meant. Most often, his work is interpreted in the light of later commentators. He is credited with writing a number of works, including devotional verses, but his key treatise (śāstra) is the Mulāmādhymakārikā ('Fundamental Verses on the Middle Way', hereafter the MMK). This complex work comprises 448 verses, arranged in 27 chapters and its main objective is to show that shunyata may properly be applied not only to all things but even to itself.

Nagarjuna is especially revered as the master of a method of philosophical analysis known as prasanga (consequence), which involved scrutinizing a proposition put forward by an opponent and showing that it was ultimately self-contradictory and so absurd. He claimed not to put forward any philosophical thesis (pratijña) of his own, but simply to point out the flaws in the claims of others.[21] Although perhaps puzzling to us, this perspective is radically traditional given that the Buddha himself claimed to have renounced all philosophical opinion (dṛṣṭi).[22] The prasangika is said to proceed like a man who, lacking his own weapon, kills his opponent with the opponent's own sword.[23]

The MMK is partly written in a dialogue format, with Nagarjuna presenting the viewpoints of his critics and then answering them. The focus

---

[20] MMK XXIV:14; cited in Garfield 1995: 301.
[21] See Vigrahavyāvartanī: Averting the Arguments, 29 in Streng 1967: 224.
[22] See, for instance, DN I.497ff.
[23] Nagao 1991: 47.

of the work is very specific; it does not address practical issues of spiritual life but concentrates exclusively on the philosophical problem of existence. Through applying shunyata as a deconstructive, analytical procedure, Nagarjuna aims to demonstrate that nothing has 'inherent existence' (*svabhāva*); in other words, nothing exists independently of conditions. The target of this critique was the views held by some Abhidharmikas, as well as other non-Buddhist philosophers.

Nagarjuna goes much further than just criticizing the notion of dharmas. In the course of the MMK, he carries out a series of attacks on the reality of many basic ideas, including causation, motion, time, and especially personal identity. Using the prasangika method, he attempts to shows that these ideas are ultimately nonsensical. In the very first verse of the treatise, he appears to deconstruct the basic Buddhist doctrine of dependent origination when he rejects the idea that anything can arise.

> Neither from itself nor from another
> Nor from both,
> Nor from a non-cause
> Does anything whatever, anywhere arise.[24]

The emphasis here is on 'thing'. Nagarjuna did not deny the reality of experience but, in line with Nikaya Buddhism, affirmed that nothing has an irreducible self that comes into being and then disappears again. There may be a more subtle point here too. When expressed conceptually, the teaching of dependent origination seems to imply that there are 'things' that arise and then 'cease', but this is only a way of talking. Even the revered formula of dependent origination is a finger that points to the moon of reality, not the moon itself, and an over-literal understanding of it is likely to prove spiritually limiting.

Nagarjuna later confirms that his teaching on shunyata is not new, simply a restatement of the basic Buddhist view of reality.

> Whatever is dependently co-arisen
> That is explained to be emptiness.
> That, being a dependent designation
> Is itself the middle way.[25]

For Nagarjuna, shunyata equates with dependent origination and so upholds the Middle Way (*Mādhyama-mārga*) between the extreme metaphysical views of eternalism and nihilism, which were criticized by the Buddha.[26]

---

[24] MMK I.1; Garfield 1995: 3.
[25] MMK XXIV:18; Garfield 1995: 69.
[26] At MMK XV: 7-11, Nagarjuna cites the *Kaccāyanagotta Sutta* (SN II.16) to support his view.

The passage quoted above also makes it clear that shunyata is itself a 'dependent designation' (*upādāya-prajñaptir*). In other words, emptiness is itself empty of ultimate existence. This means that it is not some metaphysical reality to be seen or grasped apart from the world of things, but a heuristic concept, a means of analysing experience so as to avoid taking ordinary language too literally. It is a tool for untying philosophical knots, an analytical procedure that may be *applied* to any object of awareness, such as a dog, a dream, an emotion. Nagarjuna emphasizes that emptiness is not itself a view; rather, understanding it consists in the abandoning of *all* views.

> The victorious ones have said
> That emptiness is the relinquishing of all views.
> For whomever emptiness is a view,
> That one will accomplish nothing[27]

Nagarjuna uses a scheme of *two truths* to explain the relationship between appearances and reality, which recalls the earlier Abhidharma distinction between conventional and ultimate truth but interprets them rather differently.[28] Responding to a criticism that his viewpoint entailed nihilism, he writes:

> The Buddha's teaching of the Dharma
> Is based on two truths:
> A truth of worldly convention [*lokasaṁvṛti-satya*]
> And an ultimate truth [*paramārtha-satya*].
>
> Those who do not understand
> The distinction drawn between these two truths
> Do not understand
> The Buddha's profound truth.
>
> Without a foundation in the conventional truth
> The significance of the ultimate cannot be taught.
> Without understanding the significance of the ultimate,
> Liberation is not achieved.[29]

This distinction between the conventional and ultimate truth is crucial to understanding Nagarjuna's concerns, but their precise meaning is a matter of some controversy.[30] One interpretation sees the conventional

---

[27] MMK XIII.8; Garfield 1995: 36.
[28] For an influential interpretation of Nagarjuna's two truths theory, see Candrakīrti's *Mādhyamikavatāra* as analysed in Huntington 1989: 48ff. See also Huntington 1983.
[29] MMK XXIV:8–10; Garfield 1995: 68.
[30] For a discussion, see Huntington 1983. For instance, one view sees the two truths as not *ontologically* but *epistemologically* distinct; they embody two ways of seeing things — one

truth, embodied in the Buddha's teachings, as the necessary means through which the ultimate truth of Awakening is to be realized. The ultimate truth itself is said to be beyond words. The formula of the two truths could be seen as a conceptual formulation of the Buddha's parable of the raft; the conventional truth is the raft, which takes us to the other shore of Awakening, which is the ultimate truth. Thus the true nature of things is not some metaphysical absolute standing behind the world of conventional experience; rather it is revealed within its midst.[31]

Later in the MMK, Nagarjuna goes on to make some controversial claims. Perhaps one of the most contentious is this.

> There is not the slightest difference
> Between samsara and nirvana.
> There is not the slightest difference
> Between nirvana and samsara.
>
> Whatever is the limit of nirvana,
> That is the limit of samsara.
> There is not the slightest difference between them,
> Or even the subtlest thing.[32]

From the point of view of early Buddhism, this seems a startling and somewhat alarming claim since Nagarjuna seems to suggest that samsara (the world of suffering) and nirvana (spiritual Awakening) are *the same*. This wipes out the Buddhist path in a stroke. If nirvana and samsara are the same, what is the point of spiritual practice? But the situation may not be as drastic as it first seems. Samsara and nirvana are the same only in the sense that they are ultimately shunya or empty; they are conceptual constructs. Nagarjuna is perhaps also asserting that nirvana is not some other world apart from this one but, in fact, this very world of pain viewed in its true light, as it really is. In other words, by means of the conventional truth (samsara), we realize the ultimate truth (nirvana). In fact, the two are nondual; the ultimate *is* the conventional seen free of distorting thought.

What is problematic about Nagarjuna is that he does not specify when he is speaking from the point of view of ultimate truth and when he is speaking from the conventional point of view. However, it is likely that his verses were designed for memorization and discussion with a teacher who would clarify the difference. Moreover, they may well have been written to

---

limited, the other Awakened; see Crittenden 1981. Understood this way, the two truths form a similar epistemic structure to that of the Yogachara notion of the three natures (*see* Chapter 6). This perspective appears to downgrade the value of the conventional truth and is criticized by, among others, Garfield (Garfield 1995: 296–99).

31   See Garfield 1995: 299, especially note 110.

32   MMK XXV.19–20; Garfield 1995: 75, modified by author.

be used in the context of meditation.[33] In terms of experience, samsara and nirvana are not the same at all. Nagarjuna's intention may be to discourage a literal, other-worldly view of nirvana but — considered in isolation — his method risks dissolving vital spiritual distinctions and so may undermine the Buddhist path.

Nagarjuna's MMK amounts to an attempt to prove the Buddha's spiritual insight into dependent origination and no enduring self using logical argument to demolish all claims to the contrary. But it is questionable whether or not such a rational method can result in the spiritual transformation needed to abandon attachment to self. Using words to go beyond words may be self-defeating and was certainly seen as such by some of his critics. But it is vital always to bear in mind that the application of Madhyamika analysis forms part of an integrated spiritual regime and cannot be divorced from it without distortion. The Madhyamika is much more than clever talk; ultimately it is concerned with liberating our minds from the conceptual traps that we catch ourselves in. In this sense, it resembles Wittgenstein's understanding of the function of philosophical thought: 'Philosophy unties knots in our thinking; hence its result must be simple, but its activity must be as complicated as the knots it unties.'[34]

The Influence of the Madhyamika

Although his immediate influence was slight, so revered did Nagarjuna later become that in Tibet he is widely seen as the second Buddha.[35] Details of the historical development of Madhyamika thought are sketchy but two figures that stand out are Bhāvaviveka (c.500–570 CE) and Chandrakirti (Candrakīrti, c.600–650 CE).[36]

Bhavaviveka argued that the truth of emptiness needed to be established through independent argumentation, not simply by refutation. To do so, he adopted Indian epistemological approaches (pramāṇa), which allege positive grounds for knowledge, to lend weight to Nagarjuna's conclusions.[37] This approach was strongly criticized by Chandrakirti, who re-emphasized the prasanga method. For this reason, the tradition associated with Chandrakirti has become known as Prāsaṅgika-mādhyamaka, in contrast to Svātantrika-mādhyamaka which follows

---

33 Williams with Tribe 2000: 150–1.
34 Cited in Kenny 1994: 272.
35 Richard Hayes argues that 'Nāgārjuna's writings had relatively little effect on the course of subsequent Indian Buddhist philosophy'. His explanation for this is that 'Nāgārjuna's arguments, when examined closely, turn out to be fallacious and therefore not very convincing to a logically astute reader'. (Hayes 1994: 299)
36 Precise dates for these thinkers are not known and estimates vary.
37 For an overview of this approach, see King 2000: 128-46.

Bhavaviveka. Chandrakirti not only wrote an extensive commentary on the MMK but also combined Madhyamika philosophy with the practical aspects of the Mahayana spiritual path. In particular, he emphasized the six perfections.[38]

5.4 Meditating on Emptiness

Besides its philosophical meaning, the truth of *emptiness* is something to be realized spiritually through meditation. There are many approaches to meditating on emptiness.

For instance, within visualization meditations the blue sky that forms the backdrop to the coruscating vision of a Buddha or bodhisattva represents emptiness. All images emerge from and dissolve into this blue sky; everything resolves back into emptiness.

Another approach outlines a series of progressive stages of meditation on emptiness. This begins with reflecting on the emptiness of the individual self, recognizing that there is no fixed identify but an ever-changing flux. Then one reflects that the difference between awareness and its object is empty and so one goes beyond the duality of self and other, realizing that such distinctions are ultimately empty. Next one reflects that all phenomena are empty of fixed nature; they have no enduring identity but are conceptual constructs.

In the fourth stage, one lets go of conceptual reflection about the nature of emptiness and rests the mind in an open, relaxed state in which it becomes vast and clear, like empty space. Finally, one dwells in the luminous, self-aware nature of the mind. This state is characterized by openness, clarity, and sensitivity and is seen as identical with true reality.[39]

The Madhyamika became the dominant philosophical framework for Buddhism in Tibet, underpinning not only its scholastic thought but also its meditative and ritual practices as well. The Prasangika approach is still very much alive and is especially revered by HH the Dalai Lama's Gelugpa sect, where Nagarjuna's work is interpreted in the light of Chandrakirti's commentaries. Further strands of Madhyamika thought have also been influential, in particular a tradition that incorporated insights of the Yogachara school.[40]

---

[38] Huntington 1989.

[39] This scheme comes from Gyamtso 1988. It embodies a Tibetan perspective in which insights from Buddha-nature and Yogachara thought have been integrated into an understanding of emptiness.

[40] See Chapter 6.

Madhyamika philosophy spread to China in a piecemeal fashion, giving rise to the Sanlun (Three Treatises) school.[41] A number of the Indian Madhyamika commentaries later judged seminal by the Tibetan tradition (including those of Chandrakirti and Bhavaviveka) were not translated into Chinese. In fact, in East Asia the Sanlun developed somewhat earlier than and independent from its Indian 'parent'. The most significant Chinese Sanlun master was Jizang (549–623 CE).[42]

Jizang was influenced by the *Vimalakirti Sutra*, which emphasizes nonduality, a state of spiritual realization that goes beyond emptiness considered as a conceptual construct. He pursued an approach of 'deconstructing what is misleading and revealing what is corrective'.[43] Rather than advance a system of his own, he — perhaps not unlike the contemporary thinker Jacques Derrida (1930–2004) — was concerned to analyse texts as a means of illumination. His comments reveal meaning not through assertion but through critique; they thus function as a kind of antidote to misunderstanding, rather than as an attempt to establish a set of claims of his own. The Sanlun did not survive as an independent school beyond the 9th century but some of its insights were absorbed by other sinitic schools, including Chan/Zen.

Conclusion

The Madhyamika embodies a tradition of 'negative' philosophy in the sense that it is concerned to reject all claims rather than put forward any of its own. While this may be technically sound, it left many people rather cold and still does. In principle, emptiness is prescribed as a medicine to heal the illness of clinging to metaphysical theories. Its purpose is thus therapeutic and, if applied correctly, aims to inspire 'the calming of all representations, the calming of all verbal differentiations, peace'.[44] According to the *Perfect Wisdom in 8000 Lines Sutra*, in just the same way that the Buddha and his immediate disciples wandered possessionless, homeless, not attached to anything, so bodhisattvas wander through the world without attachment to any fixed views, completely free of dogmatism, using ideas merely as skilful means to help mature others.[45] They use concepts to free others but never become trapped in them.

---

[41] The three treatises were the *Zhonglun* (*Mādhyamaka-śāstra*, T.1564), which incorporated the MMK and a commentary of uncertain provenance; the *Shiermenlun* (T.1568), an anthology of verses possibly by Nagarjuna, again with a commentary; and finally, the *Bailun* (T.1569).

[42] For more on Jizang, see Ming-Wood 1993.

[43] *Po xie xian zheng*; translation by Fox 1992.

[44] MMK XXV:24; translated in Williams 2008: 75.

[45] AP, 35-7; Conze 1994: 13.

But the Madhyamika sword of wisdom is double-edged: its strategy of using words to go beyond words led to highly technical debates which appear to stray a long way from the needs of the practising Buddhist. Divorced from a living context of spiritual transformation, Madhyamika thought can give the impression that Buddhism is narrowly intellectual. Rather than a method for transcending conceptual discrimination, at times it seems to descend into philosophizing for its own sake. Besides this, it can give the impression that Buddhist Awakening consists in developing a surgical, analytical kind of knowledge which may seem to downgrade the importance of compassion. This impression is made the more likely when the pragmatic role of Madhyamika ideas and procedures is obscured; they are strategies for freeing the mind, to be applied especially in the context of meditation.

The absence of a positive account of human experience — and especially of its potential — which was chacteristic of Madhyamika thought, resulted in a conceptual vacuum that many Buddhists clearly felt the need to fill. This state of affairs opened the way for the emergence of Yogachara and Buddha-nature thought, which we will turn to in the next chapter.

6

Mapping the Dimensions of Mind: The Yogachara and Buddha-nature

IN TERMS OF OUR EPIC JOURNEY towards Awakening, the Madhyamika is concerned to prevent us from taking a wrong turning, from going down a dead end and so getting stuck. But to succeed on any quest, it is not enough simply to know where we are going wrong; we require an understanding of our starting point, our target, and of the route towards it. Perhaps more than anything, we require reassurance that our goal is reachable. Besides the Madhyamika, the other two main streams of thought to emerge within Indian Mahayana are the Yogachara (Yogācāra) and Buddha-nature. Both constructed detailed models of human experience in order to aid the process of spiritual transformation. The Yogachara seeks to clarify the crucial role of the mind in shaping our world, while Buddha-nature ideas emphasize that, deep within our minds, we have an innate potential for liberation.

These later developments are often interpreted as correctives to the Madhyamika's apparent nihilism, but in fact there is a great deal of continuity. While the Madhyamika was more concerned with ontology — what *is* (or isn't) — the Yogachara and Buddha-nature gave more attention to human psychology, including our mechanisms for understanding — most especially, *why* we experience delusion and so *how* we can be freed from it. Far from being opposed to the Madhyamika, these later developments could be seen as complementary.

While the Yogachara evolved into a recognisable school and took part in elevated debates with the Madhyamika, Buddha-nature thought never really got off the ground in India. But it did become important in Tibet and especially East Asia, where it combined with Yogachara ideas to provide the dominant Buddhist model of human consciousness.

The Yogachara

Yogachara means the 'practice of meditation', which gives a clue to some of its main concerns.[1] Many of the key Yogachara doctrines are presented in

---

[1] This system of thought is also known by a few other names, including *Vijñaptimātra* (cognition-only), *Vijñānavāda* (doctrine of consciousness), and *Cittamātra* (mind-only).

the *Samdhinirmocana Sutra*[2] ('Elucidating the Hidden Connections') and then elaborated in a number of treatises, especially those written by two brothers Asanga (Asaṅga) and Vasubandhu (4th century CE). It is important to note that the Yogachara encompasses a wide range of thought and by no means have all Yogacharin writers shared the same ideas or interpreted leading doctrines in the same way. Any general account must simplify and necessarily gloss over more refined differences. Having said this, key metaphors, concepts, and points of departure make some broad generalizations possible.

The emphasis that Yogachara thought places on mind and the use of terms like mind-only (*cittamātra*) have led to a widespread view that it claims *only* the mind exists. In Western philosophy, this perspective is known as idealism and was put forward by Bishop Berkeley (1685–1753), among others.[3] But it is far from certain that the Yogachara makes such a bold claim, at least in its early period. As noted previously, applying Western philosophical assumptions to Mahayana philosophy can lead to distortion, because Buddhist thought is ultimately underpinned by the goal of spiritual liberation. This should make us cautious about assuming that the Yogachara is making a claim about what ultimately *is* (ontology). It may just be saying that all we can *know* is the mind; all our experience is of mind and mind alone. Not just this but all our problems, especially the problem of delusion, arise from the mind. For this reason, it is towards the mind and its workings that the Yogachara directs its attention. This also explains its close link with meditation, since meditation practices are tools for understanding and transforming the mind.

Yogachara philosophy addresses three key spiritual questions: 1) Why are we deluded?; 2) How does the deluded mind work?; and 3) How do we move from delusion to Awakening? In dealing with these questions, the Yogachara puts forward a model of how the mind functions in relation to experience and describes a spiritual psychology that explains both how we perpetuate our ignorance of reality and how this can be overcome.

Key Ideas of the Yogachara

The SMS, dating from around the 3rd century CE, introduces many of the core Yogachara doctrines.[4] These include the notion of 'cognition-only' (*vijñapti-mātra*), the doctrine of three natures (*trisvabhāva*), the psychology of eight consciousnesses, including the store consciousness (*ālaya-vijñāna*), and the 'revolution at the basis' (*āśraya-parāvṛtti*), which signals the dawning of Awakened perception.

---

2 *Saṃdhinirmocana-sūtra* (Ch. *Jie shen mi jing*, T.676–9), hereafter SMS.
3 See Berkeley 1710.
4 For a translation, see Powers 1995.

The SMS presents itself as a 'Third Turning of the Wheel' of Dharma; the first turning refers to Shakyamuni Buddha and his teachings, while the second refers to the Madhyamika. According to the SMS, the earlier teachings were incomplete and are now fully clarified through the teachings it presents. Importantly, the sutra does not reject the Madhyamika perspective as wrong but claims to bring out its full significance. 'The ultimate doctrine of the Mahayana is, no doubt, taught in the Prajnaparamita, but its way of exposition is "with an esoteric meaning"', or "with a hidden intention".'[5]

The aim of the SMS is to make this hidden intention explicit. Far from being a wholesale rejection of the Madhyamika teaching of emptiness, the Yogachara contribution is perhaps better understood as a 'tidying up' of earlier thought. Asanga, for instance, sensitive to nihilistic interpretations of shunyata, emphasized that 'emptiness is only logical if something exists'.[6] This is a 'container' conception of emptiness; there may, for instance, be no wine in an empty glass but the glass is still there. Similarly, our perceptions may be empty of ultimate existence but they are undeniably present before us.

The doctrine of three natures (trisvabhava)

Yogachara thought tries to tread a fine line — a middle way, no less — between, on the one hand, falling into a nihilistic interpretation of emptiness and, on the other, turning experience into some ultimate existent. Its viewpoint is presented through the doctrine of three natures.[7]

1. the imagined nature (*parikalpita-svabhāva-lakṣana*)
2. the interdependent nature (*paratantra-svabhāva-lakṣana*)
3. the perfected nature (*pariniṣpanna-svabhāva-lakṣana*)

There are several ways of interpreting the three natures doctrine but what is called the 'pivotal model' seems to me the most helpful.[8] The pivotal model takes the interdependent nature as what is ultimately present and real; it is what gives rise to our experiences of both inner and outer sense. The other two natures are different ways of *relating to* reality (*see* diagram below). The imagined nature is how deluded beings experience things. Under the sway of defilements (*kleśas*), they fabricate a world that

---

5   SMS VII.30; cited in King 1994: 660. See Powers 1995: 139–41.
6   *Bodhisattvabhūmi-śāstra*, cited in King 1994: 666.
7   SMS VI; Powers 1995: 81-91.
8   For this account I am indebted to Sponberg 1981. I have also drawn on unpublished work by Robert Morrison. Understood according to this model, the three natures may be correlated with the Madhyamika notion of two truths (at least in some interpretations); see Chapter 5, note 27.

distorts reality. The imagined nature is the lens of the deluded mind and its presence explains why we don't see things as they are. It also explains why we suffer, since reality constantly frustrates our expectations and desires.

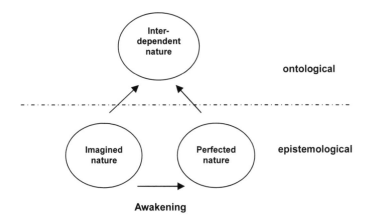

The perfected nature, on the other hand, represents 'seeing' and experiencing the interdependent nature purified of the distorting influence of the imagined nature; it characterizes Awakened consciousness. This is sometimes described in terms of breaking free of the delusory, dualistic structure of the 'grasper' (*grāhaka*) and 'grasped' (*grāhya*) relationship, or in terms of seeing the nonduality of this distinction. While grasper/grasped is sometimes interpreted to mean subject/object, it is perhaps better seen as a psychological description of our basic relationship with experience, which is one of desire and attachment. The SMS describes the perfected nature as 'like the unerring objective reference, the natural objective reference of the eyes when that person's eyes have become pure and free from the defects of clouded vision'.[9]

The interdependent nature is 'neutral' in the sense that it may either give rise to distorted experience (imagined nature) or Awakened experience (perfected nature). It is the 'reality pivot' on which both the imagined nature and the perfected nature revolve. The SMS illustrates this using the analogy of a pure crystal. When a clear crystal comes into contact with the colour blue, it appears like a sapphire; when it comes into contact with the colour red, it appears like a ruby, and so on. When the interdependent nature comes into contact with our habitual ways of seeing things, it appears as the imagined nature. When seen truly, the interdependent nature *is* the perfected nature.[10]

---

[9] Powers 1995: 83.
[10] See Powers 1995: 85-7.

To summarize, the basic Yogachara metaphor sees experience as covered over by distorting psychological material: desires, aversions, projections, and expectations. The spiritual goal is to strip away this overlaid material and so reveal experience as it is. What is left is an experience of 'suchness' (*tathatā*); things as they are. This is sometimes described as 'nondual awareness', free of conceptual fabrication. But while this may describe an elevated state of meditation, it is difficult to think that human beings can really function without concepts as we generally relate to them. The key here is about *how* we use concepts; it's not about getting rid of them but about using them more freely and consciously. Then we are not trapped in the conceptual fabrication discussed above, especially our fabricated sense of self. It is about developing a new relationship to concepts, one that is free from grasping.

The eight consciousnesses

Besides the model of the three natures, the Yogachara developed a system of eight consciousnesses to provide a more detailed psychological portrait of deluded experience. This model also accounts for the workings of karma, the ethical principle that governs human conduct.[11] The eight consciousnesses comprise: the *five* senses (*pañca-vijñāna*) considered as distinct consciousnesses; the *mind* (*mano-vijñāna*), which as well as synthesising sense experience also witnesses events of inner sense, such as visions, dreams, and so on; the *defiled mind* (*kliṣṭa-manas*); and the *store consciousness* (*ālaya-vijñāna*). The final two consciousnesses are especially important in the Yogachara system. The store consciousness, also known as the substratum consciousness, is an ever-flowing stream that underlies and informs our conscious experience. The defiled mind mistakes this store consciousness for a true, enduring self which leads to attachment, fear of losing this 'self', and so to suffering.

The Yogachara adopted a seed (*bīja*) metaphor to explain how the store consciousness works and combined this with a further metaphor of 'perfuming' or 'permeation' (*vāsanā*). Our ethically charged acts 'perfume' the store consciousness and result in the depositing of 'seeds' — or karmic potential — which then reach fruition from time to time as feelings, thoughts, and volitions. These seeds shape both the content of our inner experiences and how we experience the world in general. They are understood to be momentary, constantly replaced by similar seeds in keeping with our changing karmic stock. So the store consciousness is a kind of 'experiential warehouse in which are kept all the potentials for future experiences'.[12] Not only is it ever-flowing, informing our conscious experience, but it connects our perceptions with these seeds. The store consciousness could be understood as the structure of the ordinary self, that which — in our delusion — we come to believe makes up a real, enduring self.[13]

Karmic seeds are of two kinds: wholesome and unwholesome. Wholesome seeds take us in the direction of spiritual development, whereas unwholesome ones feed our ignorance. Besides this, our seed stock can be positively or negatively influenced by external conditions; for instance, hearing the Dharma would positively transform our seeds.

The concept of a store consciousness is useful because it helps to explain how we can reap our karma despite the fact that we have no enduring self; our karmic potential lies dormant in the store consciousness and 'bears fruit' when conditions are ripe. For instance, I have a tendency to get irritable in slow traffic and, when I find myself behind a tractor on a winding lane, frustration will arise. This is the ripening of a karmic seed. The store consciousness also accounts for our continuity of experience and explains why we have (relatively) stable characters and habit-patterns. It's important to recognize that, in view of the Yogachara emphasis on the primacy of mind, the store consciousness does not just determine ethical feedback; it informs the entire 'flavour' of our subjective world. It helps to explain why some of us experience life as threatening, even sinister while for others it seems full of joy and opportunity.

Revolution at the basis

While it may seem as though the store consciousness is something like a self, the Yogachara denies this.[14] It is mistaken for a self by the defiled mind but is in fact an ever-changing stream. Importantly, according to Vasubandhu, the store consciousness disappears at Awakening, leaving behind a radiant awareness.[15] This occurs through the evocatively termed *revolution at the basis* (*āśraya-paravṛtti*). The revolution at the basis brings about an end not only to the store consciousness but to all eight consciousnesses, which are replaced by Awakened awareness (*jñāna*). The defiled mind, which related to experience in terms of desire, or 'grasper' and 'grasped', is replaced by the wisdom that sees the equality of all things (*samatā-jñāna*). The store consciousness itself is replaced by the mirror-like wisdom (*mahādarśa-jñāna*), which sees everything just as it is, free of distortion and free of conceptual overlay (*nirvikalpa-jñāna*).

Yogachara psychology shows how our desires, investments, and prejudices colour the way we experience life. We see the world through the lens of our own habits, expectations, fears, and aspirations. This creates the

---

[13] Williams 2008: 98.
[14] See, for instance, the SMS; Powers 1995: 77.
[15] See *Triṃśika* 4; translated in Anacker 1984: 186.

unique lifeworld that we inhabit. The aim of Yogachara thought and practice is to overturn this habitual way of seeing things and replace it with Awakened cognition.

Later Yogachara Developments

Yogachara thought continued to evolve in India for more than 500 years and became the dominant strand of Mahayana thought there. When transplanted to Tibet, it continued to be highly valued, and was even combined with Madhyamika in a scholastic synthesis known as Yogachara–Svatantrika.[16] In this system, the Yogachara perspective is understood as a staging post on the way to establishing the 'more advanced' Madhyamika position.

Yogachara thought was also carried to China in a number of guises as it continued to develop in India. The busiest period of Yogachara activity in China was during the 6th and 7th centuries. One of the early Yogachara schools of thought to develop there drew inspiration from Vasubandhu's commentary on the *Ten Stages Sutra,* known in Chinese as the *Dilun*.[17] This school split into two camps which followed opposing interpretations of that treatise, the second of which synthesized Buddha-nature thought with Yogachara ideas. A further ingredient was added to the mix when Paramartha (Paramārtha, 499–569) translated another Yogachara treatise, this time written by Asanga.[18] Following the Chinese title of this treatise, the school of thought subscribing to this approach became known as the Shelun. In his analysis, Paramartha posited that when the store consciousness dissolves away (following the revolution at the basis), there remains a *ninth*, immaculate consciousness (*amalā-vijñāna*). This shows the deep influence that Buddha-nature ideas had on his thought (*see* below).

It was partly to resolve such differences of interpretation that the celebrated pilgrim-monk Xuanzang (c.600–64) was inspired to undertake his epic journey to India to collect and bring back all the relevant Buddhist treatises with the aim of translating them and then establishing an

---

[16] The basic text for this tradition is Śāntarakṣita's *Mādhyamakālaṅkāra*. For a translation, see Padmakara Translation Group 2005. Śāntarakṣita uses the Yogachara perspective to posit that in conventional experience, objects are not external to the perceiver; from an absolute perspective (Madhyamika), they have no intrinsic existence.

[17] *Shidijing lun* (Skt. *Daśabhūmika-sūtra-śāstra*), T.1522. The *Ten Stages Sutra* has no particular bearing on the Yogachara but in his commentary, Vasubandhu makes a few passing remarks about the nature of the *ālaya-vijñāna*. The concept is not explained systematically and he appears to offer two conflicting interpretations of it. Without access to the more systematic works known to Vasubandhu, Chinese scholar-monks had to piece together their own understanding. This fragmentary transmission of Indian doctrinal systems prompted the creative recasting of some key doctrines.

[18] *Mahāyāna-saṃgraha* (Ch. *She dasheng lun,* T.1593); translated in Keenan 2003.

'orthodox' interpretation. Xuanzang is a curious figure in Chinese Buddhism since, although revered as the archetypal pilgrim, the tradition he inspired was somewhat out of step with established trends and so did not endure. When Xuanzang returned to China, laden with precious texts, his prestige was such that he benefited from considerable court patronage, which meant that his school, the Faxiang ('dharma characteristics' or Weishi; 'consciousness-alone'), prospered instantly and enjoyed disproportionate influence. But some of its emphases were strongly resisted by more settled traditions, which had already begun to evolve independently of their Indian sources.

For instance, one Faxiang doctrine asserted that the store consciousness contained seeds which set boundaries to human potential. Accordingly, some people were thought to have limited spiritual capacities, while others, known as *icchantikas* (incorrigibles), were believed incapable of *ever* realizing Awakening. This view runs contrary to the basic Buddhist attitude that no matter how wretched our present state, we can always change for the better, and proved unpopular with Chinese Buddhists. Faxiang also rejected the notion of Buddha-nature, already a core concept in Chinese Buddhism. Besides this, its highly scholastic orientation helped to ensure that Faxiang was not destined for long-term success. Nevertheless, Xuanzang's school enjoyed modest influence in Korea and then Japan (where it was known as Hossō).

Yogachara insights were gradually incorporated into a number of indigenous Chinese Buddhist schools, including Huayan and Chan,[19] as well as being combined with Buddha-nature thought.

Buddha-nature

'Buddha-nature' is an umbrella term that incorporates several Mahayana doctrines but in essence it presents a profoundly affirming model of human spirituality, emphasizing that, deep within us, we all have the potential for Awakening — and even that Awakening is our real nature. While its roots are in India, it had no great impact there, perhaps partly because some of its insights were absorbed into Yogachara philosophy. Its real significance was felt in Tibet and especially in East Asia, where it became a cornerstone of many Mahayana-inspired traditions. On its pilgrimage eastward, Buddha-nature underwent several profound transformations, as it was adapted to meet new cultural assumptions and expectations.

Origins of Buddha-nature thought

The origins of Buddha-nature are in the concept of *tathagatagarbha* (*tathāgatagarbha*). This deeply resonant term means something like 'embryo

---

[19] See Chapters 7 and 8.

of Awakening' or 'womb of the Buddha' and refers to the potential for each and every human being to gain spiritual liberation. Rather than emphasizing human imperfection, as Nikaya Buddhism often did, it encapsulates an optimistic vision of human possibility; despite our failings, we have within us a precious seed that may flower into Awakening. Buddha-nature thought could be understood as a response to two key spiritual questions: first, if we are ignorant beings, how can we ever overcome this? And secondly, where does the aspiration and motivation for Awakening come from?

The Buddha-nature teaching first appears in a short and philosophically uncluttered text called the *Tathagatagarbha Sutra* (c. 3rd century CE).[20] At its inception, Buddha-nature was not the highly abstract, metaphysical idea it was later to become but a metaphor which underlined that all people, no matter how degenerate, have the potential for liberation. The Buddha of the sutra declares:

> [W]hen I regard all beings with my buddha eye, I see that hidden within the defilements (kleshas) of greed, desire, anger, and stupidity there is seated augustly and unmovingly the tathagata's wisdom, the tathāgata's vision, and the tathāgata's body. Good sons, all beings, though they find themselves with all sorts of kleshas have a tathagatagarbha [Buddha-embryo] that is eternally unsullied, and that is replete with virtues no different from my own.[21]

The Buddha-nature is then illustrated using a series of nine similes, which play on the ambiguity of the term *garbha*. In its widest use, 'garbha' can mean the inside, middle or interior of anything; it is this meaning that the author draws on when he describes it as the gold hidden inside a pit of waste, honey inside a swarm of angry bees, and a golden statue wrapped in dirty rags.[22] Most of the similes emphasize the presence of something extremely precious contained within something foul. The last of the similes compares the presence of the Buddha-nature to an impoverished, ugly, and hated woman who bears a noble son in her womb. We are left with a highly affirming message: despite all our imperfections, we are still a womb of Buddhahood.

Later conceptions of Buddha-Nature

As the notion of Buddha-nature evolved, it came to be seen not just as a positive impulse that underlies our imperfections but even as the ground of reality as a whole. The beginnings of this shift can be traced to the *Shrimala*

---

[20] *Tathāgatagarbha-sūtra* (Ch. *Dafang guang rulaizang jing*, T.666–7); translated in Grosnick 1995.

[21] Grosnick 1995: 96, modified by author.

[22] Grosnick 1995: 96-102.

Sutra (3rd century CE), which equates Buddha-nature with the dharmakaya ('body of truth' or the Buddha in Eternity; *see* p.65–6).[23] According to this seminal text, Buddha-nature is empty of defilements but full of all the Buddha qualities.

> [T]he knowledge of emptiness of that tathāgata-embryo is of two kinds. What are the two? The first is the knowledge that the tathagata-embryo is empty: that it is apart from all defilements and apart from knowledge which does not lead to liberation. The second is the knowledge that the tathagata-embryo is not empty: that it contains inconceivable Dharmas more numerous than sands of the Ganges, which embody the Buddhas' wisdom of liberation.[24]

Buddha-nature is seen as the ground of *all* phenomena.[25] It has two modes: an obscured or defiled mode, which equates to the world of samsara or spiritual ignorance, and a revealed mode, which is the dharmakaya and is equivalent to Buddhahood.[26] In its purified aspect, Buddha-nature is described as permanent, blissful, true self, and pure.[27] Albeit in practice stained by defilements, Buddha-nature is intrinsically pure. This paradox was to fascinate and perplex East Asian Buddhists for centuries. How can something be pure in princeiple but corrupt in practice? The *Shrimala Sutra* asks the same question and admits that only a Buddha can understand it.[28] This suggests that there was confusion about this new spiritual vision even among its supporters, and that its logical shortcomings were difficult to resolve. This problem only got worse as the tradition developed.

In solving the problem of the origins of our spiritual impulses, Buddha-nature seems to have replaced it with a new one: where does our delusion come from? The *Shrimala Sutra* resorts to an idea of 'beginningless ignorance' in order to explain why we don't experience the Buddha-nature as it truly is.[29] But if the underlying reality of experience is intrinsically pure, how could ignorance ever arise?

It is not easy to see why the *Shrimala Sutra* made such a radical move from Buddha-nature being a spiritual impulse to its being the ground of all

---

23 *Śrīmālādevī-siṃhanāda-sutra*, T.353. For a translation, see Wayman and Wayman 1974. Also see T.310 translated in Chang 1991: 363-86.

24 See Chang 1991: 378, modified by author.

25 Chang 1991: 380.

26 Chang 1991: 380–1.

27 See Paul 1979: 197. See also Chang 1991: 379-80. Despite this affirmative account of Buddha-nature, the *Shrimala Sutra* is at pains to deny that the Buddha-nature is an eternalistic soul. (Chang 1991: 380) Perhaps not always successfully, the sutra steers a delicate course between its affirmation of the Buddha-nature and the consequent danger of reifying it. This tension seems intrinsic to Buddha-nature type perspectives.

28 Chang 1991: 381.

29 See Paul 1979: 194-5.

existence, especially given the philosophical problems this shift creates. It may be that in his enthusiasm to present a positive account of human potential, the author failed to foresee all the philosophical implications they were committing to. I am inclined to interpret the notion of Buddha-nature sympathetically, seeing it as a practical encouragement rather than a tight-knit theory.

6.1 The Three Stages Sect: A Buried Gem

A distinctive perspective on Buddha-nature was developed by the Three Stages sect (*Sanjie jiao*).[30] This was one of the most important religious movements in China in the 6th and 7th centuries, yet until the 20th century its teachings and practices had been virtually forgotten, buried beneath the debris of history for hundreds of years. Founded by Xin-Xing (540–594), it emphasized that beings lived in the third and final age of the Dharma (Ch. *mofa*, Jp. *mappō*), when the Buddhist sangha was in a state of terminal decline and the teachings at their lowest ebb.[31]

An important teaching of the sect is that of the 'perceived Buddha' (*foxiang fo*).[32] Since all beings possess Buddha-nature, they are, in their deepest aspect, identical with Buddhas. Moreover, owing to the decline of the Dharma, the Three Stages sect believed it was impossible to make reliable distinctions between the Awakened and unawakened, and so taught that all beings — including animals — should be reverenced as Buddhas without distinction. Treating all beings as Buddhas in this way was known as the practice of 'universal respect'.[33]

The sect emphasized giving as the key practice and dissolved the widely upheld hierarchy between monk and lay. Its most distinctive institution was an 'inexhaustible treasury' to which the faithful contributed and which was distributed to the needy.[34]

The Three Stages sect was repressed around the beginning of the 8th century and its teachings disappeared. The discovery of the horde of manuscripts at Dunhuang in the early 20th century (*see* Feature 1.3) furnished scholars with the necessary material to reconstruct its teachings.

While Buddha-nature sounds rather like a permanent self, since it is described as unborn and undying, the *Shrimala Sutra* is at pains to deny

---

[30] For a study of this movement, see Hubbard 2001.

[31] For more on *mappō*, see pp.180, 207.

[32] See Hubbard 2001: 118ff.

[33] Hubbard 2001: 119-20.

[34] See Hubbard 2001: 168ff.

this, albeit not convincingly.[35] Another Buddha-nature text, the *Nirvana Sutra*, is not so circumspect.[36] This sprawling and at times inconsistent work, which survives in a number of versions, came to be highly revered in East Asia partly because it reasserts Buddhahood as a universal ideal open to all.

Radically — and certainly controversially — the *Nirvana Sutra* claims that Buddha-nature *is* a true self. While this seems to flout a basic Buddhist premise, the sutra draws on the teaching of skilful means to bolster its position. It argues that the Buddha taught non-self as a provisional teaching only, in order to counter specific points of view. In other contexts, the Buddha taught that there *is* a self and this is embodied in Buddha-nature.[37] The *Nirvana Sutra* argues that Buddha-nature teachings can help convert non-Buddhists who regard Buddhism as nihilistic — perhaps owing to the general Buddhist emphasis on no enduring self (*anātman*) and the Mahayana concern with shunyata. It thus adopts a radically pragmatic stance; teachings are addressed to particular people in specific contexts, always with the aim of bringing about Awakening. No teaching (except of course Buddha-nature) is seen as ultimate.

Ideas from the *Shrimala Sutra* were further developed in a number of other texts which were to become influential, especially a complex treatise called the *Ratnagotravibhāga*.[38] While not influential in East Asia, it provided the philosophical basis for Buddha-nature thought in Tibet. This treatise emphasizes the shift away from seeing Buddha-nature as a *psychological* principle that underlies our present spiritual ignorance towards a *cosmological* principle, which is an all-pervading, intrinsically pure mind that is the ground of all reality.

Yogachara–Buddha-nature Synthesis

Scholars are divided over whether or not Buddha-nature and the Yogachara began as separate streams or emerged from a common source. Whatever the truth of the matter, a number of texts attempted to synthesize their respective ideas. This synthesis later became a hallmark of East Asian Mahayana thought. For example, the *Lankavatara Sutra*, a miscellaneous and inconsistent text of uncertain date, gestured in this direction by identifying Buddha-nature with the store consciousness.[39]

---

[35] See note 28 above.
[36] *Nirvāna-sūtra* (Ch. *Da ban niepan jing*, T.374). For an online translation, see http://www.nirvanasutra.net/.
[37] Chapter 12; http://www.nirvanasutra.net/nirvanasutrae.htm.
[38] For a translation from Tibetan, see Kongtrul et al 2000.
[39] *Laṅkāvatāra-sūtra* (Ch. *Leng qie a bo duo luo bao jing*, T.670–2). For a translation, see Suzuki 1932.

[T]he tathāgatagarbha holds within it the cause for both good and evil, and by it all the forms of existence are produced. Like an actor it takes on a variety of forms, and [in itself] is devoid of an essence and what belongs to it … Because of the influence of habit-energy that has been accumulating since beginningless time, what here goes under the name of the Alaya-vijnana is accompanied by the seven vijnanas which is like a great ocean in which the waves roll on permanently but the [deeps remain unmoved; that is, the Alaya] body itself subsists uninterruptedly, quite free from fault of impermanence, unconcerned with the doctrine of ego-substance, and thoroughly pure in its essential nature.[40]

The *Lankavatara Sutra* does not present a consistent position on the relationship between the store consciousness and Buddha-nature, which perhaps reflects both its patchwork nature and a set of ideas still being worked through.

Paramartha, *The Awakening of Faith*, and Original Awakening

Perhaps the single most important figure in relation to synthesising Yogachara and Buddha-nature ideas for an East Asian audience was Para-martha, an Indian missionary monk who arrived in China around 546. Paramartha ranks as one of the greatest ever translators of Buddhist texts. Although more than 30 of his translations survive, many more are believed to have been lost.

Besides translating dozens of Yogachara texts, which he often 'corrected' and added to in the process, Paramartha also 'translated' several important texts that unified Yogachara and Buddha-nature concepts. Perhaps most remarkable is that some of these works were almost certainly not trans-lations at all but by Paramartha's own hand. The most important of these is *The Awakening of Mahayana Faith*.[41]

Written around the mid-6th century, the AMF is a seminal document in the transmission of Buddhism to East Asia and played a key role in what is sometimes called the 'sinification' of Buddhism: the assimilation of Chinese culture into Buddhism. It is not an easy text since it is written in a rather terse and at times cryptic style, but its ambiguity has enhanced its mystique and allowed for a range of interpretations. Owing in large part to the influ-ence of the AMF, Buddha-nature became a central pillar of East Asian Buddhist thought and remains so even today. The text attempts to resolve the problem of the relationship between ignorance and Awakening, which arose from a belief in the mind's intrinsic purity. Put briefly, if the ground of all experience is the intrinsically Awakened mind, how can ignorance

---

[40] Suzuki 1932: 190.
[41] *Dasheng qi xin lun*, T.1666, hereafter AMF: see Hakeda 2006. T.1667 represents a different version of the treatise.

ever arise? Following the *Lankavatara Sutra*, the AMF tries to explain this by linking the store consciousness and Buddha-nature.

The AMF synthesises a number of the developments sketched out in earlier Buddha-nature thought but reworks them into a system thoroughly integrated with Yogachara ideas about mind. In a somewhat complex scheme, it establishes mind as the ultimate source of all phenomena, but this mind has two aspects. First, there is the 'mind as suchness'; this is equated with Buddha-nature in its true guise, understood as an undifferentiated ground of reality that gives rise to all things.[42] The second aspect is the 'mind as phenomena', which is equated with the store consciousness and with the ordinary mind of flawed beings.[43] This scheme thus asserts that underlying our everyday mind, which is enmeshed in samsaric habits, is a primordially pure reality: Buddha-nature.

The AMF introduces a scheme of four levels or phases in the process of Awakening.

1. Original Awakening (*benjue*)
2. Non-Awakening (samsara/ignorance)
3. Initial Awakening
4. Final Awakening

Original Awakening expresses the insight that the human mind is ultimately grounded in Buddha-nature and is an ontological, rather than epistemological, concept. Awakening then is our essential nature, yet we do not currently experience ourselves like this but as non-Awakened, ignorant beings. Initial Awakening equates to a conceptual grasp of our true existential heritage, together with the aspiration to uncover or *recover* the original condition of our minds, and is equated with the arising of the bodhichitta (*see* pp.46–8). This process culminates in final Awakening. This scheme amounts to a radical reconceptualization of the Buddhist path.

From an ultimate point of view (ontologically), we have always been Awakened but, from an experiential point of view (epistemologically), we must go through a process of realizing this. This way of thinking is sometimes described as an immanent model of Awakening; everything we need is already present, we just need to bring it to light. Awakening is a kind of remembering of something that we have always been, a return to our true selves. This is contrasted with a transcendent model, which emphasizes that a gulf separates us from the state of Awakening and to bridge it we need to radically transform ourselves, even to become someone else. While the developmental model emphasizes what holds us back, the immanent, Buddha-nature model zeros in on the spiritual impulse — that

---

42 Hakeda 2006: 39-43
43 Hakeda 2006: 38.

part of us that moves towards the good, true, and creative — and enshrines this as the defining feature of who we are.

Following Yogachara thought, the AMF uses the evocative metaphor of perfuming or permeation to illustrate the relationship between mind in its true aspect and mind as we experience it. First of all, ignorance permeates into suchness, which produces the deluded mind.[44] This explains why we don't experience our true nature. Secondly, and crucially, the mind as Buddha-nature is not passive but is a dynamic force within us that is constantly disclosing itself. This is explained in the following terms.

> [Suchness] permeates perpetually into ignorance. Through the force of this permeation it induces a man to loathe the suffering of samsara, to see bliss in nirvana, and, believing that he has the principle of Suchness within himself, to make up his mind to exert himself.[45]

The permeation of our intrinsic purity, or 'original Awakening', into our present experience of unawakening explains the source of spiritual impulses. Besides this, it gives us the confidence to set out on the spiritual path knowing that we are returning to our original nature.

The process of Awakening consists simply in letting go of the coverings of the mind and allowing our true state to reveal itself. In a celebrated AMF metaphor, this letting go consists in allowing the waves, whipped up by the wind of ignorance, to become tranquil and so reveal the shimmering ocean of our true mind.[46] This suggests an attentive, receptive, and patient process, rather than an aggressive, striving one.

Given that Awakening is immanent, it need not take long to realize it. While the bodhisattva path was traversed over an unimaginable number of lives, East Asian Buddhism adopted a 'rhetoric of immediacy', which emphasized that Awakening is tantalizingly close. It need neither take a long time nor require superhuman efforts but can happen suddenly, in an instant, since it is really the disclosure of something that is always present. This touches on a major debate in East Asian Mahayana Buddhism: is Awakening sudden or gradual? Does it happen by slow degrees, and over a long period, or all at once, in a moment? This debate became central in the evolution of Chan/Zen.[47]

It is worth mentioning that the AMF's emphasis on inherent Awakening harmonized with indigenous Confucian ideas about the intrinsic goodness of man. This is no doubt a key reason why it caught the Chinese imagination and took hold so vigorously as a model for the Buddhist

---

44 Hakeda 2006: 59.
45 Hakeda 2006: 62, modified by author.
46 Hakeda 2006: 47.
47 See Chapters 8 and 11.

spiritual path. It also shows how, as ideas and teachings are transmitted to different places and cultures, specific elements may be teased out and assume greater importance because they mesh especially well with that culture's imagination, while others are neglected or even discarded. As with people, it is impossible for ideas to journey into a new cultural universe without being transformed in the process.

Original Awakening thought became influential throughout East Asia. It influenced the doctrines of Chan/Zen, Huayan, Tiantai, and even Pure Land devotion (*see* Feature 6.2). After its transmission to Japan, original Awakening continued to exert a powerful influence and was taken up by a number of key teachers, including Dōgen.[48]

In recent decades, a lively debate has raged over whether or not the concept of original Awakening is genuinely Buddhist. Opponents argue that it is at odds with the fundamental Buddhist concepts of dependent origination and no enduring entity since it posits a substantial self, which is the 'true nature' of the human individual. According to critics, the belief that Awakening is already present devalues spiritual practice and, consequently, undermines the motives for leading a Buddhist life. The logical outcome, they argue, is that people become deluded about the status of their accomplishments and don't bother to make efforts to transform in a positive direction. Supporters of original Awakening defend it by arguing that it is a pragmatic teaching that offers encouragement and confidence to those struggling on the spiritual path; it is a skilful means. It does not grant an exemption from spiritual practice but affirms our potential in the face of all the limitations we experience.[49]

A Note on the Death of Indian Buddhism

Buddhism eventually disappeared from India. While the hammer blows were struck by Muslim iconoclasts in the late 12th century, Indian Buddhism had long since been in decline. As early as the mid-7th century, Xuanzang noted symptoms of decay: abandoned stupas, shrinking monastic centres, the supplanting of Buddhist devotion by other Indian cults.

There were a number of reasons for this decline. First, there was a fusion of Buddhist ideas with Hinduism, and even a partial absorption of Buddhism into Hindu traditions. Secondly, Tantric Buddhism shared so much in common with Hindu cults that it became difficult to differentiate the two. Thirdly, monastic Buddhism had become increasingly specialized, scholastic, and disconnected from the general population. Consequently, as many Buddhist institutions had flourished under state patronage, they lacked the popular support to survive when this patronage was withdrawn.

---

[48] See Chapter 11.
[49] For a series of articles charting this debate, see Hubbard and Swanson 1997.

In a series of raids, Muslim invaders sacked monastic centres, culminating in the desecration of the great monasteries of Nalanda (1197) and Vikramashila (Vikramasīla, 1203). They massacred monks, burned libraries, and vandalized thousands of Buddha images and other art works. Muslim spite devastated the Buddhist heritage and ensured that its contribution to Indian culture was obscured for centuries. The Buddhist culture of many surrounding states, including the areas covered by modern Pakistan, Afghanistan, and Central Asia, was also shattered.

In small pockets, Buddhism limped along for several centuries, especially in South India, but its glory days were a distant memory. Meanwhile, the centres of Buddhist creativity had long since shifted eastward. It was not until the 19th and 20th centuries that widespread interest in Buddhism was renewed in the land of its birth.

6.2 Original Awakening

'Original Awakening' or 'original enlightenment' (hongaku) emerged in Japan in the context of Tendai Buddhism in the latter part of the Heian period (794–1885), illustrating the permeation of Buddha-nature thought. It claims not just that all beings have the potential to become Awakened, but that they are inherently so. This applies not just to human beings but animals, insects, even trees and mountains.

This approach could be understood as an affirmation of the everyday world just as it is and so appears to erode the necessary ground for spiritual practice. In turn, this may legitimate unskilful behaviour, and even sanctify it. Yet original Awakening gestures towards a nondual insight; the realm of Awakening is not apart from the realm of ordinary reality but is disclosed within it. This perspective recalls some aspects of the Madhyamika perspective; the conceptual boundaries that separate the conventional from the ultimate are 'empty'.

Original Awakening emphasizes that accomplishing this insight need not be the work of billions of lifetimes but may be fulfilled in an instant. It is realized neither through a path of ethical purification nor mastery of a ritual curriculum, but via a single, transformative insight. Such a doctrine perhaps helped reassure struggling practitioners of their capacity to realize Awakening, especially if they felt unable to fully honour the exacting standards of monastic life.[50]

---

[50] For an interesting essay that recognizes how original Awakening may be understood as a form of transformative language, rather than simply as some absolute affirmation of our present state of delusion, see Habito 1995.

1. **Great Buddha of Kamakura**
1252 CE, Kotokuin temple, Kamakura, Japan

2. **Commemorative Jizo images**
Contemporary, Hasedera temple, Kamakura, Japan

3. Head of a bodhisattva
late 2nd–early-3rd century CE;
found near Peshawar, Pakistan

4. The Begging Monk
2006, Osaka Castle, Osaka, Japan

5. Western Buddhists in meditation
Birmingham Buddhist Centre,
Birmingham, England

**6. Buddha with two attendant
bodhisattvas**; 544 CE, China

7. **Descent of Amida Buddha (Raigo)**
Kamakura period (1185–1333), Japan

**8. Bodhisattva Samantabhadra
riding on an elephant**
1350–1450, Korea or China

**9. "Monju with the Five Chignons"
Riding on a Lion**
Kamakura period (1185–1333), Japan

10. **Bodhisattvas of the Ten Stages of Enlightenment**
Ming dynasty (1368-1644) 1454 CE, China

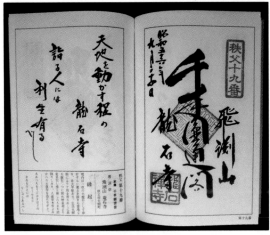

11. Pilgrim's book
Ryusekiji temple stamp and calligraphy
1981, Chichibu pilgrimage, Saitama, Japan

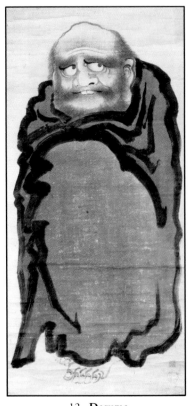

13. The five-storey pagoda at Kōfukuji
orig. 725, rebuilt 1426
Nara, Japan

12. Daruma
Ito Jakuchu (1716–1800), Japan

14. **Vairochana Buddha**
672-5 CE, Fengxian Temple, Longmen, China

15. **Buddhas and stupas at Borobudur**
8th–9th century, Borobudur, Java, Indonesia

16. **Bodhisattva as 'Guide of Souls'**
late 9th century CE, Dunhuang, China

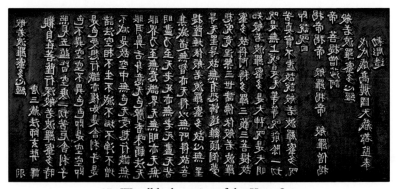

17. **Woodblock carving of the *Heart Sutra***
Madhyamaloka, Birmingham, England

7

Through the Jade Gate:
The Mahayana Enters China

WHILE MANY OF ITS EMBLEMATIC TEXTS, doctrines, and transcendent figures originated in India, Mahayana Buddhism had far greater impact in China than in its country of birth. Yet its journey from the plains of India, via the high passes of the great mountain ranges of Central Asia and across to the Chinese heartland, was long and often difficult. Notwithstanding, it evolved to become a powerful cultural force and, in the process, established China as a centre of the Buddhist world. This ascent was remarkable given that, even from the outset, the odds were stacked against the successful transmission of Buddhism to China, as shown through ongoing ideological conflict with the native Confucian tradition, and even periodic persecution.[1] But, contrary to some received opinion, China never really became a 'Buddhist country'.[2]

This chapter paints a general picture of the encounter between Buddhism and Chinese culture, identifying some of the issues central to this negotiation. It then outlines the emergence of Tiantai and Huayan, monumental systems of thought regarded by some as the apex of Mahayana development but which flourished all too briefly. In doing so, it introduces the fundamental interpretive principle of *panjiao* (doctrinal classification). The following chapter goes on to describe the most enduring manifestations of Chinese Mahayana: Chan and Pure Land.

Before proceding further, a note of caution. It would be wrong to think that China inherited a fully fledged Indian Mahayana Buddhism which was then modified according to local needs and sensibilities. Buddhism was carried to China in successive waves and even as Mahayana texts and teachings were deposited there, they continued to develop in India and Central Asia. Some of these developments were transmitted quickly, others took time, while still others never made the journey. As a consequence, the relationship between Chinese Mahayana Buddhism and its Indian and Central Asian counterparts is not one of simple, linear descent but often of parallel development.

---

[1] It should be noted that in general persecutions were directed towards the perceived excesses of the monastic sangha rather than the popular observance of Buddhist practices.

[2] Zürcher 1984: 194.

7.1 Phases of Buddhism in China

The transmission of Buddhism into Chinese culture could be seen in terms of three progressive phases of interpretation and assimilation.[3] The first phase covers the 3rd–4th centuries CE and was characterized by attempts to understand the imported religion in terms of native cultural and intellectual frameworks. However, in time more sophisticated interpreters began to recognize that this approach resulted in distortion.

The second phase, beginning around the 5th century and extending through most of the 6th, could be characterized as a 'scholastic turn', when Chinese Buddhists turned to foreign authorities and sources in order to understand Buddhism in its own terms. This laid the ground for the third phase, coinciding with the Sui (581–618) and Tang (618–907) dynasties, which saw the emergence of genuinely Chinese traditions of Mahayana Buddhism. The innovators of this period rejected the supremacy of the Indian scholastic tradition in favour of a return to the authority of scripture.[4]

To this model we might add a fourth phase: the formation of clear, sectarian lineages and institutions, associated with the Song dynasty (960–1279).[5] It is generally accepted that after this period the creative phase of Chinese Buddhism was largely over.

First Contacts

The precise date of first contact between Buddhist texts and missionaries and China is not known but it was almost certainly via one of the arteries of the Silk Route, perhaps by means of Kucha to the north or on the back of a jade caravan travelling from Khotan to the south towards the Chinese capital.[6] There is a legend that the Emperor Ming (reigned 58–75 CE) had a dream in which he saw a golden man flying towards him dressed in flowing robes. Not knowing who the man was or what the dream signified, Ming summoned his courtiers, one of whom recognized the image as the

---

3   This threefold model was suggested by Zürcher but this outline is based on Gregory's summary: Gregory 1991: 110–11.

4   Gregory, 1991: 4–5. The Tang dynasty has long been heralded as a 'golden age' of Buddhism, which was followed by a slow decline during the Song (960–1279). However, contemporary scholarship presents a more nuanced perspective, recognizing that the apparent golden age is a somewhat revisionary account of history. According to Gregory, '[F]ar from signaling a decline, the [Song] was a period of great efflorescence in Buddhism and that, if any period deserves the epithet of the "golden age" of Buddhism, the [Song] is the most likely candidate'. (Gregory 1999: 2)

5   Teiser 2005: 1165.

6   These were both oasis states, skirting the rim of the Tarim Basin, a region covered mostly by the forbidding Taklamakan Desert.

Buddha. In consequence, Ming decided to despatch envoys to find out more about this mysterious figure. Sometime during the decade 60–70 CE, the envoys are said to have returned with the first Buddhist texts and missionaries ever to be received on Chinese soil. According to this legend, Emperor Ming created a monastery for them in the capital, Luoyang.[7]

While the above story is more myth than history, a more verifiable early Buddhist influence was brought to Luoyang in 148 CE by An Shigao, a Parthian missionary.[8] He established the first of a series of translation bureaus that spanned a thousand years and which fulfilled the monumental task of translating the Buddhist scriptures from Indian and Central Asian languages into Chinese. Apart from this translation activity, little is known of the earliest sangha in China. Towards the end of the 2nd century, an Indo-Scythian monk named Lokakṣema (active c. 168–189 CE) translated several important Mahayana scriptures, including a version of the *Perfect Wisdom in 8000 Lines Sutra*.[9] While early Chinese Buddhism embraced both Nikaya and Mahayana influences, in time the Mahayana was to triumph.

Despite these translation projects, it was several centuries before Buddhism took meaningful root in China. At first it was followed mostly by refugees, traders, and immigrants but little noticed by the indigenous population, especially the cultured elite. By the end of the Han dynasty (220 CE), despite the circulation of many sacred texts, Buddhism was still primarily a religion of foreigners.

Buddhism and Chinese Culture

When Buddhism entered China, it encountered a highly sophisticated and settled culture, dominated by a scholarly elite committed to Confucian principles of efficient government, and resistant to the influence of a foreign religion. At the same time, Buddhism encountered in Daoism a native mystical tradition with a strong interest in inner cultivation and wonder-working (thaumaturgy). The encounter between Buddhism and these two native traditions was not one of simple accommodation but of mutual transformation. All three traditions evolved simultaneously, often influenced by — or in reaction to — one another.[10]

---

[7] Zürcher 1984: 196.

[8] The Parthian Empire (247 BCE–224 CE) was an Iranian kingdom, which occupied the region between the Caspian Sea and the Persian Gulf. It also expanded eastwards, controlling large sections of the Silk Route.

[9] For a summary of the texts translated by Lokaksema, see Harrison 1987.

[10] Zürcher notes that at the popular level, the three traditions were often indistinguishable, being mashed together into a soup of popular beliefs and customs. It is really only at the elite level (that is, the religious 'professionals' or the literati) that differences become clear. (Gregory and Ebrey 1993: 12)

However, there were several key emphases of Buddhism that sat awkwardly with Chinese cultural heritage. First, the monastic ideal encouraged the rejection of family ties in a culture where filial piety was a fundamental duty. One of the principal demands of such piety was to produce sons and the celibate sangha by definition shirked this obligation.[11] Secondly, monks were not supposed to work in the community. This unproductive lifestyle offended the Chinese conviction that all members of society should contribute towards its economic vitality. Even worse, monks 'begged', a practice stigmatized within Chinese society. Finally, the sangha regarded itself as exempt from secular obligations such as the duty to pay tax, provide corvée labour, enter into military service, and submit to government supervision. The sangha was an alternative society which undermined the Chinese commitment to an all-controlling, secular government guided by Confucian bureaucratrism.

As a consequence, the relationship between Buddhist institutions and the Chinese state was generally uneasy. At times, important monks and monasteries were patronized by the imperial family or other powerful officials but, on a change of leadership, this patronage might be instantly snatched away to be bestowed on a competing sect or none at all. Besides this, the Chinese state carried out periodic persecutions during which times Buddhism served as a convenient scapegoat for society's ills, such as those in 446 and 845.[12] At the same time, Buddhism was often firmly supported by non-Han Chinese regimes.[13]

For these and other reasons, Buddhism made little headway during the Han dynasty and only after it fell and China fragmented owing to a long period of political disunity (311–589) was Buddhism able to establish itself firmly within Chinese cultural life. By the end of this period of instability, Buddhist institutions had consolidated their place in Chinese society and

---

[11] Although filial piety is central to Confucianism, its Chinese origins reach back to the Shang dynasty (1766–1122 BCE). (Gregory and Ebrey 1993: 6–7)

[12] The persecution that began in 446, and lasted seven years, was the first in a series of purges of the Chinese sangha. Monks were defrocked on a large scale and monastic property was seized. Moreover, Buddhist practices were forbidden throughout the entire country. When the prohibition ended, strict limits were placed on how many monks could reside in a given prefecture, although before long the sangha began to expand rapidly. Perhaps the most notable purge occurred during 841–5. By 845, some 260,000 monks and nuns had been defrocked, while 4600 monasteries and 40,000 shrines had been damaged or destroyed. This purge has been regarded by some as marking the decline of Buddhism in China but many scholars now recognize that Buddhism recovered during the Song. (Keyworth 2003: 172–75)

[13] Eg the late Northern Wei (493–534 CE). (Teiser 2005: 1164) A notable cultural treasure initiated during this period is the series of rock-cut grottoes of Longmen, south of present day Luoyang in Henan Province. (McNair 2007.) More than 2300 of the grottoes survive. See also Feature 2.3.

the sangha as a whole had become a significant cultural force, albeit intermittently resented by Confucian literati and governmental bodies.

The Character of Early Chinese Buddhism

On arrival in China, Buddhism was still largely dressed in the garb of Indian culture; its doctrines, practices, and institutional forms bore the stamp of Indian concerns. For instance, it was framed within ancient Indian cosmology, a worldview very alien to the Chinese. For it to be assimilated within such a culturally distinct civilization, a process of adaptation or 'sinification' (assimilation of Chinese culture) was needed. This process took several hundred years and succeeded in producing uniquely Chinese Buddhist doctrines, practices, and cultural forms. But the transformation was not all one way; while Chinese culture modified Buddhism, Buddhism also modified Chinese culture in 'an extremely complicated process of convergence and hybridization'.[14] Indeed, mutual transformation was a feature common to all encounters between Buddhism and the cultural worlds in which it became immersed. For instance, through Buddhist influence the concept of merit and merit production took hold in China, ideas not previously known there. Thus a complex relationship of mutual transformation developed which was to produce what are arguably the greatest doctrinal expressions of Mahayana Buddhism.

The first few centuries of Buddhist influence in China were marked by the reception and assessment of various Indian scholastic traditions including the Abhidharma (*Jushe*), Madhyamika (*Sanlun*), and later on Yogachara (*Shelun* and *Dilun*). Another school (*Niepan*), based on the *Nirvana Sutra*, also emerged, as well as a school dedicated to monastic discipline (*Lü*).[15] But before long, indigenous Buddhist traditions began to

---

14 Zürcher 1984: 194. Teiser points out that one of the drawbacks of the model of sinification in relation to Buddhism is that during the process of assimilation, Chinese culture was undergoing constant change, some of which was inspired by Buddhist influence. Buddhism did not simply accommodate itself to Chinese culture but was an active ingredient in creatively transforming it. Moreover, to assume that Buddhism in itself was a static tradition that adapted to a new culture also distorts the dynamic nature of Buddhism as a constantly evolving phenomenon. (Teiser 2005: 1160)

15 The term *zong*, translated as 'school', has a range of meanings. According to Weinstein, it can signify: 1) a specific doctrine, thesis, or interpretation, 2) an underlying theme or teaching within a text, or 3) a religious or philosophical school. (Weinstein 1987: 482) Weinstein argues that *zong* should be understood as school in the third sense 'only when it refers to a tradition that traces its origin back to a founder, usually designated "first patriarch", who is believed to have provided the basic spiritual insights that were then transmitted through a [*sic*] unbroken line of successors or "dharma heirs"'. (Weinstein 1987: 484) This ties in with the original meaning of *zong* which refers to a clan descended from a common ancestor. Weinstein argues that early Chinese Buddhist developments are not properly schools; these began to appear only from the 8th century.

bud which were better attuned to the Chinese temperament. The most creative period of doctrinal development took place during the Sui (581–618) and Tang (618–907) dynasties, which witnessed the emergence of all the main lines of Chinese Buddhist thought and practice, including Tiantai, Huayan, and Chan. While some important developments had taken place even before this period, as embodied in texts such as the AMF,[16] distinctively Chinese Mahayana traditions emerged during the Tang.

7.2 Monastic Engineers: Building Bridges for the Dharma

From perhaps the 6th century until the fall of the Qing dynasty (1911), Buddhist monks played a prominent role in building and maintaining China's bridges. This curious function arose from the belief that the construction of bridges generates merit, or blessings, for those involved in it. The *Scripture of the Field of Blessings and Merit*, for instance, recommends seven acts which bring a heavenly rebirth, one of which is 'to establish bridges so that the ill and the weak can cross rivers'.[17]

Unlike many other merit-making activities, such as copying sutras, bridge-building served no explicit Buddhist purpose but expressed charity and compassion. Monks fulfilled several roles, serving as engineers, fundraisers, project managers, and even labourers. Besides being practical, bridges were also understood symbolically. In addition to heaping up merit, bridge construction also improved the social standing of monasteries within the local community.

Institutionalizing Chinese Buddhism

In addition to doctrinal developments, the structure of Buddhist institutions also changed as they adapted to Chinese life. One important development was a kind of monastic tenancy called a 'sangha household' (*sengjihu*). These followed a model which was similar in some respects to the medieval European monastery. They consisted of great numbers of peasant families and serfs allocated to large monasteries in order to work the fields and perform other menial tasks.[18] This system enabled monasteries to

---

(Weinstein 1987: 485) Sharf argues that while 'nominal indices such as sanlun, tilun [dilun] and shelun are often treated as discrete schools or traditions, they are better regarded as organizational categories'. (Sharf 2002a: 7)

[16] See Chapter 6.

[17] *Foshuo zhude futian jing*, T.683: cited in Kieschnick 2003: 201.

[18] Sometimes captives taken in military campaigns were installed as tenants of monastic lands. Each sangha household had to contribute sixty *shih* (2380 litres) of grain to the local monks' office. Even criminals and slaves were allocated to monastic service forming

generate tax-free income and some succeeded in becoming substantial estates, engaging in a range of business activities. While this system enabled the sangha to grow at an astonishing rate, it also became the focus for anti-Buddhist resentment, culminating in periodic persecution.[19]

Despite the existence of these sprawling, high profile monasteries, many monks lived in very small, community-based temples serving the pastoral needs of the common people. Buddhism at this level was a far cry from the world of refined philosophy and courtly influence and more or less merged into local cults and folk religion. As with many religious traditions, practice and belief at the popular level was a world away from the doctrinal sophistication and fine distinctions of the clerical elite.

As Buddhism sank its roots deeper into the Chinese cultural soil, India ceased to be revered as the holy land and was supplanted by a local spiritual geography based around Chinese holy sites, including those sacred to specific Buddhas or bodhisattvas. This process was enabled partly through the importation of the stupa cult and relic worship.[20] Related practices, such as the mummification of great masters, meant that many sites sprang up which were believed to possess sacred properties and which therefore became centres for popular devotion. This transformation of the landscape was undertaken on a more literal level by the excavation and decoration of rock-cut temples at a number of sites in China, including Dunhuang, and the Longmen grottoes near Luoyang (*see* Image 14), some of which still survive as records of the high quality that Buddhist art attained there.

In Chapter 3, we saw how, according to the classical Indian model, the Mahayana path takes aeons to traverse. The pilgrim begins in a condition of complete spiritual darkness and over inconceivably many lifetimes the light of Awakening gradually dawns. This drawn-out, developmental model of spiritual life struck many Chinese as rather remote, and it was gradually replaced by a more immanent model of Awakening as embodied in the notion of Buddha-nature. According to this line of thought, Awakening is not impossibly far away but always here and now, in the present, since it is our true condition. Given this, Awakening need not necessarily take aeons to accomplish but could be realized in this very life. This resulted in an

---

'Buddha households' (*futuhu*). Their job was to clear and cultivate the earth. Although the surplus grain was supposed to be deposited with the local monks' office, it was often used to make a profit for individual monasteries, and even for the monk-officials who administered the system. (Liu 1988: 152–3). See Feature 9.1 for more on the monastic economy.

[19] With regard to persecution, see note 12 above. Zürcher reports that in 477, the Wei Empire counted around 6500 monasteries and 77,000 monks. Just 40 years later, there were 30,000 monasteries and some 2 million monks. (Zürcher 1984: 201)

[20] For more on Buddhas and bodhisattvas, see Chapter 4. For more on stupa worship, see Chapter 2.

emphasis on the *immediacy* of Awakening, which became a hallmark of a good deal of Chinese Mahayana, and inspired original approaches to meditation.

Zhiyi and Tiantai Buddhism

Tiantai is generally regarded as the first distinctively Chinese Buddhist school and was characterized by a syncretic approach to previous Buddhist teachings and practices. It is named after the mountain where, from 575, its most seminal figure, Zhiyi (538–97) established a remote monastery at Tiantai on China's eastern seaboard (modern Zhejiang province).[21] This comprehensive and multi-faceted school later inspired influential counterparts in both Korea (Cheontae) and Japan (Tendai).

Zhiyi began Buddhist monastic training after the death of his parents at the age of 17. The first decisive development in his spiritual career came in 558 when, during a 20-day retreat, he had a spiritual insight confirming his faith in the profundity of the *Lotus Sutra* (*Fahua jing*). He later studied under Nanyue Huisi (515–77), a master himself inspired by the *Lotus Sutra* who encouraged Zhiyi to find the 'inner meaning' of the text, rather than simply to follow previous scholastic readings. This enabled Zhiyi to pursue a personal spiritual interpretation — an approach to textual inquiry that was to be widely emulated, and which led to the blossoming of Chinese Mahayana thought.

In 568, Zhiyi moved to Jinling (modern Nanjing) to begin his teaching career. Through family connections, he attracted imperial patronage and gained favour with powerful local officials. This patronage enabled Zhiyi to establish his monastic foundation on Tiantai and ensured the survival of his budding tradition.

The system of thought and practice that Zhiyi created was complex. Its broad aim was to harmonize the bewildering array of Buddhist teachings, practices, and texts as a means of healing some of the divisions that had emerged within the Chinese sangha. Zhiyi valued meditative practice and textual study equally and succeeded in incorporating both in a comprehensive spiritual regime. His syncretic, unifying approach was widely followed by later scholar-monks. Zhiyi was a prolific writer and systematizer and among his most important contributions were his system of doctrinal classification (*panjiao*), his theory of *three truths*, and his system of meditation. We will look at each of these in turn.

---

[21] In terms of Tiantai lineage history, Zhiyi is considered the third patriarch of the tradition, after the semi-legendary Huiwen (mid-6th century) and Zhiyi's master Huisi. However, Zhiyi's voluminous writings became authoritative for all later Tiantai and so he is widely regarded as the *de facto* founder.

7.3 Releasing Living Creatures

Non-violence (*ahiṁsa*) has always been a basic Buddhist principle, widely expressed through the practice of vegetarianism. In China, a practical form of compassion observed by monks and laity alike is the ceremony of releasing living creatures (*fangsheng*).[22] This practice, inspired by the releasing of fish in the *Sutra of Golden Light*,[23] is both an act of loving-kindness towards all creatures and a means of generating spiritual merit. Most commonly, fish, turtles, and birds bought from market traders are released.

Zhiyi was among those who first promoted this practice. Later, during the Tang dynasty, official ponds for releasing fish and turtles were designated, and fishing at these sites was prohibited. Ceremonies are typically carried out on special festival days, such as the day of the Buddha's birthday.

The ceremony takes the form of a conversion liturgy, which includes a Dharma sermon, the administering of the Three Refuges to the creatures due for release, and summoning various Buddhas and bodhisattvas to protect them so that they may be reborn in a higher state, even a heaven realm. Setting creatures free is associated with many benefits, including longevity, freedom from disasters, recovery from mental illness, and even Awakening. It is a practice that continues today.

Zhiyi's panjiao system

In order to understand Zhiyi's particular panjiao system, some general grasp of this idea is needed. As noted earlier, Indian Buddhist texts and teachings were transmitted to China not systematically but piecemeal. The order in which texts were translated often bore no relationship to their order of composition; later texts sometimes appeared before the earlier ones on which they were based or to which they responded. Commonly, the teachings inherited by the Chinese were shorn of their historical or doctrinal context, which placed a considerable burden on Chinese interpreters.

The complexity and diversity of this incoming Buddhist material inspired one of the most innovative features of Chinese Buddhist scholasticism: *panjiao* (doctrinal classification or taxonomy). Panjiao was a means of organizing and classifying teachings and texts with the aim of harmonizing a vast — and apparently disparate — array of material. In essence, this approach consisted in ranking texts and teachings hierarchically according

---

[22] For a discussion of this ceremony, see Stevenson 1999: 367–9.
[23] *Jin guang ming jing*, T.665. For a translation from the Sanskrit, see Emmerick 1990, especially 84–92.

to specific criteria, especially their seeming profundity and at what stage of the Buddha's teaching career they were believed to have been preached.

Gregory differentiates three main functions of panjiao schemes.[24] First, they provided an interpretive framework that conveyed order and unity upon the diverse scriptural legacy that Chinese Buddhists inherited. Secondly, they became the means by which different traditions asserted their doctrinal position, since a panjiao's hierarchical structure revealed each sect's particular judgments about which teachings and texts were the most exalted. Finally, they offered templates for individual spiritual development, as the teachings were graded according to a progressive hierarchy that rose from the most basic to the most profound.

Panjiao can be seen as an application of *skilful means* (*see* pp.15–18), enabling Chinese Buddhists to interpret each teaching as a corrective to overcome the particular shortcomings of the teaching that preceded it. This can be linked to the *Lotus Sutra* teaching of the *ekayana* or 'one way' (*see* p.44). While appearing inclusive, panjiao schemes often employed this teaching to demote — and even discredit — rival positions.

A number of panjiao systems had already been devised before Zhiyi and his general aim was to harmonize these.[25] His new approach, popularly known as the 'Five Periods and the Eight Teachings', although quite complicated, became very influential, partly because it incorporated religious practice as well as doctrine.[26] In general terms, while diplomatically recognizing the eminence of popular texts such as the *Flower Ornament Sutra* (*Huayan jing*) and the *Nirvana Sutra* (*Niepan jing*), Zhiyi's system enshrined the *Lotus Sutra* as the most exalted of all scriptures since Zhiyi believed that it presented the Buddha's message in the most accessible and universal way. It is impossible to do justice to the complexity and subtlety of Zhiyi's interpretive approach here, but his overriding concern was the relationship between provisional and ultimate truth, and so with sustaining a 'bifocal vision'. This way of seeing recognizes that, even at the outset of the spiritual path, the practitioner is identical with the Buddha — yet at the same time must progress through a sequence of stages of Awakening.[27]

---

[24] Gregory 1991: 114–5.

[25] The first notable panjiao scheme is attributed to Huiguan (dates unknown) in the 5th century. Briefly, this scheme categorizes the Buddha's teachings according to the sudden-gradual model. The *Huayan Scripture* is elevated as the sudden teaching, while all other teachings are deemed gradual and are subdivided into five categories of ascending profundity. (Kan'no 2001: 111–12) For a study of a later scheme, see Gregory 1991.

[26] Donner has shown that Zhiyi did not have a fixed panjiao scheme and used a range of interpretive categories at different times. He notes that the 'Five Periods and Eight Teachings' model was a later synthesis. (Donner 1987: 208)

[27] Donner 1987: 205–6, 209, 220. Donner uses the term 'binocular vision' (Donner 1987: 205) but I think bifocal is closer to what he means by it and expresses the notion of

The three truths teaching

Zhiyi also developed a teaching known as the *three truths*, which was a reformulation of Nagarjuna's important teaching of the *two truths* (*see* pp.94–6).[28] The precise meaning of, and relationship between, the conventional (*yu*) and the ultimate (*wu*) truth became matters of intense scholarly debate in China, partly owing to ambiguous translation. Zhiyi's solution was to adopt a model that extended Nagarjuna's twofold truth into a threefold scheme: conventional truth, emptiness, and the middle. For Zhiyi, the three truths were not different but aspects of one, integrated reality. This reality is 'subtle' (*miao*) which means that the true nature of things ultimately confounds conceptualization.[29] The basic purpose of the scheme was to uphold the Madhyamika position that nothing has inherent existence, while avoiding the trap of dissolving reality into nothingness. Another way of putting it would be to say that the threefold truth is a constant reminder not to take conceptual models too literally but to treat them as tools which may help to unravel the mystery of existence.

For Zhiyi, the threefold truth was not just a theoretical construct; it functioned as a practical tool in meditation where it became the 'threefold contemplation'. Briefly, this contemplative process involves passing through three stages: 1) realizing that things have no enduring identity (emptiness); 2) realizing that nevertheless things conventionally arise in dependence upon conditions; and 3) going beyond conceptual discrimination altogether.[30]

A meditative focus

Zhiyi devoted great attention to developing and writing about meditation. In his eminent work *Great Calming and Contemplation* (*Mohe zhiguan*), he laid out an important scheme known as the *four kinds of meditation* (*samādhi*), which became a cornerstone of the Tiantai monastic curriculum.[31] The four kinds are: constant sitting; constant walking; part-walking and part-sitting; and neither walking nor sitting.

---

seeing from two perspectives at the same time. One of the ways that this notion is articulated in Zhiyi's thought is through the 'six identities', which express the doctrinal position that we are inherently Buddhas but also that practice is required to bring this identity to full fruit. Briefly, these are: 1) *identity in principle* (Buddhahood is inherent); 2) *verbal identity* (an intellectual understanding of inherent Buddhahood); 3) *identity of religious practice* (one's behaviour begins to accord with an understanding of identities 1 and 2); 4) *identity of resemblance* (one begins to look like a Buddha in one's conduct); 5) *identity of partial truth* (one partially realizes one's identity with Buddhahood experientially); and 6) *ultimate identity* (complete Buddhahood). (Donner 1987: 204)

[28] A detailed account of this teaching is found in Swanson 1989. Swanson argues that the three truths can be used to explain Zhiyi's entire system.

[29] Swanson 1989: 15.

[30] Swanson 1989: 117.

[31] This account is based on Stevenson 1986.

Under the heading of constant sitting, Zhiyi introduces the 'one-practice samadhi' (*yixing sanmei*), where the practitioner applies himself to sitting meditation for a period of 90 days. He may either contemplate reality directly or follow a practice of Buddha reflection and recitation. Constant walking refers to the *pratyutpanna samādhi*, whereby over a period of 90 days, the devout meditator circumambulates an altar dedicated to the Buddha Amitabha, practising visualizations and recitation.[32] The ultimate goal of the practice is to enter a transcendent vision-world where one sees directly all the Buddhas of the ten directions.

The part-walking and part-sitting category is associated with two practices: the *fangdeng* repentance and the lotus samadhi.[33] Both practices are structured around cycles of walking and seated meditation. The fangdeng repentance is a purification practice that involves making ritual ablutions three times a day and regular changes of clothes, as well as periods of sitting meditation, circumambulation, and recitation. According to Zhiyi, a minimum of seven days is recommended for this practice but this may be extended to several months — or even years! The lotus samadhi or lotus repentance has two basic forms. First, there is a 21-day practice which cultivates a vision of the bodhisattva Samantabhadra and a host of Buddhas who materialize to purify the practitioner.[34] This involves intensive worship and recitation, confession, offerings, prostrations, and repetition of a repentance formula. There is also the 'practice or course of ease and bliss' (*anlexing*), which has the same objective but emphasizes the cultivation of deep meditation without time limits or ritual obligations.[35]

Under the final heading, cultivation while neither walking nor sitting, Zhiyi describes a further repentance, this time associated with Guanyin (Avalokiteshvara), as well as a practice called 'cultivating samadhi wherever mind is directed' (*suiziyi*). The latter seems to be intended for advanced practitioners and has the aim of seeing the nature of reality in every moment without resorting to formal meditation practices. This practice could be seen as a forerunner of Chan silent sitting meditation.

---

[32] This derives from the *Pratyutpanna-samādhi-sūtra* (*Sutra on the Samadhi of Seeing All Buddhas*; see p.63.). Translated into Chinese, this is the *banzhou sanmei*; *Banzhou sanmei jing* (T.418).

[33] 'Fangdeng' is a translation of the Sankrit *vaipulya*, which means 'extensive'.

[34] This practice is based on chapter 28 of the *Lotus Sutra* (*Fahua jing*, T.261), 'The Chapter on the Exhortations of the Bodhisattva Samantabhadra', and a short scripture known as *The Sutra on the Practice of Visualizing the Bodhisattva Samantabhadra* (*Guan puxian pusa xingfa jing*, T.277). Samantabhadra is one of the four great bodhisattvas in East Asian Mahayana (see Image 8). In the *Lotus Sutra* chapter, he pledges that if a practitioner single-mindedly focuses on the scripture for three weeks, he will appear before them on a white elephant with incalculable bodhisattvas to preach, bless, and confer all kinds of benefits. (Hurvitz 1976: 333–4)

[35] This second form derives from Chapter 14 (*anlexing pin*) of the *Lotus Sutra*.

7.4 Korean Monks and the Tiantai Revival in China[36]

Owing to the brutal persecution of the mid-9th century, the Chinese Tiantai tradition stagnated. Many key texts — as well as sacred artefacts — had been destroyed, disrupting its intellectual development. In the second half of the 10th century, however, a number of Korean monks contributed towards its restoration.

Uitong (927–88) travelled to China in 948. Some years later, he began to study Tiantai teachings and eventually established an influential monastic community. He attracted hundreds of students and thousands of followers. While Uitong's writings have been lost, his teaching had a formative impact on the revival of Tiantai — so much so that he was declared its 16th patriarch.

A second notable figure was Chegwan (fl. 961–71). From 961, he studied Tiantai in China and subsequently wrote an influential introduction to its teachings. Chegwan is also credited with restoring some key Tiantai texts to China, which had been preserved in Korea.

While Korean monks had travelled to China before the 10th century to study Tiantai, during this period they influenced its development. The influence went both ways: Uicheon (1055–1101) carried his new knowledge back to Korea to revive Tiantai studies there as Cheontae-jong.

Developments of Tiantai

Zhiyi's teaching and the Tiantai school embodied several key principles that came to characterize Chinese Buddhism as a whole. First, there was an emphasis on religious practice as much as doctrinal and scriptural study. For Zhiyi, meditation without study leads to self-inflation, whereas study without meditation is like a pauper counting other people's money.[37] Secondly, there was a tendency to creative interpretation of scripture, less constrained by commentarial precedent. Next was the affirmation that all beings, without exception, can gain Awakening. And finally — and perhaps most radically — was the recognition that Awakening is possible within the present lifetime.

After Zhiyi's time, his school went through a number of ups and downs. It had been founded through forging close links with the Sui imperial regime, an association not looked on favourably by the subsequent Tang rulers. Consequently, patronage was withdrawn and during the 7th century the school declined. Around the mid-8th century, Zhanran (711–782) revived it, partly through incorporating aspects of Huayan thought (*see*

---

[36] This material is drawn from Chan 2005.
[37] Donner 1987: 203.

below). Saichō (767–822), a Japanese monk, later transmitted the Tiantai teachings to Japan where they became central to the Tendai school. The persecution of the 840s noted above decimated Tiantai but it recovered to a position of significant influence during the Song dynasty.

Inherent Evil (xing e)

In the first part of the 11th century, an intriguing, and at times arcane, debate erupted between rival Tiantai factions over the true nature of the mind and Awakening.[38] What became the orthodox group, represented by Siming Zhili (960–1028) and centred on Mt. Tiantai, termed itself Home Mountain (*Shanjia*). Its opponents were dubbed Off Mountain (*Shanwai*).

The debate focused on whether Buddha-nature, inherent in all beings, was intrinsically pure. The Off Mountain group, influenced by Huayan thought, asserted that Buddha-nature is inherently pure, and this purity is the proper object of contemplation. Moreover, since evil is not intrinsic to our essential nature, it can be eliminated; this happens through Awakening.

The Home Mountain group dismissed this perspective as dualistic since it involved discriminating the mind as experienced from the mind in itself; in their view, these are not two separate things. Following earlier teachings from Zhiyi, Zhili maintained that even though a Buddha ceases to follow evil impulses, his 'inherent evil' nevertheless remains.

Inherent evil implies a profound revisioning of the nature of the goal. No longer is there an absolute disjunction between the Awakened and the unawakened; both possess ignorance and wisdom, good and evil, purity and defilement. This flatly contradicts the Nikaya Buddhist view that the Awakened person is completely free of selfish, ignorant, and harmful impulses. According to the doctrine of inherent evil, the Awakened person *retains* such impulses but does not act upon them. Thus Awakening does not consist in a fundamental change in our nature but in developing a liberated perspective upon it. In consequence, Zhili emphasized the ordinary, deluded mind as the portal through which Awakening is realized; liberation is not distinct from delusion but is revealed within it.

Huayan Buddhism

Huayan has been widely acclaimed as the crowning glory of Chinese Mahayana thought. It laid out an holistic, mind-expanding vision of the universe as conceived from the point of view of the Awakened mind that can seem bewildering and inspiring in equal measure.

The Huayan school took its inspiration from the scripture after which it is named, although much of its philosophical vocabulary was derived from

---

[38] This brief outline is based in part on Chan 1999.

Chinese commentaries. The *Huayan Scripture* (*Flower Ornament Sutra*) is a monumental work, really a collection of texts,[39] but its climax records the entrance of the pilgrim Sudhana into the miraculous treasure tower of the cosmic Buddha Vairochana (Vairocana), the 'Illuminator'. The tower is as vast as space itself and festooned with canopies, banners, pennants, and jewels — every kind of decoration. Mysteriously, inside the tower are hundreds of thousands of other towers, all *equally* large and equally embroidered. Despite this, each of the towers appears perfectly distinct, while appearing to be reflected in each and every object of all the other towers.[40] This vision became the basis for Huayan's teaching of the mutual interpenetration of all phenomena.

A series of important scholar-monks, later canonized as patriarchs, contributed towards the development of Huayan thought but Fazang (643–712), considered the third patriarch, is perhaps the most important since he systematized what had gone before and popularized the tradition's main ideas.[41] The school became especially influential during the brief Second Zhou dynasty (690–705) when Empress Wu Zhao (or Zetian, 624–705) seized the imperial seat. Empress Wu sponsored not only a new translation of the *Huayan Scripture* in the 690s but supported Fazang's own religious activities as well. By all accounts, Empress Wu was a nasty piece of work, bent on total power and ruthless in its pursuit. It is perhaps ironic that she should have had a hand in the development of such a refined system of Mahayana thought.

Like Zhiyi, Fazang studied widely and consequently his Mahayana synthesis was influenced by several strands of thought, including the Madhyamika and Yogachara, and perhaps especially Buddha-nature. He also developed a panjiao system, this time enshrining the *Huayan Scripture* as the most profound revelation of the Buddha's Dharma. While Zhiyi had also acknowledged the lofty content of this text, he felt that its vision was too elevated for the average Buddhist to understand. There is no doubt that Huayan metaphysics can be abstruse — but the same could be said of Tiantai.

The key notion in Huayan thought is the *dharmadhatu*. This complex and deeply resonant term means something like 'realm of reality' but more specifically it is a way of talking about the world of everyday experience understood as revealing the nature of truth. For Huayan, all experience is epiphanic, which means that everything reveals or discloses reality and so

---

[39] See Chapter 2, note 9 for detail.
[40] Cleary 1993: 1489–90.
[41] Huayan recognized only five patriarchs in total: Dushun (557–640); Zhiyan (602–668); Fazang (643–712); Chengguan (738–839); and Zongmi (780–841). The first four patriarchs were all recognized posthumously, as the notion of spiritual lineage emerged as a key organizing principle, partly influenced by developments in Chan.

functions as a gateway to Awakening. Although it recognizes the value of negative language as embodied in the shunyata doctrine, Huayan emphasizes positive ways of characterizing experience. It discloses an holistic vision where ultimately nothing is separate but all exists as an indivisible, interconnected totality. This is not to say that experience is a vague oneness where no distinctions are possible but rather that, on further analysis, nothing exists independently of anything else since everything is supported by conditions.[42]

7.5 Monks as Wonder-workers

Chinese monks like Fazang were revered by the general public as ritual specialists and were relied upon to exercise various skills of sorcery, including prophecy, spell-casting, and divination. In order to compete with the popularity of Daoist sages, Buddhist monks had to show superior wonder-working abilities. An especially eminent monk might exude a numinous aura and so would be credited with all kinds of miracles. This helped convince the masses that the Buddhist teachings had tangible benefits.[43]

From early on in his religious training, Fazang had been attracted to Daoist practices believed to promote longevity — even immortality — and his interest in these continued throughout his career. For instance, it is reported that in 711, and at the request of the emperor, he conducted a ritual to pray for snow to avert an imminent drought. This ritual involved inscribing a magical spell taken from a Buddhist scripture on strips of bamboo and then dropping these into a 'dragon-pool'. It was almost certainly based on a Daoist precedent.[44]

So while the received image of Fazang is as a deeply erudite philosopher, in hagiographical records he appears more like a shamanic wonder-worker.

This perspective is in perfect harmony with the early Buddhist notion of dependent origination; the difference here is that rather than isolating one

---

[42] Similar holistic concepts are found in Tiantai, also inspired by the *Huayan Scripture*, including the notion of 'the three thousand worlds in an instant of thought' (*yinian sanqian*) and 'inherent inclusion/entailment' (*xingju*), which signify that each and every phenomenon is a prism through which the entire cosmos is revealed. This line of thought seems to emphasize not only that all things are interconnected but ultimately that all things are *identical*. This implies, for instance, that ignorance and Awakening are identical. However, while they may be ontologically identical (in the sense that all things are part of a whole), they are surely not ethically so, otherwise the Buddhist path becomes meaningless. This complex area has been explored in Ziporyn 2000.

[43] For more on this topic, see Faure 1991: 96–131 and Kieschnick 1997: 67–111.

[44] Chen 2006.

factor within the context of a single, direct causal chain (a simplification necessary for the purposes of exposition), the whole of existence is instead conceptualized as an interconnected totality — a web. Ultimately, everything affects everything else, however subtly. This vision of interconnectedness has recently inspired Buddhist environmentalists and its application to modern problems, such as climate change, is alluring.[45]

More than this, the dharmadhatu is equated with the cosmic Buddha Vairochana, which means that ultimately all experience reveals the Buddha mind or Buddha-nature; every atom is a Buddha. This does not mean that there is literally a little Buddha inside every atom but that all experience is numinous, and so radiates the light of reality. Huayan thus embodies a supremely positive account of human nature and a radically immanent vision of Awakening: every moment is a revelation. Rather than conceiving of the spiritual as purely transcendent, it sees the present world itself as a sacred realm. It also emphasizes our unity with all existence, which implies a care and concern for all things since we are not separate from them.

After the late 9th century, Huayan insights and teachings were absorbed by other schools, including Tiantai and Chan (and consequently their Japanese cousins Tendai and Zen), as it petered out as a distinct Chinese tradition. But Huayan enjoyed rather longer-lasting prestige in both Korea (Hwaeom) and Japan (Kegon). The figure of Li Tongxuan (635–730), a Chinese lay hermit and contemporary of Fazang, while obscure in his own lifetime, was cited as an influence by a number of later East Asian masters.[46] While Fazang's approach to scriptural interpretation was set within a cumbersome traditional framework, Li's approach was more individual. This resulted in a number of novel insights that inspired later practitioners, including the Korean monk Jinul (1158–1210), founder of the Korean Seon (Zen) tradition (see pp.164–6). Above all, Li seemed concerned with the practical application of Huayan thought rather than its theoretical refinement.

One way that Li emphasized the practical side of spiritual life was through his radical understanding of the relationship between faith and Awakening. For Li, the experience of faith prefigures, and so guarantees, the unfolding of Awakening since in essence they are not different.[47] This way of thinking makes the goal seem more reachable, since it is the fulfillment of something already present within the average follower's life, unlike the classical bodhisattva ideal which may seem like a pipedream, almost infinitely remote and impossibly arduous. Here, Awakening is inherent within the first humble flutterings of faith; faith *encapsulates* Awakening.

---

[45] A notable example is Joanna Macy (b. 1929); see Macy 2007.
[46] This account is largely based on Gimello 1983.
[47] Gimello 1983: 337.

But is this really true? In commenting on Li's teachings, Jinul emphasizes their practical and transformative nature. They are perhaps best understood not as attempts to describe a philosophical system but as interventions that may inspire direct spiritual change within his follower.[48] This practical spirituality may explain why Li's teachings have continued to inspire Buddhists even into modern times.

Having explored some of the general issues governing the transmission of Mahayana Buddhism to China and its subsequent evolution there as well as having considered the great metaphysical systems of Tiantai and Huayan, we will next turn to two further members of the Chinese Mahayana family, those which have proved the most enduring: Chan and Pure Land Buddhism.

---

[48] Gimello 1983: 347–9.

8

Separate Transmission and Other-Power: The Emergence of Chan and Pure Land Devotion

HAVING EXPLORED SOME OF THE head-spinning metaphysical ideas that emerged within Chinese Buddhist thought, we now come to its two most enduring practical forms: Chan and Pure Land devotion. Both created distinctive spiritual universes: one populated by unpredictable masters whose seemingly madcap antics served to trigger Awakening; the other filled with light, colour, and compassion, and within which the Buddha functions as an active source of liberation reaching out to all beings.

Chan and Pure Land devotion incorporate profoundly different assumptions about the nature of Awakening and the path to its realization from those found in early Buddhism — and even in the early Mahayana. Notwithstanding, their innovations became central to the subsequent evolution of Mahayana Buddhism in East Asia and were widely adopted, most notably in Korea and Japan. While Chan was generally associated with the religious elite, Pure Land practice had broad appeal both within monastic circles and at the popular level. It is worth noting, however, that Pure Land devotion never settled into a distinct institutional structure in China but was absorbed over time into a number of other traditions, including Tiantai and Chan.[1] This chapter explores the emergence and subsequent development of these two streams of thought and practice.

The Emergence of Chan Buddhism

A monk asked Yunmen: 'What is the Buddha?' Yunmen answered: 'A dried shit-stick.'[2] Such irreverent, iconoclastic, and even comic stories are popularly used to illustrate the character and teaching methods of Chan Buddhism. Known more widely in the West through Japanese Zen,[3] Chan originated in China during the Tang dynasty (618–907). Its doctrines,

---

[1] Getz 1999: 479. The issue of a separate Pure Land tradition is a subtle one. Getz describes the evolution of Pure Land societies, which had varying degrees of autonomy, but were often inspired or controlled by Tiantai monks. (Getz 1999: 480–503) These societies attained an 'informal institutional validity'. (Getz 1999: 505) See also Sharf 2002b.

[2] *The Gateless Gate*, case 21; Sekida 2005: 77–8.

[3] See Chapter 11.

practices, and institutions continued to develop at least until the end of the Song dynasty (960–1279), which is now widely regarded as its peak.[4] During this period, Chan became the mainstream of Chinese Buddhism and, along with Pure Land devotion, has remained so into modern times. Chan has been influential throughout East and Southeast Asia, including Korea, Japan, and Vietnam.

Chan is a Chinese transliteration of the Sanskrit term *dhyāna*, which in general denotes meditation and in particular refers to a range of super-conscious states that may be cultivated by the adept. This offers a hint as to at least one of Chan's main emphases. The history and evolution of Chan is extremely complex and there is space here for only a rough sketch. Our understanding is not made easier by the fact that Chan followers, especially in the Song dynasty, rewrote earlier records in order to reflect their sectarian affiliations.[5] In recent decades, the study of manuscripts recovered from the sealed cave at Dunhuang has enabled scholars to substantially revise early Chan history.[6]

In the popular imagination, Chan (or more usually Zen) appears as a mystical, paradoxical, seductive tradition which throws off convention and cuts straight to the heart of spirituality. But we will see that this persistent image owes as much to creative fiction as it does to reality. There is a much-repeated set of four Chan 'slogans', which tells us at least as much about how Chan followers wanted to portray Chan as about how Chan has been practised.

> A separate transmission apart from the teachings;
> Not setting up scriptures;
> Pointing directly at the human mind;
> Seeing the nature and attaining Buddhahood.[7]

---

[4] See Chapter 7, note 4. In addition, Welter, 'the so-called T'ang "golden age" must be treated as a product of Sung revisionism.... The fundamental "myths" of Ch'an's founding masters were crystalized in the Sung imagination'. (Welter. 2000: 99)

[5] Teiser summarizes the situation: 'Claims about transmission ... were always executed retroactively. The tradition, which claimed its own content to be a non-content, was not so much handed down from past to present as it was imagined in the present, a willful projection into the future, against the reality of a heterogeneous past.' (Teiser 1996: 20) This topic is examined in detail in McRae 2003: 1ff.

[6] For instance, documents were found relating to the Northern School of the 7th–8th centuries. This has enabled historians to gain a more accurate understanding of the teachings and emphases of this school. Previously, knowledge of its key tenets was distorted through the sectarian lens of its opponents. See McRae 1986.

[7] This translation is taken from Foulk 1999: 265. These four 'slogans' are often attributed to the semi-mythical Bodhidharma (late 5th–early 6th century) but Foulk points out that the entire list does not appear before the 12th century, although the first three had been in wide circulation earlier.

By considering these four tenets in turn, we can learn as much about Chan *rhetoric* as about Chan *reality*. One scholar has suggested that in approaching Chan, we may do well to observe this maxim: 'It's not true and therefore it's more important'.[8] For instance, many Chan texts mythologize past masters to the point where they become archetypes rather than historical figures. But this is not to dismiss the importance of such accounts; while they may not be historical, they nonetheless disclose crucial facets of the Chan spiritual imagination.

Separate transmission

Chan is portrayed as a 'separate transmission apart from the teachings'. This raises the fundamental issues of Chan lineage, transmission, and historical origins. An important tool adopted by Chan followers to both define Chan identity and bolster its legitimacy was the lineage system.[9] So powerful did this device become that other Chinese schools also adopted it. The Chan lineage myth reaches right back to the Buddha himself who is said to have given a secret transmission to his disciple Mahakashyapa (Mahākāśyapa). According to some versions of this legend, the Buddha held up a golden flower before his assembly of monks and, knowing the meaning of it, Mahakashyapa smiled. Supposedly, this was the first transmission of Chan; consequently, Mahakashyapa is known as the first in an unbroken line of 'patriarchs'.[10]

This construction of lineage history served not only to guarantee Chan's credentials but also to elevate it to an unrivalled position. It defined itself as *true* Buddhism, direct from the source and so superior to any other tradition. The lineage system, still in use today, serves to confirm spiritual realization on the part of the disciple and so confer authority. Spiritual Awakening is 'proven' through authentication by the master, whose own Awakening has been guaranteed in the same way.

But there is more to this than meets the eye. Chan patriarchal lineages simplify the actual historical relationships between masters and their

---

[8] McRae 2003: xix.

[9] The development of lineage systems within Buddhism was nothing new. Lineage has played an important role in many traditions, including those in India and Tibet. However, in relation to Chan:

Earlier literature had portrayed connections between masters and disciples as contending lineages that could coexist simultaneously. Song sources, however, advance the claim that the orthodox tradition originated at a single point ... and continued in a mind-to-mind transmission with only one patriarch per generation. (Teiser 2005: 1165)

[10] The earliest known account of this Chan transmission myth is found in the Baolin Record (*Baolin zhuan*) of 802. In this account, the Buddha gives Mahakashyapa a robe, symbolizing the Dharma transmission. Foulk explores the subsequent evolution of the legend in satisfying detail. (Foulk 1999) It is also examined in Welter 2000. The first account to mention a flower appears in the *Tian sheng guang deng lu* (*Extensive Record of the Flame*) completed in 1036. (Foulk 1999: 257)

138 / VISIONS OF MAHAYANA BUDDHISM

disciples and were often constructed much later. In reality, a Chan master may have studied under a number of teachers and inspired many disciples. The idea that Chan has been handed down from patriarch to patriarch in a transmission as neat as a string of pearls, while an important part of Chan mythology, has served to write out certain Chan teachers from the mainstream while placing others centre-stage. In the early centuries of its development, Chan was a disparate movement and a number of factions with distinct styles of practice rose to some prominence. There was no central Chan authority and legitimacy was often bestowed in retrospect.

This theme is well illustrated in the legend of Huineng (638–713), whose spiritual career is the focus of the *Platform Sutra of the Sixth Patriarch*, a celebrated early Chan text written at least a century after the events it claims to describe (and which therefore can be seen as serving sectarian aims in its emphases).[11] The *Platform Sutra* dramatizes a lineage dispute between the seemingly illiterate Huineng, working in the monastery kitchen, and the more conventional monastic Shenxiu (606?–706). According to the sutra, Huineng was secretly confirmed as the sixth patriarch of Chan at the expense of Shenxiu, the heir apparent. The Chan tradition that traces itself back to Huineng later identified itself as the 'Southern School' and eventually became mainstream Chan, whereas Shenxiu was the seminal figure of the so-called 'Northern School', which eventually petered out.[12]

While this narrative seems to confirm the unconventional, anti-establishment image of Chan, in reality Huineng was probably a regular monk practising in an orthodox manner. The events and teachings recorded in the sutra were concerned to elevate a specific sectarian perspective, while — via misrepresentation — downgrading a rival. Interpreted mythically, the Huineng story shows that realization transcends education or rank and defies convention — important Chan emphases.[13] But while this story portrays the Chan succession system as a spiritual meritocracy, perhaps inevitably, worldly factors informed the selection of patriarchs.[14] Significantly, though, the genealogical structure of Chan — that is, its

---

[11] *Liu zu da shi fa bao tan jing*, T.2008. Note: a variant edition was discovered at Dunhuang: T.2007. This is the earliest extant copy of the *Tan jing*, perhaps dating back to within a century-and-a-half of the death of Huineng (713). For a comparison of various redactions of the scripture, see Bielefeldt and Lancaster 1975.

[12] The term 'Northern School' has a pejorative tone and was coined by the 'Southern School'. It implies that the Northern School's teachings were inferior. Another name for the school is East Mountain teaching. The Northern School is examined in McRae 1986. See also Faure 1998. Among the criticisms made of the Northern School was that it taught a gradualist, as opposed to a sudden, approach to Awakening (sudden being widely accepted as superior). This turns out to be a view fabricated by its opponents.

[13] See McRae 2003: 60–9.

[14] See McRae 2003: 69.

conception of itself as a dynastic family (or group of families) — may have been a significant factor in its popularity, since this reflected the social structure of Chinese society.[15]

Not setting up scriptures

The lineage system spiritualizes the encounter between master and disciple, which came to be seen as a crucial tool in triggering Awakening (although it is important to remember that sitting meditation and many other conventional practices were also widely followed). The consecration of the master–disciple relationship highlights Chan's second 'slogan': 'Not setting up scriptures'. Chan folklore has become infamous for stories of monks tearing up and burning scriptures, chopping up Buddha images for firewood, and even the suggestion that if one should meet the Buddha on the road, one should kill him![16] While this apparent iconoclasm has been an important theme in Chan's self-mythology, it should not be taken at face value; such stories are better interpreted metaphorically as cautions against literalism and the dangers of following authority and tradition blindly. In reality, reverence for spiritual masters and for a wide range of sacred traditions has always been integral to Chan life.

Moreover, texts have been important to Chan practice throughout its history. For instance, early Chan drew inspiration from the *Lankavatara Sutra*,[17] while later the *Diamond Sutra* and the *Heart Sutra* were highly regarded and widely studied, as well as being used in liturgy. In addition, Chan developed its own unique and extensive literature, especially that known as 'encounter dialogue'.[18] This literature laid the ground for the development of the celebrated and highly complex koan (*kōan*, Ch. *gong'an*) or legal case or precedent tradition, in which a 'critical phrase' (huatou) was selected from a dialogue record for intensive contemplation by the student. This approach is explored in detail in the next chapter (*see* pp.166–8).

Encounter dialogues purport to record meetings in which a master awakens a disciple — or sometimes just baffles him — through striking him a blow, by means of a shout, a gesture, or through a pithy rejoinder. The records of these dialogues are vivid, creative, often funny, and even endearing. But the Chan Master is no cuddly father figure; rather he is elusive, often spiky, and usually disconcerting. For instance:

---

[15] McRae 1992: 359.

[16] The saying about killing the Buddha is attributed to Linji (d. 866?), revered as a founder of his own school of Chan, which later became the source lineage of Japanese Rinzai Zen. The legend of Linji is examined in Welter. 2008. Linji himself wrote nothing but over time a tradition associated with him consolidated into a 'biography' in which he emerges as a powerful master.

[17] *Laṅkāvatāra-sūtra*, T.670.

[18] For a detailed examination, see McRae 1992: 339–69. Encounter dialogue is also explored in McRae 2003: 74–100.

8.1 Certificating Awakening

Dharma transmission between master and disciple within the medieval Chan tradition was confirmed through the issue of an 'inheritance certificate' (*sishu*), a diploma that authenticated the ritual transmission of the Dharma. The certificate not only verified that the holder was a genuine member of the Chan lineage but also that he was an Awakened being. Mythically, Chan transmission attested to an unbroken line of Awakened practitioners stretching back to the Buddha Shakyamuni. The holder of the certificate was thus 'institutionally Awakened', even if not literally so, and functioned as a repository for the accumulated spiritual charisma of the lineage.[19]

Inheritance certificates were of great symbolic importance. They comprised a list of the important figures in a given lineage, ending with the owner of the document. When the Japanese monk (and future founder of Sōtō Zen) Dōgen visited China in the early 13th century, he saw a number of certificates that he later described. One of these was inscribed on a white silk scroll with a front cover of red brocade and a roller made of jade. It was approximately ten inches wide and seven feet long.[20] As sacred objects, the certificates were carefully guarded and rarely displayed. The opportunity to see one and to prostrate and make offerings to it was considered very auspicious.

Inheritance certificates also served a critical institutional role. During the Song period, the government restricted the abbacies of many public monasteries to monks belonging to Chan lineages. A lineage certificate was thus a passport to ecclesiastical promotion. This meant not only were the certificates highly valued but they were even subject to occasional abuse through forgery.[21]

The system of Dharma transmission and the bestowal of inheritance certificates were imported to Japan where they continue as a feature of Zen today. Dōgen wrote: 'No one but a Buddha can bestow the seal of approval upon a Buddha, and no one is a Buddha without receiving the seal of approval.'[22]

A monk asked Yunmen, 'What is talk that goes beyond Buddhas and Patriarchs?' Yunmen said, 'Cake.'[23]

---

[19] Foulk and Sharf 2003: 131–2.
[20] Kodera 1980: 42–6.
[21] Foulk 1993: 160.
[22] Cited in Kodera 1980: 45.
[23] *Blue Cliff Record* (*Biyan lu*, Jp. *Hekiganroku*, T.2003), case 77, 'Yun Men's Cake', translated in Cleary and Cleary 1977: 424–27 (transliteration of names modified).

Significantly, encounter dialogue shifts the focus of spiritual practice away from individual cultivation towards the transformative communication that may occur between master and student. The Chan master catches the student napping, frustrates him, turns him upside down, all with the aim of liberating the student from his habitual way of seeing things. Through his dynamic encounter with the master, who embodies Awakening, the student's Awakened nature is activated, even rediscovered. The koan later built on this principle by substituting contemplation of a key phrase spoken by a past master for live dialogue with him.

Supposed records of master–student encounters gradually became formalized until they were written up in important collections. Two of the most popular are the *Blue Cliff Record* and the *Gateless Gate*.[24] In one case from the *Blue Cliff Record*, for example, the master Nanquan (784–834) found two groups of monks fighting over a cat. He seized hold of the cat and told the monks: 'If you can say it, I won't kill it!' Stunned, no one answered and so Nanquan cut the cat in two.[25] Such an anecdote must strike a Buddhist as especially shocking — and it was designed to — since it seems to record an eminent master transgressing the most basic of all precepts, that of respecting life. Such a record serves to confirm the Chan master's spontaneity, and his freedom from conventional morality, guided as he is by a higher principle. It can also be linked to the principle of skilful means (*see* pp.16–18). The Chan master is depicted not as a remote expert but as a *communicator* who intervenes spontaneously and pragmatically in the thought processes of his students with the sole aim of catalyzing Awakening.

Dialogue records like the story of Nanquan were used by generations of Chan masters to instruct their disciples by offering interpretations or commentaries.[26] It is worth pointing out that the written versions of the encounters were produced long after the events they claim to describe and

Following the main case, there is a commentary, part of which reads:
Some can no longer tell right from wrong — they draw a circle, adding mud to dirt, putting on chains while wearing stocks. "His gap opens — see it?" What a big gap there is in this monk posing his question! Yunmen saw it opening up in his question, so he said "Cake"to block it up tight. But this monk still wouldn't agree to stop — instead, he went on asking. Xuedou says, "Even the cake stuffed in doesn't stop him." (Cleary and Cleary 1977: 427)

[24] *Blue Cliff Record*, compiled by Yuanwu Keqin (1063–1135); *The Gateless Gate* (Ch. *Wumen guan*; Jp. *Mumonkan*) compiled by Wumen Huikai (1183–1260); for a translation, see Sekida 2005.

[25] *Blue Cliff Record*, case 63: see Sekida 2005: 319–20. The use of this story in relation to *kanhua* Chan is examined in McRae 2003: 128–30.

[26] A Chan master might expound a sermon based on an encounter dialogue in the context of the formal ceremony known as 'Ascending the Dharma Hall' (*shangtang*). For an account of this ritual, see Poceski 2000.

thus represent idealizations of past Chan masters, especially those of the Tang dynasty seen through the eyes of their Song descendents. The spontaneity, simplicity, and seeming irrationality of early Chan was rooted at least as much in the creative imagination of later followers as it ever was in fact. In the words of McRae, encounter dialogue records 'are literary re-creations of how the enlightened masters of the past must have spoken and acted'.[27] Nanquan almost certainly never decapitated any cat — at not least literally!

Pointing directly at the human mind

Chan presents itself as 'pointing directly at the human mind', which underlines that mind is its primary focus and also signifies the importance of meditation. Chan broke with Indian models of meditation to develop new forms of practice and distinctive understandings of its purpose. For instance, the *Platform Sutra* describes the practice of 'no mind' (*wuxin*) or 'no thought' (*wunian*), which is concerned with breaking free from attachment to thoughts in order directly to reveal the nature of the mind. The aim of 'no thought' is not to get rid of all thought and make the mind go blank but rather to relinquish obsessive thought and so restore the mind's radiant clarity.

Some Chan masters were suspicious of meditation, particularly when pursued in the belief that it would bring about Awakening. For instance, there is a well-known story about Master Huairang (677–744) and his student, Mazu (709–88).[28] Huairang challenged Mazu about why he spent so much time meditating. Mazu replied that his goal was to reach Awakening. Huairang then picked up a piece of tile and began grinding it on a rock. Puzzled, Mazu asked what he was doing. Huairang replied, 'I'm grinding this into a mirror.' 'But that's ridiculous,' said Mazu, 'how you can you make a mirror by grinding a piece of tile?' Huairang retorted sharply, 'How can you possibly become a Buddha by sitting in meditation?'

This story further confirms Chan's apparent iconoclasm; even a practice as central as meditation is called into question. But this anecdote does not signify a rejection of meditation as a whole. Rather, it embodies a critique of a *gradualistic* approach. For Chan, Awakening is not achieved incrementally through a process of continual effort but is in fact the true nature of the human mind — and so ever present. This underlines its 'direct' approach. A hallmark of Chan, therefore, is its 'rhetoric of immediacy' embodied in the notion of *sudden* Awakening, which emphasizes that Awakening is not something pursued over infinite lifetimes but is immanent here and now.[29] This does not necessarily mean, however, that it

---

[27] McRae 1992: 340.

[28] See McRae 2003: 80.

[29] The term 'rhetoric of immediacy' is borrowed from Faure's groundbreaking work, *The*

will be realized *quickly*. Chan thus sacralizes everyday events; Awakening is not something that happens apart from the world of ordinary experience but is revealed within it. This insight became central to later developments in Chan and also proved potent in attracting prestige, patronage, and disciples.

Seeing the nature and attaining Buddhahood

In Chan, the mind is identified with Buddha-nature, which links in with the final 'slogan': 'Seeing the nature and attaining Buddhahood'. To see into one's own nature is to realize that one is *already* a Buddha, that one is inherently awakened. Chan thus speaks proleptically; it anticipates the *future* Awakening of the disciple by declaring it to be *present* right here and now. This rhetorical strategy underscores the sudden Awakening model, although masters differed in how they understood this state of affairs and what it meant to realize it. For some, Awakening was sudden but was consolidated by gradual cultivation through practice, while for others Awakening was sudden and practice followed spontaneously.

But how does one come to realize that one is inherently Awakened? Mazu, for instance, maintained that no amount of practice could ignite Awakening; instead, one should simply allow one's innate Awakening to reveal itself spontaneously.[30] While such a view could be read as a charter to abandon spiritual practice as unnecessary, Chan instruction usually took place in the context of a strict monastic regime where daily life was punctuated by ritual and study, as well as meditation.[31] The seemingly puzzling and anti-rational teachings of some Chan masters may be understood as calculated spiritual interventions in the context of such a life, with the aim of shaking the disciple out of a limited conception of practice. In this sense, they could be likened to skilful means, exemplifying that Awakening transcends conventional understanding.

While factions or loosely organized 'houses' had existed before the Song dynasty (the so-called 'Five Houses of Chan'), it was during this latter period that Chan settled into its two most enduring forms.[32] The first of

---

Rhetoric of Immediacy: A Cultural Critique of Chan Buddhism (Faure 1991). The phrase reflects that Chan controversies over sudden and gradual Awakening exemplify 'theoretical one-upmanship'. Immediacy implies 'that which works, arises or is reached without intermediary'. (Faure 1991: 36) This expresses the idea that Awakening cannot be accommodated — or dumbed down — to the level of the unawakened. Faure points out that, in spite of this rhetorical posture, Chan perspectives inevitably incorporated a degree of gradualness in relation to practice and generally acknowledged the vital role of spiritual guidance (which implies meditation).
  A range of fascinating articles relating to the sudden/gradual (*dunjian*) debate can be found in Gregory 1987.
30 See Buswell 1987: 340.
31 This theme is explored extensively in Foulk 1993.
32 The five houses (*wujia*) were a way of stratifying a complex set of lineage-based Chan

these, Linji, emphasized the practice of 'viewing the phrase' (*kanhua*), whereby direct encounter with the master was replaced by meditative contemplation on a 'critical phrase' (*huatou*) selected from a koan. This might mean, for instance, reflecting on the phrase 'Nanquan then cut the cat in two'.[33] This approach emphasized the importance of individual effort as well as the institutional validation of Awakening, and was later exported to Japan as Rinzai Zen (*see* pp.197–202). It was also adopted in Korea as *kanhwa* Seon.[34]

The second tradition, known as Caodong, emphasized 'silent illumination' (*mozhao*). This approach assumes that the brilliance of Awakening *underpins* our experience and appears to reject conscious effort. One of its exponents wrote:

> Without taking a step, you should constantly sit in your room and just forget about the teachings. Be like dried wood, or a stone, or a wall, or a piece of tile, or a pebble.[35]

This tradition emphasizes that Awakening is *immanent* but downplays its temporal expression. It was also transmitted to Japan where it formed the basis of Sōtō Zen.[36]

The Chan lineage system proved extremely effective as a propaganda tool since it convinced the imperial authorities to appoint many Chan masters as abbots of public monasteries.[37] This enabled Chan to establish itself as the mainstream of Chinese monastic Buddhism and it has remained so into contemporary times.

Pure Land Buddhism in China

In Chapter 4, we encountered the concept of cosmic Buddhas and their buddha-fields — or Pure Lands — and saw that a number of cults emerged associated with them. In China, and then Japan, Amitabha (Amituo in Chinese, Amida in Japanese) became the preeminent cosmic Buddha and millions of Buddhists came to aspire to rebirth in his land, Sukhavati, widely regarded as *the* Pure Land (Ch. *Jingtu*). They still do. Devotion to Amitabha is expressed by means of Buddha reflection (Sk. buddhanusmrti, Ch. *nianfo*) which may take many forms, ranging from elaborate visualizations of Amitabha, his Pure Land, or both, to the simple recitation

---

traditions, which seemingly never coexisted except in written summaries. (McRae 2005a)
[33] Cited in McRae 2003: 129.
[34] See Chapter 9.
[35] Zhenxie Qingliao (1089–1151); cited in McRae 2003: 135.
[36] See Chapter 11.
[37] This theme is examined in Schlütter 2005.

of his name. These various forms of Buddha reflection activate or call forth Amitabha's compassionate intervention and are means by which the faithful may enter directly into his presence. Pure Land devotion relocates the source of Awakening away from us as individuals towards the liberating intervention of cosmic Buddhas — a shift from self-power to other-power.

8.2 Storehouse of Spiritual Capital: The Patriarchs Hall

A distinctive architectural feature of Chinese Mahayana monasteries was the Patriarchs Hall (*zutang*) or Portrait Hall.[38] In a Chan monastery, this was dedicated to the veneration of key patriarchs of the Chan lineage, including former abbots of that monastery. This practice was influenced by Confucian ancestor worship.

When an abbot died, his portrait was moved to the Patriarchs Hall and special memorial services were observed on the anniversary of his death.[39] These included making offerings to the portrait, such as food, tea, incense, and prayers. The rituals were based on the model of receiving an honoured guest and their purpose was to help raise the Awakened spirit of the abbot to an even more exalted status.

The Patriarchs Hall served as a storehouse of spiritual capital, which helped to guarantee the monastery's integrity and prestige. Through the presence of their portraits, the monastery sustained possession of the charisma of deceased abbots. The abbots remained ritually present, functioning as fields of merit capable of inspiring donations and patronage.

An especially revered abbot might be mummified and his gilded body placed in the Patriarchs Hall or other memorial building. He thus served as a 'flesh icon' whose Awakened charisma continued to bless and enrich the monastery even beyond the grave. This might be especially important if a new abbot lacked the spiritual stature of his predecessor. A mummified 'Buddha' was a priceless spiritual asset that could transform a monastery into a thriving pilgrimage centre attracting all kinds of benefits both spiritual and material.

Monastic and lay orientations

Pure Land Buddhism is often regarded as a 'popular' Buddhist phenomenon and not one widely followed by the monastic elite. While this became true of some strands of Pure Land, especially in Japan, in China it was influential in monastic circles too. In fact, it began there. Establishing an historical overview of Pure Land practice in China is not easy since much of the knowledge that we have is framed by Japanese Pure Land

---

[38] Foulk 1993: 173–7.
[39] For a detailed analysis of the ideology and practices associated with Chan portraiture, see Foulk and Sharf 2003.

schools, which have tended to reorganize the historical record in ways that conform to their sectarian interests.[40] With this warning in mind, it may be helpful to understand Chinese Pure Land in terms of two orientations: monastic and lay.[41]

Although there are no hard distinctions, the monastic orientation made use of more complex forms of Buddha reflection, including visualization, and its understanding of Amitabha and his Pure Land was underpinned by sophisticated Mahayana philosophy, including shunyata. The Pure Land and Amitabha were often understood as not separate from the mind of the individual; Amitabha was not seen crudely as a being 'out there' (or 'up there') nor was his Pure Land seen as a distant, physical world. Rather the Pure Land was in the present, it was one's own mind, understood in its true aspect.[42] Moreover, within monastic circles, Amitabha devotions tended to function as one among a number of practices.

For lay people, on the other hand, Amitabha was likely to have been revered as a more literal saviour who could intervene in their lives, and the Pure Land understood as a place where they could really be reborn after death. For some, Amitabha devotion became the primary expression of religious practice since it could be fulfilled in simple ways, such as sponsoring the carving of a stone image of Amitabha or a painting or through the recitation of the mantric formula 'Homage to Amitabha Buddha' (*Nanwu Amituo fo*), which, through popular use, came to be identified with the more general notion of *nianfo*.[43]

The monastic Pure Land orientation could be summed up as 'immanental, earned and elitist': immanental because it seeks immediate Awakening; earned because it requires individual effort; and elitist because it assumes only a privileged minority are capable of this type of realization.[44] The lay orientation, on the other hand, is 'posthumous, bestowed, and universalist': posthumous because it is oriented towards a liberation that will be accomplished after death; bestowed because it relies on the compassionate work of Amitabha, who delivers those incapable of liberating themselves; and universalist since it assumes both that everyone is in need of salvation and that Amitabha is willing and able to save us all.[45]

---

[40] Sharf attributes the clear delineation of a Pure Land lineage to the Japanese monk Hōnen (1133–1212). According to Sharf, Hōnen's conception of a Pure Land school was a creative reimagining of the past, conferring identity on a disparate array of past masters and teachings, at least in part to demonstrate the legitimacy of his own spiritual enterprise. (Sharf 2002b: 298)

[41] This is a distinction made in Andrews 1993.

[42] Chappell explores how a series of Chinese thinkers understood the nature of the Pure Land. (Chappell 1977)

[43] The invocation is also found in the form *Namo Amituo fo*; '*namo*' meaning 'homage to'.

[44] Andrews 1993: 19–20.

[45] Andrews 1993: 19.

Huiyuan's Pure Land fellowship

While there is evidence of Amitabha devotion in China as early as the 3rd century, accounts of Pure Land Buddhism usually begin with the monk Huiyuan (334–416). Although he never established a self-consciously defined sect, many centuries later he was honoured as the first Pure Land patriarch.[46] Huiyuan had already been trained in Madhyamika philosophy when, around 380 CE, he moved to Lushan in the south-east (now Jiangxi Province) to establish a mountain retreat. Soon, he began constructing a large monastery, called Donglinsi, which still survives, albeit in a much truncated form.

On a momentous day in 402 CE, Huiyuan gathered together 123 of his monastic and lay followers before an image of Amitabha and led them in a vow to be reborn in the Pure Land. In addition, he guided them through a practice of Buddha contemplation (*guanfo*), which included visualizing an image of Amitabha.[47] Huiyuan almost certainly took his inspiration from the *Sutra on the Samadhi of Seeing All Buddhas* (*see* p.63), which had been translated into Chinese in the late 2nd century.[48] While the significance of this text was later superseded by the three Pure Land sutras (the shorter and longer *Sukhavati Sutras* and the *Visualization Sutra*),[49] it fulfilled a key role in establishing the Amitabha cult in China. Although Huiyuan's followers included both monastics and lay people, his model of practice was adopted primarily by clergy. His group, later named the White Lotus Society, served as a model for subsequent Pure Land rebirth fellowships.[50]

Following Huiyuan, other figures contributed towards the evolution of Pure Land devotion in its monastic guise, the most notable of whom was Zhiyi, who incorporated Amitabha devotion into his meditation curriculum.[51] Mention has already been made of the constantly walking meditation, which centres on the circumambulation of an image of

---

[46] On the construction of the Pure Land patriarchate in the Song dynasty, see Getz 1999.

[47] Andrews differentiates Buddha contemplation (*guanfo*) from what he calls invocational Buddha-reflection (which became identified with the term *nianfo*). The first begins with visualizing an image of the Buddha and culminates in a 'buddhophany' — a manifestation of the actual Buddha; the second consists in the simple recitation of the Amitabha invocation. He associates *guanfo* with the monastic orientation and *nianfo* (in its restricted sense) with the lay. (Andrews 1993: 18–19)

[48] See Tanaka 1990: 13.

[49] See Chapter 4.

[50] This theme is explored by Getz 1999. Elsewhere, Getz points out that the society created by Shengchang (959–1020), which has been widely regarded as the first Song dynasty Pure Land society, had only a tenuous link with Pure Land practice. 'Shengchang's primary intellectual, devotional, and liturgical orientation was grounded not on the cult of Amitabha but in the Huayan tradition.' (Getz 2004: 53)

[51] Some of these are discussed in Chappell 1977. One of these was also called Huiyuan and is known as *Chingying* Huiyuan to differentiate him from *Lushan* Huiyuan (discussed above). For a study of Chingying Huiyuan, see Tanaka 1990.

Amitabha Buddha. The aim of this practice, however, is not rebirth in the Pure Land; rather, Buddha reflection is used as a means to a seemingly higher end — the realization of Perfect Wisdom. After Zhiyi, masters of other schools also assimilated elements of Pure Land devotion into their spiritual programmes.[52] Pure Land devotion continued to play a significant role in Tiantai and, around the late 12th century, it was Tiantai monks who manufactured for it a patriarchal lineage, partly in recognition of Pure Land's growing autonomy.[53] When Tiantai was transmitted to Japan — as Tendai — it was from within its ranks that a more self-consciously defined Pure Land school emerged.[54]

Tanluan and other-power

Tanluan (c.488–554) is lauded as the first systematizer of Pure Land thought and also for popularizing Pure Land devotion outside the cloister.[55] While his theoretical work had little immediate impact in China, it was later a formative influence upon the Japanese Pure Land thinker Shinran (1173–1262).[56] According to an official biography, Tanluan was converted to Pure Land practice from Daoism, when searching for practices to help extend his life.[57] He was an original and rigorous scholar, steeped in Mahayana scriptures and Madhyamika philosophy — a far cry from the soft-headed faith follower, as Pure Land enthusiasts were sometimes dismissed. This learning informed Tanluan's Pure Land commentaries, the most notable of which is known as the *Commentary on the Treatise on Birth*.[58]

---

[52] Andrews 1993: 25.

[53] Getz also suggests that the construction of the patriarchate may have been a response to the proliferation of Pure Land societies and the increasing autonomy of lay oriented groups; creating a patriarchate was a move concerned to reassert monastic control. (Getz 1999: 502)

[54] See Chapter 11.

[55] Traditional dates given for Tanluan are 476–542. For an introduction to Tanluan, see Corless 1996. A range of accessible resources on Tanluan can be found in a special issue of the journal *Pacific World* (2000, 2), available at http://www.shin-ibs.edu/academics/_pwj/three.two.php.
The selection of figures who contributed to the evolution of Pure Land thought recognized here may owe as much to Japanese sectarian emphasis as to their intrinsic value. Sharf points out that many other Chinese monks contributed to the development of Pure Land doctrine and practice. (Sharf, 2002: 296). Nevertheless, the inclusion of these figures in part acknowledges their later significance for the Pure Land traditions of Japan.

[56] On this topic, see Bandō 1971. See also Corless 1988. Also see Chapter 11 for more on Shinran.

[57] Corless casts doubt on several elements of the traditional biography, including the notion of an exclusive conversion from Daoism to Buddhism; he notes that Tanluan's Buddhist writings show Daoist influence. (Corless 1996: 108–9)

[58] *Wangsheng lun zhu*, T.1819. This a commentary on an earlier treatise the *Wangsheng lun*

Tanluan differentiates two types of path or practice: easy and difficult.[59] The difficult path, known as 'self-power' (*zili*), relies on one's own efforts, whereas the easy path, known as 'other-power' (*tali*), consists in placing faith in Amitabha and aspiring to be reborn in his Pure Land, which then provides ideal conditions for realizing full Awakening. It is called 'other-power' because it is owing to Amitabha's merits and grace — and not our own ethical purity — that we are born in the Pure Land. For Tanluan, the difficult path is 'like walking painfully overland on foot', whereas the easy path is likened to 'riding happily over water in a boat'.[60]

Tanluan divides the easy path into Five Mindfulness Gates (*wu nianmen*), which can be seen as 'portals through which one approaches the Pure Land and then leaves it to re-enter samsara so as to continue the bodhisattva practice of liberating all beings'.[61] Collectively, they represent a comprehensive spiritual regime. Reminiscent of aspects of supreme worship (*anuttarapūjā; see* p.47), the Five Gates are: 1) worship or bowing; 2) praise or chanting (especially the invocation of Amitabha (*nianfo*)); 3) resolution (to be reborn in the Pure Land); 4) visualization (*guan*) of the wonders of the Pure Land; and 5) 'turning towards' (*huixiang*), which refers to the transfer of merit.

The latter two gates warrant some explanation. Tanluan devotes a great deal of attention to describing the visualization gate and clearly regarded the contemplation of Amitabha and his Pure Land as a highly meritorious practice. Amitabha's land is characterized by purity, boundlessness, and total satisfaction of the senses. Amitabha himself is described in terms of his unrivalled magnificence, power, wisdom, and compassion. Contemplating the profound virtues of Amitabha and his paradise is regarded as a transformative exercise, instilling joy, tranquility, and confidence. Moreover, it is the gateway to a vision-world in which Amitabha reveals his transcendent presence (sambhogakaya). The final gate, 'turning towards', refers first to transferring the spiritual merit that we have accrued towards the benefit of other suffering beings, and secondly — once we have been liberated in the Pure land — it means turning *back* to be reborn in samsara in order to free others.[62]

According to Tanluan, even the most depraved of people can be saved by invoking Amitabha 10 times at the moment of death, since his name has

---

(T.1524) attributed to the Indian master Vasubandhu.

[59] This general distinction is drawn from a work attributed to Nagarjuna known as the *Commentary on the Ten Bodhisattva Stages* (*Daśabhūmi-vibhāṣā-śāstra*, Ch. *Dazhidu lun*, T.1509); see Williams 2008: 244. Tanluan's innovation is to equate the easy practice with the Pure Land path.

[60] Translated in Andrews 1993: 23.

[61] Corless 2000: 8.

[62] Corless 1996: 113–4.

the power to counteract untold evil. Amitabha is fully present through this invocation, which is equivalent to his light and so illuminates the darkness of ignorance. Tanluan conceives of the name as a kind of wonder-working spell, which has the power to release all beings from suffering.[63] Through intoning the name, Amitabha's inexhaustible spiritual virtues pour forth.

Daochuo and Shandao

The next significant figure in the development of Pure Land practice was Daochuo (562–645), who was influenced by Tanluan's teachings.[64] Daochuo became convinced that the Dharma had entered its last age (*mofa*), and so was in terminal decline (*see* also pp.180). As a consequence, he believed that the traditional means of gaining Awakening — what he called 'the path of sages' (*shengdao*) — was no longer realistic, and that the 'gate of the Pure Land' (*jingtumen*) was the only reliable means of salvation. He simplified Tanluan's approach, emphasizing verbal *nianfo* using a rosary as the key practice for the common people (though he personally valued Buddha contemplation too).

Shandao (613–681) was Daochuo's most important disciple.[65] He further crystalized Pure Land teachings and also spread their message among ordinary folk. Shandao continued to emphasize the age of degeneration and, along with it, a decline in human spiritual capacity — and he included himself in this.[66] We must all acknowledge that we are:

> common sentient beings, utterly laden with ignorance and passion, shallow of good roots, transmigrating through the triple world and never escaping from the burning house…[67]

He emphasized that the Pure Land sutras were proclaimed *especially* to meet the needs of his degenerate age and was particularly concerned to engage those who felt spiritually impoverished, including the unlettered. Consequently, Shandao's message is sympathetic to the lay orientation, emphasizing the urgency of seeking rebirth in the Pure Land through the power of Amitabha's vows. He promoted verbal *nianfo* as the method most suited to degenerate beings of the final age.[68]

Besides stressing the practice of recitation, Shandao also emphasized the importance of unshakable trust in Amitabha's saving powers. Following a

---

63   Corless 1996: 124–5.
64   On Daochuo and Shandao, see Chappell 1996. On Daochuo, see also Chappell 1977: 36–48.
65   For a study of Shandao and his teachings, see Pas 1995.
66   Pas 1995: 143–6.
67   Cited in Andrews 1993: 25.
68   As Pas documents, Shandao also gave considerable attention to Buddha contemplation (*guanfo*) but its application was likely to be more at the elite level. (Pas 1995: 163–206)

passage in the *Visualization Sutra*, this trust or faith is described in terms of cultivating a 'threefold mind': 1) a most sincere mind; 2) a profound or deep mind; and 3) and a mind which vows to direct all actions towards rebirth in the Pure Land.[69]

Shandao explains the sincere mind in terms of being genuine, even humble: 'one should not outwardly manifest the aspects of being wise, good, and diligent while inwardly embracing vanity and falsehood'.[70] Without this spirit of authenticity, the value of our outward religious acts is degraded, if not nullified. Shandao analyses the profound mind according to two aspects. First, we must cultivate the profound conviction that we are 'an ordinary sinful being involved in transmigration … tumbling in this stream of cyclic rebirth, unable to find the karmic conditions for escape'.[71] Secondly, we must nurture a deep faith that Amitabha can — and will — exercise his compassionate power to grasp us, if we entrust ourselves to him 'without doubt or reservation'.[72] The final aspect of the threefold mind invokes the economy of merit transfer; but, here, merits are transferred specifically towards rebirth in the Pure Land rather than to any other end.

Shandao also formulated a celebrated parable of the existential predicament known as the 'Parable of the White Path'.[73] This concerns a lone traveller who is assailed by bandits and wild beasts on the east side. Running towards the west, he sees two rivers: one, flowing south, is a torrent of fire; the other, snaking north, is a river of water. Both rivers are just a hundred steps wide but forbiddingly deep and long. The only way to safety is across a narrow, white path, just a few inches wide, between the rivers. How to cross over?

Left to his own devices, the traveller will die but, in his darkest despair, he resolves to try the narrow path. At this moment, the Buddha Shakyamuni's voice urges him forward and the Buddha Amitabha calls to him from the west bank. Thus reassured, the traveller steps across via the white path. The parable repays repeated reflection but the central message seems to be that the darkest hour will call forth Amitabha's compassionate light. Unfailingly, Amitabha responds to the needs of the spiritually destitute.

Pure Land–Chan Relations

As already noted, the appeal of Pure Land devotion was widespread, so much so that it became 'an ubiquitous feature of Chinese Buddhism'.[74]

---

⁶⁹ See Pas 1995: 216–19. The 'threefold mind' (*sanzhong xin*) comprises: 1) *zhicheng xin*; 2) *shenxin*; and 3) *huxiang fayuan xin*.

⁷⁰ Hōnen 1998: 99.

⁷¹ Cited in Hōnen 1998: 101.

⁷² Hōnen 1998: 101.

⁷³ Pas 1995: 147–9. The parable is recorded in Shandao's *Commentary on the Visualization Sutra* (*Guan wuliangshoufo jing zhu*, T.1753).

⁷⁴ Sharf 2002: 301.

There is some debate as to how far Chan affirmed Pure Land devotion and how far it condemned it.[75] On the face of it, the two orientations seem very different, yet there is plenty of evidence to indicate that Chan incorporated a variety of Pure Land practices, including *nianfo*, and — far from being opposed — the two approaches were often integrated. However, the Chan understanding of the nature and purpose of Pure Land practices was underpinned by key Mahayana philosophical insights such as emptiness, nonduality, and nonattachment.[76] As early as the 7th century, one Chan master wrote:

> Apart from mind there is no Buddha, apart from Buddha there is no mind. To contemplate the Buddha is to contemplate the mind; to seek the mind is to seek the Buddha.[77]

The object of *nianfo* then is the mind itself, which is non-different from the Buddha or Amitabha. Attaining the Pure Land or uttering the name of Amitabha is none other than realizing the innate purity of the mind. Thus rather than conceiving of the Pure Land dualistically, in terms of a world beyond this one, Chan integrated it within an immanent vision of Awakening. This perspective is known as 'mind-only Pure Land'. But this way of interpreting the Pure Land was not really a Chan innovation, since it can be found in earlier Mahayana texts, such as the *Vimalakirti Sutra*, and was also highlighted by Tiantai.

Later Chinese Buddhism

It is generally accepted that after the Song dynasty ended in 1279, the creative phase of Chinese Buddhism was largely over.[78] But this does not mean that post-Song Buddhism was a story of unremitting decay; recent scholarship indicates that the fortunes of the sangha continued to wax and wane as they always had done.[79]

In the course of the 13th century, China fell under the control of the Mongols as the mighty Kublai Khan assumed the Imperial seat of the Yuan dynasty (1271–1368). This period saw an increased influence of Tibetan-style Vajrayana Buddhism. From the Ming dynasty (1368–1644) onwards, Chinese Buddhism was characterized by an increased syncretism, especially of Pure Land and Chan elements, as well as an incorporation of tantric teachings and practices.[80] In addition, aspects of Buddhism were often

---

[75] See, for instance, Chappell 1986.

[76] Sharf 2002: 308–9.

[77] This was Daoxin (580–651); cited in Sharf 2002: 304.

[78] The condition of Buddhism during the Ming dynasty is explored in some detail by Yu 1981: 138–91.

[79] Yu 1998.

[80] Sharf argues that the 'synthesis' was not one of two opposed systems of thought and

combined with Confucianism and Daoism in various configurations of the principle 'the three teachings are one' (*sanjiao heyi*).[81] This resulted in a more thoroughgoing integration of Buddhist elements into mainstream Chinese culture.

8.3 Delivering Creatures of Water and Land

The *shuilu fahui* (rite for deliverance of creatures of water and land) is perhaps the most elaborate and spectacular Chinese ritual still regularly enacted in contemporary times. For more than 1000 years, large monasteries have staged what is really a mega-ritual incorporating a number of other popular ceremonies into a seven-day ritual marathon. The overall aim is to save all sentient beings and deliver them to nirvana, or at least to Amitabha's Pure Land, from where they may achieve complete liberation.

Central to the ritual is a vegetarian feast, to which all sentient beings are invited, including departed spirits. Besides this, many scriptures and mantras are recited and sermons delivered. A complex sequence of rituals is performed, including confession, offerings to deities, and food bestowal to hungry ghosts.

Owing to its scale, the ritual requires a major investment of both human and material resources. Dozens of monks are needed to perform it, besides potentially thousands of others who may participate. Each enactment also requires the creation of papier-mâché figures, various paintings and banners, thousands of hand-painted paper placards, and large volumes of vegetarian food.

The ritual produces not only spiritual merit but also large sums of money through donations made for the setting up of 'spirit tablets' on behalf of departed relatives. Profits from the ritual not only go to fund the running of the monastery but may also be donated to charitable causes.[82]

The fortunes of the sangha during the Ming period were very mixed. For convenience, this period could be characterized in terms of three phases: the early period (roughly the first 150 years until the mid-15th century), in which detailed legislation concerning every aspect of clerical life was imposed and Ming emperors took a close interest in Buddhism; the middle period (mid-15th to mid-16th century) when governmental regulation broke down and there was a serious decline in the spiritual integrity of the sangha; and the late period (1573–1620), which fostered some Buddhist renewal.[83]

---

practice but rather of lay and monastic orientations to practice. (Sharf 2002: 322)

[81] Yu 1981: 64.

[82] For a study on the contemporary observance of this ritual, see Chan 2008.

[83] Yu 1998: 898–9.

Ostensibly, government regulation in the early Ming period was concerned to purify the sangha by purging 'secularized monks', who lived outside the cloister, married, and had families. However, the desire to control a powerful — and potentially threatening — cultural force no doubt also influenced policy.[84] Popular literature suggests that Buddhist clergy in general were not held in high esteem, being depicted as 'greedy and licentious'.[85]

By the mid-Ming period, elite Buddhism was in serious decline. A significant factor here was the government's policy of selling blank ordination certificates to raise revenue; at its peak in 1466, a staggering 130,000 were sold.[86] An ordination certificate was a valuable commodity since it exempted the bearer from taxes, government labour, and military conscription. While many of those purchasing certificates saw them simply as passports to avoid these obligations, their indiscriminate sale no doubt undermined the prestige of the sangha and enabled anyone — regardless of their motives — to join it, inevitably degrading its spiritual vitality.

But the causes of decline were also *internal*. Yunqi Zhuhong (1535–1615), a notable reformer, identified the degeneration of Chan practice, the neglect of monastic discipline (vinaya), and an increased preoccupation with worldly benefits as key factors.[87] In short, many monks became decadent, caring little for their spiritual vocation, and being motivated instead by material reward.

Despite this general climate of decay, the late Ming period also witnessed some notable reformers, of whom Zhuhong, a Chan monk, is the most celebrated.[88] His approach was characterized by the fusion of Chan and Pure Land elements, the revitalization of monastic discipline, and the standardization of some important Buddhist rituals, especially those for delivering creatures of water and land (*shuilu fahui*; *see* Feature 8.3) and bestowing food on hungry ghosts with burning mouths.[89]

There was also a rise in lay Buddhist groups which generally emphasized devotion to Amitabha along with practical compassion, exemplified in releasing animals, and acts of social welfare. Zhuhong adopted a conciliatory attitude towards Confucianism and Daoism and this helped in his efforts to spread the Dharma among the educated classes. He promoted nonkilling (*busha*) and the release of life (*see* Feature 7.3), practices which

---

[84] Yu 1998: 909; Brook 2005: 146.

[85] Yu 1998: 910.

[86] Brook 2005: 151.

[87] Yu 1981: 172ff.

[88] Yu discusses four key reformers (1998: 992–7), collectively known as 'dragons and elephants'. (931). Besides Zhuhong, they were Zibo Zhenke (1544–1604), Hanshan Deqing (1546–1623), and Ouyi Zhixu (1599–1655).

[89] Yu 1998: 933. On the hungry ghost ritual, see Orzech 1996.

were widely taken up. These efforts ultimately produced a more 'this-worldly' Buddhism, better accommodated to Chinese society, although perhaps lacking the critical edge of traditional monasticism. But Zhuhong's efforts were not universally welcomed. Among his critics was Matteo Ricci (1552–1610), a Jesuit missionary who landed in China in 1582.

The 20th century inspired renewal within Chinese Buddhism, as reforming figures, such as the influential monk Taixu (1890–1947), aimed to revitalize Buddhist institutions, resist the creeping influence of Christian missionaries, and reduce governmental interference.[90] However, the Communist victory of 1949 and the subsequent 'Cultural Revolution' (1966–76) in particular led to the widespread dismantling of Buddhist institutions, the 'decimation of the sangha', and thus signalled the effective demise of Chinese Buddhism, at least at the elite level.[91] By 1957, 90 percent of all monks and nuns had either died or returned to lay life.[92] In 1966, every remaining Buddhist monastery and temple in China's metro-politan areas was closed and all monks and nuns were ordered to disrobe, return to lay life, and become 'productive'.[93] For the Communist regime, the sangha was a parasite, a drain on resources, enmeshed in superstitious rites that had no place in its brave new world.

Communist China created an atmosphere in which the Dharma could not thrive. Some leading monks crossed the water to Taiwan in the hope of a more clement environment. This diaspora led to the renewal of Buddhism in Taiwan, as reformist organizations like *Foguangshan* (Buddha Light Mountain) launched worldwide missions (*see* pp.215–16). Since the 1980s, signs of the rebirth of Buddhism in China have become increasingly visible. In particular, Buddhist studies academies (*foxue yuan*) have sprung up, dedicated to training a new generation of clerics.[94]

---

[90] On Taixu, see Pittman 2001. By his own admission, Taixu was not especially successful in his efforts to inspire radical change within the sangha. (Pittman 2001: 2) See also Welch 1968: 51–71.

[91] Welch 1972: 80, 341.

[92] Welch 1972: 81.

[93] Welch 1972: 342, 346.

[94] Birnbaum. 2003a.

9

Interpenetrated Buddhism:
The Mahayana in Korea

WHILE IN CONTEMPORARY TIMES Korea has become famous for its 'Asian tiger' economy, in which blue-chip electronic companies like Samsung and LG produce all manner of consumer goods, its rich Buddhist heritage is less widely known. Given their geographical contiguity, it would be natural to think that Chinese Buddhism stamped its influence firmly on Korea — and so it did. Yet Korean Buddhism is much more than a footnote to Chinese forms; Korea exerted significant counterinfluences — or countercurrents — upon mainstream Chinese Buddhism, especially during the first millennium.[1] It was also central to the dissemination of Buddhism to Japan. Thus it was an important hub in the development of East Asian Mahayana. Overall, Buddhism has had a huge impact on the development of Korean culture; this chapter explores some of this influence.

The basic character of Korean Buddhism was already settled by the 12th century, a fact linked to the end of the creative phase of Chinese Buddhism.[2] Perhaps its most outstanding feature has been its syncretism. This has involved not only reconciling divergent schools of Buddhist thought but also exchanging ideas and practices with other religious traditions — especially Confucianism, Daoism, and Korean shamanism.[3] A further notable feature has been the close relationship between Buddhism and the state; it became the duty of monks to entreat Buddhas and bodhisattvas to safeguard the welfare of the nation. In return, the government funded religious projects, including — in the Goryeo period — ambitious woodblock editions of the Buddhist canon.

Early Korean Buddhism

Mahayana teachings were first introduced to Korea in the late 4th century when it was divided into the three separate kingdoms of Baekje, Goguryeo and Silla, although it was some time before they had any great impact. As is probably true for most religious transmissions, the acceptance of Buddhism

---

[1] This theme is explored in Buswell 2005.
[2] Keel 2005: 430.
[3] Park 1999: 57.

within Korean culture depended upon a range of factors besides any inherent spiritual value it offered: political expediency, social prestige, and wonder-working powers were all significant reasons for its successful assimilation.[4]

The most notable early developments of Buddhism in Korea were within the kingdom of Silla, in the southeast corner of the peninsula. While the kingdoms of Baekje and Goguryeo accepted Buddhism in the late 4th century, it was not officially recognized in Silla until 527. Yet, just a few decades later, it had been embraced as the state religion, with the king taking a Buddhist name.[5] Buddhism was endorsed as a unifying force and as a mechanism for underscoring the legitimacy of the Silla regime. During this period, substantial monasteries were constructed, relics and texts imported, and Buddhist ordination was authorized.

Buddhist ideas and myths were also amalgamated with local tribal traditions, in particular, snake and dragon cults. Owing to the shamanic tenor of indigenous Korean religion, there was great interest in the early centuries in the magical properties of Buddhist rituals which were sponsored as means of state protection; monks were regarded as shamanic wonder-workers, able to subdue demonic spirits through their mastery of esoteric spells and rituals. However, in time, this interest and understanding broadened to incorporate many aspects of Buddhist thought and practice.

One eminent monk from this early period, Won Gwang (d. 630), travelled to China where he studied widely. Upon his return, he introduced a set of five precepts for lay people.

First, serve the king with loyalty, second, serve your parents with filial piety, third, be faithful to your friends, fourth, do not retreat in battle, and fifth, do not kill indiscriminately.[6]

These precepts show the blending of Buddhist, Confucian, and native concepts and were widely influential.

But Won Gwang was not the only monk to travel west; many others went to study in China too. Some of them never returned, instead contributing towards the vitality of Chinese Mahayana traditions.[7] Besides this, a remarkable feature of this early period was the number of monks who undertook the extremely long, arduous, and perilous pilgrimage to

---

[4] Best 2005: 15.
[5] Ahn 1989: 3.
[6] Cited in Ahn 1989: 19.
[7] Perhaps the most notable émigré monk was Woncheuk (613–96), who travelled to China and became a disciple of Xuanzang. His influence on 7th-century Chinese Mahayana is considered significant. While Woncheuk never returned to Korea, his Yogachara approach did gain some influence there. For more on Woncheuk, see Cho 2005. Also see Feature 7.4.

India.[8] Besides other eminent monasteries, Nalanda was one of their favoured destinations.

A further notable feature of this early period is Korean missionary activity in Japan; Buddhist monks were sent there to evangelize, especially by the Baekje and Goguryeo courts. One of these, Hyeja, worked as tutor to Prince Shōtoku (573–622) and is regarded as having been influential in his adoption of Buddhism.[9] Moreover, some Japanese came to Korea to study Buddhism. Korean monks thus played a significant role in the early developments of Japanese Buddhism.

Besides interest in its ritual and philosophical elements, there was also enthusiasm for the devotional traditions of Buddhism, especially the Maitreya cult. While devotion is often dismissed as the province of folk religion, it was in fact the elite who sponsored Maitreya worship in the early centuries of Korean Buddhism.[10] Through commissioning imposing sculptures of Maitreya, the aristocracy underlined their cultural supremacy and displayed their wealth and power. After the 7th century, Amitabha, Avalokiteshvara, and Bhaisajyaguru became increasingly popular focuses of patronage and devotion.[11]

Silla Buddhism

During the Unified Silla period (668–935), the fortunes of Buddhism took a dramatic upturn when the major scholastic schools that had emerged in China were introduced to Korea. Huayan teachings, later consolidated in the Hwaeom school, became particularly influential and remained a guiding influence on all subsequent Korean Buddhist philosophy. A distinctively Korean school known as Beopseong-jong (Dharma-nature) also emerged, emphasizing a synthetic approach to Buddhist history.[12] This school set the tone for what became the characteristically ecumenical outlook of Korean Mahayana Buddhism, a far cry from the sectarianism that was to become endemic to Japanese Mahayana Buddhism and which had also divided some strands of Chinese Buddhism.

The middle third of the 7th century has been described as the 'golden age' of Silla Buddhism. During this period, a series of remarkable scholar-monks made lasting contributions to the development of Korean Buddhist thought and practice. The first of these was Jajang (590–658), a nobleman.[13] In 636, Jajang travelled with ten disciples to Mt. Wutai, the

---

8 Grayson 2002: 39–40.
9 Grayson 2002: 30.
10 This theme is explored in McBride 2008.
11 Lancaster 1988: 135.
12 This tradition is associated with the thought of Wonhyo.
13 These dates are from Huntley 2002; other sources give different dates or simply

famous pilgrimage centre in China associated with Manjushri. There he is said to have had a vision of the sacred bodhisattva. Jajang won considerable prestige in Chinese Buddhist circles, inspiring many monks to study with him. Upon his return to Silla, his eminent status was confirmed when the Queen invested him with the title of 'supreme cleric'. Jajang's devotion to Manjushri was further underlined when he had an additional vision of the bodhisattva in the mountains of eastern Korea. Following this experience, he named the range of mountains Odae-san (Mt. Wutai in Korean), believing that they were the abode of Manjushri and that his vision proved that in a former time Silla had been a Buddhist nation.[14] In this way, Buddhism began to transform the sacred landscape of Korea.

Following his vision of Manjushri, Jajang was inspired to spread the Dharma among the wider public. Besides this, he reorganized Buddhist practice at the elite level, emphasizing four principles: 1) study of the sutras; 2) attendance at twice-yearly seminars on Buddhist doctrine, followed by exams; 3) the establishment of a central ordination temple; and 4) the establishment of a government department to ensure the maintenance of temples, images, and other Buddhist heritage.[15] Jajang was also influential in the development of the Vinaya school (*Yul-jong*), which stressed the importance of monastic discipline.

Wonhyo and Ecumenicism in Korean Buddhism

The ecumenical tendencies of Korean Mahayana were best exemplified in the work of the influential scholar Wonhyo (617–86), who initiated the Beopseong school and who has been described as 'the greatest thinker in Korean Buddhism'.[16] As with the biographies of many East Asian masters, the details we have of Wonhyo's life are framed within a mythologized narrative, which is concerned to demonstrate his spiritual accomplishments. Besides this, such narratives served as teaching devices, illustrating what the life of an exemplary Buddhist should be like. Through the influence of his mythic biography, Wonhyo became the personification of the spiritual ideal, and so the archetype upon which later Korean monks modeled themselves.[17]

With this proviso in mind, it is worth noting one or two features of Wonhyo's biography before examining his thought more closely. One noteworthy circumstance is Wonhyo's unsuccessful attempts to undertake a pilgrimage to China with his friend Uisang (*see below*). On their first

---

estimates. Tanaka, for instance, gives 608–677. (Tanaka 2004: 45)
[14] Huntley 2002: 42.
[15] Huntley 2002: 42–3.
[16] Keel 2005: 431. For more on Wonhyo, see Buswell 2007.
[17] Buswell 1995: 553.

journey, around 650, the hapless pilgrims were supposedly arrested as spies before reaching China and then repatriated to Silla. On their second trip, around 661, the companions had reached a port in Baekje territory, from which they intended to catch a boat to China, when they were caught in heavy rain. They took shelter in what they initially thought was an earth sanctuary but, with the following dawn, realized was in fact an ancient tomb, littered with skulls. This experience is said to have had a profound effect on Wonhyo; recognizing the power of his mind to transform a grisly scene into an apparently welcoming shelter, he awakened to the fact that his world was mind-made.

> [B]ecause thoughts arise, all types of dharmas [things] arise; but once thoughts cease, a sanctuary and a tomb are not different. Furthermore, the three realms of existence are mind-alone; the myriads of dharmas are mere-representation.[18]

This Yogachara-type Awakening meant that he no longer needed to go abroad to deepen his insight and it infused all his subsequent philosophical writings.

A second important circumstance of Wonhyo's life was that, having taken the tonsure at a relatively young age, in later life he disrobed, married, and had a son. This down-to-earth image is further exemplified through his work as an itinerant preacher among the common people. He is said to have sang, danced, and played a zither as means of communicating his spiritual vision to ordinary folk. According to Wonhyo:

> The attitude of staying in a deep valley while avoiding great mountains, or loving emptiness while hating existence is just like the attitude of going into a forest while avoiding trees.[19]

This perspective seems to dissolve the apparently insoluble boundary between monk and lay and to recognize that reality is not to be sought *apart* from experience but in its *midst*. Moreover, it demonstrates a reconciliation of apparent opposites that was characteristic of all of Wonhyo's work.

Wonhyo was an especially prolific writer, authoring more than 100 works, of which some 20 survive, and, in doing so, treating virtually every aspect of Mahayana thought. He was especially inspired by Huayan teachings and the AMF and drew on these to create a syncretic approach to Buddhist thought, which became known as 'interpenetrated Buddhism' (*tong bulgyo*) or 'Buddhism of the one vehicle' (*Ilseung bulgyo*).

---

[18] Cited in Buswell 1989: 66.
[19] Cited in Muller 1995.

9.1 The Monastic Economy

Running a monastery crammed with economically unproductive monks wasn't cheap. Not only was there food and clothing to provide, but texts were needed, as were ritual images and objects, and buildings had to be maintained. Regular fires meant an ongoing need for rebuilding and expansion demanded additional works.

In Korea as well as throughout East Asia, the primary source of income came through temple landholdings, built up through donation, reclamation, and even purchase. These lands, generally farmed by tenants or indentured serfs, produced food, rental income, and additional funds from the sale of surplus produce. In some early Chan communities, monks worked the land, while it was not unknown for prisoners of war, or even criminals, to be 'donated' as monastic labour.

In addition, monasteries received generous donations from wealthy patrons, especially for high-profile developments like new buildings, prestigious religious images, or merit-generating rituals. Monasteries also charged for various services, including memorial rites, and some gained profit from milling grain and pressing oil. In China, some monasteries formed the hub of a network of small businesses.[20]

Throughout his voluminous writings, Wonhyo's underlying interpretive principle was the harmonization (*hwajaeng*) of doctrinal disputes; through drawing on the Huayan doctrine of mutual interpenetration, he aimed to show that Buddhist teachings were all ultimately manifestations of a single truth or reality — the One Mind.[21] He did this through introducing two pairs of inter-related concepts: 'doctrine' (*jong*) and 'essence' (*yo*); and 'unfolding' (or 'opening'; *kae*) and 'folding' (or 'sealing'; *hap*).[22] Doctrine refers to the expressions of the Dharma — the glittering array of Buddhist teachings, which often appear to conflict, at least on the surface. Essence, on the other hand, refers to the underlying unity of these teachings, the metaphysical truth towards which all these concepts point. When, by means of doctrinal elaboration, this truth is 'unfolded', it becomes both a means of conceptual understanding and a stimulus for deeper reflection. However,

---

[20] For a summary of the Korean monastic economy, see Grayson 2002: 89-90. For a detailed discussion of the monastic economy in general, see Collcutt 1981: 249ff. This discussion focuses mainly on Japan but there is a review of the Chinese monastic economy. See also Xinru 1988: 152-4.

[21] This approach is introduced in Wonhyo's *Reconciliation of Disputes in Ten Aspects* (*Simmun hwajaeng non*, 1.838–841: *Hanguk Bulgyo Jeonseo* (*Complete Works of Korean Buddhism*)). Muller 2009 offers an online translation of this commentary.

[22] Park 1999: 63.

indirectly this gives rise to disagreement and even conflict because doctrine is inevitably partial and limited; those committed to one doctrine will tend to dismiss others who follow a different one.

The purpose of Wonhyo's textual commentaries is to exemplify the process of 'folding' the many doctrinal expressions back in to their shared essence, thus demonstrating that, from a higher perspective, they are not really in conflict at all but in harmony. In other words, he aims to show how all Buddhist teachings reveal the essential truth of Awakening. This approach can be seen as a distinctive formulation of the key Mahayana interpretive principle of skilful means.

Unlike some of his Chinese (and later Japanese) counterparts, Wonhyo was less concerned with arranging the Buddhist teachings in a rigid hierarchy than with showing their mutual containment or interpenetration. His approach was thus ecumenical rather than sectarian. Wonhyo's inclusive methodology ensured that doctrinal classification (*panjiao*) did not become as dominant in Korea as it was in China. He likened panjiao analysis to 'using a snail shell to scoop out the ocean, or trying to see the heavens through a narrow tube'.[23] Following Wonhyo, Korean thinkers were more likely to understand the Buddhist teachings as a unity, all pointing in the direction of Awakening.

One of Wonhyo's most influential works was his commentary on the AMF in Mahayana (see pp 112–5).[24] Here he adopts the widely known East Asian philosophical formula of essence–function (Ch. *ti-yong*; Kor. *che-yong*) as a tool with which to interpret the text.[25] Essence signifies the deeper, more hidden, even intrinsic character of something, whereas function refers to its dynamic, expressive, and visible manifestations.[26] In principle, the formula can be applied to anything but, importantly, its two components operate together as different ways of looking at the same thing — essence is not something that exists apart from function.

An original element of Wonhyo's interpretation is his application of essence–function analysis to the notion of faith, the core concept of the AMF. In order to do this, he examines the title of the treatise. But this is no mere preliminary; in the tradition of East Asian commentary, the analysis of a text's title may reveal its essential message.[27] According to Wonhyo, the

---

[23] Muller 1995. Some later commentarial texts attribute a panjiao scheme to Wonhyo but none of his surviving works incorporate it; see Park 1999: 66-7. See also Muller 1995.

[24] *Taesung kisillon so*, T.1844.

[25] This formula is also used by the author of the AMF, specifically to contrast the intrinsic characteristics of the One Mind with its external functioning; see Hakeda 2006: 38–9.

[26] For a detailed examination of this analytical formula, see Muller [no date].

[27] Park 1983: 38. This use of a text's title is perhaps best exemplified in the Nichiren Buddhist belief that the title of the *Lotus Sutra* incorporates all the qualities of the entire scripture (see Chapter 11). It could be understood in terms of the literary device of

text does not imply that we should aspire to develop faith in the Mahayana; rather, he identifies the Mahayana as the underlying essence of the One Mind (*yixin*) — the intrinsically Awakened nature of all beings — whereas faith represents its observable function. Faith, then, is not about believing in some external object; it is simply the mind's organic way of functioning.[28] Thus, in the unfolding of faith, the primordial nature of our mind is revealed.[29] While faith is understood crudely as 'faith in', it remains a preliminary stage of development, a precondition for Awakening. But seen as the natural activity of our intrinsic nature, it serves to reveal Awakening; the two are not separate.[30]

Wonhyo was one of the first commentators to recognize the importance of the AMF, which became a seminal text in East Asia. His thought had a profound impact on Fazang, the Chinese Huayan patriarch (*see* p.131), who incorporated many of its insights into his own, more widely known, commentary. Within Korean Buddhism itself, Wonhyo's harmonizing approach established the guiding pattern for later thought. But he was not simply concerned to ease sectarian tensions; he assembled a hermeneutic toolbox that could resolve the apparent divisions between theory and practice, study and meditation, even language and experience. Wonhyo's genius was to gather up a sprawling mass of teachings, practices, and orientations and to harmonize them in the light of an inclusive, holistic vision.

Before moving on to the next phase of Korean Buddhism, it is worth noting a third eminent figure of the 7th century: Uisang (625–702), credited as the founder of Korean Hwaeom (Ch. Huayan). Unlike his friend Wonhyo, Uisang did go and study in China, specializing in Huayan philosophy with Zhiyan (602–668), when he also met and befriended the young Fazang. After nearly ten years there, he returned to Korea where in time he began to share his insights. The syncretic tendencies of Huayan thought proved attractive to Korean thinkers and were to play a key role in the reconciliation of the doctrinal schools with the increasingly powerful Korean Seon (Chan/Zen) tradition.

Goryeo Buddhism (937–1392)

As Silla eventually crumbled, it gave way to the Goryeo dynasty, which continued to patronize Buddhism. It sponsored religious works, supported

---

synecdoche, where a part of something is seen as representing the whole (or vice versa), eg 'Friends, Romans, countrymen: lend me your ears.' (Shakespeare, *Julius Caesar*, 3.2).
28 Park 1999: 71–2.
29 Park 1999: 73.
30 For more analysis of Wonhyo's conception of faith, see Park 1999: 73–6. Tanaka 2004 examines Wonhyo's approach to faith in the context of Pure Land thought and practice.

the clergy, and encouraged popular expressions of devotion. But Korean Buddhism was in conflict. The emerging Korean Seon tradition, thwarted by the the doctrinal schools in its ambition to spread its new approach, became openly antagonistic, especially to Hwaeom. Broadly speaking, this was a quarrel over the relative value of meditation (*seon*) as opposed to doctrine (*kyo*) — study against practice. The Korean sangha was split.

But this wasn't all. So illustrious was the status of monks and nuns in Korea that ordination afforded valuable opportunities for political and financial advancement. These possibilities became increasingly tempting, and the fact that the clergy was also exempt from military and agricultural service made it an attractive career option.[31] This state of affairs resulted in an influx of clergy lacking in spiritual vocation. Two outstanding figures emerged who attempted to heal and revitalize the Korean sangha, using very different approaches: Uicheon and Jinul.

Uicheon

Uicheon (1055–1101) was a member of the royal family but was ordained as a Hwaeom monk at the age of 11. In his early thirties, he travelled to Song China where he studied for more than a year. While deepening his knowledge of Huayan, Uicheon also studied Tiantai, which had a profound impact upon him.

Upon returning home, he formally instituted a Korean Tiantai order (Cheontae-jong), which he hoped would unify the sectarian divisions within Goryeo Buddhism. Tiantai's dual emphasis upon study and meditation appeared to offer a solution to the disunity; Uicheon developed a systematic curriculum that guided the student through a series of key texts drawn from a range of Buddhist philosophical traditions, with the aim of resolving doctrinal conflict. Uicheon also emphasized meditation, albeit within a predominantly scholastic framework.

Uicheon's prestige, and the vigour of his new order, proved attractive and he recruited monks from existing orders, including Seon and Hwaeom. Ultimately, however, his venture compounded the problem; his scholarly instincts made him critical of Seon's anti-scriptural rhetoric and, consequently, rather than resolving sectarian conflict, he added to it. In response, the Seon sects began to coalesce and were eventually consolidated into a unified order (known as Chogye-jong).

Jinul and Seon

As the Goryeo period advanced, the spiritual vitality of Buddhism continued to decay. The Seon tradition expanded, both numerically and

---

[31] Buswell 1999: 79.

geographically, but increasing numbers of monks were tempted into secular careers which took them away from meditation practice. It was from within this context that Jinul (1158–1210), perhaps the single most important figure in Korean Buddhism, emerged.[32] Jinul was ordained as a Seon monk at a young age, but later supplemented his meditation instruction with considerable self-study of Buddhist scriptures.

Disgusted at the 'degenerate' Buddhism that he witnessed, Jinul vowed to set up a retreat society devoted to intensive practice, although it was some years before this materialized. In the meantime, in the context of studying the *Platform Sutra*, Jinul experienced an important insight that shaped his approach to teaching and practice: both the practice of meditation and the study of doctrine were essential keys to spiritual Awakening. Sometime later, Jinul enjoyed a further insight that convinced him that the sectarian splits between Seon and the scholastic schools could be healed and led him to emphasize an inclusive approach to spiritual practice. Eventually, Jinul was able to establish his practice community, which proved both popular and deeply influential.

Jinul's key teaching can be summed as 'sudden Awakening, gradual cultivation' (*tono cheomsu*, Ch. *dunwu jianxiu*).[33] What does this mean? Jinul followed Chinese Chan in emphasizing that Buddha-nature was inherent within the mind. This will be realized if 'we empty ourselves of passion and simply trace back the radiance of the mind'.[34] This procedure results in 'sudden Awakening'. But for Jinul, this is not the end of the story. This initial Awakening must be consolidated and refined through constant practice so that it permeates every aspect of thought, speech, and behaviour. Jinul's teaching follows the Chinese Chan thinker Zongmi (780–841), who argued that 'Awakening from delusion is sudden; transforming an ordinary man into a saint is gradual'.[35]

But once Awakened, why should there be any need to practice? Sudden Awakening here might be seen as analogous to the arising of the bodhichitta, which provides the initial stimulus for the aspirant to set out along the bodhisattva career, and which must be fulfilled through the cultivation of the six (or ten) perfections and their corresponding spiritual stages.[36] Jinul thus follows the general Chan approach of using proleptic language to speak about Awakening: its culmination is seen as already present in its first dawning. While in one sense this may seem misleading and even false, its psychological impact is to encourage the individual who

---

[32] For a detailed study of Jinul, see Buswell 1991.
[33] For a detailed analysis of Jinul's meditation system, see Buswell 1986.
[34] Cited in Buswell 1991: 170.
[35] Cited in Buswell 1989: 166.
[36] See Chapter 3.

may otherwise doubt his capacity to reach the heady goal of Buddhahood.

Jinul grounded his understanding of Awakening on the Huayan teaching of mutual interpenetration, arguing that any spiritual insight is directly connected with all possible insights; they are not ultimately distinct. Practice thus takes place on a supremely positive ground: Awakening is inherent, and all that needs to happen is that this Awakening must be fully expressed through the whole of one's life. This deeply affirming starting point is likely to give faith and strength to those struggling with their personal faults. This indicates how Jinul is concerned not simply to describe the structure of spiritual Awakening but to inspire and encourage his students along the path.

The balanced structure of Jinul's teaching can be appreciated through his emphasis on gradual cultivation. In China, and also in Korea, sudden Awakening had been associated with sudden cultivation. This was expressed in the belief that in gaining realization, practice followed spontaneously. However, Jinul recognized that reality did not seem to bear this out and that many monks continued to act in ways that did not reflect Awakened consciousness; not only this but some of them also felt that practice was superfluous. After all, if we are inherently Awakened, why bother? This objection was an ongoing problem for Buddha-nature thought.

Jinul followed Zongmi in emphasizing the need for the ongoing cultiva–tion of Awakening through practice. He saw sudden Awakening and gradual cultivation as like the two wheels of a cart, neither of which can be missing if the cart is to move forward.[37] Without sudden Awakening, practice would be blind, since it was based on the deluded mind. Further, because the goal seemed so impossibly distant, practice might also lead to despair. At the same time, gradual cultivation was needed to maintain spiritual vitality and to sustain concern for the needs of others. Zongmi explained gradual cultivation in the following way.

> Since your habits have become second nature, it is extremely difficult to abandon them suddenly. For this reason you must, while relying on your awakening, cultivate gradually. If after reducing defilements and reducing them again, you have nothing left to reduce, this is called achieving Buddhahood.[38]

The Use of Koan in Korea

Jinul's approach to practise was somewhat eclectic since he believed that many Buddhist practices could serve the cause of Awakening, depending on the needs of the individual. At the same time, he was convinced that some

---

[37] Buswell, 1989: 107.
[38] Cited in Buswell, 1989: 169.

practices were more effective than others. For more advanced practitioners he emphasized *hwadu* ('critical phrase', Ch. *huatou*), better known as koan practice (Kor. *kongan*, Ch. *gong'an*), which he had learnt through studying the writings of the Chinese Linji master Dahui (1089–1163). Instead of reflecting on the entire exchange between master and disciple, as recorded in the koan, the student contemplates a 'critical phrase'. For instance, take the following koan.

> A monk asked Zhaozhou, 'Does a dog have the Buddha-nature?' Zhaozhou answered, 'No!' (*wu*)[39]

The critical phrase selected for contemplation here is the response 'No!'. Through intense, meditative reflection on this phrase, the student traces back the radiance of his own mind to its Awakened source. Once this source has been restored, he will understand the intention behind the master's response and also the Awakened mind that inspired it. Rather than seek to explain the meaning of remarks made by previous masters, using the *hwadu* method the student aims instead to emulate their Awakening. As Buswell puts it, 'It is as if the student were instructed to pattern his mind after that of the enlightened master who appears in the koan, until they think as one'.[40] In terms of its ritual and genealogical function, the hwadu method served as a means of 'entering a particular moment in ancestral time', enabling the student to encounter the masters of the past and receive their blessings and wisdom.[41]

The critical phrase serves as a catalyst to spark awareness of the student's intrinsic Buddha-nature. This occurs by instigating confusion, which builds into a great ball of doubt. This 'great doubt' results from the student's inability to solve the kongan conceptually. This doubt becomes so intense that the student can feel as if he is gnawing on an iron bar.[42] In time, the doubt fuses with the critical phrase and the mind eventually becomes trapped in a state of perfect concentration. When the ball of doubt explodes, the mind opens out into a new, all-inclusive perspective, as self-referential habits dissolve away and the innate radiance of the mind is restored.

The hwadu method became known as the 'shortcut approach' to Awakening since it was believed capable of transcending ordinary thought in a single moment of insight, without the need for a series of steps or stages. Dahui compared it to slicing through a spool of thread: all of its

---

[39] *The Gateless Gate*, case 1. See Sekida 2005: 27–8. This translation is from McRae 2003: 74.
[40] Buswell 1987: 347, modified by author.
[41] McRae 1992: 359.
[42] Buswell 1987: 352.

strands are cut with just one stroke.[43] But this does not necessarily mean
that Awakening comes quickly. Dahui used the analogy of an archer
shooting arrows at a target; he may take thousands of attempts to hit the
bullseye. Significantly, Jinul modified Dahui's approach to hwadu practice
by emphasizing the importance of continuing cultivation after Awakening.

9.2 Miaodao: A female Chan Master in Song China

Miaodao (12th century) was one of the first nuns to be certified within
the full Chan lineage in Song-dynasty China. Moreover, in 1134, she
was the first disciple of Dahui of either sex to realize Awakening
through the application of the 'critical phrase' in the context of koan
meditation. Miaodao's Awakening convinced Dahui that his novel
method of introspective Chan was effective.

Following her Awakening, Miaodao went on to fulfil the post of
abbess at several nunneries. In his sermons, Dahui regularly referred
to the spiritual accomplishments of his female disciple and also
formed dharma relationships with her own students. These students
sponsored sermons at his monastery, while Dahui encouraged them
in their Dharma practice. The example of Miaodao, and her endorse-
ment by Dahui, served to inspire generations of Buddhist women.[44]

Through Jinul and his disciples, hwadu practice became central to Seon
and remains so. His unique synthesis of Seon and the scholastic schools
(especially Hwaeom), which was institutionalized as the Chogye-jong,
became the mainstream of Korean Buddhism.

Other Goryeo Developments

Also during the Goryeo period, one of the great feats of Korean Buddhism
was accomplished: the compilation and publication of not just one but two
versions of the Buddhist scriptural canon. The first of these projects began
around 1011 and took some 40 years to complete. Facing an invasion force,
the king was moved to pledge that, should the attack be repulsed, he would
have the entire available canon inscribed on woodblocks and then printed.
Ten days later, the raiders withdrew. As a consequence, the canon was seen
as having a protective, talismanic power. Later in the century, Uicheon
collected many other texts not initially included in the primary canon and,
in 1090, published a supplement. Sadly, the woodblocks of the entire
canon, together with its supplement, were destroyed by the Mongols, who

---

[43] Buswell 1987: 350.
[44] See Levering 1999.

invaded in 1231. In part, this was a symbolic act, designed to nullify any special powers the texts may have had, and to crush Korean resistance.

The destruction of the Korean canon was a national insult, deeply humiliating for the elite. In the mid-13th century, work began on a new version (now known as the *Tripitika Koreanum*), which would serve as a means of national protection. This revised canon incorporated more than 1500 works but did not include Uicheon's supplement, resulting in the loss of many of its texts from the historical record. Each block was made from cured hardwood, to protect against the dangers of warping, and was 2' 3" long, 10" wide, and 1" thick. Text was carved on both sides and illustrations were also included. Remarkably, the 81,258 woodblocks suvive today, offering a priceless record of Buddhist texts of the period. The work was done to exacting editorial standards and its accuracy was such that it formed the basis of the standard canon used in contemporary times.

Joseon Buddhism

During the Joseon dynasty (1392–1910), the fortunes of Buddhism waned, partly owing to the resurgent influence of Confucianism on government policy.[45] Over time, tighter controls were placed on Buddhist organizations, which reduced the number of sects, monasteries, and monks. Moreover, the social status of the Buddhist clergy was downgraded to the lowest level.[46] Despite occasional displays of royal patronage, Buddhism was marginalized.

In the 15th century, pressure from the Confucian elite led to the exclusion of Buddhist monasteries from the major cities, while temple lands were confiscated. Moreover, not only was ordination made more difficult but many existing monks were also defrocked. In the light of such stringent regulation, Buddhism lost ground not only to Confucianism but also to Christianity, which has since become a major religious influence in Korea.

Hyujeong

The most important Buddhist figure of this period was Hyujeong (1520–1604), who further consolidated the syncretic trend of Korean Buddhism.[47] Besides this, he continued earlier efforts to reconcile the three teachings of Buddhism, Daoism, and Confucianism. By Hyujeong's time, the doctrinal traditions had merged into a single, scripture-oriented school (*kyo*), while Seon was unified as the Chogye-jong. Like Jinul before him, Hyujeong aspired to unify Korean Buddhism. However, he regarded Seon as the

---

45 For an overview of Korean Buddhism during this period, see Sørensen 1999.
46 At this time, Joseon society was divided into four classes: 1) the aristocracy (*yangban*); 2) the professional middle class (*chungin*); 3) the peasants (*yangmin/sangmin*); and 4) the servant or slave class (*cheonmin*).
47 Hyujeong was also known as Seosan Taesa (Great Master of the Western Mountain).

superior perspective and so aimed to incorporate the doctrinal schools within its overall programme. For him, Seon points directly to the mind of the Buddha, whereas the doctrinal schools expound the Buddha's words only. Essentially, he regarded the study of doctrine as a necessary but preliminary stage that is ultimately transcended in favour of the more 'direct' approach of Seon. He dismissed the possibility of attaining Awakening through an exclusively doctrinal approach.

Besides his hierarchical analysis of Buddhism, Hyujeong aimed to show that Confucianism, Buddhism, and Daoism constituted 'three gates' that all led to the same ultimate truth.[48] Unlike previous thinkers, he did not assert the superiority of Buddhism over the other two; rather, he drew on a higher perspective to reconcile their differences within a context of intrinsic unity. His approach recalls Wonhyo's method of 'folding' diverse teachings back into a single essence of truth.

Hyujeong also valued Pure Land practices, especially Buddha invocation, which he conceived as a means of 'gradual cultivation' to be pursued alongside Seon meditation practice. After Hyujeong, Pure Land practices began to dominate the spiritual landscape, for a time even overshadowing Seon.[49]

Later Korean Buddhism

With the final collapse of the Joseon dynasty, Japan began sending Buddhist missions to Korea from the 1870s, ostensibly to minister to Japanese immigrants who were settling there.[50] In 1895, pressure from these missions forced the government to lift the ban excluding Buddhist monks from the capital, Seoul. During the period 1910–1945, Korea fell under Japanese colonial dominance and, among other things, this led to the sanction of clerical marriage, following the example set in Meiji Japan.[51] The colonial government then privileged the married clergy in terms of preferment.

When Korea regained independence, the sangha was divided between the Taego, a liberal sect of Seon headed by married clerics, and a new Chogye Order, committed to monasticism and celibacy.[52] In 1970, the two formally split, by which time other denominations had also become influential. Over time, the Chogye Order has asserted itself through a process of renewal but both remain significant. Since the partition of Korea

[48] For a translation of a work by Hyujeong that addresses this theme, see Lee 1995.
[49] Sørensen 1999: 114.
[50] For a discussion of Korean Buddhism in the modern period, see Grayson 2002: 184–97.
[51] See Jaffe 2002.
[52] This was not the same *Chogye* Order that existed in the Goryeo period but the name does recall that tradition.

in 1953, information about the state of Buddhism in the Communist North has been scant but it seems certain that it has been severely depleted if not obliterated.[53]

9.3 A Korean Seon Meditation Retreat[54]

Seon meditation retreats are not for the faint-hearted, since they often follow a punishing schedule. During intensive retreats, which last as long as three months, monks may meditate for 12–14 hours a day. The morning begins around 3.00am with the gong and a leading monk intoning a wake-up chant.

The monks don't have to walk to the meditation hall because they have slept there. After folding away their bedding, there is a brief opportunity to wash and use the toilet before morning prostrations. Meditation then continues until 5.30 or 6.00am. This will be followed by three further three-hour meditation blocks later in the day.

A meditation block is divided into 50-minute sessions of sitting meditation, punctuated by ten-minute periods of walking meditation, during which the monks circumambulate the hall. Silence is maintained at all times. Between blocks, the monks eat and attend to their personal needs. They may also have light cleaning duties.

The day ends with lights out around 9.00pm; the monks unfold their beds again to sleep. An enthusiastic monk may continue sitting till late in the night. During the winter retreat, the monks pursue a week of 'ferocious effort' (*yongmaeng cheongjin*), during which they do not sleep at all, only breaking off from meditation for meals and toilet breaks.

A further development worth noting is the emergence of Won Buddhism (Consummate Buddhism), a new religious movement founded in the early 20th century.[55] There is some debate over whether or not this movement is truly Buddhist, since its founder Pak Chung-bin (1891–1943), known by his posthumous title of Sotaesan) identified his insights with Buddhism only retrospectively. Moreover, Won does not ground its authority in Buddhist history but in the teachings of its founder, who is considered the equal of the Buddha.

The central symbol of Won Buddhism, and main object of worship, is *Ilwonsang* ('the form of one circle'). This is depicted as a simple, black circle and represents the ultimate truth or reality of the cosmos. It is also equated with the *dharmakaya* ('truth body'), which is the essence of all Buddhas.

---

53 Jorgensen 2000: 720.
54 This information is summarized from Buswell 1992. This book offers a valuable insight into how a contemporary Korean monastery operates.
55 This brief account is drawn from Pye 2002 and Chung 2003.

Won Buddhism teaches universalism, holding that all religions are in principle one and, for this reason, engages in enthusiastic interfaith dialogue. Won does not feel bound by or indebted to historical Buddhism but free to innovate and bears traces of influence from several religious traditions, including Confucianism. By 1995, Won had more than one million adherents in Korea alone, as well as several hundred practice centres and even its own university. Around the same time, approximately 10 million Koreans identified themselves as Buddhists.[56]

---

[56] Grayson 2002: 191.

10

From State Protection to Universal Liberation: The Mahayana Enters Japan

THE NEXT TWO CHAPTERS EXPLORE the introduction of Mahayana Buddhism to Japan and its subsequent development there. This transmission represents the end of its long pilgrimage eastwards. Japanese Mahayana traditions have proved to be among the most enduring and some, notably Zen, have become universally known. This chapter sketches out the reception of Buddhism in Japan and describes some of its early forms, especially Tendai. It then goes on to explore the religious landscape of the Kamakura period (1192–1333), including a detailed discussion of Pure Land traditions.

Early Japanese Buddhism
By the time Buddhism reached the shores of Japan, the Buddha had been dead for about a thousand years. Buddhist doctrines, practices, and cultural forms had been transmitted ever further eastward and in the course of this journey, they had been translated, added to, reformed, often misunderstood, and at times even neglected. The Buddhism that Japan inherited had thus been framed by Chinese and Korean cultural lenses. For Japanese Buddhist monks, 'going back to the source' meant travelling not to the Buddha's birthplace but to the Chinese mainland. Consequently, the Buddhist traditions that Japan inherited were confined to those which had flourished in China and Korea, and these were mostly Mahayana in character. From this, Japan was to develop its own distinctive Mahayana traditions, especially during the Kamakura era (1192–1333) — perhaps the most spiritually creative period of its history.

In contrast to China, the culture of Japan was not especially sophisticated at the time Buddhism arrived there. The indigenous religious customs associated with reverence for the *kami* (sacred spirits or deities), which later became known as Shintō ('way of the gods'), did not form a major obstacle to transmission, partly owing to the fact that Buddhist teachings did not require their rejection. Nor did *kami* worship exclude the presence of Buddhism. In time, the *kami* were even partially assimilated to the Buddhist pantheon through the principle of *honjaku* ('essence–trace').[1] This development could be understood in terms of the teaching of skilful means as communicated in the *Lotus Sutra*, which declares that the Buddha may appear in many different forms in order to teach the Dharma.[2] This enabled the Japanese to regard the *kami* as manifestations of Buddhas and bodhisattvas and so to create a Buddhist–Shintō synthesis.

Buddhism was officially introduced to Japan from the Korean kingdom of Baekje in the mid-6th century as part of an effort to create an alliance against its rival Korean states.[3] Even before then, immigrants from the Chinese mainland had begun to establish temples. The Soga family, a powerful aristocratic clan, was an early sponsor of Buddhist clerics, practices, and buildings while Prince Shōtoku (574–622) is credited with the establishment of Buddhism as the state religion.[4] By the late 7th century, the government had begun to build temples on a wide scale.[5]

During this early period, Buddhism was valued primarily for the worldly benefits it supposedly conferred through enacting its elaborate rituals, including curing illness and granting protection. Interest centred more on safeguarding the established order and the state than it did on personal liberation. Two notable scriptures, the *Sutra of Golden Light* and the *Benevolent King Sutra*, were regarded as 'state protecting sutras' and used in liturgies as well as being enshrined in temples.[6] Buddhas and bodhisattvas were regarded as similar to *kami* in their capacity to provide practical aid. At this stage, limited attention was directed towards the doctrinal and existential aspects of Buddhist teaching.

Nara Buddhism

During the Nara period (710–794 CE), Buddhist institutions began to take serious hold in Japan. Nara was the seat of the newly established capital and it was here that the first central temple was established at Tōdaiji, completed in the 750s. The cementing of Buddhism in the Japanese imagination was perhaps best exemplified in the unveiling of the Great

---

[1] More fully, *honji-suijaku* (true nature-manifestation) but the term *honjaku* is widely used. See, for instance, Matsunaga and Matsunaga 1974: 238–41.

[2] See Hurvitz 1976: 238. See pp.16–18 for more on skilful means.

[3] The exact date is uncertain but the years 538 CE or 552CE are widely cited.

[4] It is unclear whether or not Shōtoku was himself a Buddhist follower; see eg Matsuo 2007: 19. For more on the early Buddhist activity in Japan, see Sonoda 1993: especially 370–97.

[5] Weinstein reports that by the end of the 7th century, some 200 or more monasteries had been founded, mostly in the Yamato Province (present-day Nara prefecture): Weinstein 1999: 449.

[6] *Sutra of Golden Light* (*Suvarṇabhāsottama-sūtra*, T.663); *Benevolent King Sutra* (*Kāruṇika-rāja-prajñāpāramitā-sūtra*, T.245); Sonoda 1993: 392–4.

Buddha of Nara (*Daibutsu*), a 16-metre tall sculpture of Vairochana (the 'Illuminator', Jp. Dainichi nyorai), who symbolizes the Huayan (Jp. Kegon) vision of the universe as an interconnected whole. The colossal Buddha, weighing some 500 tonnes, was completed in 752 and housed at Tōdaiji, where it still stands today.[7] Its construction served both to highlight the emperor's power and to act as a symbol of national unity. Above all, it offered a compelling image of the transcendent possibilities of human existence.[8]

Tōdaiji was the head temple of what became known as the *kokubunji* system.[9] This was a network of government-controlled temples distributed throughout the country, partly serving a bureaucratic function. Each province was obliged to establish an official temple attended by 20 monks and a corresponding convent housing 10 nuns. The kokubunji system served to further institutionalize Buddhism, as well as to ensure that it remained under state control. In time, these temples amassed substantial estates and considerable wealth.[10]

Nara Buddhism is usually characterized in terms of the emergence of the 'Six Sects': Kusha (abhidharma); Jōjitsu (based on the *Satyasiddhi Sastra*);[11] Ritsu (vinaya or monastic discipline); Sanron (Madhyamika); Hossō (Yogachara); and Kegon (Huayan).[12] These were sects in only a very loose sense and might better be regarded as lineages; the boundaries between them were often very soft. Kusha and Jōjitsu, for instance, did not have individual followings but functioned as schools of thought only.

The major contribution of the Nara lineages to Japanese Buddhism was their introduction of formal academic study. With a few honourable exceptions, they made little contact with the general population, mainly appealing to the aristocracy from whom their members were recruited.[13] It

---

[7] Sections of the statue have been recast over time, partly owing to earthquake damage. The temple building in which the Buddha stands is credited as the largest wooden building in the world.

[8] Sonoda argues that the construction of the Vairochana statue signalled a shift away from a primary concern with the magical properties of Buddhism towards the notion of individual Awakening. He sees the development of interest in the *Huayan Scripture* as also connected with this. (Sonoda 1993: 400–2)

[9] For more on this system, see Matsunaga and Matsunaga 1974: 120–3.

[10] According to Matsunaga and Matsunaga, the Tōdaiji complex eventually housed 4000 families and 100 slaves. (Matsunaga and Matsunaga 1974: 123)

[11] The *Satyasiddhi-śāstra* ('True Attainment Treatise') is attributed to the Indian scholar-monk, Harivarman (fl. 4th century CE). The Sanskrit original has been lost, and so it is known through its Chinese translation (*Cheng shi lun*, T.1274; Jp. *Jojitsu ron*).

[12] Ruppert indicates that a very small percentage of monks who resided in the great temples actually belonged to these lineages; for instance, out of some 3000 monks at Tōdaiji, only 2% were affiliated with them. (Ruppert 2005: 1175)

[13] Gyōki (668–749) was one monk who served the wider population, especially through bridge construction and water projects. For more on Gyōki, see Sonoda 1993: 403–9.

became common for monks to make their livings as ritual practitioners and chaplains for aristocratic families, performing healing, fertility and other rites to prevent misfortune and promote well-being, especially that of the 'nation' (that is, the imperial court).

During the Nara period, the monastic ordination process was also formalized, especially through the influence of the Ritsu sect, which was the primary guardian of priestly ethics and etiquette. Following Chinese practice, a *kaidan* (ordination platform) was constructed. In order to become a fully-fledged monk, each postulant needed to ascend the kaidan in the context of the requisite, state-sanctioned rituals.[14] For this reason, its control became a politically charged issue and was later to be challenged when the emerging Tendai sect petitioned for its own kaidan (*see below*).

The close relationship between Buddhist institutions and the state in the Nara period resulted in some Buddhist clerics becoming powerful as well as rich through accumulating temple landholdings. These temptations inevitably resulted in a degree of corruption, with some monks vying for political influence.[15] Eventually, the government reasserted control, placing greater restrictions on the clergy and supervising their landholdings more closely.[16]

Heian Buddhism and the Emergence of Tendai

In 794, the seat of government settled at Heian (later known as Kyoto).[17] Heian Buddhism (794–1185) was characterized by the rise of two major sects: Tendai (from Tiantai) and the esoteric tradition of Shingon, a form of Vajrayana or Tantric Buddhism.[18] The key figure in the introduction of

---

[14] Weinstein reports that during the Nara period, a total of 27 ordination ceremonies were conducted, in which 18,520 people were ordained. (Weinstein 1999: 452) Three monastic centres were officially licensed to carry out ordinations during this period: Tōdaiji from 754; Kanzeonji (in present-day Fukuoka prefecture on the island of Kyushu); and Yakushiji (in present-day Tochigi prefecture, north of modern Tokyo). The latter two began granting ordinations in 761 and were oriented to regional — as opposed to metropolitan — monks. Matsuo suggests that these latter kaidan were regarded as inferior by Tōdaiji and monks ordained there had lower status. (Matsuo 2007: 28–9)

[15] A notorious monk-politicker was Dōkyō (700–72). He became the trusted adviser of Empress Kōken (later known as Shōtoku) and exploited this influence to advance his political ambitions. He was eventually appointed her chancellor — the highest government office — and was later appointed 'King of the Buddhist Faith' (*Hōō*). He even plotted to become emperor, although he did not succeed. (Matsunaga and Matsunaga 1974: 125–8)

[16] See Weinstein 1999: 454–62 for a more detailed discussion of attempts to discipline the Buddhist clergy.

[17] Moving the capital from Nara to Heian served partly to prevent the continued influence of monks on the political structure.

[18] A detailed consideration of Shingon goes beyond the scope of this book. See instead Abe

Tendai to Japan was Saichō (767–822).[19] Early in his monastic career, Saichō moved to Mt. Hiei (Hieizan), not far from the capital, where he lived in a small hermitage and began studying the teachings of Zhiyi (see pp.124–9). After gaining favour with the emperor, in 804 Saichō was permitted to undertake the dangerous passage to China with the aim of studying and then transmitting teachings to Japan, including those of Zhiyi's Tiantai school.

Saichō studied for several months on Mt. Tiantai, the home of the Tiantai tradition, and also received instruction in various meditation practices. Before leaving China, he was introduced to Tantric or esoteric (*mikkyō*) Buddhism, which affected him profoundly. Besides being influenced by esoteric teachings, Saichō's Tendai was characterized by a broad syncretism which differed from its Chinese parent in several respects. In the course of his studies, Saichō had been influenced not only by Chan meditation but also by Pure Land devotion and vinaya teachings as well. Above all, the *Lotus Sutra* was enshrined as the most sacred of all texts. All of these influences were thrown into the melting pot that became Tendai.

Saichō established a 12-year training programme on Hieizan which had two parallel streams: one pursued esoteric studies while the other focused on the system of Zhiyi. His vision was to incorporate esoteric elements into a comprehensive Mahayana scheme. To do so, Saichō was partly reliant on the help of his contemporary Kūkai (774–835), who had also visited China but had studied esoteric Buddhism much more thoroughly. Saichō studied Tantric initiation under Kūkai and borrowed many texts from him. Regretfully, their relationship later soured.[20]

Partly to secure the independence of his movement, Saichō instigated a campaign to establish a new kaidan with an ordination based exclusively on bodhisattva precepts as drawn from the Mahayana *Brahma Net Sutra*, rather than the traditional vinaya precepts.[21] While this move was bitterly opposed by the Nara establishment, posing as it did a challenge to its dominance, shortly after Saichō's death the court granted his wish. Tendai could now carry out ordinations in its own name without reference to the Nara hierarchy. The following year, the main temple on Hieizan was granted the

---

2000. For a brief account of Kūkai, the founder of Shingon, and his teachings, see Watt 1999.

[19] For a brief overview of Saichō, see Weinstein 1999: 462–73. For a detailed study, see Groner 2001b.

[20] On the relationship between these two figures, see Abe 1995.

[21] The *Brahmā Net Sutra* (*Fanwang jing*, T.1484) is an apocryphal scripture compiled in the mid-5th century which attracted wide interest. Before Saichō, there had been no specifically Mahayana ordination; procedures and monastic rules were based on the *shibunritsu*, the vinaya of the Dharmaguptaka school of Nikaya Buddhism. For a discussion of this issue, see Groner 2001b: 107ff. See also Feature 3.2 on Mahayana ordination and Feature 10.3 on Eison.

title of Enryakuji and the first ordinations were witnessed. This move signalled the emergence of monasteries dedicated exclusively to a single sect — a feature of later Japanese Buddhism. Before this, followers of different schools lived together in the larger foundations.[22]

It is difficult to exaggerate how radical this establishment of a new ordination system was. While it may seem little more than an administrative detail, Tendai's new ordination pattern was revolutionary, raising fundamental questions about lineage, orthodoxy, and legitimacy. Ordination has always been a conservative element of Buddhism and great care has been taken over the precise ritual procedures required for its authentic transmission. Opening up as it does the path to Awakening, its control has been jealously guarded. At a stroke, Saichō's new procedures redefined the basis and meaning of formal ordination. Moreover, in styling his own ordination system as exclusively Mahayana, he was making a political move, effectively declaring the orthodox system to be inferior.

After Saichō's death, the esoteric profile of Tendai was boosted through further visits by some of its leading monks to Tantric masters in China, partly as a response to the growing influence of Kūkai's Shingon, whose thorough knowledge of esoteric theory and practice made Tendai seem amateur.[23] Owing to its capacity to enact dramatic rituals and ceremonies, which were believed to have wonder-working results, Shingon attracted considerable prestige and patronage. Its system of individual transmission, use of ritual implements and diagrams, arcane knowledge, and its 'secret' character all lent it an aura of mystical power which proved seductive to the ruling elite. Through enhancing its esoteric credentials, Tendai consolidated its own position, growing into a powerful institution with branch temples across the country. Its ritual specialists were regularly called upon to conduct esoteric ceremonies on behalf of the court.

A charismatic Tendai abbot, Ryōgen (912–85), rose to prominence by outwitting eminent Nara monks in a high-profile debate.[24] He attracted the patronage of the ruling Fujiwara clan, which helped to advance his career and subsequently to elevate the status of Tendai. Ryōgen is credited with rebuilding Enryakuji, which had been devastated by fire, and with reviving

---

[22] Weinstein 1999: 471.

[23] Leaders who visited China include Ennin (794–864), who studied there during 840–7, and Enchin (814–89) during 853–8. Ennin's diary of his travels offers priceless glimpses of life in Tang China (see Reischauer 1955). His mastery of esoteric Buddhism resulted in a significant upturn in Tendai fortunes. (Weinstein 1999: 481–2) Annen (841–89/98?) was responsible for systematizing the role of esoteric teachings within Tendai. On Tendai and the development of esotericism, see Matsunaga and Matsunaga 1974: 163–6.

[24] For a detailed study of Ryōgen, see Groner 1997.

Tendai scholarship through introducing annual debates. By the end of the 10th century, there were several thousand Tendai monks living on Hieizan.[25]

10.1 'Marathon Monks': The *Kaihōgyō* of Hieizan

A celebrated feat of spiritual endurance practised by elite priests of the Tendai sect is a series of daily pilgrimages around a 19-mile circuit of Hieizan. The full discipline, known as *kaihōgyō*, consists in the completion of a thousand circuits over the course of seven years; a shorter version involves completing 100 circuits in 100 days. Five or six priests complete the short course every year but the full programme is only rarely accomplished. The pilgrimage involves making offerings, reciting mantras, and saying prayers at approximately 260 halls, shrines, and sacred places along the route. A carefully prescribed ritual uniform is worn throughout the pilgrimage, the most distinctive feature of which is a special, oblong-shaped hat made from woven strips of wood, representing the lotus of Awakening.

The full discipline requires 100 days of walking during each of the first three years. During years four and five, this is increased to 200 days. During the sixth year, the route is extended to a 36-mile circuit. Finally, in the last year, the pilgrim walks for 200 days, of which the first 100 days consists of a 48-mile route which takes in the city of Kyoto as well as Hieizan. The pilgrimage culminates in a nine-day ceremony where the priest goes without food, water, or sleep. Perhaps, not surprisingly, those who observe the full regimen are regarded as living Buddhas.[26]

Kamakura Buddhism

While Tendai continued to grow throughout the Heian period, with success came in-fighting, corruption, and degeneration. At the end of the 10th century, an especially bitter dispute came to a head in violent confrontations between rival Tendai factions.[27] Over time, Tendai splintered into many sub-sects, each allied to a different bloc and vying for power and aristocratic patronage. Shingon suffered a similar fate. The

---

25 Groner 1997: 2.
26 For a film study of this pilgrimage, see *Marathon Monks of Mount Hiei* 2002. For written considerations, see Stevens 1988a and Rhodes 1987.
27 Weinstein 1999: 489–92. The Tendai sect fractured into the Sanmon and Jimon factions, both within the vast Enryakuji complex. The Sanmon pursued a feud with the Jimon for almost five centuries, razing their main temple, known as the Miidera (Onjōji) and located at the base of Hieizan, on several occasions. (Weinstein 1999: 495–7) See also Matsunaga and Matsunaga 1976: 284–7.

violent rivalries among these Japanese schools testify that Buddhism has not always been a peaceful religion. Contrary to utopian stereotypes of 'eastern spirituality', Buddhist institutions have not been immune to the destructive poisons of greed, hatred, and delusion; at times they have exemplified them.

It was from within an increasingly fragmented Tendai tradition that many of the now renowned Buddhist figures of the Kamakura era (1192–1333) emerged: Hōnen, Shinran, Eisai, Dōgen, and Nichiren. During this politically unstable period, many new Buddhist forms appeared which began to cater to the needs and aspirations of the common people, not just the elite.[28] This was a significant departure. For this reason, the Kamakura period is sometimes described as the Japanese Reformation although this analogy should not be taken too far. Besides the advent of new schools and forms of practice, there was significant continuity with the late Heian period. Notwithstanding their later prominence, the new developments were rather the exception than the rule. It is all too easy to assume that historically significant figures and schools exploded on the scene, over-turning everything overnight. In reality, change is usually more gradual, and it may take centuries before a new development attracts widespread support. The revolutionary thinker may cut an obscure figure in his own time. Not only this, but figures judged important by their peers may be sidelined by later historical developments, and even be written out of the story.[29]

A key theme that informed the new developments within Kamakura Buddhism was *mappō*; the idea that the Dharma had entered into its final, degenerate phase before disappearing completely (*see* p 186).[30] Given the kind of mob behaviour described above, which was mirrored at the national level by warring nobles, it is easy to see why this view might seem an acceptable explanation of 'how things are' — and of use to people like Shinran and Nichiren. Despite, or perhaps because of, these unpromising circumstances, dynamic new forms of Buddhist thought and practice emerged which further established the pattern of Japanese Buddhism into the modern era. Like lotuses growing out of the mud, Pure Land, Zen, and Nichiren traditions all sprang up during the troubled Kamakura era. These new traditions reached outside the educated elite, partly through establishing simplified forms of practice that could be understood and observed without requiring years of intensive study and secluded practice. No longer was monastic ordination regarded as a prerequisite for salvation.

---

[28] Foard 1980: 267.

[29] Some of these figures are considered in Morrell 1997.

[30] For a detailed study of *mappō*, see Nattier 1991. This concept also played a part in Daochuo's thinking (see p.150).

For the first time, universal Awakening was seen not just as a theoretical idea but as a *practical* teaching.

10.2 *Sōhei*: 'Monk-warriors'

During the Heian period a number of sects, including Tendai, established militias, popularly known as *sōhei* or 'monk-warriors', who served to protect clerical interests during an unstable and often vio-lent period.[31] Sometimes these militias fought one another; at other times, they banded together against common enemies. In time, the Tendai sōhei became increasingly belligerent, flexing their power by stamping on breakaway movements perceived as damaging to Tendai power.

The sōhei also turned their anger on the new Kamakura lineages. In 1227, for instance, Tendai sōhei confiscated and then burnt the original woodblocks upon which the Pure Land monk Hōnen's *Singled-Out Collection* had been carved.[32] They also desecrated his grave and destroyed key writings, which as a consequence have not survived. In 1465, they destroyed the main Shin (Pure Land) Buddhist temple, while in 1536 they razed all 21 main Nichiren temples, burning down half of Kyoto in the process.

At its height, the Hieizan militia may have numbered several thou-sand, making it a threat to the warlords battling to gain control of medieval Japan, as much by their alliances with clans as by their own strength. In 1571, the temple complex of Enryakuji was decimated by one of the foremost warlords, Oda Nobunaga; in the process, as many as 3000 monks and lay people were killed. Even though Enryakuji was later rebuilt on a smaller scale, the main Tendai faction never fully recovered.

Official and reclusive monks

The differences between the established schools and the new traditions and movements that emerged during the Kamakura period are characterized in various ways.[33] One model distinguishes between what it terms 'official monks' (*kansō*) and 'reclusive monks' (*tonseisō*).[34] These two groups are seen

---

31 For a detailed study, see Adolphson 2007. The precise identity of the sōhei is a matter of some dispute. Adolphson claims that few of the sōhei could properly be described as 'monk-warriors'; rather, they mostly comprised secular warriors recruited from temple estates and monastic workers. He proposes replacing the term sōhei, which he considers misleading, with the term *jihei* ('temple warriors'). (Adolphson 2007: 85) Monastic warriors were simply warriors serving temple interests. Nevertheless, their violent campaigns were carried out at the bidding of the monastic establishment.

32 See note 48 and associated text below.

33 For a useful summary see Dobbins 1998.

34 This theory is laid out in Matsuo 1997. It is expanded upon in his 2007 work.

as having radically different orientations, concerns, and obligations. While perhaps an oversimplification, this model nevertheless draws out significant trends. The official monks represent the schools that emerged in the Nara and Heian periods, whereas the reclusive monks belong to reforming or breakaway movements of the Kamakura era (although they mostly began their clerical careers as official monks).

Official monks were under the control of the state, and their function was to perform a range of offices and rituals to promote the welfare of the nation, the emperor, and the community as a whole. Owing to a need to preserve their ritual purity, they were restricted in how they could minister to the needs of women and the sick (especially lepers), to participate in funerals, and to raise religious funds. Their purity was expressed in their wearing a white surplice.

Reclusive monks, on the other hand, were not state-sponsored, which meant that they were not at the beck-and-call of the emperor, and that their ordination procedures could be governed by their individual orders. Their activities focused on the needs of ordinary believers, although they some-times prayed for the welfare of the nation too. Reclusive monks commonly pursued activities concerned with the salvation of women and outcastes (*hinin*; including lepers), conducted funerals, and often raised religious funds. They were not subject to the same stringent obligations with regard to ritual purity as the official monks, and this was expressed through typically wearing a black surplice. In essence, 'the Buddhism of the official monks focused on the community while that of the reclusive monks focused on individuals'.[35]

The notion that ministering to the needs of women or the sick, or conducting funerals, or raising funds for a religious project brings about impurity may well strike you as strange, if not repugnant. With regard to women, despite the fact that a nun's order emerged fairly early in the development of Japanese Buddhism, over time the belief that their status was inferior hardened. Within Japanese society, women were commonly regarded as 'defiled', especially in relation to menstruation and childbirth. This had many implications for religious matters,[36] including the exclusion of nuns from official ordination platforms, which meant that they could not be ordained as nuns (*bhikṣuṇī*).[37]

---

[35] Matsuo 1997: 183.

[36] See Faure 2003, especially Chapter 2.

[37] The issue of female ordination in Japan is a complex one. It was only relatively recently that it became clear that the full *bhikṣuṇī* ordination disappeared during the Heian period. However, 'private ordinations' continued (that is, a type of initiation not sanctioned by the state), as did self-ordinations. New forms of ordination were intro-duced by Tendai and then by the emerging new groups of the Kamakura period.

A related belief, also widely upheld, was that women could not attain salvation before becoming men. Even while adopting a more accommodating stance, many reclusive monks continued to believe that women were inferior. A refreshing exception was the firebrand Nichiren (1222–82), who openly preached that women could become Buddhas in their female form.[38] Despite the general view, reclusive monks were responsible for reviving and establishing many nunneries as well as creating new ordination platforms for women. A notable example here is Eison (1201–90; *see* Feature 10.3).[39]

Another significant minority marginalized by the official monks were the *hinin* (lit. 'non-people'). Primarily, the hinin comprised people suffering from Hansen's disease (leprosy) and the physically handicapped who survived by begging and grave-digging. For the official priests, proximity to such people was polluting but a number of important reclusive monks, who were themselves regarded as outcastes by some, took up the cause of the hinin through precept-giving (*jukai*), alms, and medical treatment. Notable again are the activities of Eison's Ritsu Order, which emphasized salvation through reciting the name of Manjushri, the bodhisattva of wisdom, and set up images of him in hinin neighbourhoods.[40]

The official monks' concept of purity also restricted their involvement in funerals; when they did engage in them, they were then required to enter a period of quarantine during which they could not participate in official ceremonies. Reclusive monks did not regard themselves as being similarly contaminated by death and so came to play a central role in funerals, even establishing cemeteries within their temple precincts.[41]

It is clear that the role, status, and vision of the new religious orders and movements that emerged during the Kamakura era departed in important respects from earlier models. But it would be wrong to think that the emerging traditions rejected the existing religious order wholesale; organizational, doctrinal, and ritual links were often maintained with mutual benefit. Moreover, the new traditions were not homogenous. Kamakura Buddhism is perhaps most characterized by its creative diversity, some of the more notable innovations of which we will now consider.

However, while a tradition of nuns did emerge within Tendai, the sect was not especially progressive in its consideration of the ecclesiastical role of women (they were excluded from Enryakuji, for example). Eison (*see* Feature 10.3) went on to reinstitute a full ordination for nuns. This topic is discussed in the context of Tendai by Groner 1997: 245ff.

[38] Nichiren is discussed at length in Chapter 11.

[39] Eison is also transliterated as 'Eizon'. On this topic, see Groner 2005: 221ff.

[40] See Groner 2001a. Eison focused on the compassionate aspect of Manjushri rather than his wisdom.

[41] See Matsuo 2007: 149–59.

Japanese Pure Land Buddhism

We have already seen that Pure Land thought and practice was a significant strand within Chinese Mahayana Buddhism, although not really a distinct sect. In Japan, the Pure Land orientation was initially followed within the context of Tendai, which explains why many of the significant figures in Japanese Pure Land began their spiritual careers as Tendai monks. In addition, there was some interest in Pure Land practices within the Shingon sect and even from the Nara schools.[42] Over time, there emerged institutions dedicated to Pure Land study and practice, which were unprecedented in the history of Mahayana Buddhism.

Japanese Pure Land Buddhism is an umbrella term that covers a wide range of developments. These were all united in their devotion to Amida (Ch. Amituo, Skt. Amitābha), the Buddha of Compassion, and their aspiration to be reborn in his Pure Land through faith in the *nembutsu*, as the recitation of Amida's name came to be known (*Namu Amida butsu*). However, these elements were understood in many different ways. While the schools associated with Hōnen and Shinran eventually became the mainstream, for several centuries there was a broad Pure Land movement that encompassed a wide range of doctrines and lineages.[43]

An early propagator of Pure Land belief was the Tendai monk Ryōnin (1072–1132) who, following a profound spiritual vision, founded the *Yūzū Nembutsu* (permeating nembutsu) sect, which still survives.[44] Ryōnin taught that each individual's recitation of the nembutsu exerted a positive influence on the entire world; at the same time, that individual benefited from all the recitations performed by others. This philosophy reflected the Kegon (Ch. Huayan) principle of universal interconnection.

Ryōnin lived an itinerant life, travelling round the country and keeping a register of those who agreed to recite the nembutsu, which constituted 'proof' that they had committed to the practice and that their rebirth in the Pure Land was consequently assured. For Ryōnin, the number of repetitions was crucial; it was therefore not unusual for subscribers to commit themselves to a daily regime of 100, 1000 or even more recitations.

Hōnen and the *Jōdo Shū* (Pure Land School)

Perhaps the key moment in the emergence of Pure Land as a distinctive form of Mahayana practice was when Hōnen (1133–1212) began to propagate nembutsu recitation as the *exclusive* means of attaining birth in the

---

[42] One example is the 'secret nembutsu' (*himitsu nembutsu*) pursued within Shingon; see Sanford 2004.

[43] For a useful overview of earlier developments in Pure Land thought and practice in Japan, see Weinstein 1999: 507–16.

[44] On this tradition, see Matsunaga and Matsunaga 1976: 12–19.

Pure Land; quite simply, the exclusive nembutsu (*senju nembutsu*).[45] This move triggered an earthquake in the Japanese Buddhist establishment, the aftershocks of which still reverberate today. He rejected the received wisdom that complex and difficult practices were more spiritually advantageous and that monastic life was essential for salvation, so opening a practical religious path for the ordinary person. In doing so, he dimmed the aura of monastic supremacy. The inclusive nature of his approach is expressed in the following passage.

> It is therefore clear that since the *nembutsu* is easy, it is open to *everyone*, while the various other practices are not open to people of all capacities because they are difficult. Was it not in order to bring all sentient beings *without exception* to birth that he [Dharmakāra/Amida] in his original vow cast aside the difficult practice and selected the easy one?[46]

Orphaned at an early age, Hōnen entered a local temple before training as a Tendai priest on Hieizan and, notwithstanding his later thought and practice, he continued to regard himself as a faithful monk for the rest of his life, even dying in his Tendai robes.[47] On Hieizan, Hōnen followed a pattern of Pure Land practices, including visualization nembutsu (*nembutsu zammai*). He also studied the writings of the Chinese master Shandao (*see* pp.150–1), which convinced him that nembutsu recitation (as opposed to visualization and related ritual ceremonies) should be observed above all other practices.[48] Hōnen is himself known to have intoned some 70,000 recitations faithfully per day.[49]

In 1175, Hōnen's spiritual Awakening caused him to leave Hieizan after a 25-year stay and set up a hermitage near Kyoto, where he began to attract followers. During this period he compiled his main literary work, the *Singled-Out Collection*,[50] which collected passages from scriptures and commentaries, arranged to reflect his particular vision of Pure Land

---

[45] Hōnen is also known as Genkū, which was part of his Tendai ordination name of Hōnen-bo Genkū. For an overview of Hōnen's life and teaching, see Dobbins 2002: 11–20. For a detailed study, see Machida 1999.

[46] Hōnen 1998: 77, emphasis added.

[47] Blum 2002: 13.

[48] Recent scholarship indicates that Shandao's apparent emphasis on the exclusive practice of recitation is an oversimplification of his approach. Nevertheless, he did promote it for those of low spiritual capacity. This is a complex issue treated in Pas 1995: 266–75 (see also p.150 above). Moreover, the exclusivity of Hōnen's own approach and his apparent rejection of Tendai orthodoxy are far from clear. He continued to observe the monastic precepts and participated in esoteric rituals. (Matsunaga and Matsunaga 1976: 60–1)

[49] Matsunaga and Matsunaga 1976: 61. Blum suggests he observed as many as 84,000 recitations per day. (Blum 2002: 31)

[50] *Senchakushū*. Its full title is: *Senchaku hongan nembutsu shū* ('Collection of Passages on the Selection of *Nembutsu* of the Original Vow', T.2608). This has been translated into English in Hōnen 1998.

doctrine and practice. In it, Hōnen declares that the Pure Land way is the *only* valid means of salvation given the realities of mappō. In this period of the decline of the Dharma (which according to some calculations began in 1052), Hōnen believed that it is virtually impossible for beings to gain spiritual liberation entirely through their own efforts (or self-power, *jiriki*). In other words, it is not possible to pursue the classical bodhisattva path — what Daochuo called the 'path of sages' (*see* p.150). In the time of mappō, this is the 'difficult path'. Teachings belonging to the 'gate of the Pure Land', on the other hand, preach reliance on the other-power (*tariki*) of Amida. Through Amida's transfer of merit, as embodied in his bodhisattva vows, the believer is assured of immediate rebirth in the Pure Land at death, which provides a perfect environment for attaining full Awakening. This is the 'easy path' and is ideally suited to the degenerate age.

More distinctively, Hōnen argues that the practice of nembutsu recitation is the *exclusive* means to accomplish liberation; moreover, it works universally for all beings.

> Why should anyone cast aside the exclusive and right practice, by which a hundred out of a hundred obtain birth, and stubbornly cling to the miscellaneous practices, by which not even one out of a thousand attain birth? Practitioners ought seriously to ponder this.[51]

Interpreting a passage from the *Visualization Sutra*, he glosses the instruction to 'single-mindedly concentrate' on the Buddha as indicating that we must leave aside all other spiritual practices and *only* recite the nembutsu.[52] The simplicity of recitation, as opposed to visualization or other formal practice, means that everyone can be blessed by Amida's salvific light, including — and perhaps especially — the lowly and spiritually destitute.[53] But those who continue to pursue other practices will remain in darkness.[54] Hōnen's position then amounted to a rejection of *all* other forms of practice besides nembutsu recitation and was, consequently, highly inflammatory.

Hōnen used Chinese records to construct an imagined history of Pure Land tradition, which until then had not previously existed as a coherent, doctrinal school.[55] As a distinct tradition then, we might say that Hōnen

---

[51] Hōnen 1998: 71.
[52] Hōnen 1998: 84–5.
[53] Referring to people who have committed the 'five heinous sins' (killing one's father; killing one's mother; killing an arhat; injuring a Buddha; and causing schism in the sangha), Hōnen writes: 'Only the power of the nembutsu can destroy these kinds of sins. Therefore, it was for the sake of the most wicked and inferior people that the highest Dharma of the supremely good practice [ie the nembutsu] was expounded.' (Hōnen 1998: 122)
[54] Hōnen 1998: 98.
[55] This theme is explored in Andrews 1987.

invented Pure Land Buddhism. This move was necessary to establish legitimacy for his new emphasis on the exclusive nembutsu, since without a continental heritage his teachings would lack authority. Hōnen also delineated a canon for his tradition comprising the three Pure Land sutras (see p.70–1), as well as a patriarchal lineage stretching back into Chinese history.[56] The latter aspect of his system was flimsy since he could not point to any direct transmission of the Pure Land lineage to Japan; this lack of institutional continuity was one of the grounds upon which he was later criticized.

Hōnen's new theological vision and his evangelism brought him followers from all walks of life but also provoked an aggressive response from the Japanese Buddhist establishment, which saw its position as under threat. Owing at least partly to its exclusivity, Hōnen's new movement was fiercely condemned as heretical and attempts were made to suppress it.[57] Hōnen's cause was not helped by some of his disciples being publicly critical of established schools, engaging in heated disputes with rival clerics, as well as converting their followers to the nembutsu. More dangerously, some of them came to believe that they could flout ethical precepts since they were assured of rebirth in the Pure Land.[58] The campaign against Hōnen eventually succeeded and in 1207 he was defrocked, then exiled to the island of Shikoku, only returning to Kyoto shortly before his death in 1212. This was the first of a series of persecutions of Pure Land believers that took place over the next century or so.

Hōnen's germinal movement diversified into a number of lineages, each emphasizing slightly different approaches to Pure Land teaching before they eventually settled into ordered, institutional forms as the Jōdo Shū.[59]

---

56 Hōnen excluded from his canon the *Sutra on the Samadhi of Seeing All Buddhas*, which was the source of both Zhiyi's constantly walking samadhi (see Chapter 7) and of the corresponding practices followed on Hieizan and pursued by Hōnen prior to his departure. The emphasis in this sutra on complex visualization may have been one of the reasons it was left out. By excluding it from the canon, Hōnen downgraded the prestige of visualization in favour of recitation.

57 In 1204, Tendai monks moved to expel Hōnen's followers from Hieizan. The following year, Kōfukuji, a powerful Hossō temple in Nara, petitioned the retired emperor to curb Hōnen's activities, putting forward nine specific charges, including:
7. Misrepresenting Pure Land by denying that diverse religious practices lead to birth there
8. Misunderstanding the Nembutsu by claiming that uttering it is superior to using it in meditation. (Dobbins 2002: 14–15)

58 This refers to claims that Hōnen's (and later Shinran's) teachings amounted to 'licensed evil' (*zōaku muge*). Hōnen issued a *Seven Article Pledge* (*shichikajō kishōmon*) condemning behaviour that did not accord with his teaching, which suggests that some of his disciples had got rather out of hand. (Dobbins 2002: 17)

59 The institutional organization of the Jōdo Shu has a complex history but the two largest branches which survive today are known as the Chinzei Jōdo Shu and the Seizan Jōdo Shu. There are numerous sub-sects.

Interestingly, the disciple who was to have the greatest impact on subsequent Pure Land thought and practice was not one of the better known early leaders but a relatively obscure one: Shinran.

Shinran and the *Jōdo Shinshū* (True Pure Land School)

While Shinran (1173–1262) stands today as the most celebrated figure in Japanese Pure Land Buddhism, he was not widely known in his own lifetime.[60] It was several centuries before the movement he initiated reached a settled institutional form as the Jōdo Shinshū (True Pure Land School or Shin Buddhism), but it has since grown to become the largest denomination in the whole of Japanese Buddhism.[61] Shinran could be understood as taking Hōnen's teachings to their logical extreme and, in doing so, developing a radical theology of faith, one that some have seen as even falling outside the boundaries of genuine Dharma.

Shinran entered the Tendai cloisters of Hieizan at the tender age of nine. As a priest, he later served a temple dedicated to the perpetual nembutsu. In 1201, after 20 years on the mountain, he experienced a crisis in which he began to doubt the value of his religious career thus far, and to despair of his own salvation. This acute sensitivity to his personal shortcomings was to become a signature of Shinran's thought. As a consequence, he left the monastery and soon after became a disciple of Hōnen.

During his time with Hōnen, Shinran gained faith that, in spite of his failings (or, as he later believed, *because* of them), he was assured of rebirth in the Pure Land. After only six years, he was separated from his master when in 1207 they were both defrocked and banished from the Kyoto region. Shinran was sent to Echigo, a remote fishing region where he married and began a family.[62] From this time onward, Shinran referred to himself as neither monk nor layman, concluding that the only thing that mattered was salvation through the nembutsu. Much later, this example created the pattern for a married clergy in Shin Buddhism, as well as other sects.

During his exile, Shinran began to reformulate Hōnen's teachings and some time after his ban was lifted in 1211, he began a ministry in the eastern provinces, eventually returning to Kyoto in his later years to pursue

---

[60] Gyōnen (1240–1321), a Tōdaiji monk, wrote a history of Pure Land devotion (*Jōdo hōmon genrushō*, 1311). In it he identifies seven notable disciples of Hōnen and selects two — Kōsai (1163–1247) and Shōkū (1177–1247) — for detailed treatment. Shinran is not even mentioned. (Blum 2002: 26–40) On Shinran's life, see Bloom 1968.

[61] As with the Jōdo Shu, the Jōdo Shinshū has a number of branches, although these reflect administrative differences more than theological ones.

[62] It is not certain whether Shinran married in Kyoto before his exile (in which case it may have been a contributory cause) or afterwards in Echigo. He may also have married more than once. (Bloom 1968: 13–16)

his writing work. Shinran was imbued with the deep pessimism of mappō thought, which matched his own experience. He concluded that in such a degenerate age, there was nothing that the individual could do to liberate himself. Even reciting the nembutsu was useless because it expressed self-power. In this, Shinran differed from Hōnen.

Shinran believed that whatever practice we might take up is ultimately self-defeating because it will be the product of 'calculation' (*hakarai*).[63] Any belief that our individual practice can make us worthy of salvation is, in Shinran's eyes, an expression of deluded pride. Since we are ignorant beings, everything we do simply enmeshes us deeper in the mire of Samsara.[64] While this picture may seem depressing, for Shinran the acceptance of our hopeless situation is the beginning of the true spiritual life.

Other-power and shinjin

Shinran's solution to our existential predicament is other-power, which means 'to be free of any form of calculation'.[65] When we finally exhaust our own efforts to liberate ourselves and give up in despair, we may surrender to the other-power of Amida's Primal Vow, the 18th vow of the *Longer Sukhavati Sutra*.

> May I not gain possession of perfect awakening if, once I have attained buddhahood, any among the throng of living beings in the ten regions of the universe should single-mindedly desire to be reborn in my land with joy, with confidence, with gladness, and if they should bring to mind this aspiration for even ten moments of thought and yet not gain rebirth there. *This excludes only those who have committed the five heinous sins and those who have reviled the True Dharma.*[66]

This vow promises birth in Amida's perfect buddha-field, the Pure Land, to anyone who entrusts himself to him with sincerity. Confirmation that birth is assured comes in the arising of *shinjin* (true entrusting or faith),

---

63 CWS: 526.

64 CWS: 312, 525–6.

65 CWS: 537.

66 Gomez 1996: 167. The scope of this exclusion clause is a complex matter. *The Visualization Sutra* allows for those who fall within the excluded critieria to still be reborn in the Pure Land, but at the lowest of nine grades of development. They will be reborn inside a golden lotus flower which will not open for 12 kalpas. Ultimately, however, they will fulfil their spiritual potential. (*Guan wu-liang-shou jing*, T.365) Following Shandao, Shinran understands the exclusion clause of the 18th vow as a warning to desist from evil rather than as a definitive exclusion. According to Shinran, Shandao wrote: 'The [Buddha], fearing that we would commit these two kinds of faults [i.e. the five heinous sins and slandering the Dharma], seeks to stop us through compassionate means by declaring that we will then not be able to obtain birth. This is not to mean that we will not be grasped.' (cited in CWS: 148)

the transformative moment in Shin Buddhism. Shinran describes this condition in the following way.

> The compassionate light of the Buddha of unhindered light [Amida] always illumines and protects the person who has realized *shinjin*; hence the darkness of ignorance has already cleared, and the long night of birth-and-death is already dispelled and become dawn … Know that when one realizes shinjin, it is as though dawn has broken.[67]

In shinjin we experience a dual realization: on the one hand, our mind is identical to that of Amida, but on the other, we are a foolish being (*bombu*) and always will be. In shinjin we gain confidence not only that our birth in the Pure Land is now assured but that it always has been. This also guarantees that we will gain full Awakening in the future.[68] The experience of shinjin leads to great joy as well as gratitude towards Amida and a keen humility owing to an awareness of our incorrigible shortcomings.

However, shinjin is not something that may be cultivated through individual effort; rather, according to Shinran, it is entrusted to us by Amida through his compassionate transfer of merit (*ekō*). In other words, Amida grants not only rebirth in his Pure Land but the confidence to trust in that fact.[69] Shinjin is not something that the individual nurtures, it is a blessing *bestowed* by Amida. In fact, it is precisely at that the moment that we truly abandon believing that we can liberate ourselves, that Amida's light shines upon us.[70] For this reason, it arises 'altogether without one's own working'.[71]

Owing to his emphasis on the centrality of shinjin, Shinran places less importance on the mechanical recitation of the nembutsu; it is no longer the practice that accomplishes salvation but shinjin that gives rise to practise. The believer intones the nembutsu not in the hope of gaining salvation but out of gratitude for already having been 'grasped never to be abandoned' by compassionate Amida.[72] Nembutsu recitation thus becomes a joyful *expression* of salvation rather than the *means* to earn it. Reciting the nembutsu is neither a spiritual practice nor a 'good act'; rather, it arises wholly from other-power. In other words, spiritual effort, such as it is, is gifted by Amida, who practises *through* us.[73] Ultimately, the function of this 'practice' is not to accomplish our salvation but to reveal it to us.

---

[67] CWS: 519.

[68] CWS: 523, 528.

[69] The structural similarities between the theological position stated here and that of Martin Luther are striking and have been have been noticed by a number of scholars. See, for instance, Ingram 1971.

[70] CWS: 79–80.

[71] CWS: 525.

[72] CWS: 527.

[73] CWS: 665.

Owing to his radical emphasis on other-power, Shinran came to believe that the individual's moral failings were not an impediment to salvation; far from it. While some masters had excluded from Amida's Vow those who committed serious ethical breaches, Shinran argued that such individuals were precisely the focus of Amida's concern and that they were more likely to be saved because they were not deluded into thinking that their own goodness would save them.

> It is impossible for us, who are possessed of blind passions, to free ourselves from birth-and-death through any practice whatever. Sorrowing at this, Amida made the Vow, the essential intent of which is the evil person's attainment of Buddhahood. Hence, evil persons who entrust themselves to Other Power are precisely the ones who possess the true cause of birth.[74]

For Shinran, believing in one's own righteousness was an obstacle that prevented full acceptance of the scope of the Vow. He firmly believed that '[e]ven the good person is born in the Pure Land, so without question is the person who is evil'.[75] A watchful sensitivity to our moral failings is thus central to Shin spirituality, as Shinran himself exemplified.

> I have no idea whether the nembutsu is truly the seed for my being born in the Pure Land or whether it is the karmic act for which I must fall into hell.... [I]f I could attain Buddhahood by endeavoring in other practices, but said the nembutsu and so fell into hell, then I would feel regret at having been deceived. But I am incapable of any other practice, so hell is decidedly my abode whatever I do.[76]

Is Shin Buddhism Buddhist?

Shin Buddhism appears to erode the foundations of the Buddhist spiritual path: since we are all equally destined for the Pure Land, what is the point of practice? The total rejection of self-power seems to affirm things exactly as they are and so invite passivity. But at the heart of Shin Buddhism is a mystery: we have all been blessed by Amida and yet we may not experience shinjin. If no individual effort makes any difference, how then does shinjin arise? Shinran's own life offers a clue here; he practised according to self-power until this approach exhausted itself, enabling trust in the other-power of Amida to arise. Paradoxically then, although Shin Buddhism offers a sudden path, it is not necessarily quick since our attachment to self-power may be very persistent.

---

[74] CWS: 663.
[75] CWS: 663.
[76] CWS: 662.

Moreover, while good works do not earn salvation, the person of shinjin experiences a 'change of heart' that expresses itself through the transformation of his entire life. Ethical conduct becomes a spontaneous expression of humility and especially of gratitude towards Amida. While unethical conduct cannot compromise salvation, this does not amount to a license for bad behaviour. It just does not occur to a person of shinjin to transgress the ethical precepts.[77]

10.3 Eison's Vinaya Movement

A lesser known Buddhist tradition to emerge during the Kamakura period was Eison's (1201–1290) Shingon Vinaya movement, which combined esoteric teachings with scrupulous clerical discipline. Eison came to believe that his monastic ordination was invalid, owing to a lack of spiritual purity within his lineage. This inspired him to undertake a process of self-ordination and then propagate a new ordination lineage based on bodhisattva precepts.[78] As an extension of this initiative, Eison revived full monastic ordination for women.

Eison placed great emphasis on following the precepts and on ethical purity. He engaged in charitable public works such as ministering to prisoners, giving to the poor and sick, and even repairing bridges. His movement attracted wide-ranging support, not only among the poor but also from the government, which hoped that he might help restore discipline to a fragmented society.[79]

Shin Buddhism expresses a humble acceptance of human frailty, recognizing that all people are inevitably flawed. This view serves as an antidote to the poison of spiritual pride, which may arise in those who believe they have made spiritual progress. At the same time, it seems to offer hope for those who experience themselves as spiritually destitute, unable to break their limiting habits and beliefs. While in one sense Shin Buddhism seems simple and undemanding, the compassionate acceptance of human limitation expresses a profound spiritual realization.

Shin Buddhism may seem ultra-pessimistic; after all, it maintains that there is *nothing* that we can do to ensure our own liberation; in a sense, we are helpless. Yet it also affirms the possibility of being guided from a higher dimension. Other-power represents the transcendence of the deluded mind, fettered as it is by self-obsession, to a new, compassionate mode of

---

[77] On this issue, see CWS: 547.
[78] Eison's ordinations were not accorded the official status of those conducted by the Nara schools and Tendai.
[79] For more on Eison, see Groner 2005.

awareness which arises from seemingly beyond it. It does not replace or erase our deluded mind but contains it within an infinitely larger universe — the bodhisattva ideal. The person of shinjin becomes a conduit for the Primal Vow,[80] a visible manifestation of Amida's compassionate working on earth.

Ippen and the *Jishū*

Ippen (1239–89) founded another Pure Land lineage called the *Jishū*, which had some similarities to Ryōnin's movement. Rather than belonging to the conventional monastic establishment, Ippen lived as a *hijiri* (itinerant preacher). Shingon influence led him to believe that once the believer has taken refuge in Amida and agreed to recite the nembutsu, he or she becomes *identical* with the Buddha in both mind and body. Moreover, this identity is constantly reconfirmed as the devotee lives in a moment of perpetual transcendence in which he is transformed by Amida's grace.[81] Following a further spiritual insight, Ippen also became convinced that the nembutsu brought about salvation regardless of individual faith or ethical purity; all power was in the name.

Ippen converted passers-by through a single recitation of the nembutsu, after which they were encouraged to repeat it back. He then bestowed a *fuda* (a slip of paper printed with the nembutsu), which confirmed their rebirth in the Pure Land. Ippen also kept a salvation register and by the time of his death had taken more than 250,000 subscriptions.[82]

Ippen founded a mendicant sangha, which eventually became the Jishū sect, practising an itinerant ministry for the common people in groups of around 20 members. His movement became celebrated for its performance of the dancing nembutsu (*nembutsu odori*), a devotional practice in which ecstatic followers danced in a circle chanting the nembutsu to the accompaniment of gongs and impromptu percussion. After reaching a peak of popularity in the mid-14th century, the Jishū declined and was later eclipsed by the Jōdo Shinshū, although it still survives today.

Having examined some of the major developments within the early phases of Japanese Buddhism, and considered some of the leading features of the important Kamakura era, including the emergence of Pure Land traditions, we can now explore other traditions which appeared during this richly creative period: namely, Zen and Nichiren Buddhism.

---

[80] See p.71.
[81] Ippen adapted a quote from Shandao to express this: 'Completely turning about at heart, moment to moment be born in the Land of Peace.' (Hirota 1986: 153)
[82] Hirota 1986: 20.

11

Zen and the Militant Prophet:
Further Developments in Japanese Mahayana

WE HAVE SEEN THAT THE KAMAKURA ERA was a time of creative ferment within Japanese Buddhism. This chapter describes further developments that occurred during this period, including the emergence of two powerful traditions that have now become widely known in the West: Zen and Nichiren Buddhism. More specifically, it explores in detail the thought of Dōgen (1200–53), the founder of Sōtō Zen, and Nichiren (1222–82), the inspiration for Nichiren traditions.

Owing to its accessible message, the Nichiren tradition attracted widespread support among the common people; Zen, on the other hand, proved alluring to the more privileged classes who supported it on a grand scale. The rigorous demands of Zen training were beyond the practical constraints of ordinary people, while its highbrow cultural activities excluded them. We should also note that, alongside all the innovations, the more established schools continued to flourish, producing some notable scholars and reformers.

Reforms within the 'Old' Schools

In the previous chapter, we saw that the emerging schools of the Kamakura era did not immediately become the mainstream of Japanese Buddhism; rather, the established traditions continued to dominate for some time. Far from being in decline, the established schools inspired renewal and innovation of their own, sometimes as a critical response to the emerging alternatives.

The reforming activities of Eison have already been mentioned but a further eminent figure to emerge from within these schools was the prolific scholar-monk Jōkei (1155–1213).[1] Jōkei was trained at the prestigious Kōfukuji in Nara, affiliated to the Hossō lineage, and is perhaps best known for drafting a petition to the court, appealing for the censure of Hōnen's exclusive nembutsu (senju nembutsu) teaching.[2] He is also revered as a reviver of strict adherence to the monastic precepts. Besides valuing a broad

---

[1]   On the life of Jōkei, see Ford 2002: 76ff.
[2]   This was the Kōfukuji sōjō; see Morrell 1987: 66–88.

range of spiritual practices, including Zen meditation, Jōkei emphasized reliance upon other-power, but for him it signified devotion to Kannon (Avalokiteshvara) and Miroku (Maitreya). He believed that the attainment of rebirth in their celestial worlds as opposed to Amida's was easier because the requirements are less stringent.[3] Clearly, Shinran would not have agreed.

Jōkei advocated highly accessible practices including the invocation of Miroku (*Miroku nembutsu*), of Shaka (Shakyamuni; *Shaka nembutsu*), and the reverence of relics as means to accomplish birth in a celestial world and, in turn, Awakening.[4] Thus, he promoted a form of spirituality that the common people could fulfil, besides advocating more exacting practices for the monastic elite. Moreover, his inclusive approach to practice — as opposed to the exclusivity of Hōnen and Shinran — reflected a belief that because the karmic inheritance of beings differs, so diverse teachings and paths are needed to address their spiritual condition.[5] In this, we can detect the perennial teaching of *hōben* (skilful means).

Everyday Awakening: Zen in Japan

The term 'Zen' has become an everyday English word. It evokes a mood of simplicity, profundity, beauty, and perhaps mystery. Above all, it suggests something numinous — the disclosure of a higher reality via a seemingly mundane object or experience.[6] This vision finds exquisite expression in the haiku of Bashō (1644–94).

> On a bare branch
> A rook roosts:
> Autumn dusk.[7]

---

3   Ford 2002: 83–7. Specifically, Jōkei argued that because Miroku will be the next Buddha, he is the most fitting focus for devotion in the degenerate era. (Ford 2002: 84) With regard to Kannon, he seems to have regarded Fudarakusen (Mt Potalaka) as an intermediate step towards the Pure Land of Amida. (Ford 2002: 86) Neither Fudarakusen nor Totosu-ten (Tushita, Maitreya's realm) are, strictly speaking, buddha-fields but celestial worlds under the influence of advanced bodhisattvas.

4   Ford 2002: 91.

5   Ford 2002: 95.

6   Perhaps nowhere is this better exemplified than in the famous painting *Six Persimmons* (1270) by Muqi Fachang (fl. 13th century), a Chinese Chan monk.

7   Bownas and Thwaite 1998: 111. Poetry, especially *haiku*, has been closely connected with Zen. Haiku is a very disciplined form, typically comprising seventeen syllables (5–7–5) and following a number of other strict rules. A successful haiku conjures a vibrant scene in just a few words, often focusing on the observation of impermanence, especially as seen in the natural world. While in general Buddhist doctrine tends to regard impermanance as painful, haiku also celebrates the exquisite beauty of transience.

Yet we should not get carried away by this rarified image of Zen. As understood in the popular Western imagination, Zen is the product of a handful of influential thinkers and writers who had their own reasons for projecting a specific, tradition-free version.[8] Consequently, it may be that our assumptions about Zen don't quite match the reality. Specifically, while Zen is widely characterized as an uncompromising pursuit of individual Awakening, historically, its meditation and ritual forms, as well as its institutional structures, have served broader cultural functions, especially the needs of the ruling classes.[9]

We have seen how Zen originated in China (as Chan), beginning as a disparate movement that gradually coalesced into distinct lineages and forms of practice. In Japan, some of these early developments were absorbed into Tendai, and it was not until the late 12th century that Zen began to assume a distinct identity. During this period, a number of Japanese monks travelled to China and studied the forms of Chan that were flourishing under the Song dynasty.[10] This was followed by an influx of émigré Chan monks who further contributed to the formation of a fully fledged Japanese Zen tradition. In time, Zen consolidated into two main sects known as Rinzai and Sōtō, both of which survive in contemporary times. In the 16th century, a further sect, known as Ōbaku, was introduced, although this remains of less prominence.[11]

The tradition that later condensed into Rinzai Zen was introduced to Japan in the Kamakura period by the monk Eisai (1141–1215), while the founding of Sōtō Zen is generally credited to Dōgen. Today these two sects are strictly differentiated. Rinzai is usually defined by its pursuit of koan practice (*see* pp.166–8), while Sōtō is seen as rejecting this in favour of 'just sitting' (*shikantaza*). In their formative periods, however, they were less clearly delineated, and there was — and indeed still is — a great deal of doctrinal as well as practical overlap. Fairly early on, the two traditions gravitated towards different clientele. Rinzai gained a following in the urban Kyoto and Kamakura areas, attracting patronage from the military regime,

---

8 For a discussion of this issue, see McMahan 2002: 218–29.

9 For example, the shoguns who patronized Rinzai Zen did not do so from purely spiritual motives. Collcutt describes the role of the medieval Zen clergy in the following way. 'Their principal function was to conduct invocations and prayers for the memory of the deceased or the intention of the living, and to make appropriate incantation in time of warfare, drought, or natural disaster.' (Collcutt 1981: 40)

10 According to Collcutt, by the mid-13th century at least 30 Japanese monks had journeyed to China in search of Chan/Zen instruction. (Collcutt 1990: 590)

11 Introduced to Japan by the Chinese master Yinyuan Lonqi (1592–1673), Ōbaku shares many features with Rinzai but emphasizes nembutsu recitation, including nembutsu koan. It also demands rigorous monastic discipline. Mampukuji, its first temple (and present-day headquarters), was constructed in the 1660s in Uji, Kyoto prefecture. For a study of the founding of this tradition, see Baroni 2000.

while Sōtō spread in more rural, agricultural regions to the point where it was disparagingly dubbed 'farmer's Zen'.[12]

The Emergence of Rinzai Zen

Eisai is revered not only as the founder of Rinzai Zen but also for introducing tea into Japan.[13] Ordained as a Tendai monk, he visited China on two occasions. On his second trip (1187–91), he studied Linji Chan, which emphasized koan study. The pattern of practice that he developed integrated a range of Tendai practices, including esoteric ritual, meditation (*zazen*), and the observance of strict monastic discipline.

His method quickly drew opposition from the Tendai establishment, which persuaded the court to ban the propagation of Zen. In order to justify his approach, Eisai wrote a tract defending it.[14] In it, he put forward four main arguments in support of Zen: first, it was the essence of Buddhism; secondly, it had been accepted by Saichō and other Tendai leaders; thirdly, it strictly observed the monastic precepts; and fourthly, its adoption would rejuvenate Japanese Buddhism and ensure prosperity and security for the state. But his defence did little to calm the hostility of the Buddhist establishment. Nevertheless, with the backing of a local shogun (military commander), in 1202 Eisai was able to establish Kenninji monastery in Kyoto. Initially a broad-based institution, it later became a high ranking monastery of the Rinzai network. Eisai himself did not establish Zen as an exclusive sect but his example helped prepare the ground for later developments.

The gozan system

Under the patronage of the military and courtly elites, the Rinzai school grew rapidly, settling into an organizational pattern known as the *gozan* (Five Mountains) system.[15] By the end of the 14th century, this had become

---

12 Welter argues that the widespread claim that the military leadership was attracted to Zen for spiritual reasons, and especially its discipline, is mistaken. Instead, he suggests that early Zen patrons were interested in the same things that sponsors of Tendai and Shingon were: honouring the dead, ensuring victory in war, and alleviating natural disasters. (Welter 2005: 115)

13 For a brief account of Eisai, see Collcutt 2005: 2741–2.

14 *Kōzen gokokuron* ('Promoting Zen for Protecting the Country'). For more on this text, see Welter 2005.

15 This followed a Chinese model. Not all Rinzai monasteries were assimilated to the gozan system; moreover, it incorporated a small number of monasteries that were designated Sōtō. (Collcutt 1990: 610–23) A second coalition of monasteries, known as *rinka*, incorporated both Rinzai and Sōtō foundations. Some of these later became powerful institutions, notably Myōshinji, which eventually established an independent network that still thrives today. (Heine 2005: 9947)

the dominant institutional structure of Japanese Buddhism, disseminating Zen throughout the country. The gozan network ranked monasteries and temples according to a three-tiered hierarchy overseen by a super-monastery, Nanzenji in Kyoto. The top ranking monasteries were named gozan, of which there were five each in Kyoto and Kamakura (each ranked in order of seniority).[16] Institutions belonging to the second tier were designated *jissatsu* ('ten temples'), while those of the third tier were termed *shozan* ('many mountains'). Despite the nomenclature, by the 15th century there were almost 50 jissatsu and more than 200 shozan.

11.1 Zen Art

Among the art forms that flourished in the Zen cloister were various genres of ink painting. One of these, known as *shigajiku* ('poem–picture scroll'), was a communal art which involved painting a small picture at the bottom of a hanging scroll, above which the assembled monk-poets inscribed original verses or quotations to accord with the subject. A common theme was the reclusive monk in his hermitage. The paintings were often presented as parting gifts or tokens of friendship. In time, ink painting established itself as a genre independent of monasticism.

A further art that became popular was a form of calligraphy known as *bokuseki* ('ink trace', Ch. *moji*), imported from China, which originated in the authentication certificate that a master might confer upon his disciple. Bokuseki characters were written with the brush in a bold and assertive style. They comprised an evocative saying, a phrase, or even just a single character written by a Zen master to educate a disciple or edify a distinguished guest. They were viewed as embodying the master's Dharma insight and were consequently highly cherished possessions. Both Ikkyū and Hakuin were notable exponents of this art form.[17]

By the mid-15th century, the gozan network had swollen to incorporate more than 300 monasteries, many of which had their own sub-temples and branch temples, making several thousand in all.[18] More specifically, sub-temples known as *tatchū* grew up around the large metropolitan monasteries. These began as hermitages for retiring abbots who might live there quietly with just a few disciples. After the master's death, his ashes would be

---

[16] For a detailed discussion of the gozan system, see Collcutt 1981: 91–129. The number of gozan evolved over time and the relative ranks of individual monasteries changed as patterns of patronage and influence shifted.

[17] Addiss 1989.

[18] Collcutt 1981: 91.

kept in the tatchū, which then became a memorial temple and a focus for his lineage. Some of the larger monasteries attracted 20–30 such sub-temples.[19] The medieval Zen monastery could thus be compared to a planet that attracts various satellites into its orbit, and whose own mass also increases with time as it accretes more buildings on its main site.

The core of monastic life comprised meditation, interviews with the Zen master focusing on the resolution of koans, lectures on the sutras and Zen texts, as well as prayers, sutra chanting, and other communal rituals. The gozan approach also incorporated a range of artistic forms, including litera-ture, calligraphy, brush painting and garden design. These creative pursuits were especially prominent in the tatchū, some of which became 'cultural salons'.[20] As the size of monasteries swelled, the *bakufu* (military government) tried to limit numbers. By 1380, the maximum number of monks permitted for a large monastery was 500 but some already had 1000 residents or even more.[21]

But not all Rinzai monks or monasteries found the gozan system to their taste. Ikkyū Sōjun (1394–1481) began Zen life in a gozan institution but left, disgusted at the class snobbery, careerism, and lack of spiritual intensity he found there.[22] Hardly a model of monastic virtue, Ikkyū is known for his sexual adventures, drinking, and partying.[23] He is also revered as one of Japan's foremost poets. Ikkyū received Dharma transmission in his late 20s but — in the spirit of the mythologized masters of Tang China — is said to have burned his certificate. In middle-age, Ikkyū was appointed abbot of a modest temple but lasted just ten days in the role.

> Only ten fussy days as abbot,
> and already my feet are tangled in red tape.
> If, someday, you want to look me up,
> try the fish-shop, the tavern, or the brothel.[24]

Notwithstanding, late in life Ikkyū accepted the abbacy of Daitokuji monastery near Kyoto (which had left the gozan system), then ravaged by war. Such was his standing, he attracted many sponsors and patrons and the monastery was restored, becoming a leading Zen and cultural institution of the 16th century. Its lineage survives.[25]

---

19 Collcutt 1990: 605–6.
20 Collcutt 1990: 615.
21 Collcutt 1990: 608.
22 For a brief sketch of Ikkyū, together with some of his poems, see Foster and Shoemaker 1996: 267–73. There are numerous anthologies of his poetry available in English.
23 Ikkyū was hardly unique in this respect. It was not uncommon for monks to have wives and children. Nor were homosexual relationships uncommon, especially those between older and younger monks within the monastery.
24 Translation by James Sandford, cited in Collcutt 1990: 614.
25 Collcutt describes the 16th century as Daitokuji's 'golden age'. Before 1500, it had only 7

By the mid-15th century, the gozan system was in decline, eclipsed by the burgeoning Daitokuji and Myoshinji monastic networks. This deterioration is explained partly through its overemphasis on cultural pursuits at the expense of primary Zen practice. Besides this, the power of its military patrons waned and, during the incessant wars of the late Muramachi period (late 15th–16th century), many monasteries were burned or lost valuable landholdings.[26] Nevertheless, many former gozan institutions survive as head temples within the 15 branches of present-day Rinzai.[27]

The Tokugawa renewal of Rinzai and Hakuin

Credited as the reviver of Rinzai and revered as a towering figure in the later history of Japanese Buddhism, Hakuin Ekaku (1685–1768) promoted an exacting variety of Rinzai.[28] His remarkable biography and teachings recall the archetypal Chan masters of Tang China. Existentially sensitive from an early age, Hakuin feared that he was bound for hell, which inspired him to become a monk. At times itinerant, he achieved a series of spiritual breakthroughs which later drew him many followers. The passage below describes one of them.

> Suddenly a great doubt manifested itself before me. It was as though I were frozen solid in the midst of an ice sheet extending tens of thousands of miles.… This state lasted for several days. Then I chanced to hear the sound of a temple bell and I was suddenly transformed. It was as if a sheet of ice had been smashed or a jade tower had fallen with a crash.… All my former doubts vanished as though ice had melted away.[29]

The kind of spiritual intensity reflected in this experience indicates the nature of Hakuin's temperament. Notwithstanding his many accomplishments, such as being a gifted calligrapher and poet, Hakuin struggled with mental health, suffering a series of spiritual crises or 'Zen sicknesses'. He later healed himself using an introspective technique known as *naikan*.[30]

---

sub-temples but during the period 1500–1800, another 18 were established. The institution was patronized especially by the *daimyo* who were wealthy feudal lords. Prosperous men of culture also sponsored the monastery, including *renga* (linked-verse) poets and tea masters. (Collcutt 1990: 615–17)

[26] For more on Buddhism in the 16th century, see McMullin 1984.

[27] For a list, see http://zen.rinnou.net/head_temples/index.html, *Rinzai-Obaku Zen: The Official Site of the Joint Council for Japanese Rinzai and Obaku Zen.*

[28] For an accessible introduction to Hakuin's life and thought, see Yampolsky 1971. There are many other collections of various writings available. For a scholarly introduction, including a discussion of problematic aspects of Hakuin's biography, see Mohr 1999.

[29] Yampolsky 1971: 118.

[30] This is a form of energy cultivation. The basis of the practice is to feel the energy of the

Hakuin used simple language, as well as metaphor, to communicate Zen insights to the wider community. Amongst other things he wrote 'hymns' (*wasan*), such as this one.

> All beings are from the very beginning Buddhas.
> It is like water and ice:
> Apart from water, no ice,
> Outside living beings, no Buddhas.
>
> Not knowing it is near, they seek it afar, what a pity!
> It is like one in the water who cries out for thirst;
> It is like the child of a rich house who has strayed away amongst the poor.[...]
> This very place the lotus paradise, this very body the Buddha.[31]

In terms of practice, Hakuin reinvigorated the koan tradition, not least introducing the most widely known of all: 'Two hands clap and there is a sound. What is the sound of the one hand?' Hakuin emphasized the value of koan practice not only in the context of formal meditation but also as an ongoing activity amidst daily affairs. To this end, he counselled 'make the whole universe your own personal meditation cave'.[32] True meditation is not a stepping outside of life but immersing oneself in it.

> It is to make everything: coughing, swallowing, waving the arms, motion, stillness, words, action, the evil and the good, prosperity and shame, gain and loss, right and wrong, into one single koan.[33]

At the same time, he was a harsh critic of Sōtō practice, dubbing it 'dead sitting', and also of Ōbaku, which combined Zen with Pure Land practices.

> In stealth they finger the rosary hidden in their sleeves and in private call the name of the Buddha ... How pathetic this is! This is the obvious proof of their lack of capacity to see into their own natures...[34]

But Hakuin did not reject the notion of the Pure Land altogether; rather, he saw the Pure Land not as a distant world but as the true dimension of the present moment.

Hakuin is credited with establishing a progressive curriculum of koan study, which requires students to meditate on each 'critical phrase' (Jp.

---

body filling the navel, the space below it, and the loins and legs, even down to the soles of the feet. Hakuin describes this in detail in his *Yasen Kanna*; see Shaw and Schiffer 1957: 108–9.

[31] '*Zazen wasan*' ('Song in praise of *zazen*'); from Leggett 1960: 67–8.
[32] Yampolsky 1971: 58.
[33] Yampolsky 1971: 58.
[34] Yampolsky 1971: 172.

wato, Ch. *huatou*) and to 'pass' each koan by offering an appropriate response to the master in the context of a personal interview (*sanzen* or *dokusan*). This curriculum, still in use today, takes many years to complete and many practitioners do not finish it. Hakuin affiliated himself with Myōshinji school, which today stands as the largest Rinzai network. As a consequence, most contemporary Rinzai masters trace their lineage back to him.

Dōgen and Sōtō Zen

Although Dōgen is now widely acclaimed as one of the most creative thinkers of Japanese history, he remained a relatively obscure figure until the early 20th century, a little known secret wrapped within the folds of the Sōtō robe.[35] Aged 13, he began his spiritual career in the Tendai cloisters of Hieizan. He later studied Rinzai Zen in Kyoto under Eisai's disciples before going on pilgrimage in 1223 to China where he eventually received Dharma transmission in the Caodong lineage (*see* p.144). On returning to Japan in 1227, Dōgen established a new Zen community and was later joined by a maverick group known as the *Darumashū* (Dharma School), which impacted on his unfolding vision of practice.[36]

Dōgen's teachings, detailed below, are recorded in his magnum opus, *Shōbōgenzō* (*Treasury of the Eye of the True Dharma*), a collection of lectures that spans a period of two decades.[37] This is a complex work, in turns mystical, elusive, comical, and poetic. *Shōbōgenzō* reveals that Dōgen's teaching underwent significant development after his trip to China, resulting in a distinctive, even unique outlook. He came to advocate a simplified spiritual regime, emphasizing just one practice: sitting meditation. For Dōgen, the practice of zazen *was* Awakening.[38] As he so simply but forcefully put it: 'To practice the Way singleheartedly is, in itself, enlightenment. There is no gap between practice and enlightenment or zazen and daily life.'[39]

In consequence of this stark simplicity, Sōtō is characterized by strict discipline and an austere but exquisite minimalism — its signature image is perhaps black-robed monks sitting in zazen, eyes half-open, facing the blank wall to avoid distraction. But it would be wrong to think that Dōgen

---

[35] For a study of Dōgen, see Kim 2004.

[36] For more about this, see Faure 1987.

[37] This has been translated into English several times, eg Nishijima and Cross 1994–9. Some chapters are available in translation online via the Sōtō Zen Translation project at http://scbs.stanford.edu/sztp3/translations/shobogenzo/sbgz_contents.html.

[38] For an interesting analysis of Dōgen's approach to meditation, which interprets it as a ritual practice, see Leighton 2008.

[39] Yokoi with Victoria 1990: 47.

rejected everything else since he considered monastic rules, etiquette, study, and ritual observances to be of importance too. He drew together these elements of lived practice in the work *Tenzō kyōkun* (*Instructions for the Zen Cook*).[40] Moreover, Dōgen was renowned as a gifted poet, whose subtle beauty and simplicity of writing reflected his belief in the oneness of practice and Awakening.

Dōgen's key teachings

Dōgen's distinctive approach to meditation arose from a spiritual dilemma he encountered in relation to the medieval Tendai doctrine of inherent Awakening (*hongaku*), a version of the Buddha-nature theory (*see* Feature 6.2). If we are all inherently Awakened, reasoned Dōgen, why have masters down the ages emphasized the need for spiritual practice? Dōgen resolved this apparent paradox through developing a novel understanding of the relationship between meditation and Awakening, known as the 'oneness of practice and realisation' (*shushō ittō*).

> To think practice and realization are not one is a non-Buddhist view. In the Buddha Dharma, practice and realization are one and the same. As your present practice is practice in realization, your initial negotiation of the Way is in itself the whole of original realization. That is why from the time you are instructed in the way of practice, you are told not to anticipate realization apart from practice. It is because practice points directly to original realization.[41]

For Dōgen, Awakening reveals itself through practice and not apart from it; rather than seeing Awakening as a once and for all event, it becomes something that is perpetually renewed and lived through meditation. This position expresses his resolution of the sudden/gradual debate. As a consequence, Awakening is neither a possibility in the future nor an accomplishment of the past but an ever-present dimension of the here and now. For Dōgen, each moment is epiphanic, constantly disclosing the truth of Awakening. Rather than an object to be attained, Awakening becomes a radical dwelling in the present; practice is not a means to an end but in itself *manifests* the end. Thus Dōgen's approach is an antidote to goal orientation.

More than this, Dōgen developed a unique understanding of Buddha-nature, such that, rather than all things *having* the Buddha-nature as a potential within them, he proclaimed that 'All beings *are* the Buddha-nature'.[42] Buddha-nature thus comes to be seen not as a potentiality — or

---

40 See Warner et al. 2001.
41 Waddell and Abe 2002: 19.
42 Waddell and Abe 2002: 61ff.

even actuality — within beings but as the ultimate nature of all things; dependent origination, even shunyata. It is nothing apart from the world of form: 'the Buddha-nature is a fence, a wall, a tile, a pebble'.[43] Buddha-nature then is not something transcendental, something *other*, but just *this*.

According to Dōgen, 'impermanence is the Buddha-nature'.[44] This makes realization a practical and everyday matter: in understanding impermanence, we understand Buddha-nature and so dwell in Awakening. This consists in embracing the fleeting, momentary character of experience, which is the ever-present reality. Awakening then is not an escape from impermanence but a radical embracing of its universal scope. Dōgen referred to this deep acceptance of the ephemeral present as 'body-and-mind-casting-off' (*shinjindatsuraku*).[45] This does not happen in isolation, since the activity of the meditator is intertwined with all existence:

> [which p]erforms great and wide-ranging Buddha-work and carries on the exceedingly profound, recondite activities of preaching and enlightening. The trees, grasses, and land involved in this all emit a bright and shining light, preaching the profound and incomprehensible Dharma; and it is endless. Trees and grasses, wall and fence expound and exalt the Dharma for the sake of ordinary people, sages, and all living beings. Ordinary people, sages, and all living beings in turn preach and exalt the Dharma for the sake of trees, grasses, wall and fence.[46]

This poetic vision, reminiscent of Huayan thought, suggests that all elements of the cosmos are engaged in a perpetual process of mutual Awakening. Truly an inspiring vision!

While Dōgen is widely credited with founding Sōtō Zen, its growth as an institutional network owes much to the efforts of Keizan Jōkin (1264–1325), revered as a second founder.[47] He incorporated many elements of esoteric Buddhism and aspects of native cults, including mountain religion (*shugendō*), which helped to ensure a broad base of support.[48] Sōtō grew rapidly under his leadership. His reliance on dreams and astrology to help

---

[43] From *Shōbōgenzō Busshō* (Buddha-nature); Waddell and Abe 2002: 96.

[44] Waddell and Abe 2002: 76–7.

[45] This phrase is found throughout Dōgen's writings; see, for example, Waddell and Abe 2002: 41.

[46] Waddell and Abe 2002: 13.

[47] For more on Keizan, see Faure 1996. Many accounts give Keizan's birthdate as 1268. (Bodiford 2005: 5109)

[48] Shugendō adepts offer various religious and esoteric services, including fortune-telling, divination, and exorcism. They engage in a range of shamanic rituals, including ascetic retreats in the mountains. For a series of articles that explore this tradition, see *Shugendō and Mountain Religion in Japan*, a special issue of the *Japanese Journal of Religious Studies* 1989.

direct his spiritual life perhaps contrasts with the typical image of a Zen monk but was in keeping with the times.

11.2 Post-Mortem 'Ordination'

Within Sōtō Zen, receiving the ordination precepts has been regarded as equivalent to realizing Awakening. Consequently, this means that the clergy are 'living Buddhas'. This logic was used in the development of the ritual of post-mortem ordination, which offers the promise of salvation for deceased laypeople.[49] This takes place during the funeral rites where the corpse's head is shaved, the body is washed and then dressed in a monastic robe. A lineage chart (*kechimyaku*) is placed in the coffin alongside the body.

The effectiveness of post-mortem ordination is guaranteed by the purity of the monastic order's observance of the precepts and their compassionate transfer of merit to the corpse. Conducting such funerals is a key source of income for most Zen temples, Rinzai and Sōtō alike.

Keizan's disciples spread Sōtō more widely through adopting abandoned Tendai and Shingon temples and honouring local divinities, which were invoked to protect them. Sōtō also became involved in construction projects such as bridges and irrigation canals. A further notable feature of medieval Sōtō was the role of nuns, who upheld the strict clerical discipline cherished by Dōgen but also developed healing and purification rituals.[50]

A later eminent figure associated with Sōtō Zen is the poet-hermit Ryōkan (1758–1831). Ryōkan is admired for his simple, direct, even self-deprecating verse, which evokes a life of joyous solitude.

> Returning to my hermitage after a journey
> to distant mountain villages;
> Along the fence, the chrysanthemums linger.[51]

Zen Today

Both Sōtō and Rinzai remain living spiritual traditions in Japan. Sōtō is the larger denomination, boasting in the region of 15,000 temples, while Rinzai has fewer than 6000.[52] Many of these are small, parish affairs run by a single

---

49 See Bodiford 1992.
50 Heine 2005: 9948.
51 Stevens 1988b: 71.
52 Collcutt 1981: 1. The largest Rinzai branch (Myōshinji) has some 3400 temples.

priest and his family, but a few are substantial monastic complexes serving the training needs of their respective clergy. It is worth noting that, in spite of its rhetoric of meditation, relatively few contemporary Zen priests consistently engage in its cultivation after completing their initial clerical training. In recent decades, both main traditions have been active in spreading Zen around the world, especially in North America.

The Militant Prophet: Nichiren and Nichirenism

A further key figure to emerge during the Kamakura Era was the militant prophet Nichiren (1222–82).[53] Nichiren was a passionate and creative religious thinker, a Buddhist firebrand who fiercely criticized the Buddhist establishment in his insistence that the *Lotus Sutra* was the highest and most complete revelation of the Dharma. His life and thought inspired a host of movements and lineages, some of which are highly influential today.

Like many other important Kamakura Buddhists, Nichiren took the tonsure as a Tendai priest. In his early years, he received a broad training in Tendai doctrine, including esoteric practices, and later studied other Mahayana teachings including Pure Land, Zen, and the Nara schools. He came to the conclusion that the *Lotus Sutra* represented the true teachings of the Buddha and that all other teachings were inferior, if not downright evil. Placing great emphasis on this scripture was nothing new, since it had always been central to Tendai doctrine, but Nichiren's *exclusive* promotion of it, combined with his virulent condemnation of other approaches, ensured he would attract opposition and even persecution.

In the 1250s, Nichiren began evangelizing in earnest. He adopted a distinctive, confrontational approach to conversion known as *shakubuku* ('to break and subdue'), which won him many enemies as well as friends.[54] Nichiren believed that through challenging people, he would cause them to re-evaluate their beliefs (*break* their delusion) and adopt the true Dharma (*subdue* their suffering). For this reason, his writings, sermons, and dialogues struck a strident, aggressive, and even apocalyptic tone. Like many of his contemporaries, he was deeply influenced by the notion of mappō and saw its evidence in all of the Buddhist sects around him, which he believed to be corrupt, poisoned by 'evil monks'. His critique was later summarized in a series of four slogans: 'Nembutsu leads to Avīci Hell, Zen is a devil, Shingon will destroy the nation, and Ritsu is a traitor.'[55]

Nichiren proclaimed that the *Lotus Sutra* was qualitatively superior to all others. This was especially true of the second half, known as the 'origin

---

53 On Nichiren's life and thought, see Yampolsky 1990.
54 This doctrine is explored in detail in Stone 1994.
55 Cited in Stone 1994: 233.

teaching' (*honmon*), which revealed Shakyamuni as the eternally Awakened, cosmic Buddha. For Nichiren, the *Lotus Sutra* was uniquely suited to the spiritual needs of mappō, when people no longer had the capacity to gain Awakening using 'provisional' teachings — which for him meant any teachings apart from the second part of the *Lotus Sutra*. Nichiren's stance thus paralleled the Pure Land approach but, rather than the Amida myth, he placed the *Lotus Sutra* at the centre of his religious vision. But Nichiren's overall response to the challenge of mappō was rather different from the Pure Land solution. Rather than encourage aspiration to a celestial realm, he affirmed the present world of grief and pain as the place chosen by the Buddha for the adoption of the *Lotus Sutra*. To practise here and now was more spiritually meritorious than to aspire to the Pure Land. 'A hundred years' practice in the [Pure Land of] Utmost Bliss does not equal the merit of a single day's practice in this defiled world.'[56]

Nichiren saw himself as a reformer of the Tendai sect, although in reality his approach excluded nearly all practices apart from the recitation of the *daimoku* or sacred title of the *Lotus Sutra*: *Namu-myōhō-renge-kyō* ('Homage to the Sutra of the Lotus Blossom of the Wonderful Dharma'). In simplifying Buddhist practice in this way, and offering a clear message, Nichiren established a form of practice that the common people could follow, enabling his movement to become very popular. Nichiren believed that the daimoku embodied the quintessence of the Dharma and so to combine it with other practices was 'like mixing rice with excrement'.[57] Along with the object of worship (*honzon*; usually a calligraphic representation of the daimoku and of various Buddhas and associated figures), and the place of practice (*kaidan*), the daimoku made up what Nichiren called the 'three great secret Dharmas'.[58]

Nichiren regarded all the virtues of the *Lotus Sutra* as condensed into the daimoku and so preached its constant observance, promising benefits both spiritual and worldly to those who faithfully recited it. He took the *Lotus Sutra*'s self-promoting claims literally.

> If there is anyone who can receive and keep, read and recite, recall properly, cultivate and practice, and copy this Scripture of the Dharma Blossom, be it known that that person has seen Shakyamunibuddha.[59]

---

[56] Cited in Asai 1999: 243.

[57] Cited in Stone 1994: 232.

[58] Whereas kaidan previously referred to the monastic ordination platform, in Nichiren's case, it means the place where one recites the daimoku, which can really be anywhere since the daimoku sacralizes the space around it. Nichiren correlated this trinity of honzon, daimoku, and kaidan with many other things; an obvious parallel is with the Three Jewels: Buddha, Dharma and Sangha. See Matsunaga and Matsunaga 1974: 161–4.

[59] Hurvitz 1976: 335, modified by author.

This indicates that through reverencing the *Lotus Sutra*, one encounters the Buddha directly and is taught the Dharma by him; one may even enter the spiritual realm of the *Lotus Sutra* and participate in the cosmic assembly revealed there. More than this, Nichiren discloses the influence of esoteric Tendai thought when he writes:

> [I]n the case of the Lotus Sutra, when one takes it in one's hand, that hand at once becomes Buddha, and when one chants with one's mouth, that mouth is precisely Buddha.[60]

Such an identification of practice with realization resonates both with Dōgen's emphasis on meditation as Awakening and Shinran's view that in the arising of shinjin one becomes equal to the Buddhas. So, while Nichiren's approach was undoubtedly controversial, his central teachings were not unlike those of his relative contemporaries.

While Nichiren's claim that the title of the *Lotus Sutra* is the exclusive means to realize Awakening may seem rather naive, it is underpinned by some sophisticated Mahayana metaphysics. In particular, Nichiren draws on the Tendai notion of 'the three thousand worlds in a moment of thought' (*ichinen sanzen*), which derives from Zhiyi (*see* p.132, n42). For Zhiyi, this teaching indicates the mutual inclusion of all things in each and every moment, even within our ordinary minds. Tendai combined this with elements of Buddha-nature thought and concluded that it implies that our ordinary minds *include* the Buddha realm — in other words, Awakening is inherent. As we have seen, this was a widely accepted perspective in East Asian Mahayana Buddhism.

For Nichiren, however, Zhiyi's teaching merely expressed the theoretical *potential* for the three thousand worlds in a moment of thought, not its *actuality*, which is revealed only through the daimoku.[61] How is this so? According to Nichiren, the Buddha has stored all his spiritual merit in the title of the *Lotus Sutra*.

> Shakyamuni's causal practices and their resulting merits are inherent in the five characters Myoho-renge-kyo. When we embrace these five characters, he will naturally transfer to us the merit of his causes and effects.[62]

Rather than posit the trigger for Awakening within our ordinary minds, Nichiren locates it within the title of the sutra. Insofar as we embrace the

---

[60] Cited in Stone 1999: 407.
[61] See Yampolsky 1990: 177.
[62] Cited in Asai 1999: 254, modified by author. For a different translation, see Yampolsky 1990: 165.

daimoku, Shakyamuni's merits are transferred to us and we realize our Buddha potential. Thus reciting the daimoku is the means by which we disclose and *experience* the truth that the three thousand worlds exist in each moment of thought. Without this, we remain ignorant beings unaware of the deeper reality of our lives.

In 1260, Nichiren submitted a tract to the government calling for the suppression of all sects that he judged as straying from the true message of the *Lotus Sutra*, picking out Hōnen for special condemnation.[63] A short passage will express its flavour.

> Thus [Hōnen] poured out perverted words of his own invention and took absolutely no cognizance of the explanations put forth in the Buddhist scriptures. His is the worst kind of baseless talk, a clear case of defamation.[64]

He interpreted the various calamities that befell Japan, such as drought, famine, internal conflicts, and invasion threats, as direct results of the government's indulgence of these 'degenerate' sects and its failure to adopt the *Lotus Sutra* as the exclusive teaching. Placing exclusive faith in this text would not only resolve all the current problems but also usher in the millennium, transforming Japan into a Pure Land on earth. Perhaps not surprisingly, Nichiren's prophetic declamations angered many people and his hermitage was vandalized by disgruntled Pure Land followers. The following year he was exiled but then pardoned in 1263. The year after that he was almost killed in an ambush, such bitter hostility did he provoke, and he was exiled again from 1271 to 1274.[65]

Nichiren's teachings spawned many factions and lineages but his following was initially known as the Lotus Sect (Hokkeshū). Amongst other things, believers saw it as their duty to continue his practice of shakubuku by admonishing the state for not adopting exclusive devotion to the *Lotus Sutra*, and regular petitions were submitted to the ruling party. Nichiren believed that it was the duty of the faithful to resist authority, where it obstructed 'true' practice or supported 'heretical' sects, and to rebuke opponents.

---

[63] This was his *Establishment of the Legitimate Teaching for the Protection of the Country* (*Risshō ankokuron*). For a translation, see Yampolsky 1990: 13–47.

[64] Yampolsky 1990: 27.

[65] Nichiren regarded his persecution as proof of his divine mission. In particular, he identified himself with two bodhisattvas introduced in the *Lotus Sutra*: Never Disparaging (*Sadāparibhūta*, Jp. *Jofukyō*), who appears in Chapter 20; and Superior Conduct (*Viśiṣṭacārita*, Jp. *Jogyō*) found in Chapter 15.
Never Disparaging embodies Nichiren's sense of righteous suffering for the good of the Dharma, since he is reviled and even beaten for propagating the bodhisattva path (see Chapter 3). Superior Conduct agrees to uphold and propagate the *Sutra* in future times, and Nichiren clearly saw himself in this light. (Jaffe 1986)

Life is fleeting. No matter how many powerful enemies oppose us, never think of retreating or give rise to fear. Even if they should cut off our heads with saws ... as long as we have life, we must chant *Namu-myōhō-renge-kyō*.[66]

Nichiren-inspired traditions have been especially successful in contemporary times, notably Sōka Gakkai (Value Creation Society), a lay organization that has grown out of the Nichiren movement (*see* p.218).

Later Japanese Buddhism

The new Mahayana traditions that emerged in the Kamakura period grew steadily. By the end of the 15th century, Shin Buddhism had attracted a large following among the masses, particularly owing to the evangelizing of Rennyo (1415–99).[67] Nichiren groups also became widespread, while various Zen institutions exerted powerful religious and cultural influence.

In the Tokugawa period, all Buddhist sects and sub-sects were required to create formal structures comprising central temples and subordinate branch temples, a system that continues today. Each sect also had to standardize its clerical training, vinaya, and even its clothing. Moreover, every family had to register with its local temple (known as the *danka* system), ensuring that the influence of Buddhism in Japanese cultural life became all-pervasive.[68] In return for support, the temples increasingly offered a range of ritual services to their parishioners, including funeral and memorial rites.

At the beginning of the Meiji period (1868–1912), when imperial power was restored, Buddhist institutions suffered serious suppression. Shintō was promoted at the expense of Buddhism in a bid to consolidate Japanese national identity. Through a policy to separate the worship of the kami from the Buddhas (known as *shinbutsu bunri*), many images, temples, and texts were purged. The government also lifted the ban on clerical marriage which resulted in many monks — but not nuns — marrying. Even though monks had been marrying for centuries, it had never before been condoned officially.

In the 19th and 20th centuries, a number of 'new' and 'new new religions' emerged with varying ties to Mahayana Buddhist heritage.[69] Notable among

---

[66] Stone 1994: 235; see also the subsequent discussion: 235–40.

[67] On Rennyo, see Rogers and Rogers 1991.

[68] The danka system also placed an administrative burden on the temples; they had to register everyone in their territory. In time, they were required to register births, marriages, deaths, as well as changes of address and occupation. Effectively, they became local government offices. On the *danka* system, see Marcure 1985.

[69] For a study of Reiyūkai Kyōdan, another Nichiren inspired group, see Hardacre, 1984. Ancestor worship comprises the central practice of this group. The formation of this and

these is Sōka Gakkai, which claimed more than seven million followers by the 1970s. Around the turn of the 21st century, 75% (95 million) of all Japanese were officially registered as Buddhist, while 56 million people were affiliated with a recognized Buddhist religious organization. There were in excess of 200,000 Buddhist priests and 70,000 temples.[70] Despite these headline numbers, many Japanese traditions are in decline.[71] Many Japanese don't regard religious affiliation as a personal, spiritual commitment but rather as a cultural observance, as expressed in the slogan 'Born Shintō, die Buddhist'.[72] Since the late 20th century, Japanese Mahayana teachings have become increasingly internationalized, especially through the efforts of various Zen and Nichiren groups, as well as the work of academics. Contemporary Japanese Buddhism is discussed further in the next chapter.

11.3 Clerical Marriage

In theory, the Buddhist monastic system has generally demanded strict celibacy. In Japan, however, it was common for monks to keep wives, often in secret but sometimes openly, even housing their families at their temples.

In 1872, the Meiji government abolished various laws that restricted the conduct of clerics, including prohibitions against marriage and meat-eating. The response to this was very mixed. Some clerics saw it as a means to legitimize what was in fact already widespread, others as a signal to revive a more rigorous monasticism.

Within the Sōtō sect, for instance, while clerical marriage was officially prohibited, many monks continued to marry and have families. Owing to the unofficial nature of these families, they had few rights, especially in relation to inheritance. In the 1930s, the Sōtō hierarchy was forced to institutionalize the familial inheritance of temples. Clerical marriage remains a contentious issue.[73]

---

other new religions (*shin shūkyō*) and new new religions (*shin shinshūkyō*) has been a significant cultural phenomenon in modern Japan. (see Reader 1991)

[70] Covell 2005: 3–4. In terms of temple numbers, Pure Land sects (nearly 30,000; including Jōdo and Jōdo Shinshū) and Zen sects (21,000) remain the largest, while the Nara sects are the smallest (around 230 temples). In terms of numbers of adherents, the Pure Land (19.3 million) and Nichiren (17.5 million) sects are the largest, while the Nara lineages are the smallest (fewer than 200,000).

[71] These numbers are quite misleading. Reader, for instance, reports that while Sōtō Zen had 7 million members around 1990, fewer than 300,000 (just over 4%) could be described as active 'believers'. (Reader 1991: 9)

[72] Reader 1991: 2.

[73] For a detailed study of this issue, see Jaffe 2002.

12

An Ever Widening Circle:
The Mahayana Today

OUR PILGRIMAGE HAS TAKEN US through 2000 years of history and across the whole of Asia; while it may not have been as gruelling as that accomplished by the 'marathon monks' of Mt. Hiei, we have travelled across a vast imaginative terrain. We have journeyed from emptiness to Buddha-nature, from the heroic ambition of the bodhisattva ideal to the humble acceptance of other-power, from the extravagant imagery of Mahayana scripture to the immediacy of Zen anecdote. We have noted some of the highs and lows of Mahayana life and traced some of the ever-changing shapes of its ideas, practices, and cultural forms. This final chapter gives consideration to some recent developments within Mahayana Buddhism, notably its emergence in Western cultures.

Over the past century, many Asian traditions have suffered serious decline, but there are also examples of renewal; we will look at a selection of these. Besides this, the Mahayana has begun to take firm root in new cultural soil, especially in the United States and Europe, which has inspired unprecedented innovation, experiment, and adaptation. New developments have also been shaped by the easy availability of a dazzling array of Mahayana teachings and texts. In turn, this has informed a trend towards interpreting Buddhism as a religious and historical unity, which has had an enormous impact on how both new and old Mahayana traditions understand themselves.

In order to better explain the nature of contemporary developments, this discussion will differentiate between 'traditional' and 'modern' Buddhism.[1] Here, traditional Buddhism is the province of established Asian sects and of Asian communities scattered throughout the world. It tends to pursue an 'other-worldly' orientation, and so emphasizes the role of devotion, ritual, and merit-making. Modern Buddhism, on the other hand, emphasizes the here-and-now, which has led to a greater focus on social and economic issues, as well as on the environment. Modern Buddhism often downplays ritual and devotion and sidesteps traditional cosmology, highlighting instead the 'rational' character of the Dharma and its affinity with the

---

[1] See Baumann 2002. For a sophisticated study of the interaction of Buddhism with modernism, see McMahan 2008.

worldview of modern science and psychology. Adopting something of the Protestant mentality, it values individual experience through the personal pursuit of ethical conduct, meditation, and the study of texts. In some cases, it may even see Buddhist practices as means of accomplishing worldly aspirations.[2] What follows focuses mainly on modern Buddhism.

The Decline of Traditional Mahayana Buddhism

Over the past century, traditional Mahayana Buddhism in Asia has been assailed by a battery of political, cultural, and historical forces. This has led to a widespread weakening, displacing, and, in some cases, destruction of Mahayana Buddhist institutions. The influence of Communism has been catastrophic. Buddhism was virtually wiped out in Russia and Mongolia, and only since the 1990s have attempts begun to reinstate it there.[3]

The Chinese invasion of Tibet in the 1950s led to a large-scale destruction of Buddhist culture in that country, as well as the displacement of most of its prominent spiritual leaders and their exile across the globe. In China itself, the so-called Cultural Revolution (1966–76) decimated the Buddhist clergy, with untold numbers of monks and nuns defrocked and even killed. Many temples were closed, even destroyed, and their assets seized. Even before this period, there was an exodus of spiritual talent to more sympathetic nations.[4]

Little is known of the fate of Buddhism in North Korea since its self-imposed isolation in the 1950s but it is likely a similar story. In South Korea too, the influence of Mahayana Buddhism has been eroded, not by Communism but by rising interest in Christianity; there are now more Christians in South Korea than there are Buddhists.[5] In Vietnam, a prolonged period of pro-Catholic discrimination, followed by a long period of war from the late 1940s to the mid-1970s, led to a severe depletion of Buddhist institutions.[6] The eventually victorious Communist government was not sympathetic either and the situation remains delicate.[7]

---

[2] This has also been a feature of traditional Buddhism, especially as far as the laity has been concerned.

[3] Tibetan Buddhism was widely followed in the Buryat Republic, north of Mongolia, adjoining Lake Baikal.

[4] For a study of the effects of Communism and the Cultural Revolution on Chinese Buddhism, see Welch 1972.

[5] Grayson cites the census figures of 1995, when there were 10.3 million Buddhists and 11.6 million Christians (Catholic and Protestant combined). The figures for younger people showed a clear trend; of those aged 15–24, 17.5 percent identified themselves as Buddhist, whereas almost 50 percent declared themselves Christian (combined denominations). (Grayson 2005: 249–52)

[6] For a study of this period, see Topmiller 2006.

[7] For a passionate review of the current situation, see Roscoe [no date].

The erosion of Buddhist heritage was most darkly illustrated by the cultural terrorism of the Taliban military government of Afghanistan. In March 2001, Taliban soldiers blasted to rubble two gigantic standing Buddhas (55 and 37 metres high, respectively), which had been carved into cliffs near the town of Bamiyan on the Silk Route some 1500 years before. These Buddhas testified to a once thriving Buddhist culture in the region, the ancient kingdom of Gandhara.

12.1 Zen and the Art of Robe Sewing

A spiritual discipline that has emerged within modern Sōtō Zen is sewing clerical robes in groups (*fukudenkai*), sometimes in the context of retreats.[8] Practitioners believe that sewing robes generates spiritual merit, especially when pursued alongside other observances like meditation. Some sew robes for themselves, while others, especially women, sew robes for family members or their local temple.

Each stitch of the robe is regarded as equivalent to three bows to the Buddha, and so the more complex the sewing, the more merit accrues. Besides building merit in a transactional sense, robe-sewing also has a calming and focusing effect on the practitioners, and connects them with the Buddha, since the robe is regarded as an embodiment of his teaching.

The ethos of robe-sewing groups is to create modest, handmade robes from discarded or plain cloth in muted colours, expressing the ideals of simplicity and frugality. This is in stark contrast to the elaborate — and expensive — costumes that some priests may wear, especially for ceremonial occasions.

Robe sewing projects sometimes culminate in the practitioners ritually receiving their finished robes in the context of a precept-giving (*jukai*) ceremony or else in the donation of the robe. The committed robe sewer will then begin another one.

Mahayana Buddhism remains embedded in Japanese culture, although its traditional schools are struggling to adapt to such a rapidly changing technological age. For many modern Japanese, the traditional, local temple plays no greater role in their spiritual lives than does the local church in the life of the contemporary, secular European. Traditional Japanese Buddhism has been dubbed 'funeral Buddhism' since this is now its main function, and the only time that ordinary people are likely to have any real contact with it is when they are concerned with memorial rites.[9]

---

[8] Fukudenkai literally means 'assembly of the field of merit': see Riggs 2004.

[9] For a fascinating study on traditional Japanese Buddhism in contemporary Japan, see

But it is not all doom and gloom. There are examples of continuity and even renewal of Mahayana Buddhism in Asia. A key feature of contemporary developments has been how best to respond to the complexity of modern life, as we will see with some examples from Taiwan and Japan.

Modern Buddhism in Taiwan

The Chinese revolution of 1949 led to the displacement or repression of forces opposed to Communism. This included the Buddhist Association of the Republic of China (BAROC), which relocated to Taiwan, an island nominally under Chinese rule but in many respects an independent state.[10] The influx of high-ranking Chinese clerics stimulated Buddhist renewal in various directions, which gathered pace after the 1970s. Taiwanese Buddhism has revived Chinese Mahayana, incorporating modern assumptions into its institutional, doctrinal, and practical structure.

Perhaps the most significant Buddhist organization to emerge from Taiwan in recent decades has been *Foguangshan* (Buddha Light Mountain), established by the Chinese monk Hsing Yun (b. 1924) in the late 1960s.[11] While the uninformed visitor to a Foguangshan temple will assume that it represents traditional Chinese Buddhism, this is far from true. While following a well established Chan–Pure Land model, Foguangshan has embraced key features of modernity in characterizing itself as 'humanistic Buddhism' (*renjian fojiao*).[12] Hsing Yun has drawn on contemporary themes including democracy, equality, women's rights, capitalism, modernization, and globalization in articulating a renewed vision of Buddhist practice with the aim of 'establishing a Pure Land on Earth'.

Central to Hsing Yun's humanistic Buddhism is an emphasis on the living not the dead, so long the focus of traditional religious activity through funerary and memorial rites.[13] It is the living who can practise Buddhism, create merit, and even realize Awakening. Rather than encourage followers to aspire to a Pure Land after death, Hsing Yun believes in the transformation of the present world into an ideal spiritual environment. The focus is not some ethereal future but the concrete present; Awakening is not realized through fleeing the mundane world but by living

---

Covell 2005. Reader notes that a survey from the 1980s indicated that 78 percent of people were most likely to visit a temple for reasons connected with mortuary rites but only 8 percent would go there for 'spiritual reasons'. (Reader 1991: 89)

[10] For a study of Buddhism in Taiwan, see Jones 1999.

[11] For an overview of this movement, see Jones 1999: 185–98. For a detailed study, see Chandler 2004.

[12] While embracing modernity, Foguangshan also acknowledges the power of lineage, describing Hsing Yun as the 48th patriarch of the Linji School. (http://www.fgs.org.tw/english/index/index.htm). See also Chandler 2004: 216.

[13] For more on Hsing Yun's vision see, for instance, Hsing Yun 2003.

creatively within it. To this end, he emphasizes the importance of education, economic prosperity, and social service as means towards his ideal society. Unlike traditional Pure Land Buddhism, which regards the present age as spiritually degenerate, Hsing Yun takes an optimistic view and sees contemporary life as offering great opportunities for fulfilling Dharma practice and serving humanity.

Hsing Yun has established both a monastic order and a broader organization open to lay followers, known as Buddha's Light International Association (BLIA). His monastic order is open to men and women, and nuns are generally accorded a high level of respect. There are in fact significantly more nuns than monks (about six to one).[14] Not only this, but Foguangshan has played a leading role in extending monastic ordination to women in a number of Asian traditions where it has either become extinct or was never present in the first place. This radical ecclesiastical gesture has stirred controversy, especially among traditional Asian Buddhists.[15] With regard to lay followers, Hsing Yun follows a more conservative line, seeing the primary role of women as being to support their husbands and look after their families. Even so, women are eligible for leadership positions in the BLIA.

Foguangshan has become a global Buddhist organization with more than 150 centres, temples, and other institutions distributed across more than 30 countries. Moreover, the BLIA is active in more than 50 countries.[16] While it is fair to say that it generally ministers to émigrés from mainland China and Taiwan, Foguangshan has nevertheless gathered approximately one million followers worldwide.[17]

Besides Foguangshan, there are two other large, modernizing Buddhist organizations in contemporary Taiwan; these are *Ciji Gongde Hui* ('Buddhist Compassion Relief Tzu Chi Foundation', generally known as Tzu Chi) founded by the inspirational nun Zhengyan (b. 1937), and Dharma Drum Mountain (DDM), founded by the Chan master Sheng-yen (1930–2009).[18] Unlike Hsing Yun, Zhengyan has not prioritized the

---

[14] According to Chandler, in 1998 there were 188 monks and 1117 nuns (Chandler 2004: 195). He also notes that there is a high drop-out rate (nearly 40 percent overall, and 60 percent among men). (Chandler 2004: 207–8) This growth in the number of nuns is reflected more generally in the Taiwanese sangha; between 1953 and 1986, BAROC ordained more than 6000 women, as opposed to 2000 or so men. (Jones 2000)

[15] Chandler 2004: 161–5.

[16] Chandler 2004: 264–5.

[17] This is Chandler's upper estimate (Chandler 2004: 266). He indicates that there may be around half a million followers in Taiwan but notes that it is much more difficult to determine worldwide numbers. Despite the fact that Foguanshan has more centres abroad than it does in Taiwan, Chandler points out that its devotional base is likely to be much smaller in these outposts. He concludes that the BLIA probably has no more than 60,000 members whose main residence is outside Taiwan. (Chandler 2004: 267)

[18] For biographical information on Zhengyan and the founding of her movement, see Jones

creation of a monastic clergy but instead has grown a spectacularly successful lay organization, which emphasizes compassionate works. Amongst other social welfare projects, Tzu Chi has built a hospital, a nursing school, and supported relief for various natural disasters. By 1994, it had 3.5 million members worldwide, the majority of whom were women. Zhengyan's vision is inspired by the Buddhist principle of compassion, and especially the bodhisattva Guanyin (Avalokiteshvara), but commitment to Buddhism is not a requirement for membership of Tzu Chi.

Through DDM, Sheng-yen has promoted Chinese Chan throughout the world and has been noted especially for revitalizing the practice of Chan meditation through retreats and a series of influential publications.[19] Moreover, DDM has been concerned to address many contemporary social issues, including environmentalism, gender equality, and world poverty.

New Religious Movements in Japan

For the average Japanese, traditional Buddhist sects are increasingly redundant, their temples little more than quaint museums. Their main role is to perform funeral and memorial rites, which are vital sources of income, rather than to offer guidance and inspiration.[20] Many people may struggle to recall the name of their family temple or even what sect their ancestors have traditionally belonged to.[21] Priests are seen not as role models and mentors but as 'funeral businessmen'.[22] Far from exemplifying the world-renouncing ideal of traditional Buddhism, they follow secular lifestyles; many of them marry, some have regular jobs, and so on.

A number of new religious movements (NRMs), with varying links to Buddhism, have sprung up to fill the apparent spiritual vacuum left by a Buddhist establishment regarded as lacking in vitality. Risshō Kōsei-kai (founded 1938) is a lay movement inspired by devotion to the *Lotus Sutra* which emphasizes bodhisattva-like activity through positive social action.[23]

1999: 198–217. Also see the Tzu Chi website http://www.tzuchi.org.tw/. For more information on Dharma Drum Mountain, see http://www.dharmadrum.org/.

[19] See, for instance, Sheng-Yen 2005.

[20] According to figures cited by Covell, 72 percent of temple income derives either from funerals or memorial rites. The average payment made to the local temple for a funeral in 2003 was 486,000 yen (over £3000 or nearly $5000). (Covell 2005: 144–5)

[21] Covell 2005: 35.

[22] Covell 2005: 9.

[23] Its founder was in fact inspired through the help of a Nichiren-affiliated organization called Reiyukai; see http://www.rk-world.org/. In 2009 Risshō Kōsei-kai claimed to have more than 2 million member households. One of its branch websites renders the name of the organization as follows.
"'Rissho" means to stand on the right teachings of the Buddha. "Kosei" means to interact among people to try to perfect our character through mutual support and encouragement. "Kai" means a group of people of the same belief. Therefore, Rissho Kosei-kai

Shinnyo-en (originally founded in 1936 and re-organized under this name in the early 1950s) focuses on the cultivation of Buddha-nature, with the *Nirvana Sutra* as its guiding light and practices a form of meditation linked to ancestor worship.[24] The most significant Buddhist-inspired NRM is Sōka Gakkai ('Value Creation Society'), which began as a lay organization under the direction of Nichiren Shōshū, a monastic sect devoted to the *Lotus Sutra* and the teachings of Nichiren.[25]

Sōka Gakkai

Founded in the 1930s, Sōka Gakkai expanded rapidly after the Second World War and reached a peak of 8–10 million believers in the 1980s.[26] It places great value on education and has established a successful university, besides many other educational initiatives. In addition, it has spawned an influential political party, called Komeito ('Clean Government Party'), and has a vigorous peace movement. Besides this, it has been active in international welfare programmes, including refugee relief and environmental conservation. But it is not without controversy; some of Sōka Gakkai's views have been denounced as not Buddhist, while its rapid expansion was achieved partly through what many have judged to be aggressive conversion tactics.

Sōka Gakkai has been very successful in international evangelism; its global mission, Sōka Gakkai International (SGI), has established groups in nearly two hundred countries, easily making it the most successful Japanese Buddhist export.[27] In the early 1990s, differences over doctrine and practice resulted in Sōka Gakkai splitting from its Nichiren Shōshū parent and becoming fully independent. This has resulted in an exclusively lay organization with no ordained clergy, which believes in the power of the individual to gain Awakening through faith in Nichiren's teachings.

In terms of doctrine, Sōka Gakkai is exclusive, insisting that only reliance upon the saving power of the *Lotus Sutra* will resolve the problems of the world and accomplish the liberation of the individual. The main spiritual practice is recitation of the name of the scripture (daimoku). The *Lotus Sutra* promises untold rewards for those who protect it: 'His wishes shall not be in vain. He shall also in the present age gain his happy recompense.'[28] These assurances underpin the chanting of the daimoku for

---

means a community of believers that strive to perfect their character by interacting with others, basing their actions on the Dharma (teaching) taught by the Buddha.' (http://www.rkhawaii.org/)

24 For more information, see http://www.shinnyo-en.org/ and Clarke 2000.
25 For an overview, see Metraux 1996.
26 Metraux 1996: 372.
27 For more information, visit http://www.sgi.org.
28 Hurvitz 1976: 336.

the fulfillment not only of spiritual aspirations but also material desires, such as a new job or car. While pursuing religious activities in the hope of mundane reward is clearly at odds with the emphasis Buddhism generally places upon renunciation, it is nothing new. In fact, the pursuit of this-worldly goals is a key motivation for joining NRMs in contemporary Japan.[29]

Global Mahayana

Mahayana Buddhism has now circumnavigated the globe; from India, it travelled east and it has kept on going, reaching Japan, North America, and then Europe. It has also been carried to Africa, Australasia, and South America. Global Mahayana Buddhism is a rapidly evolving phenomenon, with new groups emerging all the time while more established ones consolidate and expand. This means that information, particularly with regard to numbers of centres and followers, falls rapidly out of date.

In the past century, knowledge and practice of a range of Mahayana traditions has spread throughout the world. First, diasporic Asian communities have established temples across the globe. While many of these cater primarily to the needs of ethnic Buddhists, some — most notably Tibetan groups — have consciously reached outside their traditional communities. At the same time, Asian missions have sought to implant Buddhism in new cultural soil. Finally, Western converts have initiated a host of new Buddhist movements and institutions. In many major cities, it is now possible to visit a temple or centre inspired by Mahayana Buddhist principles, even several.

We can walk into a medium-size bookstore and pick up obscure Mahayana philosophical works that we could not even have dreamt of reading a few decades ago. At the click of a mouse, we can order a Buddhist text that, until its reconstruction and translation by modern scholars, may not have been read for centuries. We can google the Pure Land sutras and read an online translation of them without even leaving the comfort of home. Some can even pop into their local Tibetan temple and receive initiation into the ritual service of a Buddha or bodhisattva, no questions asked. Mahayana Buddhist materials are almost universally available and in quantities never before seen, not even in the largest temple library.

For the first time in world history, the entire intellectual and spiritual heritage of Mahayana Buddhism has become available for study, including

---

29 For a study, see Reader and Tanabe 1998. It is worth noting that the fulfilment of mundane goals has always been a key reason for engaging in religious activities: sponsoring a ritual to protect the state, praying for a child, or petitioning a Buddhist statue to bring good luck are just a few examples. Reader and Tanabe note that key to the expansion of Sōtō Zen in the Muromachi period was its promise of this-worldly benefits through prayer formulas. (Reader and Tanabe 1998: 9)

the recovery of large volumes of material that had been lost or simply over-looked for centuries. This increasing availability of diverse Buddhist ideas and practices has stimulated unprecedented adaptation, experiment, and innovation. Alongside this, Buddhism has been constructed as a conceptual and historical unity, which has helped to create the idea of a global Buddhist community, prompted intra-faith dialogue between formerly disconnected traditions, and encouraged greater ecumenicism and conver-gence with regard to core teachings and practices.

Globe-trotting Lamas

The Chinese invasion of the 1950s catapulted leading Tibetan lamas into exile. HH the Dalai Lama set up his headquarters in Dharamsala, India but other leaders traveled further afield, especially to Europe and the United States. In a very strange way, the Chinese did both Tibetan Buddhism and the wider world a favour. The scattering of lamas across the globe forced what was a feudal religious tradition to confront the challenges of modernity and, at the same time, enabled the spiritual teachings of Tibetan Buddhism to reach a world audience.

While the intricacies of the Tibetan Buddhist system can seem arcane, many émigré lamas have emphasized core Mahayana teachings above complex Tantric elements, placing greater store on fundamental principles like the bodhisattva ideal. Moreover, the dispersal of Tibetan texts through-out the world has led to the widespread translation and publication of many Mahayana scriptures and treatises in Western languages.

Zen in the West

Perhaps the most established form of Mahayana Buddhism in the West is Zen. In the early 20th century, the Japanese scholar D.T. Suzuki played a key role in 'repackaging' Zen for Western consumption.[30] To do this, he stripped away its institutional, cultural, and religious context, arguing that it was a universal mystical experience and so 'the ultimate fact of all philoso-phy and religion'.[31] For him, Zen was not only the essence of Buddhism but of *all* meaningful religion. This deracinated version of Zen became attractive to the American Beat Generation of the 1950s, and then to the hippy culture of the 1960s and '70s. Writers like Suzuki and the English mystic Alan Watts helped to create a climate in which Zen — whether properly understood or not — was seductive. This helped to pave the way for more rigorous engagement with Zen traditions, especially in their Japanese form.

---

[30] See McMahan 2002.
[31] Suzuki 1927: 254 (italics added).

While Zen has attracted quite a few European converts, especially in France and Germany, it has proved especially popular in North America where it has inspired groups too numerous to list, with Western students now recognised as 'roshis' (revered teachers) in their own right. Probably the most high-profile Zen institution in the United States is the San Francisco Zen Center, inspired by the Japanese Sōtō priest, Shunryū Suzuki Roshi (1904–71).[32] The White Plum Asanga, a loose affiliation of students of Taizan Maezumi Roshi, is also influential, following a rich combination of Sōtō and Rinzai forms.[33] Thich Nhat Hanh's Vietnamese Zen (*Thien*) has also become widely known.[34]

While in Asia, practitioners of Zen meditation have generally belonged to the clergy, and even then only a select band, meditation in the West has proven to be a big draw for lay practitioners.[35] Owing partly to controversies surrounding influential teachers but also to the prevailing democratic climate, Western Zen has moved away from the strictly hierarchical teacher–student relationship of traditional Zen. For instance, Charlotte Joko Beck (b. 1917), an American Zen practitioner, writes: 'There is only one teacher ... life itself.'[36]

These factors have led to the creation of a Western style of Zen practice that differs significantly from its Asian parent. Primarily lay in composition and focused on meditation, it is less stratified and more democratic, pursued not by renunciates but by people living more or less conventional Western lifestyles with families and jobs. Traditional ritual structures have been simplified — or even dispensed with — while personal spiritual experience has become central.

Also significant has been the increased prominence of women, including female teachers, in Western Zen, contrary to Asian traditions where women are often marginal. A remarkable — and somewhat eccentric — example is the Englishwoman Jiyu-Kennett (1924–96), who inspired the Order of Buddhist Contemplatives (OBC), which has 'Westernized' Zen, drawing on the Christian monastic tradition and especially its liturgy.[37] In the United States, notable women Zen teachers include Joko Beck and Cheri Huber (b. 1944).[38]

---

[32] For a disciple's account of Suzuki Roshi, see Chadwick 1999.
[33] See http://www.whiteplum.org/.
[34] See http://www.interbeing.org.uk/about/Order.html.
[35] With regard to contemporary Japanese Sōtō Zen, Reader comments that priests will pursue a fairly rigorous meditation curriculum during their training period but, once appointed to run a regular temple, relatively few maintain systematic practice. (Reader 1991: 83, 88) Moreover, he notes that for many priests, their role is not vocational; rather, they are simply following in their father's footsteps. (Reader 1991: 88)
[36] Beck 1989: 15.
[37] For a study of Jiyu-Kennett and the OBC, see Kay 2004: 117–226. See also http://www.obcon.org/.
[38] For Cheri Huber, see http://www.cherihuber.com/index.html.

Western Mahayana Traditions

Modern Buddhist traditions, including Mahayana-inspired movements, tend to share a number of key features, several of which are prominent in examples discussed here. These features include: a syncretic approach to Buddhist heritage; a softening — and even dissolving — of the monk/lay split; the decentralization and democratization of spiritual authority; increased individualism; greater opportunities for women; a stress on meditation; an emphasis on the psychological as opposed to the religious; and social engagement.[39] There is not room here to examine each of these features systematically; instead, they will be illustrated through the consideration of specific Buddhist movements.

Western Buddhist syncretism

Western Buddhist groups are often syncretic, sometimes drawing on the entire Buddhist tradition in the process of creating a new synthesis of Buddhist thought and practice. One example of this is the Amida Trust, based in the United Kingdom. Its name suggests some link with Pure Land Buddhism and this is true. At the same time, the Trust incorporates many insights from Zen as well as contemporary Western psychology into an eclectic system.[40]

Another self-consciously ecumenical movement is the Friends of the Western Buddhist Order (FWBO) — the tradition that I belong to — founded in 1968 by Sangharakshita, an English Theravada monk.[41] At its heart, the FWBO has a non-monastic clergy (the Western Buddhist Order (WBO)), open to men and women equally. Having abandoned the traditional monk–lay structure, members are known simply as 'Dharmafarers' (m. Dharmachari, f. Dharmacharini) and make individual lifestyle choices that best express their commitment to the Three Jewels.

While many of the core teachings of the WBO are drawn from the Theravada's Pali Canon, these are framed within the Mahayana mythic story of the 1000-armed Avalokiteshvara. Each member is regarded as a hand of Avalokiteshvara and the Order collectively is conceived as functioning as a bodhisattva.[42] Besides its Mahayana affinities, the WBO also draws on Tantric elements, especially in relation to its rituals and the personal meditation practices often transmitted to members at ordination. The WBO asserts the unity of Buddhism and encourages the broad-based study of traditional teachings, as well as wider cultural enquiry, as means to spiritual transformation. In India, where it is known as TBMSG, the

---

[39] This analysis is based in part on Baumann 2002: 55ff and Wallace 2002: 35ff.
[40] For more information, see http://www.amidatrust.com/index.html.
[41] For an introduction to the FWBO, see Vishvapani 2001.
[42] See Sangharakshita 1991: 4–5.

FWBO has had considerable success in ministering to the followers of the late Dr. B.R. Ambedkar (1891–1956), an important leader of the Dalit communities who — along with millions of his followers — converted to Buddhism in the 1950s.[43]

Engaged Buddhism

Engaged Buddhism is not a specifically Mahayana phenomenon but key Mahayana ideas and teachers have influenced its development.[44] The term itself was coined by the émigré Vietnamese Zen teacher, Thich Nhat Hanh (b. 1926), whose Order of Interbeing is based in Bordeaux, France.[45] Engaged Buddhism has been used to describe a diverse range of activities and organizations but typically manifests in peace movements, programmes of economic and social uplift, ecological initiatives, and social welfare projects. Unlike traditional Buddhism, which has tended to focus on inner cultivation, engaged Buddhism also pursues the transformation of the outer world, and often prioritizes it. For some engaged Buddhists, traditional Buddhism is part of the 'problem', owing to its seeming lack of social engagement, its rigid hierarchies, and marginalization of women.

Philosophically, engaged Buddhism draws on notions such as interdependence to encourage social and environmental responsibility. Joanna Macy, a leading theorist, argues that we are not only connected to one another but to the world as a whole. In her suggestively titled book *World as Lover, World as Self*, Macy writes, 'self, society, and world are reciprocally modified by their interaction'.[46] Engaged Buddhism emphasizes not only the reciprocal relationship between people but also between the inner and the outer world: to achieve world peace, we must find inner peace; to attain personal liberation, we must accomplish social liberation.

Nhat Hanh has himself been in the forefront of peace activism, especially in relation to his homeland of Vietnam, and was nominated for the Nobel Peace Prize in 1967 by Martin Luther King, Jr. He has produced a string of influential publications with evocative titles such as *Being Peace* and has also been active in cross-religious dialogue, another focus of engaged Buddhism. Much like HH the Dalai Lama, Nhat Hanh's books, as well as his public profile, have been instrumental in introducing Buddhist values to a mass audience.[47]

---

[43] For more on this, see Sponberg 1996.

[44] Queen has argued that it can be seen as a fourth *yāna* (way or vehicle) of Buddhism. (Queen 2000: 17–26)

[45] For more information, visit http://www.orderofinterbeing.org/.

[46] Macy 2007: 99.

[47] *The Miracle of Mindfulness*, for instance, has sold in excess of 125,000 copies. (Tweed 2002: 21)

Owing to his Zen monastic training and personal study, Nhat Hanh's teaching is steeped in Mahayana themes. He emphasizes the teachings of Buddha-nature and shunyata, and has coined the term 'interbeing' as a way to refer to the inter-subjective nature of human experience. Nhat Hanh has cultivated a radically pacifist stance that emphasizes inner change as the organic trigger for social progress. Some engaged Buddhists have criticized this position as naive, arguing that it ignores how oppression is sustained by social structures. Notwithstanding, Nhat Hanh is widely respected.

12.2 Glassman Roshi: An Engaged Western Buddhist

Tetsugen Bernard Glassman Roshi (b. 1939), a disciple of the late Zen master Taizan Maezumi Roshi,[48] has pioneered a series of engaged Buddhist projects. After founding the Zen Community of New York (ZCNY) in the 1970s, he went on to establish the Greystone Mandala which, amongst other things, now runs a bakery, a low-cost housing project, and an HIV clinic. Greystone projects serve the needs of the economically and socially disadvantaged.

In 1996, Glassman founded what is now known as the Zen Peacemakers Sangha (ZPS),[49] an international, interfaith network that stresses the integration of spiritual practice and social action through commitment to three principles.

Not-knowing, thereby giving up fixed ideas about ourselves and the universe
Bearing witness to the joy and suffering of the world
Loving action toward ourselves and others[50]

ZPS arranges unconventional spiritual activities, including pilgrimages to the Nazi death camp of Auschwitz–Birkenau to 'bear witness' to the suffering experienced there, and 'street retreats', during which participants live for several days as homeless beggars.

Amongst other initiatives, Glassman Roshi has established an Order of Disorder, which has the motto: 'Don't be here now!'[51], and an Order of Minstrels, whose role is 'to help bring mirth and joy to the Zen Peacemakers'.[52]

---

48 See the White Plum Asanga noted above.
49 On its website, this organization is variously referred to as Zen Peacemakers, the Zen Peacemaker Order, the Zen Peacemaker Community, and the Zen Peacemaker Sangha (http://www.zenpeacemakers.org/zps/). For more on Glassman's approach, see Glassman 1998.
50 http://www.zenpeacemakers.org/about/vision.htm, Mission and Vision tab, [accessed 09.03.09].
51 http://www.orderofdisorder.com/.
52 _http://www.zenpeacemakers.org/zps/om.htm.

Conclusion: The Postmodern Bodhisattva

In past centuries, Mahayana Buddhism has been central to the spiritual life of many Asian countries and has bequeathed a lasting cultural legacy. But I think it unlikely that, in our global era, large numbers of people will embrace it explicitly. This is partly because religions tend to implant best when the governing regime sponsors them, and it is improbable that a contemporary state will adopt Mahayana Buddhism as its official religion. Another important factor is that religious affiliation in general is on the decline in many contemporary Westernized cultures, especially those where Buddhism has become attractive. A diffuse impact of Buddhist ideas, practices, and cultural forms seems more realistic; far more people are likely to read a book by HH the Dalai Lama, perhaps even go and hear him speak, than would declare themselves as Buddhists. And this is no bad thing.

Many Western people have a positive appreciation of Buddhism in general, even if this view is often over-simplified. Buddhism evokes peace, calm, contentment, and a general atmosphere of spirituality. Buddha heads and other icons are used widely as domestic ornaments, and Buddhist imagery and ideas are regarded as assets in selling consumer products. I have seen images of Tibetan monks used to sell washing powder, IT solutions, and paper tissues. Buddhist ideas like nirvana, karma, Enlightenment, and Zen are now embedded in the Western vocabulary and regularly pop up in TV shows, newspapers, and popular literature; there has even been a perfume (not to mention a rock band) named Nirvana.

While these phenomena represent a relatively low level of knowledge or understanding of Buddhism, they underline a general view that Buddhism is seen as a good thing. HH the Dalai Lama has been awarded the Nobel Peace Prize, as has another high profile Buddhist, the Burmese political leader Aung Sang Suu Kyi (b. 1945).[53] Books by leaders such as Thich Nhat Hanh and HH the Dalai Lama sell in the tens of thousands — and there are many of them. According to one survey, two million French people declared that Buddhism was the religion they liked best.[54]

Rather than making exclusive commitments to Buddhist practice, contemporary Western people are more likely to be 'sympathizers'.[55] They may read Buddhist texts, meditate, participate in online chatrooms, perhaps even attend a Buddhist group, but they may also take an interest in other religious traditions, value the insights of Western psychology, and be regularly found browsing through the Mind/Body/Spirit section at the bookstore. Rather than adopting a formal, religious framework, they may

---

[53] For more on 'The Lady', visit http://www.dassk.com/index.php.
[54] Tweed 2002: 20.
[55] This term is borrowed from Tweed 2002: 20.

combine many elements into a personal, self-growth philosophy. Such activity fits a growing trend in which inner spirituality is replacing explicit religious identity.[56] Religions are mined for the insights they can offer, but conversion is seen as unnecessary, limiting, or even dangerously exclusive. To coin a slogan: spirituality good, religion bad.

12.3 Toni Packer: A 'Post-Buddhist' Teacher?

Toni Packer (b. 1927) trained in Zen under the American-born roshi, Philip Kapleau (1912–2004), then abbot of the Rochester Zen Center. In 1981, after being named his successor, she became disillusioned with traditional Zen and left to form her own community, now based at the Springwater Center for Meditative Inquiry and Retreats in upstate New York.[57]

While her teachings are deeply indebted to Zen, Packer has abandoned traditional affiliation and many of the formal trappings that go with it. She teaches a non-denominational approach to meditation that emphasizes awareness of the present moment, attentiveness to habitual thoughts and feelings, and a non-grasping state that she calls 'the stillness of not knowing'.[58] Her retreats tend to be informal, enabling curiosity and attention to arise in an organic, rather than forced way. According to Packer: 'The emergence and blossoming of understanding, love and intelligence has nothing to do with any tradition... It happens completely on its own when a human being questions, wonders, listens and looks without getting stuck in fear, pleasure and pain.'[59]

Packer's post-Zen meditative enquiry represents the logical end point of a view of Zen that sees it more as an inner process than a historical tradition. It may also embody the future profile of Buddhism in the West, at least in one guise.

If this process continues — and I think it will — is there any future for formal commitment to Buddhism, Mahayana or otherwise? I believe there is. Above all else, Mahayana Buddhism frames ordinary human life within a cosmic story, the bodhisattva ideal, which, by amplifying the significance of everyday acts of kindness — or cruelty — lends gravity to routine ethical choices. The bodhisattva ideal projects a backdrop of meaning, purpose, and value onto our seemingly unremarkable lives by reminding us that we are sons and daughters of the Buddha. It connects our daily travails with an infinitely larger spiritual struggle: the Awakening of the entire cosmos. In

---

56 For an interesting study of this apparent trend, see Heelas et al. 2005.
57 http://www.springwatercenter.org/.
58 Packer 2007.
59 http://www.springwatercenter.org/teachers/packer/ [accessed 09.03.09].

the terms of one traditional reflection, we have been granted this precious human birth, and it is our obligation to live it out compassionately.

Mahayana Buddhism exemplifies the transformative power of the imagination, a faculty that is infinitely creative, forever generating new visions, ideas, and possibilities for human experience. It offers a sequence of portals opening out to the infinite. Stepping through one of these portals can, like Alice stepping through the looking glass, open up new universes of meaning, value, and purpose. While daily life is beset by petty frustrations and obsessions, Mahayana Buddhism reminds us that we also dwell within a boundless sphere, and each moment offers an opportunity to explore it.

The history of Mahayana Buddhism teaches us that even the most sublime teachings can be distorted, abused, and used to harm rather than to liberate people. They can be used to serve the cause of self or to transcend the self. They can be used as tools of oppression as well as freedom. At the same time, Mahayana Buddhism teaches us that despair can give rise to hope, that destruction can give rise to renewal, and that no gesture of the creative imagination is futile. Even if it goes unnoticed in the present, it may lie buried, like some Tibetan *terma* (treasure text), and be rediscovered even hundreds of years later to inspire someone in another country, speaking another language, to transform themselves in the light of the bodhisattva vow.

> As long as space abides and as long as the world abides, so long may I abide, destroying the sufferings of the world.[60]

---

[60] Santideva 1995:10.55: 143.

Epilogue:
The Mahayana on My Doorstep

I LIVE IN A SMALL TOWN, formerly a mill village, in the north-west of England. To get to work, I take a 20-minute train ride into Manchester, once a heartland of the industrial revolution and centre of cotton trading, but now more famous for its music exports, bars, and clubs. It might seem that we are light worlds away from Mahayana Buddhism and yet there are Buddhas everywhere. After stepping off the train, I saunter into the Triangle, a trendy shopping mall, formerly the city's Corn Exchange, and in the flower shop, minding its own business, is a Buddha.

Passing through the Triangle, I walk past a major department store and, through the window, glimpse a row of orange, Japanese-style Buddhas – a temporary art exhibition. I then wander up Market Street — the heart of Manchester's retail district — and visit my favourite shop. Among the decorative plant holders, the vases, and the tea trays are ornamental Buddhas awaiting rescue.

I pass along High Street entering the Northern Quarter. Many of its Victorian buildings, once cotton warehouses, have been transformed into loft apartments with bars, cafes, and restaurants at ground level. Here I am more likely to enter the world of urban socialites and offbeat, designer shops than the cosmic dimension of the Mahayana – or so you might think. I enter Turner Street and am drawn to two huge turquoise banners. On one side, in golden letters, they proclaim the Manchester Buddhist Centre, on the other a rain of golden Buddhas. I climb the steps, a huge sculpture of the Three Jewels hovering above me, and then enter a Mahayana universe. There are Buddhas everywhere. In the meditation hall, I come face to face with Amitabha, the Buddha of light and compassion.

This is not my first visit. I was part of the team of Buddhists that created this place, inspired by the Mahayana and in particular the bodhisattva ideal. We hoped to create a Pure Land — an oasis of tranquillity, perfect for learning about and practising Buddhist teachings.

Manchester is home not only to the Manchester Buddhist Centre; near the university quarter, there is a Taiwanese Mahayana temple belonging to Foguangshan. In Openshaw, there is a Zen dojo (meditation hall). Gathering at the Friends Meeting House near the Town Hall, there is a Western Chan group. Around the city, there are several Tibetan groups and other spiritual centres for whom Mahayana doctrines, practices and ideas are central.

Finally, I make my way up Oxford Road towards the university quarter. Besides other things today, I am giving a lecture on the origins of the Mahayana. In doing so, I draw on contemporary Western knowledge and scholarship which enables me to understand and talk about things that had been forgotten or lost for a thousand years and more.

On completing my lecture, I retrace my steps back along Oxford Road; a Tibetan monk crosses the street in front of me. Was that an apparition? Then I see it; at first I think it is just the Manchester rain but it is strangely luminous, even golden. A rain of Buddhas pours down, saturating everything and everyone with compassion, with wisdom, with energy, and with light. I am soaked through with Buddhas.

Glossary

Most entries are Sanskrit terms and show the form used in the text. Entries from other languages are noted as such.

Abhidharma	schematic classification of Pali canon
ahimsa	non-harm
alaya-vijnana	store consciousness
Amida (Jp.)	*see* Amitabha
Amitabha	Buddha of Infinite Light; particular focus of Pure Land tradition
Amituo (Ch.)	*see* Amitabha
anatman	lack of enduring identity
anitya	impermanence
anuttarapuja	supreme worship
arhat	worthy one
asharaya-paravrtti	revolution at the basis
atman	enduring self
Avalokiteshvara	bodhisattva of compassion
Bhaisajyaguru	Medicine Buddha
bhumi	bodhisattva stage
bija	seed
bodhichitta	the Awakening mind
bodhisattva	Awakened being
buddha-field	realm overseen by a Buddha; their 'paradise'
Buddha-nature	belief that all beings have the potential to become Awakened
buddhanusmrti	recollection of the Buddha
buddhavacana	the word of the Buddha
Chan (Ch.)	Mahayana tradition that emphasizes meditation, better known as Zen (Jp.)
Cheontae-jong (Kor.)	*see* Tiantai
cittamatra	mind-only
daimoku (Jp.)	mantric formula invoking the Lotus Sutra
dependent origination	central belief of Buddhism: all things arise out of conditions
dharmadhatu	realm of reality
dharmakaya	body of the Buddha's teachings; essence of Awakening
dharma	the Truth; teaching of the Buddha; thing
dharmas	analytical categories ; atomic constituents of reality

Dizang (Ch.)	*see* Kshitigarbha
drsti	opinion, view
dukkha	suffering
Dunhuang	complex of illustrated cave-temples in China on the Silk Route
garbha	the inside, middle or interior of anything
gong'an (Ch.)	koan (Jp.)
guanfo (Ch.)	Buddha contemplation
Guanyin (Ch.)	*see* Avalokiteshvara
Hinayana	first main phase of Buddhism (pejorative), *see* Nikaya
huatou (Ch.)	critical phrase (ref. koan)
Huayan (Ch.)	Mahayana philosophical tradition that understands reality as an interconnected totality; Chinese name for the *Flower Ornament Sutra*
hwadu (Kor.)	critical phrase (ref. koan)
Hwaeom (Kor.)	Huayan
icchantikas	those incapable of accomplishing Awakening; literally 'incorrigibles'
ichinengi (Jp.)	single nembutsu
jatakas	birth stories
jiriki (Jp.)	self-power
Jizō (Jp.)	*see* Kshitigarbha
jnana	knowledge
Jōdo Shinshū (Jp.)	True Pure Land tradition
Jōdoshu (Jp.)	Pure Land tradition
kaidan (Jp.)	ordination platform
kami (Jp.)	native Japanese deities
Kannon (Jp.)	*see* Avalokiteshvara
kansō (Jp.)	official monks
klesha	defilement
koan (Jp.)	phrase or story which necessitates use of intuition rather than rational thought for understanding
kongan (Kor.)	koan
Kannon (Jp.)	*see* Avalokiteshvara
Kshitigarbha	bodhisattva who goes to the hell realms
Madhyamika	Mahayana philosophical tradition which emphasizes that all things lack a independent nature
Mahayana	second phase of Buddhism
Maitreya	future Buddha
Manjushri	bodhisattva of wisdom
mappō (Jp.)	the age of the decline of the Dharma; 'degenerate'
mikkyō (Jp.)	esoteric teachings

Mile Pusa (Ch.)	*see* Maitreya
Miroku (Jp.)	*see* Maitreya
Monju (Jp.)	*see* Manjushri
nembutsu	recitation (recollection) of the Buddha's name
nianfo (Ch.)	recollection of the Buddha
Nikaya	term used to describe early sects of Buddhism
nirmanakaya	manifestion of a Buddha in a physical body
nirvana	Awakening; literally 'blown out'
panjiao	doctrinal classification
paramita	bodhisattva 'perfection'
prajna	wisdom
prajnaparamita	Perfect Wisdom
pratitya-samutpada	dependent origination
punya	merit
Pure Land	a buddha-field (often of Amitabha)
Pure Land tradition	Buddhist tradition focusing on Amitabha
Rinzai Zen	tradition emphasizing use of koan
samadhi	vision-world; meditation
Samantabhadra	bodhisattva associated with meditation, patron of the *Lotus Sutra*
sambhogakaya	a luminous, apparitional body of the Buddha
samsara	round of birth, death, and rebirth
sangha	spiritual community, often the monastic community only
sanjie jiao (Ch.)	Three Stages sect
shastra	treatise
shikantaza (Jp.)	just sitting
shinjin (Jp.)	true entrusting, faith
Siddhartha Gautama	historical Buddha
Shingon (Jp.)	esoteric tradition related to Vajrayana Buddhism
shunyata	emptiness; absence of inherent existence, *see* svabhava
Silk Route	extensive network of trade routes through Asia and reaching the Mediterranean
skandhas	schema analyzing the human being into five categories
seon (Kor.)	meditation; also Zen
Sōtō Zen	tradition emphasizing meditation, esp. shikantaza
Sukhavati	the buddha-field of Amitabha
svabhava	inherent existence
Tantric Buddhism	tradition emphasizing direct experience through body, speech, and mind
tariki (Jp.)	other-power
tathagatagarbha	embryo of Awakening

tathata	suchness
Tendai (Jp.)	Japanese interpretation of Tiantai, also incorporating esoteric elements
Theravada	doctrine of the Elders; form of Buddhism found throughout southern Asia
Tiantai (Ch.)	tradition emphasizing meditation and study, with belief in conventional, subtle and ultimate truth
tonseisō (Jp.)	reclusive monks
trisvabhava	doctrine of three natures
Tushita	the Buddha-field of Maitreya
upaya-kaushalya	skilful means
Vajrayana	the third phase of Buddhism, also known as Tantric Buddhism
vinaya	clerical code
Yogachara	system of belief emphasizing the mind in determining our experience
Zen (Jp.)	tradition with emphasis on meditation

Image Descriptions

Images follow page 116.

1. *The Great Buddha of Kamakura (Kamakura Daibutsu)*. Kōtokuin temple, Kamakura, Japan, 1252 CE. Courtesy: Marie Wintzer, 2007.

2. *Commemorative Jizō images*. Hasedera temple, Kamakura, Japan, contemporary. Courtesy: Marie Wintzer, 2007.
   These images, approximately 40cm in height, are purchased from the temple and then offered in remembrance of lost or aborted children.

3. *Head of a bodhisattva*. Found near Peshawar, Pakistan, late 2nd–3rd century CE. Schist with traces of pigment and gold. 23cm (h), 15cm (w). Courtesy: Victoria and Albert Museum.
   The fine carving of the head indicates that it belonged to a standing bodhisattva image of high quality. It has an elaborate headdress, constructed of ribbons and jewels. The central cockade (now missing) originally slotted onto the raised tapering tenon on a disc prominently displayed at the centre of the turban and bejewelled diadem. This probably displayed the attribute identifying the specific bodhisattva this head belonged to.
   The beautifully carved head has an auspicious forehead mark ('urna') and the wavy moustache much favoured in the Gandharan school of Kushan Buddhist art. The head in not worked fully in the round. This suggests that it was intended to be displayed against a temple structure or in a wall niche.

4. *The Begging Monk*. Osaka Castle, Osaka, Japan, 9 October 2006. Courtesy: Alex Masters.

5. *Western Buddhists in meditation*. Birmingham Buddhist Centre, Birmingham, England, contemporary. Courtesy: Alokavira/Timm Sonnenschein.

6. *Buddha with two attendant bodhisattvas*. China, 544 CE. Stele: carved limestone. 92.5 cm (h). Courtesy: Victoria and Albert Museum.
   This stele probably stood in a public place for passers-by to worship.

7. *Descent of Amida Buddha (raigō)*. Japan, Kamakura period (1300s). Hanging scroll: ink, color and gold on silk. 170.2cm (h), 84.8cm (w). Courtesy: Cleveland Museum of Art.
   This scroll represents the vision of the dying believer who is received and welcomed into the Pure Land by Amida Buddha. He is attended by the bodhisattvas Kannon, offering the lotus throne, and Seishi, clasping his hands in prayer (at the bottom of the scroll).

8. *Bodhisattva Samantabhadra riding on an elephant*. Korea or China, 1350–1450. Water-based colours and gold (*kirikane*) on silk mounted on paper. 139cm (h), 56cm (w). Courtesy: Victoria and Albert Museum.

9. *'Monju with the Five Chignons' Riding on a Lion (detail)*. Japan, Kamakura Period (1185–1333). Hanging scroll: ink and colour, gold pigment and cut gold (kirikane) on silk. 102cm (h), 42.6cm (w). Courtesy: Cleveland Museum of Art.

    Monju is often portrayed with the Sutra of Wisdom in the left hand, a sword in the right hand to cut through illusion (to shed light on the unenlightened mind, to disperse the clouds of ignorance), and sitting atop a roaring lion, which symbolizes the voice of Buddhist Law and the power of Buddhism to overcome all obstacles. This riding-lion form is also known as the 'Kishi Monju Bosatsu' in Japan. Monju is frequently represented with five curls or knots (chignons) of hair, indicating the five-terraced mountain (Ch. Wutaishan) in China where Monju is venerated, or the Five wisdoms.

10. *Bodhisattvas of the Ten Stages of Enlightenment*. China, Ming dynasty (1368–1644), 1454. Hanging scroll; ink and colour on silk. 141cm (h), 79.4cm (w). Courtesy: Cleveland Museum of Art.

11. *Pilgrim's book; Ryusekiji temple stamp and calligraphy*. 1981. Courtesy: Ian Reader. Author's photograph.

    Ryusekiji is temple 19 of the 34 temples on the Chichibu pilgrimage route (Saitama area, Japan), dedicated to Kannon. Together with the Saikoku (Kansai area) and Bando (mostly in the Kanto region) pilgrimages, it makes up a 100-temple mega-pilgrimage.

12. *Daruma*. Japan. Painter: Ito Jakuchu (1716–1800). Hanging scroll: ink on paper. Courtesy: British Museum.

    Daruma is a Japanese representation of the semi-mythical Chinese figure Bodhidharma, the supposed founder and embodiment of Chan/Zen.

13. *The five-storey pagoda at Kōfukuji*. Nara, Japan, 1426. Courtesy: Kryptos86, 2008.

    First constructed in 725, the current building is a restoration completed in 1426. It is the second highest pagoda in Japan, rising 50.1 metres. Inside the pagoda, enshrined around the central pillar are a Yakushi triad (to the east), a Shaka triad (to the south), an Amida triad (to the west), and a Miroku triad (to the north). It is now a world heritage site.

14. *Vairochana Buddha*. Cave 19, Fengxian Temple, Longmen, China, 672–5 CE. Cut into grey limestone rock. Courtesy: Glynnis Ritchie, 2007.

15. *Buddha and stupas at Borobudur*. Java, Indonesia. Courtesy: Fabian Foo, 2005.

    Borobodur is a monumental stupa complex dating from the 8th and 9th centuries CE. Its construction comprises a pyramidal base, the trunk of a cone with three circular platforms, and, at the apex, a crowning stupa. The walls and balustrades are decorated with reliefs. Around the circular platforms there are 72 openwork stupas, each containing a statue of the Buddha. Perhaps as early as the late 10th century, Borobudur was abandoned, and then lost in jungle growth. Rediscovered by colonial Europeans in the early 19th century, it was reinvigorated as a pilgrimage site after restoration work in the 1970s. (*see also* Feature 2.2)

16. *Bodhisattva as 'Guide of Souls'.* Cave 17, Dunhuang, China, late 9th century CE. Ink and colours on silk banner. 80.5cm (h), 53.8cm (w). Courtesy: British Musuem. This painting shows a bodhisattva leading a finely dressed figure to the Pure Land, depicted in the clouds at the top left-hand corner. The bodhisattva carries a hand-censer in his right hand and in his left a lotus flower, from which hangs a white banner with tail streamers. The image probably depicts Guanyin (Avalokiteshvara).

17. *Woodblock carving of the Heart Sutra.* Madhyamaloka, Birmingham, England. Courtesy: Alokavira/Timm Sonnenschein.

© Copyright of all images held by image source, unless otherwise noted.

Further Reading

The readings suggested here are most likely to benefit the general reader. Those with more specialised interests should consult the *Work Cited* section as well as the bibliographies of some of the general works mentioned below. Sources with only author name and year can be found in *Works Cited*.

General Reading
There are now dozens of general overviews of Buddhism available. The following are among the more reliable and accessible.

Bechert, Heinz, and Gombrich, R.F. 1984. *The World of Buddhism: Buddhist Monks and Nuns in Society and Culture*. London: Thames & Hudson.

Harvey, Peter (ed.). 2001. *Buddhism*, London: Continuum.

Keown, Damien. 2000. *Buddhism: A Very Short Introduction*. Oxford: Oxford University Press.

Prebish, Charles S., and Keown, Damien. 2006. *Introducing Buddhism*. London: Routledge.

Skilton, Andrew. 1994. *A Concise History of Buddhism*. Birmingham: Windhorse Publications.

For those with access to academic libraries, a wealth of articles can be found in the following encyclopedias.

Buswell Jr., Robert E. (ed). 2004. *The Encyclopedia of Buddhism* (2 vols.). New York: Macmillan Reference USA.

Jones, Lindsay. (ed.) 2005. *The Encyclopedia of Religion* (15 vols., 2nd edn). Detroit: Macmillan Reference USA.

Keown, Damien, and Prebish, Charles S. (eds.) 2007. *Encyclopedia of Buddhism*, London: Routledge.

Mahayana Buddhism
The standard academic introduction to Mahayana Buddhism is:
Williams 2008.
> This contains a wealth of information but is directed primarily at an academic readership. It emphasises doctrinal developments within Mahayana and its continuity in Tibetan Buddhism.

The development of Mahayana thought is traced in Williams with Tribe 2000.

Chapter 2: The Origins of the Mahayana
Nattier 2003.
> Although academic, this is a highly readable and fascinating study of the development of early Mahayana, together with translation of an early Mahayana scripture.

Among the more accessible Mahayana sutras are the following (in English translation).

Lotus Sutra
Hurvitz 1976.

Sukhavati Sutras
http://www12.canvas.ne.jp/horai/sukhavati-index.htm [accessed 10.03.09].
Gomez 1996.

Vimalakirti Sutra
Thurman 1976; this translation also online at
    http://www.fodian.net/world/0475.html [accessed 10.03.09].

Chapter 3: The Bodhisattva Ideal
Santideva 1995.
> The classic, devotional account of the bodhisattva path, together with a wealth of useful background information.

Chapter 4: Buddhas, Bodhisattvas and Buddha-fields
Birnbaum 2003b.
Vessantara. 2008. *A Guide to the Buddhas*; *A Guide to the Bodhisattvas*; *A Guide to the Deities of the Tantra* (three separate vols). Cambridge: Windhorse Publications.

Chapter 5: Perfect Wisdom and Madhyamika
Conze 1988.
> A translation of two Perfect Wisdom texts together with explanatory notes.

Garfield 1995.
> A translation of Nagarjuna's central work, the *Mulamadhyamikakarika*, with commentary.

Sangharakshita. 1993. *Wisdom Beyond Words: Sense and Non-sense in the Buddhist Prajñāpāramitā Tradition*. Glasgow: Windhorse Publications.
> A contemporary commentary on the *Heart*, *Diamond*, and *Ratnagunasamcayagatha* sutras.

Chapter 6: Yogachara and Buddha-nature
There are no easily accessible introductions to Yogachara or Buddha-nature thought. However, Williams 2008 and Williams with Tribe 2000 include useful introductory sketches. See also:

King, Richard. 1999. *Indian Philosophy: An Introduction to Hindu and Buddhist Thought*. New Delhi: Maya and Edinburgh University Press.

More challenging is a translation of the *Ratnagotravibhaga* from Tibetan:
Kongtrul et al. 2000.

Chapters 7–8: China
Erik Zürcher in Bechert 1984 (above, *General Reading*) offers an excellent introduction to Buddhism in China.

The standard, although dated, overview of Chinese Buddhism is:
Ch'en, Kenneth. 1972. *Buddhism in China* (new edn). Princeton: Princeton University Press.

Books on specific Chinese schools tend to be specialised academic works. A few of the more accessible ones are these.

Huayan
Cook, Francis H. 1977. *Hua-Yen Buddhism: The Jewel Net of Indra.* University Park: Pennsylvania State University Press.

Tiantai
Swanson 1989.

Chan
McRae 2003.

For a contemporary approach to Chinese Chan, see works by Master Sheng-Yen, such as Sheng-Yen and Henderson, Dan. 2002. *Hoofprint of the Ox: Principles of the Chan Buddhist Path as Taught by a Modern Chinese Master.* Oxford: Oxford University Press.

Chapter 9: Korea
There are few general books on Korean Buddhism. Perhaps the most accessible is:
Grayson 2002.
Try also Buswell 1991.

Chapters 10-11: Japan
For a general sweep of Japanese Buddhism:
Tamura Yoshiro and Hunter, Jeffrey. 2001. *Japanese Buddhism: A Cultural History.* Tokyo: Kosei.
Bowring, Richard. 2005. *The Religious Traditions of Japan, 500-1600.* Cambridge: Cambridge University Press.
Although an academic work, this is highly readable; most content is concerned with Buddhism, and there is a useful emphasis on material culture.

Hōnen and Jōdo shū
http://www.jodo.org/ [accessed 10.03.09].

Shinran
His collected works are available in English translation at:
http://www.shinranworks.com/ [accessed 10.03.2009].

Nichiren
A number of his writings are available in English translation at:
http://www.sgilibrary.org/writings.php [accessed 10.03.09].

Pure Land Buddhism
An accessible introduction is Unno, Taitetsu. 1998. *River of Fire, River of Water.* New York: Doubleday.

Dōgen
For a developing archive of translations of his work, see
http://hcbss.stanford.edu/research/projects/sztp/index.html [accessed 10.03.09].

For a study of contemporary Japanese Buddhism:
Covell 2005.

For a contemporary view of Japanese Zen:
Suzuki, Shunryu. 1973. *Zen Mind, Beginner's Mind*. New York: Weatherhill.

For a Western approach to Zen, see for instance works by Charlotte Joko Beck, such as Beck 1989.

Chapter 12: The Mahayana Today
Useful articles on modern developments within Buddhism (not only Mahayana):
Heine, Steven and Prebish, Charles S. (eds). 2003. *Buddhism in the Modern World: Adaptations of an Ancient Tradition*. New York: Oxford University Press.
Prebish, Charles S., and Baumann, Martin (eds). 2002. *Westward Dharma: Buddhism Beyond Asia*. Berkeley: University of California Press.

For a range of articles on Engaged Buddhist initiatives:
Queen, Christopher S. (ed.). 2000. *Engaged Buddhism in the West*. Boston: Wisdom Publications.
Queen, Christopher S., and King, Sallie B. (eds). 1996. *Engaged Buddhism: Buddhist Liberation Movements in Asia*. Albany: State University Press of New York.

For other developments:
The Amida Trust
    http://www.amidatrust.com/index.html [accessed 09.03.09].
Friends of the Western Buddhist Order
    http://www.fwbo.org [accessed 10.03.09].
Soka Gakkai International
    http://www.sgi.org [accessed 10.03.09].

Other Resources
An exceptional online resource for Buddhist art is the Huntington Archive
    http://kaladarshan.arts.ohio-state.edu/ [accessed 10.03.09].

Works Cited

Books and articles

Abe Ryūichi. 1995. Saichō and Kūkai: A Conflict of Interpretations. *Japanese Journal of Religious Studies* 22(1–2): 103–37.

--------. 2000. *The Weaving of Mantra: Kūkai and the Construction of Esoteric Buddhist Discourse* (new edn). New York: Columbia University Press.

Addiss, Stephen. 1989. *The Art of Zen: Paintings and Calligraphy by Japanese Monks, 1600–1925.* New York: Abrams.

Adolphson, Mikael S. 2007. *The Teeth and Claws of the Buddha: Monastic Warriors and Sohei in Japanese History.* Honolulu: University of Hawaii Press.

Ahn, Kye-hyŏn. 1989. Introduction of Buddhism to Korea. In Lancaster, Lewis R., and Yu, C.S. (eds). *Introduction of Buddhism to Korea: New Cultural Patterns.* Berkeley: Asian Humanities Press.

Anacker, Stefan. 1984. *Seven Works of Vasubandhu: The Buddhist Psychological Doctor.* Delhi. Motilal Banarsidass.

Andrews, Allan A. 1987. The "Senchakushu" in Japanese Religious History: The Founding of a Pure Land School. *Journal of the American Academy of Religion* 55(3): 473–99.

Andrews, Allan A. 1993. Lay and Monastic Forms of Pure Land Devotionalism: Typology and History. *Numen* 40: 16–36.

Asai, Endō. 1999. Nichiren Shōnin's View of Humanity: The Final Dharma Age and the Three Thousand Realms in One Thought-Moment. *Japanese Journal of Religious Studies* 26(3–4): 239–59.

Bandō, Shōjun. 1971. Shinran's Indebtedness to T'an-luan. *The Eastern Buddhist* 4(1): 72–87, reprinted in 2000. Pacific World 2: 17–30.

Baroni, Helen J. 2000. *Ōbaku Zen: The Emergence of the Third Sect of Zen in Tokugawa Japan.* Honolulu: University of Hawaii Press.

Batchelor, Martine. 2004. *The Path of Compassion: The Bodhisattva Precepts, the Chinese Brahma's Net Sutra.* Walnut Creek: Altamira Press.

Baumann, Martin. 2002. Protective Amulets and Awareness Techniques, or How to Make Sense of Buddhism in the West. In Prebish, Charles S., and Baumann, Martin (eds). *Westward Dharma: Buddhism Beyond Asia.* Berkeley: University of California Press.

Beck, Charlotte Joko. 1989. *Everyday Zen.* London: Thorsons.

Benn, James A. 1998. Where Text Meets Flesh: Burning the Body as an Apocryphal Practice in Chinese Buddhism. *History of Religions* 37(4): 295–322.

Benn, James A. 2007. *Burning for the Buddha: Self-immolation in Chinese Buddhism.* Honolulu: University of Hawaii Press.

Berkeley, George. 1710. *A Treatise Concerning the Principles of Human Knowledge.*

Best, Jonathan. W. 2005. Paekche and the Incipiency of Buddhism in Japan. In Robert E. Buswell Jr. (ed.). *Currents and Countercurrents: Korean Influences on the East Asian Buddhist Traditions.* Honolulu: University of Hawaii Press.

Bielefeldt, Carl, and Lancaster, Lewis R. 1975. T'an Ching (Platform Scripture). *Philosophy East and West* 25(2): 197–212.

Birnbaum, Raoul. 2003a. Buddhist China at the Century's Turn. *China Quarterly* 174: 428–50.

Birnbaum, Raoul. 2003b. *The Healing Buddha* (rev. edn). Boulder: Shambhala.

Bloom, Alfred. 1968. The Life of Shinran Shōnin: The Journey to Self Acceptance. *Numen* 15(1): 1–62.

Blum, Mark L. 2002. *The Origins and Development of Pure Land Buddhism: A Study and Translation of Gyonen's Jodō Hōmon Genrushō*. New York: Oxford University Press.

Bodhicaryavatara *see* Santideva.

Bodiford, William M. 1992. Zen in the Art of Funerals: Ritual Salvation in Japanese Buddhism. *History of Religions* 32(2): 146–64.

--------. 2005. Keizan. In Jones, Lindsay (ed). *Encyclopedia of Religion*, vol. 8 (2nd edn). Detroit: Macmillan Reference USA.

Bownas, Geoffrey and Thwaite, Anthony (trans. and eds). 1998. *Penguin Book of Japanese Verse* (rev. edn). London: Penguin.

Bradbury, Ray. 1953. *Fahrenheit 451*. New York: Ballantine.

Brook, Timothy. 2005. *The Chinese State in Ming Society*. London: Routledge.

Buswell Jr., Robert E. 1986. Chinul's Systematization of Chinese Meditative Techniques in Korean Sŏn Buddhism. In Gregory, Peter N. (ed.). *Traditions of Meditation in Chinese Buddhism*. Honolulu: Kuroda Institute, University of Hawaii Press.

--------. 1987. The "Short-cut" Approach of K'an-hua Meditation: The Evolution of a Practical Subitism in Chinese Ch'an Buddhism. In Gregory, Peter N. (ed.). *Sudden and Gradual: Approaches to Enlightenment in Chinese Thought*. Delhi: Motilal Banarsidass.

--------. 1989. *The Formation of Ch'an Ideology in China and Korea: The Vajrasamadhi Sutra, a Buddhist Apocryphon*. Princeton: Princeton University Press.

--------. 1990. *Chinese Buddhist Apocrypha*. Honolulu: University of Hawaii Press.

--------. 1991. *Tracing Back the Radiance: Chinul's Korean Way of Zen*. Honolulu: Kuroda Institute, University of Hawaii Press.

--------. 1992. *The Zen Monastic Experience: Buddhist Practice in Contemporary Korea*. Princeton: Princeton University Press.

--------. 1995. Hagiographies of the Korean Monk Wonhyo. In Lopez Jr., Donald S (ed.). *Buddhism in Practice*. Princeton: Princeton University Press.

--------. 1999. The Koryŏ Period. In Takeuchi Yoshinori et al. (eds). *Buddhist Spirituality: Later China, Korea, Japan, and the Modern World*. New York: Crossroad.

--------. (ed.). 2005. *Currents and Countercurrents: Korean Influences on the East Asian Buddhist Traditions*. Honolulu: University of Hawaii Press.

--------. 2007. *Cultivating Original Enlightenment: Wonhyo's Exposition of the Vajrasamādhi-Sūtra (Kumgang Sammaegyong Non)*. Honolulu: University of Hawaii Press.

Chadwick, David. 1999. *Crooked Cucumber: The Life and Zen Teachings of Shunryu Suzuki*. New York: Broadway Books.

Chan, Chih-wah. 1999. Chih-li (960–1028) and the Crisis of T'ien-t'ai Buddhism in the Early Sung. In Gregory, Peter N., and Getz Jr., Daniel A. (eds). 1999. *Buddhism in the Sung*. Honolulu: Kuroda Institute, University of Hawaii Press.

--------. 2005. The Korean Impact on T'ien-t'ai Buddhism in China: An Historical Analysis. In Robert E. Buswell Jr. (ed.). *Currents and Countercurrents: Korean Influences on the East Asian Buddhist Traditions*. Honolulu: University of Hawaii Press.

Chan, Yiu Kwan. 2008. Popular Buddhist Ritual in Contemporary Hong Kong: Shuilu Fahui, a Buddhist Rite for Saving All Sentient Beings of Water and Land. *Buddhist Studies Review* 25(1): 90–105.

Chandler, Stuart. 2004. *Establishing a Pure Land on Earth: The Foguang Buddhist Perspective on Modernization and Globalization*. Honolulu: University of Hawaii Press.

Chang, Garma C. 1991. *A Treasury of Mahayana Sutras: Selections from the Maharatnakuta Sutra*. Delhi: Motilal Banarsidass.

Chappell, David W. 1977. Chinese Buddhist Interpretations of the Pure Lands. In Saso, Michael, and Chappell, David W. (eds). *Buddhist and Taoist Studies I*. Honolulu: University of Hawaii Press.

--------. 1986. From Dispute to Dual Cultivation: Pure Land Responses to Ch'an Critics. In Gregory, Peter N. (ed.). *Traditions of Meditation in Chinese Buddhism*. Honolulu: Kuroda Institute, University of Hawaii Press.

--------. 1996. The Formation of the Pure Land Movement in China: Tao-ch'o and Shandao. In Foard, James et al. (eds). *The Pure Land Tradition: History and Development*. Berkeley: University of California.

Chen. Jinhua. 2006. Fazang (643–712) and Wuzhensi: With a Special Reference to his Daoist Ties. *Journal of the Royal Asiatic Society* 16(2): 179–97.

Cho, Eunsu. 2005. Wŏn'chŭk's place in the East Asian Buddhist Tradition. In Robert E. Buswell Jr. (ed.). *Currents and Countercurrents: Korean Influences on the East Asian Buddhist Traditions*. Honolulu: University of Hawaii Press.

Chung, Bongkil. 2003. Won Buddhism: The Historical Context of Sot'aesan's Reformation of Buddhism for the Modern World. In Heine, Steven, and Prebish, Charles S. (eds). *Buddhism in the Modern World: Adaptations of an Ancient Tradition*. New York: Oxford University Press.

Clarke, Peter Bernard. 2000. *Japanese New Religions: In Global Perspective*. London: Routledge.

Cleary, Thomas. 1993. *The Flower Ornament Scripture: A Translation of the Avatamsaka Sutra*. Boston: Shambala.

Cleary, Thomas, and Cleary, J.C. (trans). 1977. *The Blue Cliff Record*. Boston: Shambala.

Collcutt, Martin. 1981. *Five Mountains: The Rinzai Zen Monastic Institution in Medieval Japan*. Cambridge: Council on East Asian Studies, Harvard University.

--------. 1990. Zen and the Gozan. In Kozo Yamamura (ed.). *The Cambridge History of Japan*, vol. 3: Medieval Japan. Cambridge: Cambridge University Press.

--------. 2005. Eisai. In Jones, Lindsay (ed.). *Encyclopedia of Religion*, vol. 4 (2nd edn). Detroit: Macmillan Reference USA.

Conze, Edward. 1988. *Buddhist Wisdom Books: The Diamond Sutra and the Heart Sutra*. London: Unwin-Hyman.

--------. 1994. *The Perfection of Wisdom in Eight Thousand Lines and its Verse Summary*. Delhi: Sri Satguru Publications.

-------- et al. 1999. *Buddhist Texts Through the Ages*. Delhi: Motilal Banarsidass.

Corbin, Henry. 1997. *Alone with the Alone: Creative Imagination in the Sufism of Ibn Arabi*. Princeton: Princeton University Press.

--------. 1988. Shinran's Proofs of True Buddhism. In Lopez Jr., Donald S. (ed.). *Buddhist Hermeneutics*. Honolulu: Kuroda Institute, University of Hawaii Press.

--------. 1996. T'an-luan: The First Systematizer of Pure Land Buddhism. In Foard, James et al. (eds). *The Pure Land Tradition: History and Development*. Berkeley: University of California.

--------. 2000. The Enduring Significance of T'an-luan. *Pacific World* 2: 3–16.

Covell, Stephen G. 2005. *Japanese Temple Buddhism: Worldliness in a Religion of Renunciation*. Honolulu: University of Hawaii Press.

Crittenden, Charles. 1981. Everyday Reality as Fiction: A Madhyamika Interpretation, *Journal of Indian Philosophy* 9: 325–33.

Dobbins, James C. 1998. Envisioning Kamakura Buddhism. In Payne, Richard K. (ed.). *Re-Visioning "Kamakura" Buddhism*. Honolulu: University of Hawaii Press.

--------. 2002. *Jōdo Shinshū: Shin Buddhism in Medieval Japan*. Honolulu: University of Hawaii Press.

Donner, Neal. 1987. Sudden and Gradual Intimately Conjoined: Chih-i's T'ien T'ai View. In Gregory, Peter N. (ed.). *Sudden and Gradual: Approaches to Enlightenment in Chinese Thought*. Delhi: Motilal Banarsidass.

Emmerick, R.E. 1990. *The Sutra of Golden Light*. Oxford: Pali Text Society.

Faure, Bernard. 1987. The Daruma-shu, Dogen and Soto Zen. *Monumenta Nipponica* 42(1): 25–55.

--------. 1991. The *Rhetoric of Immediacy: A Cultural Critique of Chan/Zen Buddhism*. Princeton: Princeton University Press.

--------. 1996. *Visions of Power: Imagining Medieval Japanese Buddhism*. Princeton: Princeton University Press.

--------. 1998. *The Will to Orthodoxy: A Critical Genealogy of Northern Chan Buddhism*. Stanford: Stanford University Press.

--------. 2003. *The Power of Denial: Buddhism, Purity, and Gender*. Princeton: Princeton University Press.

Foard, James H. 1980. In Search of a Lost Reformation: A Reconsideration of Kamakura Buddhism. *Japanese Journal of Religious Studies* 7(4): 261–91.

Ford, James L. 2002. Jōkei and the Rhetoric of "Other-Power" and "Easy Practice" in Medieval Japanese Buddhism. *Japanese Journal of Religious Studies* 29(1–2): 67–106.

Foster, Nelson, and Shoemaker, Jack. 1996. *The Roaring Stream: A New Zen Reader*. Hopewell: Ecco Press.

Foulk, T. Griffith. 1993. Myth, Ritual, and Monastic Practice in Sung Ch'an Buddhism. In Ebrey, Patricia Buckley, and Gregory, Peter N. (eds). *Religion and Society in T'ang and Sung China*. Honolulu: University of Hawaii.

--------. 1999. Sung Controversies Concerning the "Separate Transmission" of Ch'an. In Gregory, Peter N., and Getz, Daniel A. (eds). 1999. *Buddhism in the Sung*. Honolulu: Kuroda Institute, University of Hawaii Press.

--------. 2008. Ritual in Japanese Zen Buddhism. In Heine, Steven, and Wright, Dale S. (eds). 2008. *Zen Ritual: Studies of Zen Theory in Practice*. Oxford: Oxford University Press.

Foulk, T. Griffith, and Sharf, Robert H. 2003. On the Ritual Use of Chan Portraiture in Medieval China. In Bernard Faure (ed.). *Chan Buddhism in Ritual Context*. London: RoutledgeCurzon.

Fox, Alan. 1992. Self-Reflection in the Sanlun Tradition: Madhyamika as the "Deconstructive Conscience of Buddhism". *Journal of Chinese Philosophy* 19: 1–24.

Garfield, Jay L. (trans.). 1995. *The Fundamental Verses of the Middle Way*. Oxford: Oxford University Press.

Getz Jr., Daniel A. 1999. T'ien-t'ai Pure Land Societies and the Creation of the Pure Land Patriarchate. In Gregory, Peter N., and Getz Jr., Daniel A., (eds). *Buddhism in the Sung*. Honolulu: Kuroda Institute, University of Hawaii Press.

--------. 2004. Shengchang's Pure Conduct Society and the Chinese Pure Land Patriarchate. In Payne, Richard K., and Tanaka, Kenneth K. (eds). *Approaching the Land of Bliss: Religious Praxis in the Cult of Amitābha*. Honolulu: Kuroda Institute, University of Hawaii Press.

Gimello, Robert M. 1983. Li T'ung Hsüan and the Practical Dimensions of Hua-yen. In Gimello, Robert M., and Gregory, Peter N. (eds). 1983. *Studies in Ch'an and Hua-yen*. Honolulu: Kuroda Institute, University of Hawaii Press.

Glassman, Bernie. 1998. *Bearing Witness: A Zen Master's Lessons in Making Peace*. New York: Bell Tower.

Gombrich, Richard F. 2006. *Theravāda Buddhism: A Social History from Ancient Benares to Modern Colombo* (2nd edn). London: Routledge.

Gomez, Luis O. 1996. *The Land of Bliss: The Paradise of the Buddha of Measureless Light*. Honolulu: University of Hawaii Press.

Grayson, James Huntley. 2002. *Korea: A Religious History* (rev. edn). London: RoutledgeCurzon.

Gregory, Peter N. (ed.). 1987. *Sudden and Gradual: Approaches to Enlightenment in Chinese Thought*. Delhi: Motilal Banarsidass.

--------. 1991. *Tsung-mi and the Sinification of Buddhism*. Princeton: Princeton University Press.

--------. 1999. The Vitality of Buddhism in the Sung. In Gregory, Peter N., and Getz Jr., Daniel A., (eds). *Buddhism in the Sung*. Honolulu: Kuroda Institute, University of Hawaii Press.

Gregory, Peter N., and Ebrey, Patricia Buckley. 1993. The Religious and Historical Landscape. In Ebrey, Patricia Buckley, and Gregory, Peter N. (eds). *Religion and Society in T'ang and Sung China*. Honolulu: University of Hawaii.

Griffiths, Paul J. 1994. *On Being Buddha: The Classical Doctrine of Buddhahood*. Albany: State University of New York Press.

Groner, Paul. 1997. *Ryōgen and Mount Hiei: Japanese Tendai in the Tenth Century*. Honolulu: University of Hawaii Press.

--------. 2001a. Icons and Relics in Eison's Religious Activities. In Sharf, Robert H., and Sharf, Elizabeth Horton (eds). *Living Images: Japanese Buddhist Icons in Context*. Stanford: Stanford University Press.

--------. 2001b. Saichō: *The Establishment of the Japanese Tendai School* (new edn). Honolulu: University of Hawaii Press.

--------. 2005. Tradition and Innovation: Eison's Self-Ordinations and the Establishment of New Orders of Buddhist Practitioners. In Bodiford, William M. (ed.). *Going Forth: Visions of Buddhist Vinaya*. Honolulu: University of Hawaii Press.

Gross, Rita M. 2001. Women in Buddhism. In Harvey, Peter (ed.). *Buddhism*. London: Continuum.

Grosnick, William H. 1995. The Tathagatagarbha Sutra. In Lopez Jr., Donald S (ed.). *Buddhism in Practice*. Princeton: Princeton University Press.

Gyamtso, Khenpo Tsultrim. 1988. *Progressive Stages of Meditation on Emptiness*. Oxford: Longchen Foundation.

Gyatso, Geshe Kelsang. 2007. *Meaningful to Behold: Becoming a Friend of the World* (rev. edn). Ulverston: Tharpa Publications.

Habito, Ruben L.F. 1995. The Logic of Nonduality and Absolute Affirmation: Deconstructing Tendai Hongaku Writings. *Japanese Journal of Religious Studies* 22 (1–2): 83–101.

Hakeda, Yoshito S. 2006. *The Awakening of Faith*. New York: Columbia University Press.

Hallisey, Charles, and Keown, Damien. 2007. Nikaya Buddhism, In Keown, Damien, and Prebish, Charles S. (editors). *Encyclopedia of Buddhism*. London: Routledge.

Hardacre, Helen. 1984. *Lay Buddhism in Contemporary Japan: Reiyūkai Kyōdan*. Princeton: Princeton University Press.

Harrison, Paul. 1978. Buddhanusmrti in the Pratyutpanna-Buddha-Sammukhavasthita-Samadhi-Sutra. *Journal of Indian Philosophy* 6: 35–57.

--------. 1987. Who Gets to Ride in the Great Vehicle? Self-Image and Identity among the Followers of the Early Mahayana. *Journal of the International Association of Buddhist Studies* 10(1): 167–89.

--------. 1995. Searching For the Origins of the Mahayana: What Are We Looking For? *The Eastern Buddhist* 28(1): 48–69.

--------. 2000. Manjusri and the Cult of the Celestial Bodhisattvas. *Chung-Hwa Buddhist Journal* 13(2): 157–93.

Harvey, Peter. 2007. Buddhas, Past and Future. In Keown, Damien, and Prebish, Charles S. (eds). *Encyclopedia of Buddhism*. London: Routledge.

Hayes, Richard. 1994. Nāgārjuna's Appeal. *Journal of Indian Philosophy* 22(4): 299–378.

--------. 2007. Yogacara School. In Keown, Damien, and Prebish, Charles S. (eds). *Encyclopedia of Buddhism*. London: Routledge.

Heelas, Paul et al. 2005. *The Spiritual Revolution: Why Religion is Giving Way to Spirituality*. Oxford: Blackwell Publishing.

Heine, Steven. 2005. Zen. In Jones, Lindsay (ed.). *Encyclopedia of Religion*, vol. 14 (2nd edn). Detroit: Macmillan Reference USA.

Hirakawa, Akira. 1990. *A History of Indian Buddhism: From Sakyamuni to Early Mahayana*. Paul Groner (trans. and ed.). Honolulu: University of Hawaii.

Hirota, Dennis. 1986. *No Abode: The Record of Ippen*. Kyoto: Ryukoku University.

Hōnen. 1998. *Hōnen's Senchakushū: Passages on the Selection of the Nembutsu in the Original Vow*. Senchakushū English Translation Project (trans.). Honolulu: Kuroda Institute, University of Hawaii Press.

Hopkirk, Peter. 2006. *Foreign Devils on the Silk Road: The Search for Lost Cities and Treasures of Chinese Central Asia*. London: John Murray.

Hsieh, Ding-Hwa E. 1999. Images of Women in Ch'an Buddhist Literature of the Sung Period. In Gregory, Peter N., and Getz Jr., Daniel A. (eds). 1999. *Buddhism in the Sung*. Honolulu: University of Hawaii Press.

Hsing Yun. 2003. *Humanistic Buddhism: A Blueprint for Life*. Hacienda Heights: Buddha's Light Publishing.

Hua, H. 1974. *Sutra of the Past Vows of Earth Store Bodhisattva*. New York: Institute for Advanced Studies of World Religion.

Hubbard, Jamie. 2001. *Absolute Delusion, Perfect Buddhahood: The Rise and Fall of a Chinese Heresy*. Honolulu: University of Hawaii Press.

Hubbard, Jamie, and Swanson, Paul Loren (eds). 1997. *Pruning the Bodhi Tree: The Storm over Critical Buddhism*. Honolulu: University of Hawaii Press.

Hughes, Aaron. 2002. Imagining the Divine: Ghazali on Imagination, Dreams, and Dreaming. *Journal of the American Academy of Religion* 70(1): 33–53.

Huntington, C.W. 1983. The System of the Two Truths in the Prasannapada and the Madhyamakavatara: A Study in Madhyamika Soteriology. *Journal of Indian Philosophy* 11: 77–106.

--------. 1989. *The Emptiness of Emptiness: An Introduction to Early Indian Madhyamika*. Honolulu: University of Hawaii Press.

Huntington, Susan L. 1990. Early Buddhist Art and the Theory of Aniconism. *Art Journal* 49(4): 401–8.

Hurvitz, Leon (trans). 1976. *Scripture of the Lotus Blossom of the Fine Dharma*. New York: Columbia University Press.

Ingram, Paul O. 1971. Shinran Shōnin and Martin Luther: A Soteriological Comparison. *Journal of the American Academy of Religion* 39: 430–47.

Jaffe, Paul D. 1986. Rising from the Lotus: Two Bodhisattvas from the Lotus Sutra as a Psychodynamic Paradigm for Nichiren. *Japanese Journal of Religious Studies* 13(1): 81–105.

Jaffe, Richard. 2002. *Neither Monk Nor Layman: Clerical Marriage in Modern Japanese Buddhism*. Princeton: Princeton University Press.

Japanese Journal of Religious Studies. 1989. Special issue: Shugendō and Mountain Religion in Japan 16(2–3).

Jones, Charles B. 1999. *Buddhism in Taiwan: Religion and the State, 1660–1990*. Honolulu: University of Hawaii Press.

--------. 2000. Taiwan. In Johnston, William M., and Dearborn, Fitzroy (eds). *Encyclopedia of Monasticism*. London: Routledge.

Jorgensen, John. 2000. Korea: Recent Changes. In Johnston, William M. (ed.). *Encyclopedia of Monasticism*. London: Routledge.

Kan'no, Hiroshi. 2001. The Reception of Lotus Sūtra Thought in China. *Journal of Oriental Studies* 11: 106–22.

Kay, David N. 2004. *Tibetan and Zen Buddhism in Britain: Transplantation, Development, and Adaptation.* London: RoutledgeCurzon.

Keel, Hee-Sung. 2005. Korea. In Robert E. Buswell Jr. (ed.). *Currents and Countercurrents: Korean Influences on the East Asian Buddhist Traditions.* Honolulu: University of Hawaii Press.

Keenan, John (trans.). 2003. *The Summary of the Great Vehicle* (rev. 2nd edn). Berkeley: Numata Center for Buddhist Translation & Research.

Kenny, Anthony (ed.). 1994. *The Wittgenstein Reader.* Oxford: Blackwell.

Keown, Damien. 1992. The *Nature of Buddhist Ethics.* London: Macmillan.

Keyworth, George A. 2003. Confucianism and Buddhism. In Buswell Jr., Robert E. (ed.). *Encyclopedia of Buddhism,* vol. 1. New York: Macmillan Reference USA.

Kieschnick, John. 1997. *The Eminent Monk: Buddhist Ideals in Mediaeval Chinese Hagiography.* Honolulu: Kuroda Institute, University of Hawaii Press.

--------. 2003. *The Impact of Buddhism on Chinese Material Culture.* Princeton and Oxford: Princeton University Press.

Kim, Hee-Jin. 2004. *Eihei Dōgen: Mystical Realist* (rev. edn). Boston: Wisdom Publications.

King, Richard. 1994. Early Yogacara and its Relationship with the Madhyamaka School. *Philosophy East and West* 44(4): 659–83.

--------. 2000. *Indian Philosophy: An Introduction to Hindu and Buddhist Thought.* New Delhi: Maya and Edinburgh University Press.

Kinnard, Jacob N. 1999. *Imaging Wisdom: Seeing and Knowing in the Art of Indian Buddhism.* London: RoutledgeCurzon.

Klokke, Marijke J. et al. 2003. *Worshipping Siva and Buddha: The Temple Art of East Java.* Honolulu: University of Hawaii Press.

Kodera, Takashi James. 1980. *Dogen's Formative Years in China: An Historical Study and Annotated Translation of the Hōkyō-ki.* London: Routledge Kegan Paul.

Kongtrul, Jamgon. 1993. *The Great Path of Awakening: An Easily Accessible Introduction for Ordinary People.* Ken McLeod (trans.). Boston: Shambhala.

-------- et al. 2000. *Buddha Nature: The Mahayana Uttaratantra Shastra with Commentary.* Rosemary Fuchs (trans.). Ithaca: Snow Lion Publications.

LaFleur, William R. 1994. *Liquid Life: Abortion and Buddhism in Japan.* Princeton: Princeton University Press.

Lancaster, Lewis R. 1988. Maitreya in Korea. In Sponberg, Alan, and Hardacre, Helen (eds). *Maitreya, the Future Buddha.* Cambridge: Cambridge University Press.

--------. 1989. The Rock-Cut Canon in China: Findings at Fang-Shan. In Skorupski, Tadeusz (ed). *The Buddhist Heritage.* Tring: Institute of Buddhist Studies.

Lee, Young-ho. 1995. The Ideal Mirror of the Three Religions (Samga Kwigam) of Ch'ŏnghŏ Hyujŏng. *Buddhist-Christian Studies* 15: 139–87.

Leggett, Trevor (trans.). 1960. *A First Zen Reader.* Rutland: Tuttle.

Leighton, Taigen Dan. 2008. Zazen as an Enactment Ritual. In Heine, Steven, and Wright, Dale S. (eds.). *Zen Ritual: Studies of Zen Theory in Practice.* Oxford: Oxford University Press.

Levering, Miriam. 1999. Miao-tao and Her Teacher Ta-hui. In Gregory, Peter N., and Getz Jr., Daniel A. (eds). *Buddhism in the Sung.* Honolulu: Kuroda Institute, University of Hawaii Press.

Lewis, C.S. 1950. *The Lion, the Witch, and the Wardrobe.* London: HarperCollins.

Liu, Xinru. 1988. *Ancient India and Ancient China: Trade and Religious Exchanges: AD 1– 600.* Oxford: Oxford University Press.

Lokaksema et al. (trans.) 2006. *The Pratyutpanna Samadhi Sutra and the Surangama Samadhi Sutra* (new edn). Berkeley: Numata Center for Buddhist Translation & Research.

Luk, Charles (trans.). 1988. *Empty Cloud: The Autobiography of the Chinese Zen Master Xu Yun.* Shaftesbury: Element Books.

Machida, Sōhō. 1999. *Renegade Monk: Hōnen and Japanese Pure Land Buddhism.* Berkeley: University of California Press.

MacQueen, Graeme. 1981. Inspired Speech in Early Mahayana Buddhism I. *Religion* 11: 303–19.

--------. 1982. Inspired Speech in Early Mahayana Buddhism II. *Religion* 12: 49–65.

MacWilliams, Mark W. 1997. Temple Myths and the Popularization of Kannon Pilgrimage in Japan: A Case Study of Ōya-ji on the Bandō Route. *Japanese Journal of Religious Studies* 24 (3–4): 375–411.

Macy, Joanna. 2007. *World as Lover, World as Self.* Berkeley: Parallax Press.

Marcure, Kenneth A. 1985. The Danka System. *Monumenta Nipponica* 40(1): 39–67.

Matsunaga, Alicia, and Matsunaga, Daigan. 1976. *Foundations of Japanese Buddhism*, vol. 2. Tokyo: Buddhist Books International.

Matsunaga, Daigan, and Matsunaga, Alice. 1974. *Foundation of Japanese Buddhism*, vol. 1. Tokyo: Buddhist Books International.

Matsuo, Kenji. 1997. What is Kamakura New Buddhism? Official Monks and Reclusive Monks. *Japanese Journal of Religious Studies* 24(1–2): 179–89.

--------. 2007 *A History of Japanese Buddhism.* Folkestone: Global Oriental.

McBride II, Richard D. 2008. *Domesticating the Dharma: Buddhist Cults and the Hwaŏm Synthesis in Silla Korea.* Honolulu: University of Hawaii.

McCallum, Donald F. 1995. *Zenkōji and Its Icon: A Study in Medieval Japanese Religious Art.* Princeton: Princeton University Press.

--------. 1998. Orality, Writing, and Authority in South Asian Buddhism: Visionary Literature and the Struggle for Legitimacy in the Mahayana. *History of Religions* 37(3): 249–74.

McMahan, David L. 2002. Repackaging Zen for the West. In Prebish, Charles S., and Baumann, Martin (eds). *Westward Dharma: Buddhism Beyond Asia.* Berkeley: University of California Press.

--------. 2008. *The Making of Buddhist Modernism.* Oxford: Oxford University Press.

McMullin Neil. 1984. *Buddhism and the State in Sixteenth-Century Japan.* Princeton: Princeton University Press.

McNair, Amy. 2007. *Donors of Longmen: Faith, Politics, and Patronage in Medieval Chinese Buddhist Sculpture.* Honolulu: University of Hawaii Press.

McRae, John R. 1986. *The Northern School and the Formation of Early Ch'an Buddhism.* Honolulu: Kuroda Institute, University of Hawaii Press.

--------. 1992. Encounter Dialogue and the Transformation of the Spiritual Path in Chinese Ch'an. In Buswell Jr., Robert E., and Gimello, Robert M. (eds). *Paths to Liberation: The Marga and its Transformations in Buddhist Thought.* Honolulu: Kuroda Institute, University of Hawaii Press.

--------. 2003. *Seeing Through Zen: Encounter, Transformation, and Genealogy in Chinese Chan Buddhism.* Berkeley: University of California Press.

--------. 2005a. Chan. In Jones, Lindsay (ed.). *Encyclopedia of Religion*, vol 3 (2nd edn). Detroit: Macmillan Reference USA.

--------. 2005b. Daoxuan's Vision of Jetavana: The Ordination Platform Movement in Medieval Chinese Buddhism. In Bodiford, William M. (ed.). *Going Forth: Visions of Buddhist Vinaya.* Honolulu: University of Hawaii Press.

Metraux, Daniel A. 1996. The Soka Gakkai: Buddhism and the Creation of a Harmonious and Peaceful Society. In Queen, Christopher S., and King, Sallie B. (eds). *Engaged Buddhism: Buddhist Liberation Movements in Asia.* Albany: State University of New York Press.

Ming-Wood, Liu. 1993. A Chinese Madhyamaka Theory of Truth: The Case of Chi-Tsang. *Philosophy East and West* 43(4): 649–73.

Mizuno, Kōgen. 1982. Buddhist Sutras: Origin, Development, Transmission. Tokyo: Kōsei.

Mohr, Michael. 1999. Hakuin. In Takeuchi Yoshinori et al. (eds). *Buddhist Spirituality: Later China, Korea, Japan, and the Modern World*. New York: Crossroad.

Morrell, Robert E. 1987. *Kamakura Buddhism: A Minority Report*. Berkeley: Asian Humanities Press.

Nagao, Gadjin. 1991. *Madhyamika and Yogacara*. Albany: State University of New York Press.

Nagapriya. 2004. *Exploring Karma and Rebirth*. Birmingham: Windhorse Publications.

Nattier, Jan. 1991. *Once Upon a Future Time: Studies in a Buddhist Prophecy of Decline*. Berkeley: Asian Humanities Press.

--------. 2003. *A Few Good Men: The Bodhisattva Path According to the Inquiry of Ugra (Ugrapariprcchā)*. Honolulu: University of Hawaii.

Ng, Zhiru. 2007. *The Making of a Savior Bodhisattva: Dizang in Medieval China*. Honolulu: University of Hawaii Press.

Nishijima, Gudo Wafe, and Cross, Choto (trans.). 1994–9. *Master Dōgen's Shōbōgenzō* (4 vols). Tokyo: Windbell Publications.

Orzech, Charles. 1996. Saving the Burning Mouth Hungry Ghost. In Lopez Jr., Donald S. (ed.). *Religions of China in Practice*. Princeton: Princeton University Press.

Overmyer, Daniel L. 1976. *Folk Buddhist Religion: Dissenting Sects in Late Traditional China*. Cambridge: Harvard University Press.

Packer, Toni. 2007. *The Silent Question: Meditating in the Stillness of Not Knowing*. Boston: Shambhala.

Padmakara Translation Group (trans.). 2005. *The Adornment of the Middle Way: Shantarakshita's Madhyamakalankara* with Commentary by Jamgon Mipham. Boston: Shambhala.

Pagel, Ulrich. 2001. The Sacred Writings of Buddhism. In Harvey, Peter (ed.). 2001. *Buddhism*. London: Continuum.

Park, Sung-Bae. 1983. *Buddhist Faith and Sudden Enlightenment*. Albany: State University of New York Press.

--------. 1999. Silla Buddhist Spirituality. In Takeuchi Yoshinori et al. (eds). *Buddhist Spirituality: Later China, Korea, Japan, and the Modern World*. New York: Crossroad.

Pas, Julian. 1995. *Visions of Sukhavati: Shan-tao's Commentary on the Kuan Wu-Liang-Shou-Fo-Ling*. Albany: State University of New York Press.

Paul, Diana. 1979. The Concept of Tathagatagarbha in the Srimaladevi Sutra (Sheng-man ching*), Journal of the American Oriental Society* 99(2): 191–203.

Pittman, Donald A. 2001. *Toward a Modern Chinese Buddhism: Taixu's Reforms*. Honolulu: University of Hawaii Press.

Poceski, Mario. 2000. Chan Rituals of the Abbots' Ascending the Dharma Hall to Preach. In Heine, Stephen, and Wright, Dale S. (eds). *The Koan: Texts and Contexts in Zen Buddhism*. New York: Oxford University Press.

Powers, John. 1994. *An Introduction to Tibetan Buddhism*. Ithaca: Snow Lion Publications.

--------. 1995. The Wisdom of Buddha: Samdhinirmocana Mahayana Sutra. Berkeley: Dharma Publishing.

Price, A.F., and Wong Mou-Lam. 1990. *The Diamond Sutra and the Sutra of Hui-Neng*, Boston: Shambhala.

Pye, Michael. 2002. Won Buddhism as a Korean New Religion. *Numen* 49: 113–41.

--------. 2003. *Skilful Means: a Concept in Mahayana Buddhism* (2nd edn). London: Routledge.

Queen. Christopher S. 2000. Introduction: A New Buddhism. In Queen, Christopher S. (ed.). 2000. *Engaged Buddhism in the West*. Boston: Wisdom Publications.

Reader, Ian. 1991. *Religion in Contemporary Japan*. Basingstoke: Macmillan.

Reader, Ian, and Tanabe, George J. 1998. *Practically Religious: Worldy Benefits and the Common Religion of Japan*. Honolulu: University of Hawaii Press.

Reischauer, Edwin O. 1955. *Ennin's Travels in T'ang China*. New York: Ronald Press.

Rhodes, Robert F. 1987. The *Kaihōgyō* Practice of Mt. Hiei. *Japanese Journal of Religious Studies* 14(2–3): 185–202.

Riggs, Diana E. 2004. *Fukudenkai:* Sewing the Buddha's Robe in Contemporary Japanese Buddhist Practice. *Japanese Journal of Religious Studies* 31(2): 311–56.

Rogers, Minor, and Rogers, Ann. 1991. *Rennyo: The Second Founder of Shin Buddhism: With a Translation of His Letters*. Berkeley: Asian Humanities Press.

Ruppert, Brian O. 2005. Buddhism: Buddhism in Japan. In Jones, Lindsay (ed.). *Encyclopedia of Religion,* vol. 2 (2nd edn). Detroit: Macmillan Reference USA.

Samuels, Jeffrey. 1997. The Bodhisattva Ideal in Theravada Buddhist Theory and Practice: A Reevaluation of the Bodhisattva-Sravaka Opposition. *Philosophy East and West* 47(3): 399–415.

Sanford, James A. 2004. Amida's Secret Life: Kakuban's Amida hishaku. In Payne, Richard K., and Tanaka, Kenneth K. (eds). *Approaching the Land of Bliss: Religious Praxis in the Cult of Amitābha*. Honolulu: University of Hawaii Press.

Sangharakshita. 1987. *A Survey of Buddhism*. London: Tharpa.

--------. 1991. *15 Points for New — and Old — Order Members: Bhante's Concluding Remarks at Guhyaloka 1988*. Norwich: Padmaloka Books

--------. 1995. *Transforming Self and World: Themes from the Sutra of Golden Light*. Birmingham: Windhorse Publications.

--------. 1999. *The Bodhisattva Ideal: Wisdom and Compassion in Buddhism*. Birmingham: Windhorse Publications.

--------. 2005. *The Ten Pillars of Buddhism* (rev. edn). Birmingham: Windhorse Publications.

Santideva. 1995. *The Bodhicaryavatara*. Kate Crosby and Andrew Skilton (trans.). Oxford: Oxford University Press.

Schopen, Gregory. 1975. The phrase "sa pṛthvīpradeśaś caityabhūto bhavet" in *The Vajracchedikā*: Notes on the cult of the book in Mahāyāna. *Indo-Iranian Journal* 17: 147–81.

--------. 1997. *Bones, Stones, and Buddhist Monks: Collected papers on the archaeology, epigraphy, and texts of monastic Buddhism in India*. Honolulu: University of Hawaii Press.

--------. 1999. The Bones of a Buddha and the Business of a Monk: Conservative Monastic Values in an Early Mahayana Polemical Tract. *Journal of Indian Philosophy* 27: 279–324.

--------. 2000. The Mahayana and the Middle Period in Indian Buddhism: Through a Chinese Looking-Glass. *The Eastern Buddhist* 32(2): 1–25.

--------. 2003. Mahayana. In Buswell Jr., Robert E. (ed.). *Encyclopedia of Buddhism,* vol. 2. New York: Macmillan Reference USA.

--------. 2005. *Figments and Fragments of Mahayana Buddhism in India*, Honolulu: University of Hawaii.

Schlütter, Morten. 2005. Vinaya Monasteries, Public Abbacies, and State Control of Buddhism under the Song (960–1279). In Bodiford, William M. (ed.). *Going Forth: Visions of Buddhist Vinaya*. Honolulu: University of Hawaii Press.

Sekida, Katsuki (trans). 2005. *Two Zen Classics: The Gateless Gate and the Blue Cliff Records*. Boulder: Shambhala.

Self, Will. 2007. *The Book of Dave: A Revelation of the Recent Past and the Distant Future*. London: Penguin.

Sen, Tansen. 2004. *Buddhism, Diplomacy and Trade: The Realignment of Sino-Indian Relations (600–1400)* (new edn). Delhi: Manohar.

Shakespeare. *Julius Caesar.*

Sharf, Robert H. 2001. Prolegomenon to the Study of Japanese Icons. In Sharf, Robert H., and Sharf, Elizabeth Horton (eds). *Living Images: Japanese Buddhist Icons in Context.* Stanford: Stanford University Press.

--------. 2002a. *Coming to Terms with Chinese Buddhism: A Reading of the Treasure Store Treatise.* Honolulu: Kuroda Institute, University of Hawaii.

--------. 2002b. On Pure Land Buddhism and Ch'an/Pure Land Syncretism in Medieval China. *T'oung Po* 88: 282–331.

Shaw, R.D.M., and Schiffer, Wilhelm. 1957. Yasen Kanna: A Chat on a Boat in the Evening. *Monumenta Nipponica* 13(1–2): 108–9.

Shaw, Sarah (trans.). 2006. *The Jatakas: Birth Stories of the Bodhisatta.* London: Penguin.

Sheng-yen. 2005. *Getting the Buddha Mind: On the Practice of Chan Retreat.* Berkeley: North Atlantic Books.

Shinran. 1997. *The Collected Works of Shinran* (2 vols). Hirota, Dennis et al (trans.). Kyoto: Hongwanji International Centre.

Silk, Jonathan A. 2002. What, If Anything, Is Mahayana Buddhism? Problems of Definitions and Classifications. *Numen* 49(4): 355–405.

Sonoda, Kōyū. 1993. Early Buddhist Worship. In Brown, Delmer M. (ed.). *Cambridge History of Japan, Vol. 1: Ancient Japan,* Cambridge: Cambridge University Press.

Sørensen, Henrik H. 1999. Buddhist Spirituality in Premodern and Modern Korea. In Takeuchi Yoshinori et al. (eds). *Buddhist Spirituality: Later China, Korea, Japan, and the Modern World.* New York: Crossroad.

Sponberg, Alan. 1981. The Trisvabhava Doctrine in India and China: A Study of Three Exegetical Models. *Ryukoku Daigaku Bukkyo Bunka Kenkyujo Kiyo* 21: 97–119.

--------. 1986. Meditation in Fa-hsiang Buddhism. In Gregory, Peter N. (ed.). *Traditions of Meditation in Chinese Buddism.* Honolulu: Kuroda Institute, University of Hawaii Press.

--------. 1996. TBMSG: A Dhamma Revolution in Contemporary India. In Queen, Christopher S., and King, Sallie B. (eds). *Engaged Buddhism: Buddhist Liberation Movements in Asia.* Albany: State University of New York Press.

--------. 2007a. Buddha-Fields and Pure Lands. In Keown, Damien, and Prebish, Charles S. (eds). *Encyclopedia of Buddhism.* London: Routledge.

--------. 2007b. Vimalakirti Nirdesa Sutra. In Keown, Damien, and Prebish, Charles S. (eds). *Encyclopedia of Buddhism.* London: Routledge.

Stevens, John. 1988a. *The Marathon Monks of Mount Hiei.* Boston: Shambhala.

Stevens, John (trans.). 1988b. *One Robe, One Bowl: The Zen Poetry of Ryōkan.* New York: Weatherhill

Stevenson, Daniel B. 1986. The Four Kinds of Samadhi in Early T'ien T'ai Buddhism. In Gregory, Peter N. (ed.). *Traditions of Meditation in Chinese Buddhism.* Honolulu: Kuroda Institute, University of Hawaii Press.

--------. 1999. Protocols of Power. In Gregory, Peter N., and Getz Jr., Daniel A., (eds). *Buddhism in the Sung,* Honolulu: Kuroda Institute, University of Hawaii Press.

Stone, Jacqueline. 1994. Rebuking the Enemies of the Lotus: Nichirenist Exclusivism in Historical Perspective. *Japanese Journal of Religious Studies* 21(2–3): 231–59.

--------. 1999. Placing Nichiren in the "Big Picture": Some Ongoing Issues in Scholarship. *Japanese Journal of Religious Studies* 26(3–4): 383–421.

Streng, Frederick J. (trans.). 1967. *Emptiness: A Study in Religious Meaning.* New York: Abingdon Press.

Suzuki, D.T. 1927. *Essays in Zen Buddhism* (First Series). London: Luzac.

--------. 1932. *The Lankavatara Sutra.* London: Routledge and Kegan Paul.

Swanson, Paul L. 1989. *Foundations of T'ien T'ai Philosophy: The Flowering of the Two Truths Theory in Chinese Buddhism.* Berkeley: Asian Humanities Press.

Tanaka, Kenneth K. 1990. *The Dawn of Chinese Pure Land Doctrine: Ching-ying Hui-yüan's Commentary on the Visualization Sutra*. Albany: State University of New York Press.

--------. 2004. Faith in Wonhyo's *Commentary on the Sutra of the Buddha of Immeasurable Life*: The Elevated Role of Faith over Contemplation and Its Implication for the Contribution of Korean Buddhism to the Development of Japanese Pure Land Buddhism. *Pacific World* 6: 45–6.

Teiser, Stephen. 1996. Introduction: The Spirits of Chinese Religions. In Lopez Jr., Donald S. (ed.). *Religions of China in Practice*. Princeton: Princeton University Press.

--------. 2005. Buddhism: Buddhism in China. In Jones, Lindsay (ed.). *Encyclopedia of Religion*, vol. 2 (2nd edn). Detroit: Macmillan Reference USA.

Thurman, Robert A.F. 1976. *The Holy Teaching of Vimalakīrti: A Mahāyāna Scripture*. University Park: Pennsylvania State University Press.

Topmiller, Robert J. 2006. *The Lotus Unleashed: The Buddhist Peace Movement in South Vietnam, 1964–1966* (new edn). Lexington: University Press of Kentucky.

Tweed, Thomas A. 2002. Who is a Buddhist? Night-stand Buddhists and Other Creatures. In Prebish, Charles S., and Baumann, Martin (eds). *Westward Dharma: Buddhism Beyond Asia*. Berkeley: University of California Press.

Vessantara. 2008a. *A Guide to the Bodhisattvas*. Cambridge: Windhorse Publications.

--------. 2008b. *A Guide to the Buddhas*. Cambridge: Windhorse Publications.

Vishvapani. 2001. *Introducing the Friends of the Western Buddhist Order* (rev. edn). Birmingham: Windhorse Publications.

Waddell, Norman, and Abe, Masao (trans.). 2002. *The Heart of Dogen's Shōbōgenzō*. Albany: State University of New York Press.

Waley, Arthur (trans.) 1973. *Monkey*. London: Penguin.

Wallace, B. Alan. 2002. 'The Spectrum of Buddhist Practice in the West. In Prebish, Charles S., and Baumann, Martin (eds). *Westward Dharma: Buddhism Beyond Asia*. Berkeley: University of California Press.

Warder, A.K. 2000. *Indian Buddhism*. Delhi: Motilal Banarsidass.

Warner, Jisho et al. (eds). 2001. *Nothing is Hidden: Essays on Zen Master Dōgen's Instructions for the Cook*. New York: Weatherhill.

Watt, Paul B. 1999. Kūkai. In Takeuchi, Yoshinori et al. (eds). *Buddhist Spirituality: Later China, Korea, Japan, and the Modern World*. New York: Crossroad.

Wayman, A., and Wayman, H. 1974. *The Lion's Roar of Queen Srimala*. New York: Columbia University Press.

Weinstein, Stanley. 1987. Chinese Buddhism. In Eliade, Mircea (ed.). *The Encyclopedia of Religion*, vol. 2. New York: Collier Macmillan.

--------. 1999. Aristocratic Buddhism. In Shively, Donald H., and McCullough, William H. (eds). *Cambridge History of Japan, Vol. 2: Heian Japan*. Cambridge: Cambridge University Press.

Welch, Holmes. 1968. *The Buddhist Revival in China*. Cambridge: Harvard University Press.

--------. 1972. *Buddhism Under Mao*. Cambridge: Harvard University Press.

Welter, Albert. 2000. Mahakasyapa's Smile: Silent Transmission and the Kung-an (Koan) Tradition. In Heine, Stephen, and Wright, Dale S. (eds). *The Koan: Texts and Contexts in Zen Buddhism*. New York: Oxford University Press.

--------. 2005. Zen Buddhism as the Ideology of the Japanese State: Eisai and the *Kōzen gokokuron*. In Heine, Steven, and Wright, Dale S. (eds). *Zen Classics: Formative Texts in the Zen Canon*. Oxford: Oxford University Press.

--------. 2008. *The Linji Lu and the Creation of Chan Orthodoxy: The Development of Chan's Records of Sayings Literature*. Oxford: Oxford University Press.

Williams, Paul. 2008. *Mahayana Buddhism: The Doctrinal Foundations* (2nd edn). London: Routledge.

Williams, Paul, with Tribe, Anthony. 2000. *Buddhist Thought: A Complete Introduction to the Indian Tradition*. London: Routledge.

Yamabe Nobuyoshi. 2005. Visionary Repentance and Visionary Ordination in the Brahma Net Sutra. In William M. Bodiford (ed.). *Going Forth: Visions of Buddhist Vinaya*. Honolulu: University of Hawaii Press.

Yampolsky, Philip B. 1971. *The Zen Master Hakuin: Selected Writings*. New York: Columbia University Press.

--------. 1990. *Selected Writings of Nichiren*. New York: Columbia University Press.

Yokoi, Yūhō, and Victoria, Daizen (trans. and eds). 1990. *Zen Master Dōgen: An Introduction with Selected Writings*. New York: Weatherhill.

Yu Chun-fang. 1981. *The Renewal of Buddhism in China: Chu-hung and the Late Ming Synthesis*. New York: Columbia University Press.

--------. 1998. Ming Buddhism. In Twitchett, Denis, and Mote, Frederick W. (eds). *The Cambridge History of China, Vol. 8: The Ming Dynasty (1368–1644), Part 2*. Cambridge: Cambridge University Press.

--------. 2001. *Kuan-yin: The Chinese Transformation of Avalokiteśvara*. New York: Columbia University Press.

Ziporyn, Brook. 2000. *Evil and/or/as the Good: Omnicentrism, Intersubjectivity and Value Paradox in Tiantai Buddhist Thought*. Harvard: Harvard University Press.

Zürcher, Erik. 1984. Beyond the Jade Gate: Buddhism in China, Vietnam and Korea. In Bechert, Heinz, and Gombrich, Richard (eds). *The World of Buddhism*. London: Thames & Hudson.

Online and film resources

http://www12.canvas.ne.jp/horai/contemplation-sutra.htm [accessed 08.03.09].
http://www.acmuller.net/articles/indigenoushermeneutics.htm [accessed 09.04.09].
http://www.acmuller.net/budkor/wonhyo-chinul-kihwa.htm [accessed 09.04.09]
http://www.acmuller.net/kor-bud/simmun_hwajaeng_non.html [accessed 09.04.09].
http://www.amidatrust.com/index.html [accessed 10.04.09].
http://www.cherihuber.com/index.html [accessed 10.04.09].
http://www.dassk.com/index.php [accessed 10.04.09].
http://www.dharmadrum.org/ [accessed 10.04.09].
http://www.fgs.org.tw/english/index/index.htm [accessed 10.04.09].
http://www.interbeing.org.uk/about/Order.html [accessed 10.04.09].
http://www.maitreyaproject.org [accessed 08.03.09].
http://www.nanzan-u.ac.jp/SHUBUNKEN/publications/publications.htm [accessed 05.04.09].
http://www.nirvanasutra.net [accessed 05.04.09].
http://www.obcon.org/ [accessed 10.04.09].
http://www.orderofdisorder.com/ [accessed 10.04.09].
http://www.orderofinterbeing.org/ [accessed 10.04.09].
http://www.rk-world.org/ [accessed 10.04.09].
http://www.rkhawaii.org/ [accessed 10.04.09].
http://scbs.stanford.edu/sztp3/translations/shobogenzo/sbgz_contents.html [accessed 10.04.09].
http://www.sgi.org [accessed 10.04.09].
http://www.shin-ibs.edu/academics/_pwj/three.two.php [accessed 09.04.09].
http://www.shinnyo-en.org/ [accessed 10.04.09]
http://www.springwatercenter.org/ [accessed 10.04.09].

http://www.springwatercenter.org/teachers/packer/ [accessed 10.04.09].

http://www.taleofgenji.org/my_saigoku_pilgrimage.html [accessed 29.03.09].

http://www.tzuchi.org.tw/ [accessed 10.04.09].

http://www.whiteplum.org/ [accessed 10.4.09].

http://www.zenpeacemakers.org/about/vision.htm [accessed 10.4.09].

http://www.zenpeacemakers.org/zps/ [accessed 10.4.09].

http://www.zenpeacemakers.org/zps/om.htm [accessed 10.4.09].

http://zen.rinnou.net/head_temples/index.html [accessed 10.04.09].

Legge, James (trans.). 2006. A Record of Buddhistic Kingdoms: Being an account by the Chinese monk Fa-hsien of travels in India and Ceylon (A.D. 399–414) in search of the Buddhist books of discipline. http://www.gutenberg.org/etext/2124 [accessed 08.03.09].

Marathon Monks of Mount Hiei. 2002. [DVD] Watertown: DER (dir C.J. Hayden).

Monkey. 2002. [DVD] London: Fabulous Films.

Muller, A. Charles. [no date]. East Asia's Unexplored Pivot of Metaphysics and Hermeneutics: Essence-Function/Interpenetration.
http://www.acmuller.net/articles/indigenoushermeneutics.htm
[accessed 09.04.09].

--------. 1995. The Key Operative Concepts in Korean Buddhist Syncretic Philosophy: Interpenetration and Essence-Function in Weonhyo, Chinul, and Kihwa. *Bulletin of Toyo Gakuen University* 3: 33–48, available at
http://www.acmuller.net/budkor/wonhyo-chinul-kihwa.htm [accessed 09.04.09].

Muller, Charles (trans). 2009. Ten Approaches to the Resolution of Doctrinal Disputes, by Wonhyo (*Simmun hwajaeng non*).
http://www.acmuller.net/kor-bud/simmun_hwajaeng_non.html [accessed 09.04.09].

Roscoe, Jared. [no date] Buddhism Under Vietnam's Thumb.
http://www.tricycle.com/web-exclusive/buddhism-under-vietnams-thumb
[accessed 09.04.09].

Index

Abhidharma, 12, 85, 86, 89, 94, 121
abhimukhi, 51, 56
achala, 51, 58
adhisthana, 67
Afghanistan, 25, 116, 214
Africa, 219
ahimsa. *See* non-harm
Akshobya, 67, 68
Alan Watts, 220
alaya-vijnana. *See* store consciousness
amala-vijnana. *See* immaculate
    consciousness
Ambedkar, Dr. B.R., 223
AMF, 112, 113, 114, 122, 160, 162,
    163
Amida, 21, 22, 69, 70, 81, 144, 184,
    185, 186, 189, 190ff, , 195, 207,
    222. *See also* Amitabha.
Amida Trust, 222
Amitabha, 68, 69, 70ff, 128, 144, 146,
    147, 149, 150ff, 158, 229
Amitayus, 70
Amitayur-dhyana-sutra. See
    Visualization Sutra
Amituo, 70, 144, 184. *See also*
    Amitabha
An Shigao, 119
anatman, 87, 89, 111
anicca, 87
Annen, 178
anuttarapuja, 47, 149
arcismati, 51, 54
arhat, 26, 27, 34, 35, 40, 42, 43, 44,
    53, 56, 59
Asanga, 101, 102, 106, 224
Ashoka, 25, 38
asraya-paravrtti. *See* revolution at the
    basis
Astasahasrika-prajnaparamita-sutra, 38
atman, 54, 86
Aung Sang Suu Kyi, 225
Australasia, 219
Avalokiteshvara, 40, 75, 76, 77, 128,
    158, 195, 217, 222
    Chenrezig, 75
    Guanyin, 77, 128, 217

Avalokiteshvara (cont.)
    Kannon, 77, 195
    Saikoku Kannon, 77
Awakening
    gradual, 27, 114, 126, 143, 165,
        166, 170, 203
    sudden, 113, 114, 115, 116, 123ff,
        129, 130, 133, 135, 137, 138, 139,
        141ff, 165, 166, 192, 203
Awakening of Mahayana Faith. See
    AMF
bala, 51, 58
Bashō, 195
Beastie Boys, 10
Benevolent King Sutra, 174
Berkeley, Bishop, 101
Beopseong-jong, 158
Bhaisajyaguru, 72, 73, 158
    Medicine Buddha, 68, 72, 73, 74
    Sangye Menla, 74
    Yaoshifo, 74
Bhaisajyaguru Sutra, 73
Bhavaviveka, 96, 98
bhumi, 42, 50ff
bija. *See* seed
Blue Cliff Record, 141
Bodhicaryavatara. See Guide to the
    Buddhist Path to Awakening
bodhichitta, 42, 46, 47, 48, 54, 88,
    113, 165
bodhisattva, 10, 13, 15, 17, 19, 29,
    34ff, 97, 98, 114, 123, 125, 128,
    149, 156, 159, 165, 174, 177, 183,
    186, 192, 195, 209, 217, 219, 222
bodhisattva ideal, 13, 35, 40, 42, 43,
    45, 59, 71, 72, 74, 133, 193, 212,
    220, 226, 229
bodhisattva path, 13, 30, 35, 44, 45,
    46, 51, 52, 54, 55, 56, 59
Borobudur, 37
Bradbury, Ray, 32
Brahma Net Sutra, 49, 177
Buddha's Light International
    Association, 216
buddha-field, 61, 66ff, 75, 78, 81
    Pure Land, 66, 70, 71, 72, 76, 77

buddha-field: Pure Land (cont.)
79, 144, 146ff, 184ff, 195, 201,
207, 209, 215, 229
buddhasektras. *See* buddha-field
Buddha-nature, 1, 11, 14, 68, 90, 97,
99, 100, 106ff, 123, 130, 131, 133,
143, 165, 166, 167, 203, 204, 208,
212, 218, 224
buddhanusmrti. *See* recollection of the
Buddha
Buddhas, various, 19
buddhavacana, 31, 33
Buddhist Association of the Republic of
China, 215
Burma, 8
Cambodia, 8
canon, 11, 12, 24, 31, 187
Buddhist, 29, 156, 168
Korean, 169
Mahayana, 11, 28, 33
Nikaya, 12, 51, 85
Pali, 9, 12, 65, 222
rock-cut, 39
Taishō shinshū daizōkyō, 33
Tripitika Koreanum, 169
Caodong, 144, 202
caves, 14, 28, 39
Central Asia, 5, 9, 14, 22, 23, 27, 28,
38, 71, 74, 75, 79, 116, 117, 119
Chan, 14, 15, 20, 55, 68, 79, 85, 98,
107, 114, 115, 117, 122, 128ff,
151ff, 161, 163, 165, 168, 177,
195, 196, 197, 200, 215, 216, 217,
229
Chandrakirti, 96, 97, 98
Chegwan, 129
Chenrezig. *See* Avalokiteshvara
Cheontae, 124, 129, 164
China, 1, 3, 5, 6, 9, 10, 14, 15, 20, 22,
23, 28, 33, 37, 38, 39, 49, 55, 67,
68, 70ff, 91, 98, 106, 107, 110,
112, 117ff, 157, 158, 159, 161,
162, 163, 164, 166, 168, 173, 177,
178, 196, 197, 198, 202, 213, 216
Chogye, 164, 168, 169, 170
Christianity, 10, 76, 155, 169, 213,
221
Ciji Gongde Hui, 216
cittamatra, 100, 101
Communism, 155, 171, 213, 215
compassion, 4, 7, 9, 11, 13, 15, 17, 18,
21, 25, 26, 29, 34, 35, 43, 48, 51,

compassion (cont,)
52, 53, 56ff, 61, 66, 67, 70, 75, 76,
80
concentration. *See* meditation
Confucianism, 114, 117, 119, 120,
121, 145, 153ff, 169, 170, 172
consciousness-only, 11
Dahui, 167, 168
daimoku, 207, 208, 209, 218
Dainichi nyorai. *See* Vairochana
dana. *See* generosity
danka system, 210
Daochuo, 150, 180, 186
Daoism, 119, 132, 148, 153, 154, 156,
169, 170
Daoxuan, 49
Dasabhumi, 149
Dasabhumika-sutra, 28
dependent origination, 56, 83, 87, 89,
93, 96, 115, 132, 204
Derrida, Jacques, 98
devotion, 11, 13, 21
Dharma Drum Mountain, 216, 217
dharmabhanaka, 32
dharmadhatu, 65, 131, 133
Dharmaguptakas, 49
Dharmakara, 48, 71, 72. *See also*
Amitabha; primal vow
dharmakaya, 65, 109, 171
dharmamegha, 51, 58
dharmas, 86ff, 93, 109, 160, 207
Dharmodgata, 57
dhyana, 55, 71, 136
Diamond Sutra, 14, 85, 90, 139
Dilun. *See* Ten Stages Sutra
Dizang. *See* Kshitigarbha
Dōgen, 21, 115, 140, 180, 194, 196,
202ff, 208
Dōkyō, 176
drsti, 92
Dunhuang, 14, 110, 123, 136, 138
durangama, 51, 56
East Asia, 5, 6, 11, 23, 36, 37, 38, 40,
41, 60, 65, 70, 71, 75, 76, 98, 100,
107, 109, 111, 112, 114, 115, 128,
133, 135, 136, 138, 156, 159, 161,
162, 163, 208
eight consciousnesses, 101, 104, 105
Eisai, 180, 196, 197, 202
Eison, 177, 183, 192, 194
ekayana, 44, 126
emptiness. *See* shunyata

About Windhorse Publications

Windhorse Publications is a Buddhist publishing house, staffed by practising Buddhists. We place great emphasis on producing books of high quality, which are accessible and relevant to those interested in Buddhism at whatever level. Drawing on the whole range of the Buddhist tradition, our books include translations of traditional texts, commentaries, books that make links with Western culture and ways of life, biographies of Buddhists, and works on meditation.

As a charitable institution we welcome donations to help us continue our work. We also welcome manuscripts on aspects of Buddhism or meditation. To join our email list, place an order or request a catalogue please visit our website at www.windhorsepublications.com or contact:

Windhorse Publications Ltd.	Perseus Distribution	Windhorse Books
38 Newmarket Road	1094 Flex Drive	PO Box 574
Cambridge CB5 8DT	Jackson TN 38301	Newtown NSW 2042
UK	USA	Australia

About the FWBO

Windhorse Publications is an arm of the Friends of the Western Buddhist Order, which has more than sixty centres on five continents. Through these centres, members of the Western Buddhist Order offer regular programmes of events for the general public and for more experienced students. These include meditation classes, public talks, study on Buddhist themes and texts, and bodywork classes such as t'ai chi, yoga, and massage. The FWBO also runs several retreat centres and the Karuna Trust, a fundraising charity that supports social welfare projects in the slums and villages of Southern Asia.

Many FWBO centres have residential spiritual communities and ethical businesses associated with them. Arts activities are encouraged too, as is the development of strong bonds of friendship between people who share the same ideals. In this way the FWBO is developing a unique approach to Buddhism, not simply as a set of techniques, but as a creatively directed way of life for people living in the modern world.

If you would like more information about the FWBO please visit the website at www.fwbo.org or write to:

London Buddhist Centre	Aryaloka	Sydney Buddhist Centre
51 Roman Road	14 Heartwood Circle	24 Enmore Road
London E2 0HU	Newmarket NH 03857	Sydney NSW 2042
UK	USA	Australia

Also by Nagapriya
Exploring Karma and Rebirth

While appearing frequently in popular culture, the fundamental Buddhist themes of karma and rebirth are often misunderstood. In this guide, the author introduces and clarifies these complex concepts, revealing their relevance for practitioners across the western world.

"An excellent introduction to, and critical overview of, the complex and frequently misinterpreted Buddhist doctrines of karma and rebirth...of interest to anyone in need of a clear presentation of the strengths and weaknesses of these ideas."
Stephen Batchelor

"A cogent, knowledgeable, and penetrating discussion of this critical Buddhist theme." *Zoketsu Norman Fischer*, founder, teacher of Everyday Zen Foundation.

"For Buddhism to thrive in the modern world we need to rethink traditional understandings of karma and rebirth. This admirable book does that better than anything else I know of. Every Buddhist should read it." *David Loy*

ISBN 9781 899579 61 7
£8.99 / $13.95 / €13.95
176 pages

Satipaṭṭhāna
The Direct Path to Realization
by Anālayo

This best-selling book offers a unique and detailed textual study of the *Satipaṭṭhāna Sutta*, a foundational Buddhist discourse on meditation practice.

"This book should prove to be of value both to scholars of Early Buddhism and to serious meditators alike." *Bhikkhu Bodhi*

"...a gem. Ven. Anālayo has done a superb job of elucidating this core teaching of the Buddha. His clarity of style, nuanced observations, and depth of analysis opens many new doors of understanding. I learned a lot from this wonderful book and highly recommend it." *Joseph Goldstein*

"An indispensible guide...surely destined to become the classic commentary on the *Satipaṭṭhāna*." *Christopher Titmuss*

"Very impressive and useful, with its blend of strong scholarship and attunement to practice issues." *Prof. Peter Harvey*, author of *An Introduction to Buddhist Ethics*

ISBN 9781 899579 54 9
£16.99 / $24.95 / €24.95
336 pages

A Survey of Buddhism
Its Doctrines and Methods through the Ages
by Sangharakshita

Highly acclaimed at its first appearance and now in its ninth edition, this survey provides a comprehensive study of the entire field of Buddhist thought and practice, placing its development in an historical context.

"Without hesitation, without any reservation whatsoever, I recommend Sangharakshita's book as the best survey of Buddhism we possess at present."
Dr E. Conze, Further Buddhist Studies

"A considerable achievement of Buddhist scholarship...this book can be heartily recommended to readers of all schools of thought." *The Middle Way*

"Published some four decades ago, this book remains one of the finest introductions to Buddhist thought and practice in the English language. *The Survey* is remarkable for its comprehensive scope, its sophistication and subtlety, its fidelity to the experience of Buddhism, and its balance in treating the various schools and traditions." *Dr Reginal A. Ray*, author of *Touching Enlightenment*

ISBN 9780 904766 93 6
£19.99 / $39.95 / €25.95
576 pages

A Concise History of Buddhism
by Andrew Skilton

How and when did the many schools and sub-sects of Buddhism emerge?

How do the ardent devotion of the Pure Land schools, or the magical ritual of the Tantra, relate to the direct teachings of Gautama, the 'historical' Buddha?

Here is a narrative which offers a fascinating insight to the development of Buddhism throughout its 2,500 year history. Describing its various manifestations across Asia, the author explores ancient sutras, early Sanghas and Buddhism's new spiritual ideal, placing these all in a useful chronological structure.

A Windhorse Publications' best-seller, this overview is highly recommended to those seeking a basis for further Buddhist study, be it of doctrine or of history.

ISBN 9780 904766 92 9
£9.99 / $19.95 / €12.95
272 pages